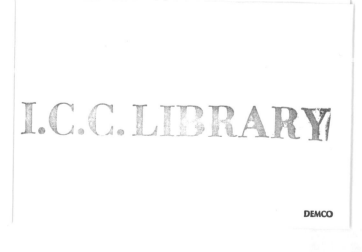

The Fall of the
House of Credit

How was it possible for problems in one relatively small sector in the global financial system – the American sub-prime mortgage market – to lead to the most serious economic crisis in living memory?

Alistair Milne untangles the complex world of modern banking and examines solutions to the crisis. He shows how the banks misused their ability to securitize loans and, by borrowing short and lending long, exposed themselves to exceptional risks when asset prices started to fall. But it has been above all a collapse in trust and confidence, rather than poor lending decisions, which has fuelled the crisis. Despite all the talk of 'toxic' assets, the book argues that most assets are sound and can be repaid. The imperative is to restore confidence through collective action involving asset purchases, guarantees and recapitalization. Failure to do so will mean that taxpayers will be carrying a crippling tax burden for generations to come.

ALISTAIR MILNE is Reader in Banking and Finance at the Cass Business School, City University, London. He has also worked for the Bank of England and HM Treasury.

The Fall of the House of Credit

What went wrong in banking and
what can be done to repair the damage?

ALISTAIR MILNE

CAMBRIDGE
UNIVERSITY PRESS

To J, K, L and all the Ms

CAMBRIDGE UNIVERSITY PRESS
Cambridge, New York, Melbourne, Madrid, Cape Town, Singapore, São Paulo, Delhi

Cambridge University Press
The Edinburgh Building, Cambridge CB2 8RU, UK

Published in the United States of America by Cambridge University Press, New York

www.cambridge.org
Information on this title: www.cambridge.org/9780521762144

First published 2009

Printed in the United Kingdom at the University Press, Cambridge

A catalogue record for this publication is available from the British Library

ISBN 978-0-521-76214-4 hardback

Contents

impact of the initial losses on US sub-prime. Structured credit markets became illiquid, resulting in write-offs of many bank portfolios. The disruption of money markets and global impact.

The narrative continued, up to the failure of AIG. A series of case studies both discusses the major losses experienced by many individual institutions (UBS, Merrill, Citigroup, Fannie and Freddie, AIG) and provides an overview of losses across the banking sector. Discusses also many of the knock-on effects on monolines and municipal bond markets.

Goes into the details of central bank monetary and liquidity operations, pointing out the limitations of central bank liquidity provision. Explains how banks use money markets to raise short-term funding. Compares orthodox and unorthodox approaches to monetary policy. Notes that there are substantial limits on the ability of central banks to provide commercial banks with new funds for lending.

The failure of Lehman and the four-week run on the global banking system and government rescues that followed. An assessment of the policy measures taken, showing how they are moving in the direction of taxpayer provision of long-term systemic risk insurance.

Explains how a global slump can be avoided and briefly considers longer-term measures to restore global prosperity.

Figures

Tables

Boxes

Acknowledgements

Writing a book is a hard slog. Writing a book on a subject that changes and evolves almost every day during the writing is an even harder slog. The final product would have been much weaker without the help of comments and discussion provided by many individuals, including Kern Alexander, Alistair Barr, Adrian Berendt, David Clark, Brandon Davies, Peter Fell, Paul Filer, Stephen Frost, Paul Hallas, Vince Johns, Esa Jokivuolle, Nick Kaufmann, Karlo Kauko, Lawrence Kotlikoff, Colin Lawrence, Gilad Livne, Perry Mehrling, Thorvald Moe, James Moser, Mark Robson, Dirk Schoenmaker, Jez Sillett, Mohan Sodhi, Jukka Vesala, Jouko Vilmunen and Larry Wall. I apologize to others whose names have been left off this list. None of these, of course, has any responsiblity for the content.

I have been greatly helped, as I have been in my research throughout the past four years, by the generous hospitality of the Monetary Policy and Research Department of the Bank of Finland. I have also had the opportunity to present parts of the text to staff of the Bank of Finland, the Helsinki branch of the Chartered Financial Analysts Association, the department of work and pensions, the conference 'The Regulatory Response to the Financial Crisis' hosted by the London School of Economics Financial Markets Group, HM Treasury, the European Federation of Financial Analysts and the Cambridge University Investment Banking Society.

The work has been assisted by a small grant from the Association of Chartered Certified Accountants that brought Perry Mehrling over to the United Kingdom in October 2008 to pursue our joint work on policy responses to the crisis, and paid for some research assistance on a paper on financial institution risks and accounting. Parts of that analysis have been incorporated into this text. Tables and charts in chapters 7, 8, and 9 were put together with help from two able research assistants, Agnes Maumus and Ivan Introna. I am also indebted to Richard Kao of HSBC for putting together Figure 7.1 at short notice.

The team at Cambridge University Press, including my editor Chris Harrison, have been immensely patient and professional. I thank Chris in particular for his suggestion in August 2008 that the title be changed from 'The House of Credit' to 'The Fall of the House of Credit'. He clearly knew better than most of us what was about to happen to the financial system!

To Rudy, I apologize that while I have been able to include the financial equivalent of a car chase, I could not satisfy your other request for some steamy bedroom scenes. Let's hope that despite this the text still has some general appeal. My children have had much less of my time over the past eight months than I would have liked. My partner has been the most long-suffering of all, putting up with many weekends and evenings when I have been devoted only to the computer screen. She tells me in no uncertain terms that this has to be a one-book relationship. On my side I am determined that this will be the only book I ever write – at least on such a topical subject and to such a tight deadline.

17 March 2009

Introduction

What this book is about

Why would anyone who does not work in the banking industry want to read a book about banking? The subject should be a bore. Savings accounts are not fashionable. Mortgages do not entertain. Most of us – well, apart from banking professionals and a few banking professors like myself – have better things to do than think about payment cards or credit transfers. All we want from banks is security and convenience: we want to trust them as the best place to keep our money and to be able to use our money without difficulty, so we can enjoy the things we desire – say a new car, a well-earned holiday, a restaurant meal, the latest DVD or the new jacket that has caught our eye. Some of us also want to be able to borrow reasonable amounts of money at not too great a cost and others – those with some cash to spare – are interested in the return that banks offer on savings. But even interest rates on bank borrowing and lending are only of passing interest, at those times when we have financial decisions to make.

Today, though, banking is attracting unusual attention. The reason is, of course, that banks are in deep trouble. Far from being boring, banks now arouse strong emotions: shock, confusion, anger and fear. Trust in banks has evaporated. Are they safe? How did they get into such difficulties? Who is responsible for their problems? How can we best prevent these spilling over into lost jobs and lower income and financial problems for all of us?

The problems originated with the bubble in US house prices, but have since turned into a global banking and financial crisis more severe than any since the 1930s. This is now producing such a sharp reversal of bank lending – the 'fall of the house of credit' referred to in my title – that the world is now facing the deepest and longest-lasting economic contraction since the great depression of the 1930s. If politicians and policymakers fail to respond appropriately, the present downturn could turn out to be even worse than that terrible economic tragedy. This book explains how and why all this happened and what needs to be done to prevent a new great depression.

The 'how' is the easy part. In these pages you will find a concise account of the key events in the crisis, as they evolved from the initial slowdown in the US housing market in late 2006 until the global banking run of late 2008. These developments are placed in their broader economic and business context. The economic context was the growing global current-account imbalances, with savings from China, Japan, Germany and other surplus countries recycled to finance the consumer credit and housing boom in the United States, the United Kingdom and other deficit countries. The business context was the rise of a system of 'parallel' banking, with credit intermediated not through traditional retail deposits but using new innovative credit instruments, held by banks and financed through short-term wholesale money markets.

The 'why' and 'what' are more difficult. The unsustainable boom of credit and house prices that preceded the crisis had its roots in psychology and culture and what has been aptly called the madness of crowds. This statement in itself is not controversial. Many others have written about the role of euphoria and of mutually self-reinforcing beliefs when the banks were building up their large exposures to household and risky corporate debt, the exposures that are now proving so difficult to manage. The controversial argument made in this book is that psychology, culture and crowd madness are playing an equally important, if not bigger, role in the crisis itself. What has been pushing many banks to the wall is not poor lending decisions but a blind panic, an overreaction to mistakes made during the boom, a panic made possible by the reliance on highly unstable short-term funding, in which professional investors are fleeing from any form of bank exposure.

This panic is being reinforced by a powerful stream of negative commentary on banks, financial markets and the economy. Media commentary and the sentiment of bankers and investors have switched in little over a year from blithe optimism and overconfidence to fatalism and extreme pessimism. Consumers and governments, especially in the English-speaking world, have borrowed far too much. There is nothing else to be done except cut back on our spending and sell off all our assets to reduce borrowing. Banks assets are worth far less than the banks pretend and they may be hiding even worse problems. They must reveal the full extent of their holdings of 'toxic' assets and revert to being cautious, riskless utilities.

Arguing against this fatalism does not mean understating the seriousness of the current financial and economic situation. This crisis has already spread to the real economy, as evidenced by falling economic output and the many millions who have already lost their jobs. This will not be a short-lived recession of a few months' duration, like those that have occurred every few years since the early 1980s. It will be deep and long lasting. Global output and income look as if they will fall by as much as 5 per cent before stabilizing. There will be no return to rapid, consumption-led growth in the deficit countries, the spending that has led the global economic expansion of the past twenty-five years. The world economy will have to adjust to a different pattern of trade and growth, something which will take years, and in the meantime growth of output and incomes will be modest at best.

This is a huge political and economic challenge. Western countries face major long-term changes, shifting the balance of economic activity from consumption and importing to investment and exporting. Politicians have had an easy time during the fat years, courting popularity and winning votes by offering spending or tax cuts paid for out of the fruits of future consumer-driven growth. Now the growth is no longer there, but most politicians continue to be under the illusion that they have the policies to restore the good times and allow the policies of high spending and low taxation to continue.

Adjusting to the new political and economic realities of lower growth and much tighter public finances would be difficult even with well-managed banks and sound bank balance sheets. The banking crisis – a crisis caused by panic and unstable funding arrangements and therefore entirely avoidable – threatens to make the economic situation far worse, triggering a cumulative collapse of credit, output, and jobs that could go as far as to fracture our society, to undermine our political fabric and destroy much of the way of life that we have enjoyed for more than fifty years. This is a far more dangerous threat to Western democracy than terrorism or even, at least within the horizon of the next decade or so, climate change.

Policymakers around the world, led by the new Obama administration in the United States, can avoid this outcome. While economic adjustment will be difficult and painful, there is no need for a collapse of bank credit to worsen the decline of economic activity. The clue to preventing such a banking calamity is to be found in the origins of the word 'credit', derived from the Latin 'credere', meaning 'to believe' or 'trust'. Bankers made many mistakes. Some risky exposures, such as sub-prime mortgages and leveraged loans, got out of control. Traders and senior management were paid outrageously large salaries for taking responsibility for and then losing a great deal of other people's money. Trust was betrayed.

But that was in the past. The task now is to rebuild trust. Despite all those mistakes banking is fundamentally sound. The problem is not, as many claim, that banks are hiding losses. Strict 'mark to market' accounting rules mean that losses have been more than fully acknowledged. The majority of bank assets are still of good quality. Many are worth far more than bank accounting statements suggest. The value of bank investments will bounce back once the economy stabilizes and markets recover. There will then be very many opportunities for banks to lend to creditworthy borrowers.

The reason this is not yet happening is the absence of trust. Panicked global investors no longer believe in banks or bank assets. Banks themselves do not trust in the future. They cannot raise money to lend, and when they can raise money they will not lend it.

This, then, is a time for leadership. The duty of government is to provide that leadership, to demonstrate that, even if right now no one else does, they still support the banks. Money, if necessary extraordinarily large sums of taxpayer money, must be placed on the table and made available to support banks and enable them to start lending again. Of course this must not be done recklessly. Blanket guarantees are not appropriate. There have to be clear arrangements for sharing both profits and losses between government and taxpayers on the one hand and banks on the other. Banks and their shareholders should still be exposed to normal business risks. Central banks, government and ultimately the taxpayer will have to take responsibility for economy-wide disasters, providing insurance against extreme 'systemic' risks. This is needed in order to allow banks to lend freely again, thus beginning the process of ending the market panic and re-establishing investor and customer trust in our banks.

What must banks do in return for this support? What we, as taxpayers and citizens, need to see in return is banks themselves beginning to take actions that demonstrate that they merit our trust. Banks are going to have to do a huge amount more than in the past to explain and communicate their activities to investors and customers. They are going to have to focus on basic simple products and services. There will still be room for some sophisticated financial engineering, such as credit derivative and securitizations, but it will be up to banks to explain exactly how they are using these tools and what they contribute to their business.

Banks are also going to have to develop a new and more persuasive vision of their future role in business and society. Once the banking system and financial markets are fixed the sources of future global economic growth will not be the same as before. We will no longer be able to rely on stimulating consumer spending in the West in order to increase output and employment. We will have to do much more in the developed countries of Europe, North America and Australasia to raise productivity both in private business and in government. Developed and emerging economies will have to work together on rebalancing the world economy, offering the citizens of the emerging world higher levels of consumption and citizens of the developed world more opportunity to earn a living supplying goods and services.

This has further important implications for Western banks. Growth in their consumer lending businesses will be in emerging markets, and not, with the possible exception of Japan and Germany, in the developed world. They need to deal with some of the gross inefficiencies that still pervade basic banking transaction and payment systems. They will need to offer much more effective banking services to the small and medium-sized enterprises that will generate the income that in turn repays the large pool of global savings borrowed by Western consumers.

Who this book is for

I have set myself the goal in writing this book of explaining the banking crisis and to outline how it can be resolved in a manner which does not oversimplify but can be read by any concerned citizen. This decision – to write for a general not a specialist audience – has posed considerable challenges. I have had to explain in straightforward language how the new credit instruments and credit markets at the centre of our financial problems operate. I have also had to provide an account of the evolution of the crisis, from its early beginnings with the weakening of US house prices in the second half of 2006 to the dramatic collapse of confidence in global banks in autumn 2008, which does not assume specialist knowledge but covers all the key developments in sufficient detail to explain not just what happened but also why it happened in this way. Along the way I have had to reveal some of the mysteries of central banking and bank funding and liquidity management, subjects which normally are of concern only to specialists but are key to understanding the current crisis.

So why go to such trouble to explain technical details which many experts will already know and understand? In part this is because such explanation is one of the pleasures of my chosen profession. There is little more satisfying to a professor than introducing students and others to subjects that at first seem difficult and challenging and showing that they are not really so hard to follow after all. But the main reason for writing this book for a general rather than a specialist audience is because I want to do my best to tackle one of the root causes of our present economic and financial difficulties, the excessive faith placed in 'experts' such as financial engineers, derivative traders, investment advisers, equity and banking analysts, fund managers, risk managers and economists, and the resulting excessive specialization that is hampering our response to the crisis.

In fact, as I shall show, the new financial instruments and our current global financial situation are not really that complicated or difficult to understand. Bankers have often preferred to conduct their business in as sophisticated and roundabout a way as possible. That way, it is not too clear when they are doing a good or a bad job; they can charge high fees and not be too worried about competition from other professionals doing the same task just as well for a smaller fee; nor, then, do they have to be too concerned about customer complaints, because few customers can tell whether they are getting good value or not.

This lack of understanding of how financial instruments and financial markets work suits the specialists in good times. But it has come back to haunt them. This is another reason why the blithe optimism of the recent credit boom has given way so quickly to confusion and excessive pessimism. The experts on banking and financial markets and global economics are themselves all so specialized and so compartmentalized that, while they have a detailed understanding of their own small part of the credit and financial system, few can join up all the dots and present a complete picture of what has been going on and how the problems of the banks can be repaired. This practice – of bankers and financial experts working in compartmentalized silos without any need to pay attention to the operation of the business as a whole – is one of the main reasons why the industry and financial markets are in such disarray.

Financial journalists who report on these events are also struggling to make sense of them and have tended – in rather herd-like manner – to run in the same direction as investors from one extreme viewpoint to its opposite, from naive faith in the efficiency and power of markets to great scepticism about market forces. The dominant voices in the media now call loudly for much closer supervision, regulation and controls of financial institutions, for the clearing out of 'toxic' assets, and for a massive 'deleveraging' – that is, reduction of private-sector borrowing and lending.

A sensible book written for a general not specialist audience can help restore some much-needed balance to these debates. Yes, there are serious problems with bank loan portfolios, but the overall quality of bank assets is far better than the broadcast media and other commentary suggest. A lack of long-term funding – in the professional jargon a lack of bank 'capital' in the form of both equity and bonds – is the main factor undermining bank balance sheets. This is a chicken and egg problem. The global downturn is being driven by shortage of bank credit. A sufficiently large injection of capital into the entire global banking system will allow banks to lend to all creditworthy borrowers looking for funds. This will stabilize the global economy and ensure that most bank borrowers are able to repay their loans. But the fear that borrowers will not repay their loans prevents investors providing banks with the necessary capital. So the cumulative global collapse of output and activity continues. The global economy will not stabilize without new bank capital and private investors will not provide banks with new capital until there is stability in the global economy. Only decisive government action on a grand scale to recapitalize banks can end this downward spiral.

This does not mean igniting another unsustainable credit boom. Many households and companies will have eventually to 'deleverage', reducing the amount of borrowing against their incomes, but there is no need for this process to take place in a hurry. On the contrary, the sooner the banks are adequately recapitalized and the supply of bank credit restored, then the slower the reduction in leverage and the more it will take place through increases in incomes rather than sale of assets and repayment of debt. Generous recapitalizing of the banks is essential if we are to have an orderly adjustment to our present financial and economic challenges.

A closely related chicken and egg problem is the closure of the new markets for mortgage-backed and other structured credit securities. These are a key source of both long-term funds and liquidity for many banks. But now, because there is no functioning secondary market for buying and selling these securities, investors will not touch even the safest versions of them. The market cannot reopen because no investors will buy these securities and no investors will buy these securities because the market remains closed. This is another fixable problem undermining bank balance sheets.

In short, this book presents a clear statement of how government support can give the banks the opportunity to recover from their present difficulties. This book, if you like, places a flag on the high ground – presenting an intellectual and practical case for the large sums of money now being offered by financial authorities in the United States and other countries to repair bank balance sheets.

There is plenty of room for debate over the exact form of this support. The media and the public, understandably, are suspicious of the apparent use of large sums of taxpayers' money to protect banks from the consequences of their own mistakes. Details of the rescue plans can be challenged. It is arguable that the authorities are doing too much to help shareholders and bank bond holders, and that the interests of taxpayers would be better served if financial support for banks were accompanied by corporate restructurings, so that shareholders receive nothing and bond holders' interests are written down to cover part of the overall costs.

But these are side issues. The priority is ensuring that enough is done to remove all concerns about the quality of bank balance sheets and the stability of the banking system. The exact way this is done is secondary. Failure to act, because of disputes over how to act, will impose ultimate costs on taxpayers, from lost output and jobs, far greater than any undeserved subsidy to bank management, bond holders or shareholders.

The curse of excessive specialism is also affecting politicians, government officials, central bankers and financial regulators. They have struggled to come up with a coherent, common approach to the crisis. As this book documents, policymakers around the world have been groping their way towards a sensible and appropriate response to our present problems. Governments and central banks worldwide have taken firm action and committed very large sums to dealing with the crisis. But these responses have been halting and sometimes inconsistent, with policymakers switching from one approach to another and giving the impression that they were trying out anything to see what works, rather than having a clear understanding of what they were trying to do. Government officials and central bankers have also struggled to present a clear account of their actions to their political masters and to the electorate, whom politicians and officials alike all serve.

Creating a bridge between these different specialisms, between credit specialists and managers and between officials and bankers, is a further reason for writing for a general rather than specialist audience. I have sought to provide a clear picture of the crisis that can be understood by all these different groups, explaining how the new banking and credit markets worked, why they have got into difficulties, and how support from taxpayers and investors will allow the new credit markets and the banking industry to recover from their present problems. If I have been successful, then this book will also help officials, politicians and industry to engage in a more constructive policy debate.

A key point is that we need to move beyond blame and accusation and think about how, as we go forward, credit and loan risks will be shared between investors and taxpayers. Taxpayers are already, implicitly, providing extreme 'disaster insurance' to banks, since if banks fail then the taxpayer must pay the bill to protect depositors and the financial system. An obvious further step – to rebuild and sustain trust in the banks and restore confidence in the new credit instruments, so avoiding an unnecessarily large economic contraction – is making this disaster insurance open and explicit. This is in fact exactly the rationale behind many current policies, such as widespread guarantees of bank assets and liabilities.

The writing of this book

The text was written over an eight-month period between July 2008 and March 2009. Figures and tables have been updated to the end of December 2008. I have not attempted to take account of the most recent developments – for example the emergence of the Madoff investment fraud – in any systematic fashion. I have, however, included references to some of the most prominent events in the weeks while I was finalizing the manuscript. Inevitably, even much of what has taken place to date has been left out. The focus is on the major banking and financial markets. Marshalling this amount of material has left no further space for discussing the truly devastating impact of the crisis on global trade and industry, on the periphery economies such as those of eastern and central Europe, or even on secondary financial centres such as Dubai, or the painful impact on the economies of Ireland and Spain.

My own background and experience impelled me to write this book. I know the new credit instruments well, from teaching courses at a leading UK business school on credit products and credit risk management, covering topics such as mortgage-backed securitizations, credit default swaps, and collateralized debt obligations. I have worked on problems of bank risk management and regulation for more than a decade. The earlier part of my career was spent in macroeconomics, during which, among other responsibilities, I worked on monetary policy and also researched and analysed the UK housing boom and bust of the late 1980s and early 1990s. This places me in an ideal position to explain both the details of how the new credit markets and instruments work and the bigger picture of how they led the industry and the wider economy into crisis.

Like most others I thought that the worst was already behind us by summer 2008. In fact many of the most dramatic events – such as the loss of confidence in the giant US mortgage institutions Fannie Mae and Freddie Mac, the failure of Lehman Brothers and the run on the global banking system that followed, and the massive interventions by central banks and by governments worldwide – took place while I was working on the manuscript.

A danger in writing any book such as this about current events is that it may date quickly. I have no crystal ball that allows me to foresee what other dramas might yet affect banks and financial markets, and I am not attempting to predict the future. Nevertheless much of this material will remain current. A central concern of this book is with the perennial debate that arises in every financial crisis and is at the heart of this crisis. On the one side are those who insist on punishing the wrongdoers, allowing financial institutions to fail and forcing shareholders and others to bear the consequences of their own decisions. On the other side are those, such as myself on this occasion, who urge government or collective support for weak financial institutions in order to prevent a financial crisis causing much wider economic damage.

My own analysis and understanding of these events continues to evolve. From September 2008 to March 2009, alongside writing this book I have been closely involved in public and professional debates on the policy response in the United Kingdom. Some of the pieces I have written can be found on our business school website at www. cass.city.ac.uk/cbr/activities/bankingcrisis.html, and I have also made a number of contributions to the *Financial Times* Economists' Forum, http://blogs.ft.com/wolfforum/. Several of my papers and posts there, arguing that governments should provide 'disaster insurance' to banks, especially my collaborations with Laurence Kotlikoff of Boston University and Perry Mehrling of Barnard College, Columbia University, can be found on these web pages. I expect to put on the Cass pages further analyses updating my views.

In thinking about these issues I have often been drawn back to a youthful experience when I was a part II undergraduate student at King's College, Cambridge, in the late 1970s. Along with the other economics tripos students of my year I was privileged to attend some special tutorial sessions with the renowned King's College fellow in economics Nikki Kaldor, one of the key contributors to the Keynesian revolution in economic analysis.

Kaldor is deservedly one of the most celebrated economists of his generation. I and my fellow students were privileged to hear him give a virtuoso exposition of a well-known argument associated with his name – his critique of the monetarist views of Milton Friedman. Kaldor's critique of monetarism, inspired by the earlier work of Keynes, is that, with modern monetary arrangements, where most money is in the form of deposits created by banks, the central bank cannot directly control the supply of money. The supply of money is instead the outcome of the lending decisions of many individual commercial banks. When banks are confident about the prospects of returns on lending or their ability to fund their lending, then they are willing to lend money regardless of the decisions of the central bank. When confidence collapses then lending and the money supply can also collapse. The 'money multiplier' – the ratio of total bank money to narrow money created by the central bank – is not stable, but rather varies hugely over the course of the business cycle, depending upon the views of banks about the prospects of returns on their lending. One implication is that Friedman's dictum, that to stabilize the economy all that is necessary is for central banks to stabilize the supply of money, is extremely difficult to put into practice.

Kaldor's analysis could not be more relevant at any time than it is today. The key challenge now facing economic policymakers is the collapse of confidence in bank assets and bank funding instruments and the consequent reductions of money and credit. The economic downturn will finally come to an end and confidence will then eventually return of its own accord, regardless of how policymakers deal with the crisis. But in order to avoid a massive collapse of money and credit, with all the consequent damage to our social and political fabric that would then result, policymakers will have to rebuild trust in banks and confidence in credit instruments.

My analysis is far from being entirely original. It has been influenced or paralleled by the arguments of several other prominent academics and practitioners. Since this book is written for general readers and not for my academic peers, I do not provide a full discussion of these other views, but I have included some chapter notes that will guide readers to what I regard as important contributions to recent debates and other reading that may help them understand the crisis and how it can be addressed.

How the book is organized

Chapter 1 is an overview of the causes of the current crisis, contrasting my own perspective – that this is to a large extent a crisis of confidence in bank loans and bank funding instruments – with other interpretations, including the predominant view that this crisis is due entirely to excessive and unsustainable levels of bank lending. It asks the question 'where did all the money go?' and finds that the main reason why money and credit began to contract, at least initially, was problems of bank funding. Because of a collapse of confidence and liquidity in traded credit instruments, banks could no longer freely access the wholesale funding markets on which they have come to rely for funding during the consumer and credit boom of the past twenty-five years – either the short-term markets for money or the longer-term bond and structured security markets. This created a dynamic of its own – what is sometimes called a 'feedback loop' – explaining why what was initially a rather small shock, at least in terms of the magnitude of the world banking system, had such a large cumulative destabilizing effect.

More recently a further, even more powerful, feedback loop has begun to play a role, with a deteriorating economic outlook making banks more concerned about the risks of loss and more reluctant to lend, in turn accelerating the decline of economic output and employment. Policymakers, to deal with this situation, must break into these feedback loops. This is not easy, but the most promising way to do this, which governments worldwide are now beginning to do, albeit rather half-heartedly, is to offer guarantees, capping bank losses in the most extreme possible outcomes, and to provide banks with enough long term equity capital to make them entirely safe from the risk of insolvency. Many banks may, as a result, end up in public ownership but this is much better than allowing these feedback loops to continue.

Chapter 2 provides an initial synopsis of the crisis itself. It begins with a short analysis of the global financial arrangements that supplied credit from savers in China, Japan, Germany and other countries to governments and especially to consumers in the Anglo-Saxon and other countries with low levels of household savings and large current-account deficits. It examines the exposure of banks to the new credit instruments. Then it reviews the losses of banks, distinguishing fundamental underlying loan losses and credit impairment from the temporary liquidity losses on credit-related securities – liquidity losses that have greatly increased the exposure of banks to the downturn in mortgage and other loan markets and cut banks off from almost all wholesale sources of funding. In order to understand the crisis properly it is essential to realize that these liquidity losses, which account for about half of all bank losses and write-downs, have been on good-quality effectively credit-risk-free securities, not on fundamentally unsound assets. This chapter also explains the key point, central to the argument of this book, that these liquidity losses are not external shocks but rather are reactions of market participants to a potential deterioration of economic fundamentals, reactions which will be reversed provided that the anticipated decline of fundamentals is itself avoided. Finally, this chapter provides a brief review of how governments and central banks have responded to the crisis.

Chapter 3 then compares the current financial crises with some previous historical episodes. Long books can and indeed have been written on the history of financial crashes and credit crises. The purpose of this chapter is to show that in past episodes of financial boom and bust both excessive optimism and excessive pessimism have played a role. In some cases – for example the grossly excessive extension of bank credit in Japan in the 1980s – the subsequent bust has been mainly due to the excesses and over-optimism of the preceding boom. In other cases – such as the US banking panic of 1907 or the Long-Term Capital Management (LTCM) liquidity crisis of 1998 – the crisis is more attributable to overreaction and panic, with a pronounced collapse in liquidity and market values prompted by a relatively small deterioration in fundamentals. Most crises result from a mixture of both these causes, both over-optimism in the boom and excessive pessimism in the subsequent bust.

Chapters 4, 5 and 6 are devoted to a detailed assessment of the new traded credit securities at the heart of the crisis and the business strategies of banks that used them. Banks used these instruments primarily as funding instruments to help finance relatively rapidly growing loan books (the common description of these new banking strategies as 'originate and distribute' is misleading, because typically banks retained rather than sold much of the risk on the positions they held). Investment banks created special credit structuring departments for assembling the new instruments, and found that they could create additional profits by conducting trading transactions in which they bought in high-yielding assets for inclusion in their credit structures. Banks held large amounts of the safest structured credit securities in their trading and investment portfolios, financed by using short-term borrowing, rather than selling these securities to long-term investors.

As long as borrower and investor appetite for credit remained strong these new activities were highly profitable. When the credit boom collapsed the structuring came to a halt and the market value of even the best-quality structured credit products collapsed. Bank portfolio strategies had assumed that the markets for structured credit products would always remain liquid, and hence that it was safe to finance portfolios of these products using short-term borrowing. But while banks individually were not exposed to liquidity risks, because they could always sell down their portfolios to meet any withdrawal of funding or decline in net worth, this exposed the banking system as a whole to substantial liquidity risk. Beginning in summer 2007 the deterioration of credit fundamentals triggered a vicious circle of falling prices for structured credit products, forced sales and further withdrawals of short-term funding.

Chapters 7 to 10 then trace the course of the crisis, from its early stirrings in US housing markets in late 2006 until the worldwide run on the global banking system and subsequent large-scale government rescue packages in September and October 2008. Chapter 7 reviews the early stages, from the initial weakening in US housing markets in late 2006 through to the run on the UK bank Northern Rock in September 2007. Northern Rock's difficulties, like that of several other banks worldwide, was a consequence of the closure of the markets for trading and issuing the new securitized credit instruments, especially mortgage-backed securities. Chapter 8 takes the story up to early September 2008, describing the growing mortgage-related losses of many banks world-wide and the impact on the industry of the rising stresses in various global financial markets, such as the money and repo markets and also the credit default swap markets for hedging of traded credit risk.

Chapter 9 addresses a particular aspect of the story, the role of central banks in providing reserves to commercial banks in order both to provide liquidity to money markets and to enforce central bank monetary policy decisions. This chapter explains how these central bank operations are conducted. It looks at the tools available to a central bank to deal with a financial crisis, including its role as lender of last resort. There is an important distinction between bank liquidity and bank funding. Central banks can provide commercial banks with unlimited liquidity (increased balances in their accounts with the central bank) but with only a limited amount of funding.

As long as central banks conduct monetary policy in the orthodox fashion, seeking to control short-term market rates of interest, then even their liquidity provision is constrained: whatever they provide at one maturity they must take away at another in order to maintain control over interest rates. But there is an alternative. If central banks are willing to stop targeting interest rates, allowing them to fall at or close to zero, then they can operate monetary policy in an 'unor-thodox' fashion, purchasing all manner of financial assets simply by expanding the central bank balance sheet.

With this background Chapter 10 then looks at the global banking run, triggered by the failure of Lehman Brothers and finally ending some four weeks later with the announcement of extensive packages of government and central bank support. Central banks played an especially important role in restoring stability, increasing their balance sheets and their loans to banks and other financial market participants to an extraordinary degree. The announcement of a commitment of major sums of taxpayer money to rebuild bank balance sheets and guarantee bank liabilities finally ended the run. Increasingly, the United States and, most recently, the United Kingdom have been moving towards using policies such as government guarantees to cap the potential losses of the banking industry. But much more can be done to clarify the purpose of these interventions and to help guide the expectations of investors and bankers, and these actions will clearly be most effective if similar support is provided on a global scale. The final passage of Chapter 10 is the key policy analysis of the book. It summarizes the case for large-scale insurance and recapitalization, referring back to the feedback loops illustrated in Figure 1.1 of Chapter 1. These feedback loops create powerful negative externalities, with the decisions of individual banks to sell assets or reduce lending having a substantial negative impact on the profitability and solvency of other banks. But the presence of these negative externalities is good news; they imply that insurance and recapitalization is a win-win policy, creating both profits for the taxpayer and substantial capital gains for bank shareholders.

A final chapter of conclusions summarizes the findings of the previous chapters. It also considers the longer-run prospects for the banking industry and wider economy after the crisis, arguing that there will have to be a thorough rethinking of the appropriate relationship between government and the banking industry. Attempts to reduce risk-taking in banking and to introduce much closer regulation will be counterproductive, leading to unnecessary restrictions on loan growth and starving households and companies of needed finance.

Notes on further reading

These are the first of the chapter notes on further reading provided in this book. The notes for this chapter are fairly lengthy, providing an overview of all that has been written about the crisis. Notes to the subsequent chapters are shorter, providing links to books and articles that are relevant to the topic of that particular chapter.

The further reading mentioned in these notes is mostly, like this book, written by professional economists for a general readership. There are only a few references to the writing of journalists. Does that mean that there is no journalism on the crisis worth reading? Far from it. I have made extensive use of many excellent newspaper and web articles, but the reason for not citing this work as further reading is that most journalists, like the 'experts' who worked in the markets, do not have their own independent expertise on the new credit arrangements; they are only reporting the views of others, and are not in a good position to explain the entire crisis. If you like, they give excellent accounts of individual trees but fail to give a clear picture of the entire forest.

Another problem with a lot of journalism about the crisis is the use of a number of loose phrases, such as 'toxic assets', or (on the monetary side) 'printing money' or 'injecting liquidity into the economy'. When journalists use such phrases, which mean little to their audience, they simply reveal that they have not gone the extra mile in order to understand and explain what has been going on. I hope that Chapters 4, 5 and 9 in particular will explain why such phrases oversimplify.

What, then, do the economic experts say caused this financial crisis and what are their views on how policymakers can bring it to an end? There is a great deal of professional consensus on these questions. As an example see the short articles collected and published on Vox in response to the worsening of the financial crisis in October 2008, at www.voxeu.org/index.php?q=node/2340, of 9 October, and also the open letter, and the many accompanying signatures, on Vox at www.voxeu.org/index.php?q=node/1729. Another useful collection, from one of the leading US business schools and again indicating a considerable agreement across a wide range of issues, is Viral V. Acharya and Matthew Richardson (eds.), *Restoring Financial Stability: How to Repair a Failed Financial System: An Independent View from New York University Stern School of Business*, due to be published by Wiley and Sons in March 2009 (for summaries of the papers in this book see http://media.rgemonitor.com/papers/0/NyuFinArch.pdf).

Yet another set of views, also illustrating the degree of consensus among economic experts but written for central bankers and not for general readers, is found in the six papers and discussants' comments from the 2008 Jackson Hole symposium, hosted by the Federal Reserve Bank of Kansas City, in August 2008 (www.kc.frb.org/home/ subwebnav.cfm?level=3&theID=10697&SubWeb=10660).

For a reader prepared to do a bit more searching I can recommend the various articles and debates in the Economists' Forum http:// blogs.ft.com/wolfforum (I provide links to several contributions to this forum, including some of my own). The European economic policy commentary site Vox (www.voxeu.org/) also contains many good articles (but the usefulness of this site is a bit limited by its clumsy archiving system). Finally, there is a lot of relevant material on Nouriel Roubini's Global Economics Monitor at www.rgemonitor. com/, but this requires registration and much of the content (often the most interesting) is available to paying subscribers only.

While economists share a framework for thinking about the crisis and agree about much of what has been going on, there is still plenty of room for differences in opinion about facts and the interpretation of facts. We are also, of course, sometimes influenced by more subjective political opinions. How, then, to summarize the range of opinion?

To put some structure on these different views, I think of my fellow economists as falling in two main groups. The first are what I describe as the mainstream. Those in this group see parallels between this crisis and previous episodes when bank credit grew at an unsustainable level, for example in the years preceding banking crises such as those of Scandinavia and Japan in the early 1990s. They focus on deteriorating standards of credit underwriting, unsustainable increase in asset prices, relaxation of supervisory oversight, expansion into new business activities without proper controls, excessive 'leverage' – that is, too much borrowing in relation to the value of their asset portfolios – and excessive risk-taking, perhaps exacerbated by undesirable remuneration arrangements which offer substantial rewards for making a big win. In short, they think that this is a crisis of poor-quality bank assets and too much borrowing by banks in order to hold those assets.

The second group – where I place myself – emphasizes a different set of problems – the excessive reliance on short-term borrowing and the resulting maturity mismatch, the weaknesses of 'mark to market' accounting rules for many of the new assets when there is no market, and the panic withdrawal of short-term funding that has created widespread market illiquidity, resulting in undervaluation of assets and the dislocation of money markets where banks normally borrow in the short term. In short, this is a crisis of confidence in the banks, whose assets are not as bad as many suppose, but who are no longer able to borrow short- or long-term and so are forced to cut back sharply on their lending.

A lively debate between exponents of these two viewpoints was kicked off on the Economists' Forum by Christopher Carroll's brilliant 'TARP and the ruin of Pompeii: an analogy', at http://blogs.ft.com/economistsforum/2008/10/henry-paulson-and-mount-vesuvius/. This short piece and the eleven subsequent comments represent most of the views expressed by the economic profession on the crisis. My own align closely with those of Max Fysh and Laurence Kotlikoff in this discussion thread.

This contrast of views between the mainstream (the problem is poor asset quality) and the alternative (the problem is confidence) is not clear-cut; the distinction is only a matter of emphasis, and many economists have expressed opinions that place them in both groups. For the reader prepared to tackle some of the more technical writing about the crisis, the Jackson Hole papers are an excellent illustration of both the overall consensus among economists and the range of individual views. Four of the six papers emphasize the 'crisis of confidence' interpretation of the crisis that I share. These are the papers by Gary Gorton, Franklin Allen and Elena Carletti, Willem Buiter, and Charles Calomiris. The other two contributions are what I call mainstream, emphasizing the poor quality of bank assets. These are by Tobias Adrian and Hyun Song Shin, and by Anil Kashyap, Raghuram Rajan and Jeremy Stein. But individual authors can stress different aspects of the crisis at different times. Another paper by Adrian and Shin ('Liquidity and leverage', at http://papers.ssrn.com/sol3/papers.cfm?abstract_id=1139857) is one of the clearest statements available of how high levels of short-term borrowing can trigger funding problems, a key part of the 'crisis of confidence' interpretation of the crisis.

The reason I refer to the first group of opinions as the mainstream view is not because it dominates professional debate (on my count it is actually the minority view of this banking crisis), but because it is this interpretation of the crisis that currently holds greatest sway with policymakers. There is a forceful expression in President Barack Obama's inauguration speech of 20 January 2009:

Our economy is badly weakened, a consequence of greed and irresponsibility on the part of some, but also our collective failure to make hard choices and prepare the nation for a new age. Homes have been lost; jobs shed; businesses shuttered. Our health care is too costly; our schools fail too many; and each day brings further evidence that the ways we use energy strengthen our adversaries and threaten our planet. These are the indicators of crisis, subject to data and statistics. Less measurable but no less profound is a sapping of confidence across our land – a nagging fear that America's decline is inevitable, and that the next generation must lower its sights.

It is an encouraging sign that the new US president has so clearly and concisely articulated the current economic problems and is also aware of the economic constraints that limit economic policy (a dangerously large number of politicians, including some who have held the post of president or equivalent office in other countries, ignore economic constraints altogether, telling voters the fairy tale that they can have lower taxes and higher government spending and need never worry about the future because rapid growth will pay all the bills). There have been criticisms of these particular words of President Obama because they are rather vague on what will be done, but that was not their purpose. They were chosen to help build a political consensus on Capitol Hill, both on the need to use fiscal policy to deal with the crisis and on the necessity of confronting the longer-term economic problems facing the United States.

This mainstream account of the crisis focuses on both the poor lending decisions made during the credit boom and the problem of over-indebtedness in economies that have devoted a large share of their resources over the past decade or more to increasing consumer spending. Similar mainstream opinions are expressed by policymakers at the highest levels. Policymakers have also committed themselves to the need for a global co-ordinated response to the crisis, a response that President Obama will now lead (see for example Dominique Strauss-Kahn, the Chief Executive of the International Monetary Fund, who provides a short and comprehensive statement of his view of the crisis in a *Financial Times* opinion piece, at www.ft.com/cms/s/0/f8c6ccae-955a-11dd-aedd-000077b07658.html).

A list of influential exponents of these mainstream views might include (even if they object to the categorization) the prolific and insightful Martin Wolf of the *Financial Times* (who has justifiably been described as the world's pre-eminent financial journalist), the economic historian Niall Ferguson of Harvard University, who writes so elegantly about financial history, and the commentator George Magnus, who has been proved to be totally correct when he described the emerging losses on US sub-prime in early 2007 as a 'Minsky moment' that would lead to sharp contracting of global credit. There are many others. I would put three of the banking economists whose work I most admire – Raghuram Rajan and Luigi Zingales, both of Chicago Business School, and Carmen Reinhardt of the University of Maryland – in this mainstream group.

There are also a number of excellent books articulating this mainstream thinking. Martin Wolf's *Fixing Global Finance* (Yale University Press, 2009), a comprehensive discussion of the macroeconomics of financial crises, persuasively argues that most recent financial crises, including that now faced by the United States, are rooted in large-scale unsustainable levels of international borrowing. Recently republished is Hyman Minsky's 1986 book, *Stabilizing an Unstable Economy* (McGraw-Hill, 2008), arguing that unregulated provision of credit creates a fundamental macroeconomic instability in the free-market economy and describing the characteristic build-up of the credit cycle. Minsky wrote for academics and students of economics, not for a general readership, but even the non-specialist can learn a lot from his Chapter 9, 'Financial Commitments and Instability', with its classic discussion of how investment financing shifts from cautious 'hedge' finance to speculative finance (where cash flows repay interest but not principal) and Ponzi finance (where new borrowing is required to repay even interest payments). It is a sign of how far professional opinion has moved in the past two years that Minsky can now be regarded as mainstream, since within the economics profession he is seen as one of the leading figures of the 'heterodox' tradition that rejects much of the standard macroeconomic analysis supporting the policies of finance ministries and central banks around the world.

Other recent informative and lively books in this mainstream tradition are George Cooper's *The Origin of Financial Crises* (Vintage, 2008), developing the thesis that asset bubbles and unsustainable credit expansion have occurred because of the failure of central banks to prick asset and credit bubbles, and Robert Shiller's *Irrational Exuberance* (Princeton University Press, 2nd edn, 2005), an admirably clear presentation of a massive body of research evidence, supporting the view that stock prices and house prices are prone to irrational

self-fuelling and ultimately unsustainable bubbles, driven by underlying cultural and psychological factors. Shiller has supplemented
this work with his short, elegant and passionate book *The Subprime
Solution: How Today's Global Financial Crisis Happened, and What
to Do about It* (Princeton University Press, 2008), stressing the irrational nature of the US housing bubble and the need for public action
to prevent a collapse of mortgage credit and avoid damaging systemic
economic consequences from the puncturing of this bubble.

Another thought-provoking contribution is Graham Turner's *The
Credit Crunch* (Pluto Press, 2008). Like Wolf, he places the credit
crisis in the context of the globalization of the past twenty years, but
he emphasizes instead the political economics of reliance on consumer
borrowing to finance the import of manufactured goods from low-
cost exporting nations, hence protecting the real incomes of domestic
wage earners from the negative impact of increasing global competition for unskilled labour.

What about the views of economists such as myself who are in the
other group, those who see this crisis as much a crisis of confidence
as a crisis of poor asset quality? There are many respected economists who look at the crisis this way. In this group I would include
Laurence Kotlikoff and Perry Mehrling (my own co-authors in some
short pieces on the crisis, developing the argument in favour of
government-backed insurance of extreme systemic credit losses as a
stabilizer in the current crisis), Viral Acharya, Michael Bordo, Marcus
Brunnermeier, Ricardo Caballero, Tim Congdon, Brandon Davies,
Harold James, Stephen King, Paul Krugman, Rick Mishkin, John
Muellbauer, Avinash Persaud, Nouriel Roubini, Luigio Spavento and
Michael Spence.

Thus it transpires that a large proportion, perhaps even a majority,
of informed economists who have closely studied the new credit instruments and their role in the crisis share my belief that this is to a large
extent a crisis of confidence, as well as of underlying asset quality.
However, this group cannot be labelled mainstream, since theirs is *not*
the view shared by most policymakers, nor does it get much coverage
in the newspapers, on television or radio or in the online media. The
media are dominated by the mainstream view that this is a crisis of
poor lending decisions and too much bank borrowing. The alternative view does not get much space, even in the specialist media. There
have been relatively few articles in this vein in the *Financial Times* or

the *Wall Street Journal*. Even *The Economist* magazine, one of whose first editors was the leading nineteenth-century analyst of such crises of confidence in banks, Walter Bagehot, has given little space to this alternative interpretation of the crisis.

One of the main goals of this book is to redress the balance, presenting and articulating the alternative view of the crisis to the mainstream but pessimistic account that dominates the general and specialist media. Policymakers, journalists and general readers should be aware of these arguments in favour of viewing the current economic situation as a *temporary* and *avoidable* collapse of confidence, one that can be reversed by appropriate government policy at little cost to taxpayers. The notes of further reading to remaining chapters are largely devoted entirely to this other point of view.

While they differ on the fundamental value of bank assets, there is greater consensus on policy. Most exponents of what I have labelled the 'mainstream' view on the quality of bank assets, for example Martin Wolf or Robert Shiller, and all those adopting the 'alternative' view stress the need to use public funds to support the supply of mortgage and bank credit. The differences are on how exactly this should be done. Proposals include government and central bank lending, guarantees of bank credit, publicly funded resolution of troubled banks imposing losses on bond and shareholders, and insurance (for some appropriate premium) of various bank assets. References to some of this work are provided after the concluding chapter.

1 | *Where did all the money go? An analysis of the causes and cure of the current global banking crisis*

A major cause of the current global financial crisis has been maturity mismatch – too much short-term borrowing in order to finance long-term bank loans. There were serious fundamental problems as well: rapid credit growth and a deterioration in standards of loan assessment, resulting in banks holding many low-quality assets. But these fundamental problems do not explain the depth of the current crisis, which has been greatly amplified by investor panic and withdrawal of these short-term funds.

This chapter is an overview of this argument. Banks have relied on mortgage and other loan-backed securities to finance their loan portfolios, either by selling these securities outright or using them as collateral for short-term borrowing. Other banks have acted as wholesale intermediaries, purchasing the new instruments for trading or investment and financing these holdings using short-term borrowing. Relatively few of these securities were sold to long-term investors.

This short-term wholesale borrowing successfully underpinned the credit boom, until rising losses on US sub-prime lending undermined confidence in the mortgage-backed and other structured securities that were used as collateral for this borrowing. Now banks can no longer 'rent' the money they need to lend. Their access to wholesale funding has declined further as the value of the structured credit instruments on bank balance sheets has collapsed, further undermining investor confidence in banks.

Central bank liquidity provision has not solved this problem. Commercial banks have substantially increased their borrowing from central banks, as a substitute for borrowing from money markets or simply to increase their reserves with the central bank, but loans from central banks are strictly rationed through regular auctions (banks cannot invite the central bank to make offers of funds in the same way that they invite money-market participants to offer funds). The result is that bank balance sheets are now extremely liquid (central bank lending means that they have ample reserves available to meet payments obligations), but their access to funding remains limited because of the illiquidity of structured credit markets. This has started a snowball of reduced credit, declining economic activity and worsening prospects for returns on lending. As a result, despite falling interest rates and the extensive financial support of governments and central banks around the world, banks have been reducing their lending as much as possible.

This is not the usual explanation of the crisis. The commonly held interpretation is that the contraction of bank lending is a reaction to a previous unsustainable credit boom, to excessive indebtedness and to the resulting poor quality of bank assets. Yes, there was too much lending and much of it was poorly assessed. But this needs to be put in a proper perspective. Provided we avoid a new great depression, most bank borrowers can service their loans. Even if we do experience an economic slump of that magnitude, the majority of the mortgage-backed securities and other new credit instruments are not at great risk of default. Their valuations have fallen because of problems of funding and illiquidity, not underlying credit losses, because of investor panic, not fundamentals. The collapse of these valuations and the resulting withdrawal of funding is a central part of the credit contraction.

This is good news for policymakers. It is very much easier for them to stem a panic than it is to deal with underlying fundamental credit impairment. To the extent that the problems of the banks are due to lack of trust, confidence and funding, they can be addressed by focusing government and central bank policy on supporting good-quality but undervalued bank assets. This is not the same as the suggestion made by many commentators of financing a 'bad bank' to take all the poor-quality assets off bank balance sheets. Purchasing bad assets exposes taxpayers to substantial risk and it is very difficult to work out an appropriate price. Much better first to restore bank balance sheets by supporting good-quality but undervalued assets, because this earns a profit instead of being a burden on taxpayers.

There are several ways of doing this. Central banks can directly purchase senior tranches of structured securities (as Chapter 4 explains, the AAA senior tranches of most of these securities even now are very safe from default). Government can provide insurance against extreme losses, either on loan-backed securities or on loan portfolios. Such support not only directly supports bank balance sheets, it also helps to restore liquidity to the markets for senior structured credit securities, which will in turn reopen bank funding markets.

Purchase and insurance of good-quality assets will not be enough on its own. There was also a lot of poor-quality lending, and the balance sheets of some banks, those that have made the worst lending decisions, are in such a poor state that taxpayers will have to bail them out in order to prevent their collapse. But, provided all banks are given liquidity and funding support, the overall costs to taxpayers will not be large and a major depression will be averted. The key lesson to learn from the crisis is something we should already have been aware of from the stock market crash of 1987, from the Asian crisis and from many other financial panics. Financial markets are inherently unstable, veering from excessive optimism to excessive pessimism. This implies that the more banks rely on short-term wholesale funding, the more protection must be in place to safeguard banks from these excessive changes in market sentiment. Banks have always tended to increase their lending too much in booms and to reduce their lending too much in recessions. Withdrawal of short-term wholesale funding has exaggerated that tendency. Government must replace the lost bank funding in order to avoid an economic collapse, and in future we need either to wean banks off short-term funding or to provide protections that will maintain that funding even when the going gets tough.

Banks create money by lending

Banks create money by lending. During the credit boom they lent a great deal and now they are lending less than before. This is why there is now less money for households and companies to spend.

A simple thought experiment illustrates this point. Consider a bank providing a customer with a loan. It does not matter much which bank; this could be Barclays in the United Kingdom, Commerzbank in Germany, BNP Paribas in France, Wells Fargo in the United States or one of many hundreds of other institutions around the world, both large and small.

Suppose, for example, that BNP Paribas is making a loan of €12,000 for a car purchase to M. Jacques Laurent, a customer in Lyon. Once the loan is approved M. Laurent's account in the Rue de la République branch is credited with the €12,000. At the same time the bank has acquired a new asset, the €12,000 loan to M. Laurent. By this routine act, approving a loan, BNP Paribas has created an additional €12,000 of money that did not exist before.[1]

All banks make loans in this way every day. The money may not necessarily appear in the customer's account as it did for M. Laurent; it might be transferred directly to someone else, for example to a retailer or to the seller of a house. But in every case by making a loan a bank creates money.

Loans are of course also being repaid all the time, reducing the stock of bank money. Customers who have borrowed money make regular repayments of the outstanding principal. M. Laurent's €12,000 loan might be repaid over five years, in which case M. Laurent will pay back the principal at an average rate of €200 per month (usually the repayment of the principal is more rapid towards the end of the lending period). Banks therefore need to keep lending to prevent a reduction of money and credit.

Funding is a key constraint on lending

One key constraint on bank lending is the prospective return on the loan. In an economic boom, when the prospects for repayment are good, banks are happy to lend money, sometimes even to quite risky borrowers. In a recession banks are much more reluctant to lend, although they may still accept some risk of default if the interest rate on the loan is high enough. What this means is that bankers' perceptions about the future (or what might also be called confidence or, in Keynes's phrase, 'animal spirits', although he was really thinking about the perceptions of returns on business investment) are a major determinant of the growth of money and credit.

There is also another key constraint on bank lending, one that has been especially important in this crisis. A bank will only offer a loan, such as the five-year loan to M. Laurent, if it is confident that it can also 'fund' the loan – that is, keep enough money on deposit in the

---

[1]   This account of money creation, which is essentially the same as that of Kaldor, is radically different from the 'money multiplier' described in all the money and banking textbooks, according to which bank money is a multiple of bank reserves. Chapter 9 explains why that textbook description, appropriate to in a world of commodity money standards such as the nineteenth-century gold and silver standards, no longer applies when, as today, money is 'fiat money', backed ultimately by the power of the state.

bank throughout the life of the loan at a cost that justifies making the loan in the first place. Normally, funding is simply a question of cost – banks routinely factor the 'cost of funding' into their lending decisions. But in this crisis banks have found themselves in a situation where they cannot be certain about obtaining funding at all.

To get a better understanding of the funding constraint, let's take this 'thought experiment' a little further. Suppose that all the banking in a country were provided by a single monopoly bank (this is not so far from the situation that pertained in the centrally planned economies of the Soviet bloc and communist China, except that then all the lending decisions were determined by the central plan). In this case the simultaneous creation of the loan and the deposit is the end of the story. Since there is only a single bank the money that has been created always remains with the bank. The loan is 'self-funding', and the only limit on this monopoly bank's willingness to lend is whether it believes the loan offers a high enough return to justify the risk of credit loss.

This point, that bank lending is 'self-funding' remains true at the level of the entire banking system as a whole, even if many banks compete for deposits. Every loan creates its own deposit and the deposit must remain somewhere in the banking system. Now, however, individual banks face an additional constraint on their lending. Not only must their loans offer a high enough return to compensate for default risk, the individual bank must also be able to attract enough funding in the markets for retail and wholesale deposits to finance the loan. This funding could be in the form of retail deposits from bank customers, wholesale money from large institutional investors or 'interbank' lending from other banks. If for any reason customers, investors or other banks are unwilling to provide these funds, the bank will be unable to fund its lending. Thus when banks compete for funds it is critical for a bank to maintain the confidence of all those on whom it relies for funding – retail depositors, 'money market' investors and other banks.

What about if banks compete in an open economy, where goods and services are both exported and purchased from abroad? This does not change matters much; it just means that, at least for countries that are substantial net borrowers from abroad, the markets for deposits and money involve governments, banks and companies from other countries, who end up holding bank deposits or other financial claims denominated in domestic currency.[2] An example would be, say, a Japanese exporter selling video gaming consoles in Canada who ends up holding balances of Canadian dollars from the sale of its consoles to wholesalers around Canada. Once again, for the banking system as a whole all the lending is self-funding. Loans made to consumers to buy video gaming consoles end up, in part, as non-resident deposits with the banking sector. But it can be difficult to persuade foreign residents to continuing holding domestic bank deposits, and so the need to obtain funding imposes a greater discipline on bank loan decisions in countries where household and corporate savings rates are low and banks raise much of their funding from foreign residents.

Renting money: how banks have come to depend on short-term wholesale funding

Banks prefer retail funding when they can get it. Retail depositors often complain about banks, but only a few are prepared to spend much time looking around for better deals. As long as the quality of service is acceptable, retail customers tend to stick with their existing banks and not investigate whether they might get a better deal elsewhere. Moreover, retail depositors rarely pay much attention to whether the bank itself is earning healthy returns on its lending or only just managing to turn a profit. As a result, retail deposits from established customers – so-called 'core' retail deposits – are a relatively inexpensive and stable source of bank funds.

While existing retail funds are inexpensive, getting in new retail funding is costly and difficult. Bringing in additional core retail funds requires substantial investment, both in marketing and in the upgrading of bank channels such as call centres or bank branches and equipment to service the depositors. As lending has outstripped the supply of deposits in many countries, banks have turned increasingly to short-term wholesale funding – that is, to renting money from global financial markets.

Banking statistics give some idea of the magnitude of the shift from retail to short-term wholesale funding. In the United Kingdom

---

[2] I am here assuming a pure floating exchange rate, so that neither government nor the central bank finances these net exports out of foreign-exchange reserves, giving foreign residents foreign currency in exchange for domestic currency.

the ratio of retail bank deposits to total bank lending fell from just over 100 per cent in 1970 to only 50 per cent by the middle of 2007 – nowadays for every £1 of lending UK banks 'rent' 50p of funding from wholesale financial markets. A similar shift has taken place in most large developed countries. Retail deposits, as a percentage of total bank lending, fell over the same period from 102 per cent to 76 per cent in France, from 110 per cent to 61 per cent in Italy and from 136 per cent to 77 per cent in Australia. Canada also experienced a large decline, from 177 per cent to 112 per cent but, as this figure for 2007 reveals, their banks still have a relatively large retail deposit base relative to their total lending.

The increasing reliance of banks on wholesale funding has a macroeconomic dimension. It is the flip side of what are known as the global current-account imbalances, with large amounts of saving in some surplus countries, such as China, Japan and Germany, matching the borrowing in deficit countries such as the United States, the United Kingdom and Spain. Wholesale borrowing by banks plays a key role in channelling this international flow of savings to borrowing households in deficit countries.

Among banks in the largest G8 developed economies, only banks in Japan and in Germany have not experienced a major shift in funding from retail to wholesale sources. The ratios of retail bank deposits to total bank lending in Germany *rose* from 87 per cent in 1970 to 94 per cent in 2007, and in Japan from 126 per cent to 143 per cent over the same period. It is no coincidence that the three G8 countries whose banks rely least on wholesale funding, Germany, Japan and Canada, are major exporters of manufactured goods or (in the case of Canada) of natural resources. Unlike the other five G8 countries, all three have enjoyed current-account surpluses.

Using loan-backed securities to raise wholesale funding

Wholesale funding is more expensive than retail and increases the risk of banking instability. Wholesale investors lend large sums of money and so will only lend when the interest rate is attractive. Moreover, and for good reason, wholesale funders are sceptical about the ability of bank management to manage their business and avoid major problems. Banks are exposed to many financial, operational and business risks, and they are also, in comparison with other large companies, rather opaque. It is not easy for an outsider to understand their financial statements or to work out where exactly they earn their profits. Serious problems do emerge from time to time, for example the notorious cases of rogue trading perpetrated by Nick Leeson (Barings), John Ruznick (Allied Irish) and Jerome Kerviel (Société Générale). Because of this opaqueness wholesale funding is therefore usually only available for short maturities of up to about three months.

Such short-term wholesale funds are 'hot money' that can be withdrawn at the slightest provocation. This is why banks turned to the new structured credit instruments – that is, loans packaged into securities. Banks were effectively using their own loans as collateral for funding. This was rather like a high street shop pledging its own shelf inventory in order to obtain credit.

The analogy is not exact. The banks created pools of loans and bundled them up inside tradable mortgage- or asset-backed securities. The owner of these securities could not seize the bank loans if there was no repayment. What they had instead was a legal claim to the interest and principal payments due on the underlying loan pool. But this still gave the investors some confidence that they would be repaid. This meant that banks could attract and keep wholesale funds by selling or lending these loan-backed securities.

Some mortgage banks such as Countrywide in the United States and Northern Rock in the United Kingdom financed a very high proportion of their lending by selling these loan-backed securities. These are extreme examples, but most banks in countries with high levels of household borrowing also relied on loan-backed securities to obtain the funds for their lending.

Other banks used these securities in a quite different way, as buyers rather than sellers, acquiring large investment portfolios of mortgage-backed and other structured securities. Very often they took a 'hedge fund' approach to these investments, financing them using short-term wholesale funds, most often using so-called 'sale and repurchase agreements' or repo.

A repo works as follows. The bank that owns a mortgage-backed or other security agrees to sell it on a temporary basis to a 'hot money' investor, with an ironclad legal agreement to buy it back at a slightly higher price, say two weeks or one month later. This is, of course, equivalent to borrowing the money for two weeks or one month on a short-term secured basis. Such repo borrowing is now by far and away the most important form of short-term finance in modern financial markets. Banks, erroneously, assumed that repo finance collateralized against mortgage-backed securities would always be available. That proved not to be the case when investors lost confidence in these securities.

Another response to the shortage of bank retail funding has been to bypass altogether the role of banks in holding and funding loans, again using structured credit securities. A pool of loans, bought from banks or brokers, is bundled within a tradable security which can then be sold to banks or investors. This bypassing of banks has happened to only a small extent with retail loans (US sub-prime mortgage lending has been the main exception), but it has become a very important tool for the funding of corporate credit. Again, most of these securities were purchased by banks and were mostly funded using short-term 'hot money'.

Borrowing short and lending long

This practice, of borrowing short-term wholesale funds to finance portfolios of mortgage-backed and other structured securities, created substantial maturity mismatch. Banks were pursuing a very old banking stratagem, using relatively low-cost but unstable short-term borrowing to hold what turned out to be illiquid long-term securities. They thought they were safe. There appeared to be liquid markets in which these instruments could be bought and sold. As long as the long-term assets were liquid, short-term repo borrowing would always be available to finance them.

Banks and regulators alike failed to recognize the fallacy of composition on which this funding strategy rested. What was safe for an individual bank – borrowing short to hold long-term safe senior marketable structured credit securities – was far from safe for the banking sector as a whole. The ability of one bank to sell always depends on the presence of other banks willing to buy.

This then set in train the crisis that followed, a crisis characterized by what engineers call a 'positive feedback loop', when an initial disturbance has an effect which then feeds back, reinforcing the initial disturbance.

Figure 1.1 illustrates the damaging positive feedback that has undermined the world's banking system. In this figure there are in

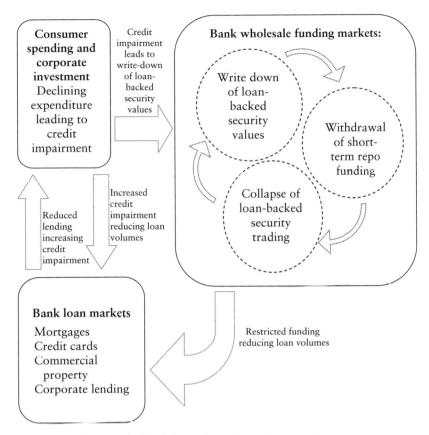

Figure 1.1. Positive feedback loops in bank funding and loan markets

fact *two* positive feedback loops, each reinforcing the other. The first positive feedback loop, on the left-hand side of the figure, is between the volume of lending and the levels of consumer expenditure and corporate investment. Lower lending leads to less consumer expenditure and corporate investment – that is, a recession. The recession increases credit impairment (the banker's shorthand for arrears on payments of loan interest and principal). Rising credit impairment makes bankers more concerned about the risk of default and so less willing to make loans. So bankers reduce lending further, deepening the recession.

The second positive feedback loop is within wholesale funding markets. Rising credit impairment leads to write-downs of the values of mortgage and other loan-backed securities. This write-down of value leads to a withdrawal of short-term repo funding. The withdrawal of repo funding leads to a collapse of trading, with no buyers and no sellers. The collapse of trading volumes leads to further writedowns in the values of the securities and further withdrawal of repo funding. The withdrawal of repo funding leads to a reduction of bank lending. The presence of this second feedback loop is what has made this banking crisis so different from previous crises.

The presence of this second positive feedback loop in bank wholesale funding markets has substantially increased bank write-downs. The initial disturbance was increasing credit impairment (arrears) on US sub-prime mortgage lending. Because of the positive feedback loop in wholesale funding markets and the consequent withdrawal of short-term funding, the value of mortgage-backed securities fell by much more than could be justified by the credit impairment. The increasing illiquidity of the markets for mortgage-backed and other structured securities meant that no one had much idea what the market value of these securities was, and accountancy procedures for 'marking to market' turned instead to using extremely conservative hypothetical valuations ('if you were to observe a trade of this security today, then what price might it trade at?'). Valuations fell markedly and investors suffered very large 'liquidity losses'. Eventually these losses will be recovered, since the valuations of most of these securities have fallen far below even the most pessimistic assessment of eventual repayment from the underlying loan pools. But banks will have to wait a long time for recovery, and in the meantime they have suffered much larger 'mark to market' write-downs on US sub-prime mortgage and other loan-backed securities than they ever thought possible.

This wholesale funding loop explains the global nature of the crisis, why the financial crisis and economic downturn is affecting banks in virtually all countries around the world at the same time. Many banks, notably in Germany, invested surplus retail funds in the high-yielding US mortgage-backed securities and the other structured credit products whose value has collapsed because of withdrawal of wholesale funding. Many other banks around the world relied on the issue of mortgage-backed and other loan-backed securities, in order to expand their lending and make up for a shortage of retail funding. Once the markets for these new issues closed, these banks with insufficient retail funds could no longer finance their lending.

This in turn created the global 'credit crunch', with banks unable to raise sufficient funding reducing lending, even to many good-quality borrowers who would normally face no difficulty in obtaining bank loans. These problems continued to mount in 2007 and 2008, causing 'runs' on banks as doubts about their ability to raise funding increased. At first this was limited to a few institutions. Then, in September and October 2008, as the macroeconomic situation deteriorated, investors began to worry about the possibility that many banks would become insolvent and the run spread to the entire global banking system. By late 2008 the only place from which many banks could borrow whole-sale funds was their central bank.

There are other feedback loops

Figure 1.1 deliberately, for the sake of clarity, oversimplifies. There are several other important feedback loops in bank lending, feedbacks referred to collectively as the 'credit cycle':

1. Lenders interpret low levels of loan default as an indication that their lending is low-risk, when in fact low defaults are due to the economic expansion and the general availability of credit, making it easier for borrowers to pay interest and also to refinance their lending and so stay current on their loans. As credit expansion and income growth slow, defaults rise and lenders suddenly realize that their lending is much riskier than they had believed. They thus begin to withdraw credit, refusing or limiting the amount of lending they provide to risky borrowers. This withdrawal of credit then amplifies the initial economic downturn. This is the first positive feedback loop, on the left of Figure 1.1.
2. This basic credit cycle was magnified by a weakening of controls and bank governance during the credit boom. Unscrupulous credit practices – for example offering loans to some US sub-prime mortgage borrowers who were clearly only able to repay this borrowing from capital gains on house price appreciation – became common. The credit cycle was also exaggerated by weaknesses of governance in some institutions, with senior management pursuing growth of earnings and stock valuations without proper regard for risk exposure.
3. A severe shortage of bank capital has amplified the credit cycle downswing. Capital is the difference between the value of bank assets and liabilities. It is the main protection against the threat of

insolvency. In the downturn losses mount, reducing bank capital, and a substantial decline in bank capital can force banks to reduce their lending further. This is partly because of bank regulations. Banks are required to have certain minimum levels of capital to support their lending. It is also because banks with low capital are at greater risk of insolvency and struggle to raise funds. This aspect of the credit cycle has been further exaggerated this time by the 'pro-cyclicality' of regulatory capital requirements, with the new Basel II measures of required regulatory capital increasing sharply as asset quality deteriorates during the credit downturn, and by the excess leverage of many banks in the upswing, especially investment banks that had come to supply a great deal of the new credit.

4. Yet further amplification of the credit cycle has come from the rise and then subsequent fall in prices of land and housing and financial assets. During the boom high-risk borrowers obtained credit against the expectation that prices would continue to rise further. As prices fall this supply of credit vanishes. Furthermore, asset price falls reduce the value of collateral that borrowers can pledge against their lending, so further reducing the supply and increasing the cost of credit.

5. Similarly, household incomes and corporate revenues rose during the economic upswing, making it easier for them to borrow money, but are now falling during the economic downturn, restricting their access to credit (a mechanism that economists refer to as the 'financial accelerator').

6. There is another, more technical, aspect of the credit cycle. Banks, regulators and rating agencies have increasingly been relying on quantitative models to assess their exposure to credit risk. These models are still in their infancy and, compared with the risks of foreign exchange, government bonds and equities, there are relatively short runs of data on which these models can be tested. Regrettably, most of these models shared a common weakness. In the data they have used there are relatively few loan defaults and low levels of loan losses, leading the modellers to assume mistakenly that it was very unlikely that many borrowers would default at the same time. The models failed to recognize that in a deep recession such as we are now experiencing, the rate of loan defaults and loan losses can rise sharply, resulting in much bigger losses than these models predict.

These factors have all played a role in the current crisis. The purpose of Figure 1.1 is to highlight a distinguishing feature of the current crisis: the much increased reliance of banks on wholesale funding. This has magnified the other feedbacks and resulted in a much more amplified credit cycle than usual. Banks face funding difficulties in every credit downturn, but the funding difficulties in this credit downturn have been much more severe than in the past.

Dealing with the aftermath of a credit cycle

How should policymakers deal with a credit cycle? It is best if financial regulation and monetary policy restrain unsustainable credit growth, so avoiding the possibility of a severe credit contraction. But it is never easy to determine, at the time, whether credit growth is unsustainable or not.

Many have accused the US Federal Reserve, under its then chairman Alan Greenspan, of having encouraged an unsustainable credit boom in the years 2002–7, when interest rates were kept at very low levels following the puncturing of the 'dot-com' stock market boom in 2000, the emergence of the accounting scandals at Enron, Worldcom and other giant firms and the 9/11 terrorist attacks on the United States in 2001. With the benefit of hindsight we can see that this policy did reignite another unsustainable asset price bubble, this time in US housing markets, but there was no obvious reason to expect as sharp a credit contraction as we have now experienced.

Financial authorities around the world have acquired considerable experience in dealing with the aftermath of such credit booms (Chapter 3 looks at some of these episodes). Not every credit cycle leads to widespread bank failure. Often credit booms and the subsequent bust are small enough to be dealt with by banks on their own without extensive intervention by the financial authorities. An example is the pronounced UK credit and house price boom in the late 1980s, followed by a sharp contraction in lending and rising bank loan losses in the early 1990s. A number of UK banks, notably Barclays, lost money, mainly on small business and property lending. But the only bank failures were a few, relatively small specialized institutions that relied on relatively expensive wholesale funding.

Sometimes, however, the financial authorities must intervene in the aftermath of a credit crisis, in order to prevent the failure of banks with substantial retail deposits or an important role in the provision of business credit. As Chapter 3 describes, the financial authorities in Sweden, Norway, Finland and Japan faced just this challenge in the aftermath of their own pronounced credit booms of the late 1980s. The usually accepted blueprint for dealing with such episodes, where bank assets turn out to be of low economic value, is a combination of transfer of the poor-quality assets such as non-performing loans into a 'bad bank' accompanied by a recapitalization of those banks that are close to insolvency.

The transfer of assets into a bad bank provides time and opportunity to recover as much value as possible from the impaired loans. New capital for recapitalizing banks might sometimes be obtained from private sources, but more often it takes the form of government funds. Once bank balance sheets are repaired then the banks can return to their normal business of lending and taking deposits.

This sounds straightforward, but it is far from being the medicine that cures all banking crises. The key practical problem is valuing the loans or other assets transferred into the proposed bad bank. Shareholder rights must be respected. If a bank remains under private control then its bad assets must be purchased voluntarily (or if there is compulsory purchase then shareholders must be compensated for the difference between the amount paid for the assets and their fair market value).

Ironically, the transfer of assets to such a bad bank is very much easier in the extreme situation when many banks have entirely failed and have to be taken into public ownership in order to continue as going concerns. Shareholder claims are then worthless and, since the government inevitably ends up protecting retail depositors and compensating wholesale creditors generously in order to maintain confidence in the banking system, the taxpayer is the only remaining claimant on the bad assets. Provided that government solvency is not in doubt, valuation of the bad assets is then irrelevant. The taxpayer can wait for recovery of whatever money can be obtained from the bad loans without needing to know a current market value.

This credit cycle is different

An important difference today from most previous banking crises, for example those in Scandinavia, is that this credit crisis has taken place at the very peak of the business cycle, resulting in a rapid shift from credit expansion to credit contraction – that is, the banking crisis has triggered the downturn rather than the downturn triggering the banking crisis. In the Scandinavian crises it was the other way around. External trade shocks and a slowdown of the previous economic boom led to falling output and rising unemployment. Only later did these problems result in high levels of losses on bank loans. By the time the governments of Finland, Norway and Sweden intervened to protect their banking systems, their economies were already beginning to recover, boosted by substantial exchange-rate depreciations.

The current credit contraction has also been surprisingly severe, relative to the size of the preceding credit expansion. This can be explained by the withdrawal of 'hot money' – the investor panic underlying the wholesale funding loop shown on the right-hand side of Figure 1.1. This mechanism was more powerful than in most previous credit contractions (although, as Chapter 3 explains, a similar run of 'hot money' greatly exaggerated the Asian banking crisis of 1997).

The wholesale funding feedback loop on the right-hand side of the figure also helps to explain why the credit downturn has been more global than any before (banks in almost every country of the globe were exposed to mortgage-backed securities and other structured instruments, as investors, as issuers or often as both).

The global nature of the crisis also made the traditional credit impairment feedback loop on the left-hand side of Figure 1.1 more powerful than usual. When this feedback loop operates in a single region or country it is relatively benign. Bank lending and economic activity in other regions or countries maintains economic activity and loan quality. A single country or region can also always devalue its exchange rate in order to offset a slowdown in domestic demand. When, as now, this feedback loop operates globally, the stabilizing impact of expenditure from other regions and countries is removed and exchange-rate depreciation does not offset a global credit slump.

Because this credit cycle is different, the Scandinavian blueprint – recognition of bad loans and recapitalization – is unlikely to end the banking problems, even if the thorny problems of valuing the bad assets of banks can be overcome. The reason is that the value of bank assets will continue falling until we reach the bottom of the downturn, and that is still many months, if not years, away. Thus without a crystal ball no one can say how much banks are going to lose, and there is no way to decide what to pay for bank assets or how much recapitalization they might need.

This time the problem is the scale of future losses, not the extent of past losses. This suggests that policy must focus on potential future losses rather than already crystallized past losses, and this would seem to require an insurance approach, capping the amount that banks can lose, not providing upfront capitalization.

The problem is lack of trust and confidence, not the new loan-backed securities

Much of the blame for the crisis has been put on the new credit instruments, including the mortgage-backed and other loan-backed securities. These are often described by the rather unhelpful and indiscriminate label 'toxic assets', because the unexpected declines in their mark to market valuations have undermined bank balance sheets.

A lot did go wrong with these new products. Banks did not understand them as well as they should have. Some of the restructured credit securities were overly complex and seem to have been created purely for the purpose of confusing traders and investors. If so, they were only too successful. Much of the losses reported by the large banks UBS and Merrill Lynch arose because they held large portfolios of these especially risky 'restructured' instruments, originally rated as AAA but which turned out to be unsound.

Structured financial innovations were also used to increase leverage for traders and hedge funds. Traders always want the greatest possible exposure to the upside. Such leverage increases returns when the economy is doing well and maximum leverage is therefore usually seen as a good thing. But this leverage also exacerbates losses when trading positions lose money. Leverage of this kind was the business justification for the various 'transaction deals' described later in Chapter 5.

Does this mean that all the new credit instruments are all unsound? Not at all. As Chapters 4 and 5 document, most structured securities are safe.

It is often asserted that structured credit products lack transparency. This is not correct either. This view confuses transparency and illiquidity. Structured credit is now very hard either to buy or sell (illiquidity). But most structures are simple and well documented (transparency). There is a wealth of information – on these securities and the performance of the underlying loan pools and credit obligations – for anyone who has access to a Bloomberg screen or similar information service.

Some suggest that the problems of structured credit are due to the failures of ratings agencies, which were paid by issuers for providing ratings and were as a result biased or even corrupted. This accusation does not square well with the facts either. In fact many ratings of structured credit securities stand up fairly well to close scrutiny. Even more than two years after the beginning of the US housing market downturn, there has been little credit impairment on the large majority of the rated structured paper measured by dollar value, the highest grade senior AAA paper issued by the more 'vanilla', that is, less complex, structures. Most of this structured paper is still very far from default. As chapters 4 and 5 explain, this is because the safe senior paper has a massive amount of credit protection. Even if as much as 20 or 25 per cent of principal on the underlying loan pool is lost, the senior AAA paper is still fully repaid.

The rating agencies did make serious rating errors on more complex restructured securities and on the lower-grade paper of the vanilla structures. Much of this suspect paper has been subject to substantial downward re-ratings. But this paper accounts for only a small part of the overall market and of overall bank write-downs. The rating agencies also failed to appreciate that their rating methodology for lower-quality mezzanine and junior tranches of credit structures yielded ratings that were much more likely to be downgraded in a recession than were equivalently rated corporate bonds. This was a mistake rather than a misrepresentation, but investors should have been warned beforehand and the failure to do so has weakened investor faith in all structured credit ratings.

Another misleading assertion is that banks were pursuing a flawed new business model, 'originate and distribute', in which they no longer retained exposure to loans packaged and sold to investors. It is suggested that there was a major deterioration in loan underwriting standards during the credit boom because banks no longer had incentives to maintain adequate underwriting standards or properly monitor lenders when they did not retain exposure. It is also suggested that this new business model is flawed, so that banks must return to traditional 'buy and hold' banking in which all loans are held on a balance sheet and funded out of retail deposits.

This interpretation, with its implication that the development of the new credit instruments and securitization markets must now be reversed, is difficult to sustain. Chapters 4, 5 and 6 provide detailed discussion and illustration of the way in which banks have used these markets and instruments. In most securitizations banks retained a large part of the risk for themselves, so that they continued to have incentives to maintain loan standards.

It is true that in the 'transaction deals' described in Chapter 5 banks did not retain very much risk, but in many of these cases they were buying tradable securitized corporate loans or bond exposure subject to pretty rigorous credit assessment by both banks and rating agencies. There was weakening of underwriting standards in some of these transaction deals, especially those used for financing sub-prime mortgage lending, resulting in the infamous NINJA (no income no job no assets) loans, but this was a relatively small problem in the broader context of the global credit boom.

So, contrary to the widespread impression conveyed by many finance and business journalists, most of the senior AAA structured securities are still extremely safe. Provided we avoid a worldwide economic collapse, almost all this better-quality paper will be fully repaid. That is, in fact, the whole point of structuring: to separate the credit risk and manufacture safe, effectively credit-risk-free securities. The central problem is not with the instruments themselves but with the flawed funding strategy, the maturity mismatch where banks have borrowed in the short term to hold long-term securities, and the resulting exposure of banks to the withdrawal of short-term 'hot money'. Thus a key step in solving the current problem of the banking system is overcoming the problems of confidence and illiquidity that currently prevent banks using these funding tools and are driving the global contraction of bank lending.

Borrowing and saving in the short and the long run

Is a pronounced credit cycle driven by funding problems really the driver of the banking crisis or are there other explanations? Another cause was the high and unsustainable levels of household borrowing in English-speaking and other current-account-deficit economies. It has been clear for some years that an increase of household savings ratios in these countries was unavoidable. Policymakers could not always rely on lower interest rates stimulating higher consumer expenditure in order to maintain growth of output and incomes.

This is correct, but it is a mistake to conclude, as many do, that we need to have *rapid* reductions of borrowing and increases of saving to deal with the crisis. This suggestion confuses the immediate short-run response to the crisis with the necessary long-run adjustment. Eventually savings ratios – that is, the proportion of household income that is saved in the form of bank deposits or other financial investments – have to rise substantially in the United States, the United Kingdom and other countries, perhaps by about 6 per cent of total household incomes. But household savings ratios do not have to rise by 6 per cent in a single year, and the adjustment does not have to be made entirely through lower consumption; it can also be achieved by increasing incomes.

Rapid reduction of consumption is in any case an ineffective way of increasing household savings ratios. The reason is the 'paradox of thrift' highlighted by Keynes in his General Theory of Employment, Interest and Money. If everyone saves more, as many are now doing, then the consequence is a sharp decline in the demand for goods and services and falling incomes and employment. The decline of income may go so far that the ratio of savings to income, the 'savings ratio', hardly changes. This paradox of thrift is another example of a 'fallacy of composition', rather like the illusion of liquidity in structured credit markets. What is true for an individual household – that saving more will help stabilize their income and borrowing – is not necessarily true for households as a whole. It is in this sense that the work of Keynes remains relevant today. To avoid a collapse of output and incomes we need, in the short term, more rather than less expenditure. This will provide the time for adjustment to higher expenditure in the surplus countries and higher saving in the deficit countries and for the damaging feedback loops in the banking system to be controlled.

Fiscal stimulus: an appropriate temporary response

The US and other governments are now turning to fiscal stimulus, reducing taxes and increasing government spending, in order to combat the global recession. This is an appropriate temporary response to large-scale falls in consumer and other private spending. Fiscal policy already responds to such spending declines through so called 'automatic stabilizers', the increased government borrowing that occurs when falls of spending and employment result in lower tax receipts and higher expenditure on social security. This increased government expenditure and reduction of taxes help to protect private-sector incomes from the decline of private expenditure. Additional discretionary fiscal stimulus packages, with further tax cuts or government spending increases, may be useful to further offset declining private expenditure.

Measures to reduce the rate of foreclosures can slow down the rate of house price falls. Now, when there is substantial overcapacity in the construction industry, is an opportunity for programmes of publicly financed social housing construction. The taxpayer will get much better value for money than at times when there is no spare capacity.

But fiscal stimulus is not a panacea. Governments, just like households finances, cannot borrow on a large scale indefinitely (as economists say, they are subject to long-run balance sheet constraints). A fiscal stimulus, whether automatic or discretionary, has only a *temporary* impact on expenditure and incomes, an impact that is subsequently reversed when, as must eventually happen, taxes are raised or temporary programmes of government expenditure ended. There are some permanent government expenditure programmes that are different – for example, spending on infrastructure or on education that has a large positive impact on future output and income and so largely pays for itself. Such programmes can be sustained for a long time, but these types of expenditure cannot be easily used to counter a temporary economic downturn; they take a great deal of time to get right and if they are worth doing at all then they should be taking place already.

Since the impact of a fiscal stimulus is temporary it is not, on its own, a sufficient policy response to a severe economic downturn. An analogy is often made between the impact of a fiscal stimulus on an economy and the effect of passengers getting out and pushing a car with a flat battery in order to start the engine. A number of politicians, including the incoming US president Barack Obama, have described the purpose of a fiscal stimulus to 'jump-start' the economy. But such a jump-start is only effective if the increased spending created by the fiscal stimulus is self-sustaining and continues once the original stimulus is withdrawn. So a fiscal stimulus must be followed up by further policy measures to fix banks and credit markets and so ensure that there is long-term sustainable growth of output and expenditure.

Restoring faith in banks and restarting bank lending

What has led the recent global economic boom to change so rapidly into global economic bust? This question is central. Politicians and journalists, just like bankers and investors, are affected by the herd instinct. Now, in the face of a big shock – the biggest economic shock of our lifetimes – they are all running in the same direction at the same time. Without pausing to consider the facts carefully, they assert that the global economic boom was a pure credit bubble, an unwise and unsustainable extension of mortgage and consumer credit by a grossly mismanaged banking system interested only in short-term profit. Yes, many loans will not be repaid, but this does not mean that all the new credit instruments were unsound, that all the lending was unwise and that all the debt must now be unwound. On the contrary government must now do all that it can to maintain credit availability, through purchase and insurance of undervalued assets and generous bank recapitalization.

There is also a great deal of understandable anger about high bank salaries and bank bonuses. There are really two separate issues here, although they are often confused. One is a concern that bank compensation packages have offered too great a reward for high returns without any offsetting penalty for poor returns, thus encouraging traders, loan officers and senior executives to take unnecessary risks. The other issue is more atavistic: jealousy of high levels of remuneration and anger that such highly paid people should have led the world economy into such a severe economic downturn. This jealousy is creating an extraordinarily damaging political dynamic, with politicians of all stripes opposing the provision of financial support to the banking system essential for limiting the scale of the economic downturn.

Shareholders and regulators have been aware of the incentive problems in bank payment and bonus packages for years. They arise not just in credit trading but in equities, corporate finance, retail savings products and all other areas of bank activities. Thus there were already steps being taken, even before the crisis, to ensure that bonuses were deferred or paid in the form of stock with restrictions on sale. If there is an underlying incentive problem that has not yet been adequately addressed it is in the asset management industry, where compensation depends entirely on short-term portfolio performance. The consequence is excessive focus on quarterly earnings, which are most easily increased in a rising market simply by increasing leverage.

The overall level of banking salaries and bonuses is a sensitive issue, and the industry has done little to respond to public concern. But it must be recognized that, while concern about bankers' remuneration is understandable and legitimate, it is a longer-term issue that is best considered carefully and at length once we have recovered from the crisis.

We must all hope that politicians and policymakers will come round to a more constructive answer than simply attacking the banks. There was nothing fundamentally wrong with most of the new credit instruments and, while there were many errors of credit assessment, much of the lending during the boom was sound. Many previous episodes of financial instability – the stock market crash of 1987, the Asian crisis of 1997, the collapse of LTCM in 1998 – illustrate the excessive overreaction of short-term 'hot money' to bad news. A similar market overreaction is behind the current economic downturn. Banks relied on unstable short-term wholesale money to finance their holdings of the new credit instruments, 'hot money' which is no longer available because of the fear of extreme loss. The consequence has been a collapse in confidence, among both investors and banks themselves, in all forms of credit exposure.

What is required in this situation is leadership. In the midst of a blind panic, in which no one will put money in many banks (except retail depositors backed by government deposit insurance) and when banks avoid any lending that appears to be associated with the slightest risk, government must take the lead and provide the long-term money that private investors are too frightened to supply. This is not money thrown away.

This is using the vast potential resources of the state to support good-quality but severely undervalued bank assets, either by outright purchase or insurance guarantees, and where necessary recapitalizing insolvent institutions to prevent a further knock-on impact on customers and financial markets.

One goal must be to break into the feedback loop between the valuation of structured credit products and short-term wholesale funding illustrated in Figure 1.1. This can be done by the government underwriting extreme risks, providing 'disaster insurance' on the now illiquid senior tranches of structured credit products. This way, although it will take time, liquidity can be restored to the markets for these securities and the outflow of short-term wholesale funding can be restored.

As the downturn of the credit cycle has intensified, especially the feedback lower lending → credit impairment → lower lending, then banks themselves as well as wholesale investors are becoming increasingly fearful of extreme losses. Banks are becoming unwilling to lend, not because of lack of funding but simply because almost all loans look too risky in such a difficult economic environment. To restart bank lending in this environment it is likely that there will have to be extensive bank recapitalization and disaster insurance will have to be taken further, applied to pools of assets that remain on bank balance sheets as well as to securitized pools of loans, and to new lending as well as to existing loans.

Does this approach not risk the loss of huge sums of taxpayer's money? No, not as long as the main focus is on guaranteeing only the good assets. There is a possibility of very large 'hidden' exposures that are not revealed in bank accounting statements, but because they are hidden if they emerge they will not be covered. For those assets that are insured, most of the risk is still carried by the banks and their shareholders; taxpayer money covers only an extreme loss. But once the situation is stabilized and banks can begin the slow and painful process of rebuilding investor trust, then there will be economic recovery, disaster will be avoided and taxpayers will not have a large bill to pay.

Is this really the correct direction for policymaking – giving money to the bankers of Wall Street who caused the crisis in the first place? Is it not better to spend the money on Main Street instead, so directly helping the victims of the crisis? This sentiment and the desire to punish are perfectly understandable. But this is not the best way to fix our current economic problems. Yes, it was a mistake to finance the structured securities using short-term funding. Mistakes of credit assessment were made. But government cannot take over the job of banks and make all the crucial commercial decisions about who gets credit and who does not. It is time to move on, to make it clear that government stands behind the banks so that they can begin the long and painful process of rebuilding the trust of customers and investors once again.

Further reading

Two recent papers, written for economists but fairly accessible, refer
to the same feedbacks as Figure 1.1. One is Marcus Brunnermeier's
superb review of the crisis, 'Deciphering the liquidity and credit crunch
2007–08', which he continues to update as the crisis has evolved (the
latest version can be found on his homepage, at www.princeton.
edu/~markus/). This paper contains many more academic references,
including his own influential work with Lasse Pederson.

The other is a recent conference presentation by Rick Mishkin of
Columbia University, former Federal Reserve Governor and author
of a market-leading money and banking textbook, which also emphasizes the role of these feedbacks and the importance of using monetary
policy to offset them: 'Is monetary policy effective during financial
crises?' (www.aeaweb.org/annual_mtg_papers/2009/author_papers.
php?author_ID=6461). Note that my own account of money creation is different from that presented in the textbooks including that of
Mishkin, being much closer to the endogenous bank-credit views of
Nikki Kaldor.

Another notably prescient account of the crisis is Nouriel Roubini's
written testimony to the House of Representatives Financial Services
committee of February 2008, 'The current US recession and the
risks of financial crisis', at www.house.gov/apps/list/hearing/finan-
cialsvcs_dem/roubini022608.pdf (Roubini continues to write a great
deal about the crisis, but most of his analysis is only for subscribers
to his webservice Roubini Global Economics Monitor). Roubini, even
though he identifies illiquidity problems as lying at the heart of the
crisis, is *much* more pessimistic than others about the ability of policymakers to deal with these problems of funding and illiquidity.

Professor Phil Davis of Brunel University provides a thorough
review of different theories of liquidity and its role in financial crises in
his paper 'Liquidity, financial crises and the lender of last resort – how
much of a departure is the sub-prime crisis?' (www.brunel.ac.uk/9379/
efwps/RBApapersemifinal.doc), with copious references to the academic literature. Note that he uses an extremely broad definition of
'lender of last resort', using the term to refer to all forms of public provision of credit to financial institutions, not in its original meaning of
the central bank providing means of payment to commercial banks.

My own policy recommendations for government-backed insurance against extreme systemic risks have been developed in co-operation with Laurence Kotlikoff of Boston University and Perry Mehrling of Barnard College, Columbia University. A detailed statement is Mehrling and Milne, 'The government's responsibility as credit insurer of last resort and how it can be fulfilled', and can be found on my school web pages, www.cass.city.ac.uk/cbs/activities/banking crisis.html. A shorter statement is Kotlikoff–Mehrling–Milne, http://blogs.ft.com/wolfforum/2008/10/recapitalising-the-banks-is-not-enough/#more-227, and see also other postings by Kotlikoff and Mehrling on the Economists' Forum.

Others have developed closely related policy proposals, notably Luigi Spaventi and Avinash Persaud. Spaventi, now at the University of Rome and formerly Italian Treasury Minister and head of the Italian securities regulator CONSOB, has put down his views in 'Avoiding disorderly deleveraging', www.cepr.org/pubs/PolicyInsights/CEPR_Policy_Insight_022.asp. This provides an overview of the crisis similar to that of Brunnermeier and of this book, and then discusses both standard policy responses (monetary policy, recapitalization) and his own proposal for a new 'Brady plan' (this was the successful response to the 1980s crisis of banking lending in Latin America, sponsored by US Treasury Secretary Nicholas Brady and described in Chapter 3) to take illiquid assets off bank balance sheets in exchange for treasury securities. This is a very similar idea to Kotlikoff–Mehrling–Milne.

The well-known UK financial economist Avinash Persaud argues for essentially the same idea in his 'What is to be done and by whom: five separate initiatives', at www.voxeu.org/index.php?q=node/2370 ('. . . the creation of long-term liquidity pools to purchase assets – rather like John Pierpont Morgan's 1907 money trusts'). For more extended discussion see also his article in the Banque de France *Financial Stability Review*, 'Regulation, valuation and systemic liquidity', of October 2008, at www.banque-france.fr/gb/publications/telechar/rsf/2008/etud8_1008.pdf.

Another proponent of insurance against systemic risk is Professor Ricardo Caballero of the Massachusetts Institute of Technology (MIT). See his Vox posting, 'A global perspective on the great financial insurance run: causes, consequences, and solutions (Part 2)' (www.voxeu.org/index.php?q=node/2828).

2 | *Build-up, meltdown and intervention*

This chapter provides a synopsis of the crisis, looking first at the build-up of financial problems, then at the subsequent meltdown and finally at interventions by the governments and central banks of the world's major economies to confront the crisis. This is not a chronological account. That task is left to chapters 7, 8, 9 and 10. What this chapter does is to assess the risk exposures that built up during the credit boom and show how government and central banks have moved to accept much of what was previously private-sector risk.

The several stages of the crisis

This crisis has emerged not suddenly, but in several stages, each stage not only unexpected but also at the same time more serious and more damaging than the stage before. At first things did not seem so bad. In August 2008 one of the best informed policymakers in the world expressed his surprise that the crisis has been so long-lasting and deep-seated. Charles Bean, deputy governor of the Bank of England, said in a radio interview from the Jackson Hole central bank governor's conference,

Last year most of us thought this was a financial crisis that with a bit of luck would be over as we got the other side of Christmas, but it has dragged on for a year and looks like as if it will drag on for some considerable time further yet. There are periods when markets look as if they are getting rather better, and then another grenade explodes, another bout of fear of sustainability, fear of problems in some financial institution, maybe of intervention by the authorities. So it is very much ebb and flow, the mood here is of considerable caution, there is still the recognition that there is still some considerable way to go yet.[1]

---

[1] Broadcast on the BBC radio *Today* programme on 25 August 2008, archived at
    http://news.bbc.co.uk/today/hi/today/newsid_7580000/7580413.stm.

His surprise was shared by many others. In early autumn 2007 most experts believed that once mortgage losses were fully acknowledged, credit and financial markets could return to normal, and steady economic growth would resume. This was certainly the belief of stock market investors. Stock prices remained very strong, despite evident financial strains in the markets for buying and selling of credit exposures and in the 'money markets' where banks raise short-term funding. The widely quoted Dow Jones industrial average achieved an all-time record closing high of 14,165 on 9 October 2007, well after the financial crisis began.

But, as Charles Bean acknowledged, hopes that the credit crisis would be short-lived were dashed. The losses reported by many major banks, for example UBS, Merrill Lynch and Citigroup, mounted far higher than anyone had expected. The strains in credit and money markets were persistent and on occasion got sharply worse, resulting, for example, in the failure of the US investment bank Bear Sterns in late March 2008. At the same time the Chinese economy continued to grow and suck in raw materials, and an increasing shortage of commodities led to sharp increases in oil, commodity and food prices (for example, the price per barrel of light sweet crude oil on the Nymex exchange doubled between September 2007 and July 2008, from around $70 to over $140).

The combination of falling house prices, reduced mortgage lending and a higher cost of living put household budgets under strain. There was a sharp slowdown in US consumption growth – not just housing-related expenditure but other categories of consumer spending as well. Stock prices, especially those of financial stocks, weakened, the Dow Jones industrial average falling to around 11,500 in the summer of 2008. Charles Bean's remarks reflected a growing realization that the financial and economic crisis would be long-lasting.

But still no one realized quite how severe it would yet become. Less than a month after Charles Bean's interview, the global credit crisis took a new, unexpected, and even more serious, turn for the worse. The failure of Lehman Brothers on 15 September 2008, and the bailout of the giant US insurer AIG the following day, marked the start of a four-week-long worldwide financial panic, with a dramatic loss of confidence in bank liabilities, a virtual free fall in bank share prices and massive withdrawals of money by professional investors from both banks and money market mutual funds.

This was nothing less than a run on the entire global banking system. Only an unprecedentedly large expansion of central bank lending to commercial banks, making up the shortfall created by this withdrawal of short-term investor funding, prevented widespread bank failure. The Federal Reserve, the European Central Bank and the Bank of England increased their loans to banks by more than $2 trillion in just four weeks, an astonishing increase that roughly doubled the size of their balance sheets. Even then, the panic only finally abated after the announcement of massive packages of government support, with first the UK and then other governments stating their intention to purchase large amounts of newly issued bank shares and to provide widespread guarantees of bank borrowing.

In early 2009 it appears that even these substantial commitments of funds in support of the world's banks will not prevent a global economic contraction deeper than any in the past seventy-five years. Share prices remain weak. B y 20 November 2008 the Dow Jones industrial average had fallen to an intra-day low of below 7,200, nearly 50 per cent below its all-time peak just over a year earlier, and had fallen even further by early March 2009. The spectre we now face is of a return to the worldwide slump of the 1930s, with all the accompanying problems of long-term unemployment, social deprivation and political instability of that time. So what, then, lay behind these dramatic events, and what can be done about them?

The macroeconomic context: structural current-account imbalances

To an important extent the financial crisis has been a response to tensions built up because of the large structural current-account imbalances in the global economy. These current-account imbalances reflect some extraordinary financial relationships. The savings of thrifty households and companies in China, Japan, Germany, Taiwan or Singapore has found its way, eventually, to the pockets of bank borrowers in the United States, Spain, Australia, the United Kingdom and other countries. The vast surpluses enjoyed by the major resource-exporting economies such as Russia, Saudi Arabia and the United Arab Emirates follow similar routes as they are channelled to the governments and citizens of the major consuming economies of the West. Banks are the intermediaries that recycle these massive global flows

Table 2.1. *Some national current-account deficits and surpluses*

Country	2007 current account deficit (−) or surplus (+)	
	$bn	% of national income
United States	−739	−5.3
Spain	−146	−10.1
United Kingdom	−136	−4.9
Germany	+185	+5.6
Japan	+213	+4.9
China	+361	+11.1

Source: International Monetary Fund

of capital, either directly on their balance sheets or indirectly through financial markets.

How big are the flows of credit between nations? The International Monetary Fund (IMF) collects statistics on current-account surpluses and deficits that generate global capital flows (some of these are shown in Table 2.1). In 2007 the government and citizens of the United States – the biggest net importer – borrowed nearly $750 billion from other countries to finance their expenditures – about $2,500 a year for every man, woman and child. Spain and the United Kingdom each also borrowed around $140 billion from other countries in 2007. Australia, Italy, Greece, Turkey and France (although not shown in Table 2.1) were also major borrowers, together borrowing a further $220 billion. At the other end of the scale are the major lending countries. The largest surpluses are those of the big exporters of manufactured goods. China, the biggest of them all, generated a surplus of income over expenditure of $360 billion, Japan of $212 billion and Germany of $185 billion. Not so far behind them are the major resource-exporting countries of Algeria, Iran, Kuwait, Norway, Kuwait, Russia, Saudi Arabia, and the United Arab Emirates which together generated surpluses totalling nearly $400 billion.

What do these large numbers mean? They reflect the balance of income and expenditure for the country as a whole. A current-account surplus of say $5 billion means that a country is generating $5 billion more income from all its economic activities than it is spending on goods and services. Any activity for export, including taking oil out of the ground or manufacturing products for shipment around the world, contributes to an external current-account surplus; and any goods or services purchased from foreign suppliers contribute to an external current-account deficit.

A current-account surplus of $5 billion is similar to the situation of an individual with an excess of income over expenditure of, say, $5 per day. Each day this individual saves $5 and over a year he or she would save around $1,800, investing this money in (for example) bank accounts, government bonds or corporate stocks. What is true for an individual is also true for a country. A current-account-surplus country is a net saver, investing in overseas bank deposits and securities and thus exporting its savings to other countries around the globe. These savings are mirrored by household and other borrowing in deficit countries, such as the United Kingdom, the United States and Spain.

It is helpful to express these current-account deficits as percentages of income. Spain's deficit of 10 per cent of national product stands out; the economic adjustment necessary to cope with a deficit of this magnitude is very large indeed and its economic situation is extremely challenging, even when compared with the United States, with its 2007 deficit of 5.3 per cent of national product, or the United Kingdom (4.9 per cent) or Australia (6.2 per cent).

Most bank wholesale funding comes, directly or indirectly, from the current-account surpluses of the savings-exporting countries. China, Japan, Germany, Saudi Arabia, Kuwait and the others are the major source of the 'hot money' that has now been scared away, and will no longer finance bank holdings of structured securities. Their surpluses provided a large share of the cash deposited with banks through short-term money markets (this can happen in many ways, through sale and repurchase or 'repo' lending, through purchase of asset-backed commercial paper, by investing in money market mutual funds or, most directly, by holding bank deposits).

There are other linkages as well. Government, companies or banks from the surplus countries also hold some bank-issued securities directly (shares, bonds or mortgage-backed and other structured securities). In addition to this direct funding surplus, country savings are invested in many non-bank securities, for example equities, government bonds, corporate bonds or short-term bills and commercial paper. This pushes down their returns and makes them less attractive.

As a result there is displacement of other domestic funds, from companies, insurance companies and pension funds into both short-term funding of bank portfolios through the money markets and bank-issued securities.

This pattern of world savings and investment, with high-saving countries, including Germany and Japan and the emerging market manufacturing exporters and resource exporters such as China, Russia and Saudi Arabia, lending large sums to the high-consuming countries has been a feature of the global economy for several years. Instead of shrinking, these imbalances have risen over the years.

Increasing global trade has opened up tremendous opportunities for growth. The rapidly growing economies of south-east Asia, including South Korea, Malaysia, Taiwan and Thailand, have all benefited, and, more recently, so have India and China. These rapidly growing economies should be the ones with the most attractive business investment opportunities. Yet the world's savings are being channelled mostly from these fast-growing economies to mature developed economies, ones where the prospects for productive investment are relatively poor.

Why have savings been channelled to governments and consumers in the West rather than to productive investment in the emerging markets? One reason is that returns to investment in emerging markets are surprisingly low, due among other reasons to weak enforcement of property rights in the courts and bankruptcy laws that provide little protection to lenders.

A further part of the answer is the different operation of their banking systems. Banks in the United States, the United Kingdom and other developed countries have been extremely skilful in persuading households to borrow freely in order to finance both house purchase and general consumption. Meanwhile banks in emerging markets have been much less successful at finding opportunities to lend in their own countries, either to companies or to individuals. This reflects both much stronger social security systems in Western countries (households worry less about saving for old age) and more effective systems of credit referencing and credit scoring to identify creditworthy borrowers – systems that have been developed over many years.

The export of savings has also been encouraged by the fiscal and monetary and exchange-rate policies in the exporting countries, for example in China, where the exchange rate has been maintained at a very competitive level to encourage export growth.

This borrowing, or 'capital importing', has not just been used for household consumption. It has also financed government expenditures, including, for example, the large increase in military expenditure, especially in the United States, because of the campaigns in Iraq and Afghanistan. Companies and governments have borrowed directly from overseas investors. But the most important destination for this flow of savings has been households, borrowing money from banks through mortgages, credit cards and other forms of personal credit, in turn financed on wholesale funding markets.

How will these global current-account imbalances correct: gradual adjustment or sudden shock?

High levels of current-account surpluses in those countries which are manufacturing exports and producing resources and correspondingly high levels of current-account deficits in the consumer-driven importing economies cannot be sustained indefinitely. Borrowing such a high proportion of income must eventually be curtailed. But there has been considerable room for difference of opinion on how and when this would happen and whether the correction, when it eventually came, would be a gradual and relatively smooth adjustment of incomes and patterns of trade or a jarringly painful forced contraction of expenditure.

To explain what is involved, it is worth recounting the views of some leading economists in 2006, before the financial crisis erupted (for me, as a card-carrying economist holding a London School of Economics Ph.D. this is a natural reference point). The media characterizes economists as being unable to agree about anything. Disagreement on economic issues among professionals is as natural as it is among non-specialists. When policy advice depends on forecasts – which are always uncertain – and on different political standpoints and judgements, then economists do indeed express a wide range of views.

What is striking about this issue is that back in 2006 leading economists, from a wide range of different standpoints, were expressing very much the same views about the world current-account imbalances. They all agreed that the level of savings by exporters of resources and manufactures and correspondingly large borrowing by the importing countries, could not be sustained indefinitely. The reason is simple arithmetic. A country, even a large and great country like the United

States, is in the same position as an individual; it cannot keep borrowing 5 per cent of its income forever, spending $105 for every $100 it actually earns.

There were arguments about the statistics. Some, for example, believed that there is hidden income on US overseas assets and that when this is included the deficit looks a little smaller. But almost no one disputed that eventually income and expenditure in the United States and other deficit countries would have to adjust, through some combination of reduced spending on imported goods and services and higher domestic production, to bring total expenditure more into line with total income.

Where there were disagreements was on how this adjustment would come about and how quickly, and on what policy measures might be needed to deal with it. Some were pessimistic about this adjustment process, anticipating what was commonly labelled as a 'hard landing'. To take one example, Paul Krugman, Professor of Economics at Princeton University and an op-ed writer for the *New York Times*, wrote on several occasions about the possibility of an abrupt slowdown in US consumption and house prices and a potentially sharp dislocation in exchange and interest rates.[2] He was concerned about both the sustainability of consumption and the role of international investors. Household consumption – which accounts for around 70 per cent of all US expenditure – might slow sharply, triggering a sharp decline in national output. There could also be a collapse of confidence by overseas investors, leading them to switch out of dollars into other currencies, and triggering a massive correction to the dollar exchange rate, far more than was required for adjustment of the external deficit, and leading to rising inflation and a major reduction in business confidence and private-sector investment.

Other commentators stressed the ability of the market to self-correct, arguing that households and taxpayers are not entirely short-sighted and would recognize when they, or government on their behalf, are spending beyond their incomes, and then gradually take steps either to reduce expenditures or to increase incomes. Savings, in other words, can be expected to rise gradually to bridge the gap. Market prices will

---

[2] His *New York Times* articles, 'The Chinese connection', 20 May 2005 (www.nytimes.com/2005/05/20/opinion/20krugman.html?pagewanted=print), and 'Debt and denial', 13 February 2006 (http://select.nytimes.com/2006/02/13/opinion/13krugman.html?_r=1), were widely debated.

also adjust to encourage this correction, so that we can expect to see a lower dollar exchange rate, at least against the Chinese renminbi and the Japanese yen. These will lead to higher US savings and to greater export growth, and to a slowdown in consumer borrowing and the growth of imports.

Many economists held these views. One elegant statement is to be found in a 2006 paper by the respected economists Guillermo Calvo and Ernesto Talvi.[3] They contest Krugman's argument that reduced investment in the United States by the Chinese government would lead to a sharp fall in US economic activity, arguing instead that the export of savings by surplus economies is unlikely to come to a sudden sharp halt; but they do acknowledge the possibility that a sharp correction in US housing markets could lead to a slowdown in US consumer spending.

It is now clear that the adjustment of the world's structural current-account imbalances is clearly not going to be smooth. But the shock is not one of those identified by Krugman or indeed by any other economic commentator before early 2007. We have not so far seen a complete collapse in household consumption in the deficit countries. Nor have we seen an uncontrolled collapse of exchange rates and withdrawal of foreign capital from the United States, the United Kingdom and other borrowing countries. What has instead happened is an entirely unanticipated major and long-lasting dislocation to credit markets and bank funding.

As a result, far from a gradual adjustment of the world's current-account balances, we now seem to be heading towards a much sharper correction through a massive contraction of credit, leading to falling household and business expenditure. If this happens it will create a cumulative downward spiral in world economic activity.

Bank exposure to structured credit markets

How did this happen? The packaging of loans into mortgage-backed and other structured credit securities has played a key role in the recycling of savings to Western consumers. Chapters 4 and 5 of this book

---

[3] Guillermo Calvo and Ernesto Talvi, 'The resolution of global imbalances: soft landing in the US, hard landing in emerging markets?', *Journal of Policy Modeling*, 28 (2006), 605–13. A working paper version can be found at www. iadb.org/res/files/Imbalances/pp/CALVO-TALVI-PAPER.pdf.

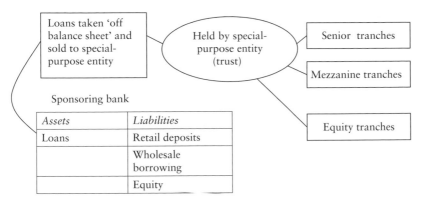

Figure 2.1. Schematic diagram for mortgage-backed securitization

look at these structures in some detail. But it is not necessary to be familiar with all the details in order to understand how loss of confidence in these instruments has undermined bank funding. Figure 2.1 is a simplified representation of how these deals work.

In a typical deal a sponsoring bank moves loans off its balance sheet and sells them to a special-purpose entity. For legal and tax reasons this is a non-profit vehicle; if it is established under US law it is usually known as a 'trust'. The special-purpose entity then sells bonds to investors, known as 'tranches' (from the French word 'tranche' – 'slice') of different seniority. The most senior tranches have the first claims on the interest and principal payments from the loans. The proceeds from the bond sales are then used to purchase the loans from the bank.

The senior tranches of these securitizations are extremely safe. They are protected in several ways: first, by 'over-collateralization' – that is, the practice of putting a larger value of loans into the special-purpose entity than the value of bonds sold – second, by the interest margin earned because the interest rate paid on the loans is always higher than the interest rate paid on the tranches; and, third, because of the seniority of the senior bonds. In a typical structure the most senior AAA tranches are only about 75 per cent of the total issue. This means that they are virtually free of any default risk; the losses on the loans would have to eat up all the interest surplus, all the over-collateralization and the 25 per cent of more junior tranches before the most senior tranches lose money. Loan losses of this magnitude would be quite extraordinary.

Sponsoring banks often keep the riskier tranches of securitizations themselves. This is a reasonable thing for them to do if the main motive for creating the structure is, as it usually is, obtaining cheap funding rather than transferring risk. They may also buy and sell loans in and out of the mortgage or other loan pool, in order to maintain the asset quality. There is often no legal obligation for them to buy bad loans and replace with good loans, but doing this helps to maintain a reputation for quality and thus helps when selling loan-backed securities in the future.

Even if the sponsoring bank retains the riskier tranches it still benefits from the securitization, because it can replace relatively expensive wholesale borrowing on its balance sheet with the relatively cheap funding from selling senior structured securities. The difference in cost can be very large; a bank might pay a spread of, say, 25 basis points above the standard London Interbank Offer Rate (Libor) on the senior tranches of a loan securitization but a spread of 150 basis points or more on floating-rate bonds issued on its own balance sheet.

Box 2.1. Some further details on bank involvement in structured credit markets

Figure 2.2 shows a bit more of the detail of bank involvement in structured credit markets (detail explained further in chapters 4, 5 and 6). This figure provides an overall picture of the various different ways in which banks were exposed to mortgage-backed and structured securities.

All these credit structures, whether backed by mortgages or other types of credit, were created by placing the selected credit assets, in this example a pool of mortgage loans (2) taken from a sponsoring bank (1), inside a special legal vehicle (3).

This special legal vehicle in turn issued securities ((4), (5) and (6)) with different claims on the interest and principal payments on the pool of loans.

The senior-grade tranches (6) have the first claim, so they are very safe and are rated AAA. Next come the mezzanine tranches (5) that carry some risk. The junior and equity tranches (4) carry all the remaining 'residual' risk, and if the loan pool performs badly they may get little repayment at all.

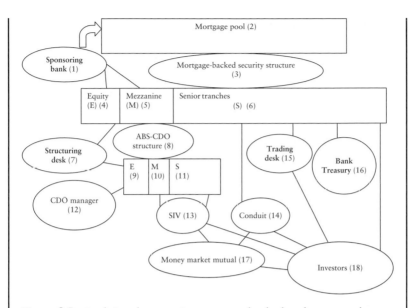

Figure 2.2. Bank involvement in mortgage-backed and structured credit

Banks have been involved in creating and holding these structures in several ways:

The sponsoring commercial bank (1) sold loan assets into the securitization structure. As Chapter 4 explains, the main reason for doing this was to obtain low-cost funding (because the funding was secured on the pool of loans, it was much cheaper than the bank borrowing in its own name). Not all structures have sponsoring banks; sometimes in the 'transaction' deals described in Chapter 5 the loan assets were bought on the open market.

The structuring desk (7), usually a division of an investment bank, was paid a fee by the sponsoring bank for creating the structure and selling tranches to other banks and investors. In the transaction deals with no sponsor the structuring desk made a profit by selling the tranches for more than the costs of assembling the structure.

The trading desk (15), again usually a division of an investment bank, held the structured securities in order to make a profit from the relatively high yield they offer. In addition the treasuries (16)

of both commercial and investment banks held liquid assets to manage their bank's cash flows, and often held structured assets because they offer higher yields than government bonds.

Structuring desks often faced difficulties finding buyers for the riskier equity and mezzanine tranches. To get round this they often restructured the riskier tranches, placing them inside a second structure (8) known as an ABS-CDO (this stands for asset-backed securitization– collateralized debt obligation – what a mouthful!) and so created more senior (11), as well as equity and junior (9) and mezzanine (10) tranches. Obtaining an investment grade rating for these restructured tranches helps to persuade investors and other banks to purchase this paper.

'Investors' (18) is a broad category including pension funds, insurance companies, large corporates, charitable bodies, and also overseas governments and the sovereign wealth funds that invest on their behalf. Most often the securities were held by banks with short-term funding from investors. Trading desks (15) financed their holdings of these structured assets by short-term collateralized borrowing from investors (18), using a contract known as a sale and repurchase agreement or repo.

Another way for banks to finance their holdings of structured securities was by placing them in off-balance-sheet funds run by banks and known as structured investment vehicles (SIVs) and conduits.

Chapter 6 explains more about these off-balance-sheet vehicles. While they are broadly similar, SIVs tended to hold riskier assets. What they both did was to issue short-term paper known as ABCP or 'asset-backed commercial paper', which was then purchased by investors (18). Just like a repo, this short-term collateralized borrowing was very cheap, creating good profits for the SIVs and conduits as long as the prices of the securities did not fall sharply.

Investors would also sometimes purchase the investment-grade structured securities themselves, but they were reluctant to hold many, especially the more complicated restructured securities because, unlike corporate bonds, none of these securities had a long historical track record and they did not feel that they really understood the risks.

The final involvement of banks in structured securities markets was the security portfolios held by bank treasuries (16), in order to manage uncertain cash flows. As the structuring of credit boomed, bank treasuries purchased more and more investment-grade tranches of mortgage-backed and structured securities, financed out of the deposit base of the bank. These were attractive securities for bank treasuries because they seemed to be safe (mostly they obtained AAA ratings). They were as liquid as government or the very best corporate bonds, they offered high yields and, until the crisis, their prices were very stable. (This is partly because they offer floating interest rates, so their prices are not much affected by interest rate changes.)

Commercial banks and the structuring departments of the investment banks created a lot of paper during the boom years of structured and mortgage-backed credit, from 2002 until 2007. While there are no comprehensive statistics, industry bodies have recently released estimates of the outstanding stock of most categories of these securities. With some further estimation of remaining stock, based on the issue flows, it is possible to get approximate figures for the overall size of the market. The results of this exercise are shown in Table 2.2.

There are many acronyms in the world of structured credit. Table 2.2 uses some of the most common, including RMBS (residential mortgage-backed security, i.e. a security backed by mortgage loans on houses), CMBS (commercial mortgage-backed security, i.e. a security backed by mortgage loans on commercial property such as offices or shops), ABS (asset-backed security, backed by retail loans other than mortgages) and CDO (collateralized debt obligation, a security backed by bonds or loans to large companies).

The table reports the relative size of the markets for the different structured credit products. The largest is for so-called 'agency RMBS' in the United States – the residential mortgage-backed securities issued by the government sponsored enterprises Fannie Mae and Freddie Mac. $5.9 trillion is a huge number. It is about half of all US mortgage lending and not far shy of half of US national income (which was close to $14 trillion in 2007). But these agency RMBS are a special case; the mortgages that back them are guaranteed by Fannie and Freddie, so they are backed at least implicitly by the US government.

Table 2.2. *Approximate magnitudes of the European and US structured credit market*

	Fourth quarter of 2007, outstanding		
	Europe	US	Total
		$ trillion	
Agency RMBS		5.9	5.9
Sub-prime RMBS		0.8	0.8
Other RMBS	1.0	0.5	1.5
ABS	0.3	1.7	2.0
CMBS	0.2	0.9	1.1
CDO	0.4	1.1	1.5
Total	1.8	11.1	12.9
Total non-agency	1.8	5.2	7.0

Sources: ESF, SIFMA. US CMBS and CDO are author's estimates of stock outstanding based on published data for issuance flow. US ABS excludes $1trillion of 'other', mostly government guaranteed ABS. European data converted to dollars using end-2007 exchange rate of $1=€0.6794. CDOs include leveraged loan, bond, and synthetic structures.

The next biggest market, especially in the United States, is the $2 trillion market for asset-backed securities (ABS). These are securitizations of retail lending of all kinds including vehicle loans, credit card receivables, student loans, equipment leases, small business loans and also home equity loans.

There are some other surprises from looking at these numbers. The sub-prime residential mortgage-backed securities, where all the credit market problems first appeared, are only around one-tenth of the entire market for mortgage-backed and structured securities, less than half of the ABS market (sub-prime RMBS are issued only in the United States, not in Europe) and less than the market for commercial mortgage-backed securities.

The broadest category here comprises 'collateralized debt obligations' or CDOs. They include a range of structures where the securitized assets are neither retail loans nor mortgages, for example restructured securities (such as the ABS-CDOs), corporate bonds, corporate loans and so-called 'synthetic CDOs', where the assets are the tradable insurance contracts known as credit default swaps.

This table reveals quite how large the market for structured credit had become by 2007. Even if we exclude the agency-backed RMBS, there was close to $7 trillion outstanding, which is about twice the size of the market for tradable US government debt, normally regarded as the biggest and most liquid securities market in the world.

Despite all the talk about 'toxic assets', the fact is that the large majority of this structured paper is at virtually no risk of default (a point developed in some detail in chapters 4 and 5 of this book). This fact should not come as a surprise. Consider for example an ABS structure containing, say, vehicle or student loans. The individual borrowers will mostly make an effort to repay, since they do not want to face the difficulties of having a poor credit record. Most will have the income to repay as well. In a pool of such loans, even in a deep recession, it would be quite out of line with all previous experience of such lending to have losses of more than say 10 or 15 per cent on the portfolio. This means that the senior investment-grade tranches, the top, say, 80 per cent of the structure, are indeed very safe. Allowing for the other forms of credit protection in these structures, overcollateralization and interest income, the losses on the portfolio have to go well above 20 per cent before these tranches are at risk. The very best investment-grade tranches, those rated AAA, have even more protection. They might be the top 70 or 75 per cent, so losses have to rise well above 25 per cent before they are in difficulties.

The big problem for the banks – the reason they can no longer fund themselves – is that investor confidence in *all* structured assets has now evaporated. Even the AAA tranches of safe asset-backed securities cannot be sold. Where there are transactions, they are at prices 10 or 20 per cent below par value – that is, so far below any sensible assessment of their fundamental value that no holders will part with them at this price unless forced to do so.

The amount of this good-quality but illiquid paper is extremely large. Some further calculations using the data in Table 2.2 as a starting point suggest that, after excluding around $600 billion of dubious restructured ABS-CDOs and CDO^2 which never deserved AAA ratings in the first place, there is still about $4.8 trillion of extremely safe AAA structured paper outstanding.

Who was holding all these securities? Regrettably, there are few statistics on who was holding what. The IMF has collected views from the market participants and reports broad estimates of holdings in its global financial stability reports. Commentary from many industry professionals makes it clear that the majority of the AAA paper was kept by banks, either in trading or treasury portfolios. My own judgement, based on this information and discussion with a number of industry professionals, is that about $3 trillion of the investment grade paper has remained with banks.

What about the riskier mezzanine and equity tranches? Much of the mezzanine tranches were sold into restructured vehicles, so were again often held by banks. Equity tranches were sometimes held by the structuring departments. It is very difficult to say where the rest have ended up.

If most of the new credit securities were sound, what then went wrong? The big weakness of the new credit arrangements was that banks assumed that there would always be a liquid market for trading these securities. If this were true – that securities could always be sold – then it was safe to finance portfolios of long-term credit securities using large amounts of low-cost short-term borrowing.

Banks pursued this flawed strategy on a huge scale. Analysis of bank accounting statements suggests that banks worldwide held at least $3 trillion (nearly a quarter of US national income) of supposedly high-quality AAA credit securities, financed short term. But this maturity mismatch, borrowing short to hold long-term assets, is an inherently risky portfolio strategy, susceptible to collapse whenever there is a loss of investor confidence.

The growing losses on US sub-prime mortgage lending triggered a loss of confidence in all forms of structured and mortgage-backed credit instruments. This had a global impact because so many banks worldwide held and manufactured different kinds of these instruments. They all tried to reduce their exposures at the same time. As a result there were now many sellers of these securities but hardly any buyers. Sellers but no buyers meant that trading slowed to a halt, and prices collapsed. The liquidity which all banks assumed they could rely on was no longer there.

Why were there no buyers from outside the banking system? Because of the market freeze, prices of senior structured and mortgage-backed securities had fallen well below any reasonable estimate of their underlying value. They should have been attractive investments at these bargain prices. But non-bank investors did not understand these instruments very well and if they did perceive opportunities they were subject to regulatory and other constraints that prevent them purchasing assets when prices are low.

A particular problem seems to have been so-called 'solvency regulations', which are supposed to help financial institutions avoid insolvency but actually have the opposite effect, exaggerating swings in market prices and making it more likely that institutions will fail in a financial crisis. These impacts are further exaggerated by the mark to market accounting rules. No one has an incentive to 'catch a falling knife' – that is, to purchase an asset that has fallen in value – until they are very sure that prices have bottomed out. Until then the asset has the potential both to add to your capital requirement if the asset is downgraded (under banking and insurance regulations) and to result in short-term losses if the price falls further (IFRS and US GAAP accounting standards). Such mispricing could be substantial and last a long time.

So the principal explanation of why this has been such a global crisis is that banks worldwide (wrongly) assumed that they were safe borrowing short to hold long-term structured mortgage assets. If funding withdrew they could always limit their exposures by cutting back on their portfolios, for example by selling loans to other banks, or taking out 'hedges' (insurance contracts) against further losses. But this idea, of active credit portfolio management, does not work when all banks are in trouble. Another analogy is with a fire in a crowded hotel lobby. Everyone tries to get out through the revolving doors, but only a few can do so at any one time, and in the crush everyone is trapped. What is required instead is an orderly exit, one investor at a time, to allow all to exit their positions without huge loss.

The spread of the crisis

The early casualties of the crisis were institutions pursuing rather unusual business models. Off-balance-sheet trading funds with large holdings of mortgage-backed securities, such as those operated by the German banks IKB and Sachsen Landesbank, were forced to close at a loss. Banks such as Northern Rock, relying on the sale of mortgage-backed securities rather than retail deposits to finance the extremely rapid growth of their loan books, were no longer able to finance their loan portfolios.

Not long after this, serious failures of governance and risk management emerged. The failure was not the emergence of losses on mortgage exposures. Banks take risks, so they must expect to make losses some of the time. Occasional losses on lending or on trading or investment portfolios are normal.

The problem was that a handful of institutions, including some very large banks such as UBS, Merrill Lynch and Citigroup, had very large exposures to this one market – sub-prime and other high-risk US mortgage lending – and had made a lot of investments in the higher-yielding but higher-risk types of securities. The losses that these banks experienced were extremely large relative to their annual earnings and the 'capital' (the difference between their assets and their liabilities) on their balance sheet.

The impact of the crisis then spread still further. The $3 billion overhang of illiquid structured assets made it impossible for banks to use mortgage-backed or other structured securities to raise funds for new lending or even for financing their existing portfolios. As the global economy weakened it became increasingly likely that very many banks would face funding problems and be forced to sell assets. Some might even turn out to be insolvent. These increasing fears crystallized with the failures of Lehman Brothers and AIG in September 2008, which were followed by a global financial panic and withdrawal of funds from across the banking system lasting for the next four weeks.

Central bank lending and government support packages have reduced the fear of bank failure, but this is still not the end of the banking crisis. Looking forward into 2009 and 2010, it is clear that even with promises of large-scale government support the squeeze on bank balance sheets will continue and may get considerably worse. As the global economy goes into a steep downturn, companies will lose revenues and households will lose income. Both companies and households will then run down their cash holdings and also turn to banks for emergency borrowing by drawing down lines of credit or increasing credit card balances. Bank funding problems will be made yet worse by the maturing of medium-term bank bonds, money which banks will be unable to refinance because of fears about future bank losses. This flow of money out of the banking system will worsen the squeeze on bank balance sheets, further reducing the availability of bank credit, reducing consumption and investment, and worsening the worldwide economic downturn.

Holding of traded credit securities has amplified bank losses, but they are still manageable

While it is difficult to know exactly how much of the structured credit was retained by banks, we do know that these holdings have amplified bank losses during the credit crisis. Table 2.3 presents some projections illustrating this point.

These projections are not predictions of the future losses. They are calculations of possible losses based on Table 2.2 and other data for bank lending to households and corporations, with specific assumptions about both loss rates on credit exposures and declines in market values of senior AAA structured credit tranches (the notes to the table specify the exact assumptions). This is similar to a widely reported exercise carried out by the IMF, with the difference that this table includes losses on European as well as US exposures. The losses are for the entire financial sector, although the majority are among banks.

This table illustrates several points. The level of bank losses, unsurprisingly, depends to a large extent on the prospects for the world economy. The central projection is close to what many forecasters are saying about the prospects for the world economy at the end of 2008. The rates of loss shown here are based on a fairly crude extrapolation of the arrears on loans that had emerged by late in 2008, similar to those used by the IMF in a similar exercise published in their October 2008 Global Financial Stability Report. Total fundamental loan losses climb to a little over $800 billion, with much of this loss concentrated in the United States.

But if we have a much more severe economic downturn, then fundamental losses could climb much higher. In this second, 'severe' projection, loss rates on the different categories of loan and the overall fundamental losses are roughly double those of the central projection.

This is the feedback from the quantity of bank lending onto credit impairment on the left hand side of Figure 1.1. If bank lending collapses much further and this results in a considerably deeper global recession than currently anticipated, then this will in turn lead to much higher levels of losses on bank lending. Fear of such an outcome is one of the main reasons why banks are not lending. But if banks are confident that other banks are maintaining their lending, or if they are

Table 2.3. *Some projections of possible credit crisis losses*

	Fundamental	Liquidity	Total
	$bn		
Central projection			
US exposure	591	551	1,142
European exposure	250	185	435
Total	841	736	1,577
Severe projection			
US exposure	1,038	1,401	2,439
European exposure	600	478	1,078
Total	1,638	1,879	3,517

Assumptions: *Central* (similar to IMF, October 2008, but includes Europe) – global fall of output of around 1% in 2009 and recovery in 2010. Fundamental loss 12% sub-prime; 5% multi-family, Alt-A, home-equity, leveraged loans; 3% on all other loans including prime mortgage, credit cards and corporate loans + liquidity losses on AAA range from 30% to 5%. *Severe* – much larger global fall of output with no recovery in 2010. Fundamental loss 20% sub-prime; 10% multi-family, Alt-A, home-equity, leveraged loans; 5% on all other loans including credit cards and corporate loans + liquidity losses on AAA range from 50% to 30%.

protected by 'disaster insurance' then the economic downturn need not be so severe and there is no reason for them not to lend.

This table also indicates that temporary losses on safe AAA structured credits, the ones that will remain safe from actual default even in the event of a severe economic downturn, roughly double the scale of overall losses. So the practice by banks of holding senior structured credit securities, either to make a trading profit or as what they thought were liquid securities that could be sold if necessary to manage their balance sheets, greatly amplified their exposure to the credit crisis.

Even on the more severe projection the losses look perfectly manageable. The second set of figures shown here assume very high rates of loss on bank credit exposures, but the total of $3 trillion of fundamental and liquidity losses is only about 5 per cent of the balance sheets of the world's largest fifty banks. This is only around half of the scale of losses, relative to the size of bank balance sheets, experienced in the Japanese and Scandinavian banking crisis in the 1990s. And much of this is a temporary loss due to the illiquidity of structured credit markets that will eventually be recovered when the undervalued assets are held to maturity.

Those who choose to panic can always envisage scenarios in which losses rise much higher still than those envisaged in these projections. But central banks and governments can take action that will avoid a complete breakdown of our economic system. There is no basis for such extreme fears and there can be a return of short-term funding and a resumption of bank lending.

A 'mark to market' accounting controversy

A great deal of concern has been expressed about the accounting treatment of these liquidity losses on senior structured securities. Many senior bank staff, including those in charge of trading books or security portfolios held for liquidity management, believe that the fall in market prices grossly exaggerates their losses, that the liquidity losses of AAA securities in this right-hand column will not result in real credit losses at all, and so should not be treated as losses for accounting purposes. There is a lot to support the view that the market prices are wrong and mark to market is contributing to the squeeze on bank balance sheets and the resulting global contraction of bank lending. Only if the losses on lending become unimaginably bad, much worse than even the severe outcome shown in Table 2.3, will many of these safe securities default. This suggests that for assessing bank performance it would be better to look only at the first column of this table, the fundamental losses, and to put the liquidity losses to one side.

How is it possible that market prices can be wrong? The reason is simple: there is no market. The markets on which these securities once traded are dead. There are no buyers, no sellers and so no market price. But accountancy rules, the International Financial Reporting Standards (IFRS, applied to most European banks from 2005) and the US GAAP, force auditors to come up with a 'market price' anyway, even when there is no market. The outcome is that banks value their trading assets and security portfolios held for liquidity management using a hypothetical substitute for the market price (the word 'hypothetical' is my own; it does not appear in the accountancy rules but this in practice is what happens).

Where there is no market, banks' staff and external auditors must use some ingenuity to come up with a hypothetical substitute for a market value. In practice what they end up doing is finding the most recent trading price for a fairly similar security or, alternatively, seeking the opinion of a trader or dealers on the hypothetical question of what the current price would be if there were a trade.[4] The outcome is that even the safest structured securities are valued using hypothetical market prices at anywhere between 5 and 30 per cent below what the value was when markets were liquid. Virtually none of this markdown reflects an underlying or even prospective impairment.

This has in turn led many – including, in a widely publicised report in April 2008, the G30, an international lobbying and research body representing many of the world's largest banks – to challenge the mark to market accounting rules, suggesting that these should be relaxed and illiquid securities should instead be assigned accounting values based on their prospective long term repayment, much like a traditional bank loan. This proposal proved to be very controversial. Not all banks agreed and one, Goldman Sachs, resigned from the G30 because of this report.

There are strong arguments for continuing to use 'mark to market' valuations, even when the prices used are hypothetical and not actual market prices. The great virtue of mark to market is that it prevents the delayed recognition of losses such as those that hindered the restructuring both of US savings and loans in the 1980s and of Japanese banks in the 1990s. For example, had there been mark to market accounting twenty years ago the US savings and loans would have had to recognize, very much earlier than they did, that the rise of short-term interest rates of the early 1980s had left many of them insolvent. The necessary restructuring would then have happened much earlier and the overall losses would have been a good deal smaller. Japan in the 1990s was similar; their banks also delayed recognition of loan losses and postponed restructuring for several years. A substantial move away from 'mark to market' could further undermine investor trust of banks and hinder, not help, their efforts to raise funds.

---

[4] A technical issue is the distinction between what US GAAP calls level two pricing, based on a correspondence with a recently observed price of a comparable asset, a level one observed market price and a level three model-based price based on market inputs. The vast majority of structured securities are valued on the level two basis.

Given such extreme differences of view, compromise was always going to be difficult. Eventually, by late 2008 there have been concessions by the International Accounting Standards Board, allowing firms to switch the classification of assets so that they are less affected by fluctuations in hypothetical market prices. US GAAP has also been amended to allow illiquid asset valuations based on anticipated cash flows.

The real issue is not the accounting rules but the illiquidity of structured credit markets. As long as the market for these securities remains closed, then new issues cannot be sold to investors and in the absence of a liquid market that reveals informative prices on a daily basis, they cannot be used as collateral for borrowing. Better to address the liquidity problem directly, through government-backed insurance to put a floor under prices.

The responses to the crisis

The financial authorities – finance ministries, central banks and financial regulators – have done a great deal to confront the global crisis. This chapter concludes with a brief discussion of these actions. (See Table 2.4 at the end of the chapter for a tabulation of the principal actions taken in response to the crisis. Note that this table excludes reductions of target monetary policy rates and programmes of fiscal stimulus.) Chapters 7 to 11 look at these actions and the events that prompted them in a little more detail and assess what still needs to be done.

These responses have been on a very large scale. A quick tally of the various measures listed in Table 2.4 indicates around $3 trillion of new central bank funding to the banking sector and to credit and money markets. This includes large-scale asset swaps – where the central bank provides banks with government bonds that are acceptable as collateral for money-market repo borrowing in exchange for AAA mortgage-backed and structured securities – directly addressing bank funding problems. It also includes the very large-scale Federal Reserve facilities to support directly money market funds, commercial paper markets, and the markets for asset and mortgage-backed securities in the United States.

Much of the expansion of the central bank balance sheets in September and October 2008 was because central banks accepted excess reserves from banks that would no longer lend in the money markets, and lent these to banks that could no longer borrow in the money markets – that is, bank-to-bank lending was being intermediated via the central bank instead of via the market. This is not included in the $3 trillion tally because it is not net new funding for the banking sector.

A similar tally yields around $4 trillion of government expenditure and guarantees. This includes injections of bank capital announced in October 2008. It also includes the substantial sums spent by the US Treasury on supporting AIG and Citigroup. Finally it includes the substantial guarantees of bank wholesale funding provided by first the UK and then other European governments.

There are notable differences of approach between Europe on the one hand and the United States on the other. In the United States the Federal Reserve has introduced several facilities, worth a total of around $1.5 trillion, in direct support of the mortgage and asset-backed security markets and to providing funding and liquidity to short-term money markets. US Treasury and the Federal Reserve are also providing around $0.5 trillion of guarantees to assets of Bear Sterns, AIG and Citigroup. These measures come fairly close in practice to the government-backed guarantees of systemic credit risk advocated in this book.

Taking the Citigroup rescue as an example, the US Treasury is guaranteeing some $306 billion of Citigroup leveraged loans and structured assets. The terms of this guarantee are that Citigroup must carry the first 10 per cent of losses and $1 in every $10 of all further losses.

These guarantees fall short of the extreme systemic credit risk insurance proposed here only because they are not transferable. The press release that announced these measures gives no indication that the insurance of these Citigroup assets or loans will transfer along with the asset or loan should Citigroup sell it to another bank or investor. This a shortcoming, because unless such insurance is transferable it will not restore the market value of the securities and support the resumption of trading.

There is as yet no parallel in Europe to the various Federal Reserve measures to purchase mortgage- and asset-backed securities. These measures are also similar to the extreme systemic insurance scheme proposed here in that they help to put a floor under the pricing.

Consider a senior structured security with a face value of $100 that because of market illiquidity is now valued at $80. It would be possible for government or central bank to provide insurance that guarantees that the asset is worth at least $90. Or it would be possible instead for government or central bank to purchase the same asset for $91 dollars. In either case the government or central bank is accepting the extreme tail of the loss distribution. If eventually the security pays back, say, only $85, then the authorities are exposed to a loss. If government or central bank is providing insurance they will get a premium of, say, $1, so their net loss insuring at $90 will be $4. If they purchase at $91 the loss is $6. But the exposure is similar.

The bigger difference is on the upside. If the security eventually pays back $95 then the government or central bank makes a profit of $4 through purchasing the asset. If it insures for a premium of $1, then its profit is only $1 and the bank keeps this 'upside' gain of $4.

Which is better: purchase or insurance against extreme losses? The advantage of insurance is that this avoids any argument between banks and government about the magnitude of the 'upside'. Banks will always argue that the upside is very large and so they should be paid a substantial sum for sale of any troubled assets. Governments on the other hand will always argue that the upside is relatively small and that the purchase price of troubled assets should be low. It is difficult to reconcile these two points of view (one suggestion is to use so called 'reverse auctions' where banks announce prices for sale of assets and the government accepts the best offers, but these are difficult to organise and the quality of the assets offered for sale may be poor).

Insurance pricing is much easier. It depends only on the exposure of the government to downside risk i.e. to large losses in the event of a systemic crisis. There can be disagreement about this too, but the difference here is that there is a large surplus that can be shared between the government and banks i.e. banks are willing to pay a high price that more than covers the expected payout by government. If policy is successful and avoids economic disaster then the expected insurance payouts are small. But banks will still be willing to pay a lot to avoid the disaster. Moreover if economic disaster does occur then government is likely to have to pick up the losses anyway, because it has a duty to protect depositors and maintain market confidence. So governments can get a good return from providing insurance against extreme

systemic credit losses, without having to make many additional payments other than those for which they are already responsible.[5]

In Europe, in contrast to the United States, policy has also emphasized guarantees on wholesale funding rather than funding of credit
and money markets. In theory this should also be effective in addressing the funding position of banks, but in practice it appears not to
have worked so well. The evidence so far is that even with government
guarantees these funding markets remain illiquid and investors are
demanding considerable spreads over government bonds of equivalent
maturity. Such direct-funding guarantees also have the serious drawback that the government is accepting far more than the extreme tail
of credit risk. They may also create a 'moral hazard', i.e. encourage
risk taking, because the bank can raise private-sector funds even when
taking very great portfolio risks (insurance of loan assets also creates
moral hazard, but this can be minimised by offering insurance only
on loans made before the crisis). This kind of behaviour might be
prevented through close supervision, but it will always be a concern
when such blanket guarantees are provided. Insurance of senior structured credits does not have this disadvantage, provided that there is
a strict quality standard applied to the securities that qualify for the
insurance.

On 19 January 2009 the UK government announced that it was
now changing its approach to supporting the banking industry, taking
up versions of the insurance measures already being used by the US
Treasury and the Federal Reserve. What is called an 'asset protection
scheme' is to be introduced, offering banks government insurance to
cap losses on a wide variety of bank assets, including mortgage loans,
structured securities and leveraged loans. It appears that corporate
and unsecured personal lending will not be covered. The scale and
coverage was not due to be revealed before March 2009, after detailed
negotiation with the banks. The same package included £50 billion of

---

[5]   There are other ways of implementing government-backed disaster insurance.
    Perhaps the simplest is for governments to conduct a large-scale mandatory
    recapitalization of banks, raising their capital ratios from, say, 10 to 30 per cent
    of risk-weighted assets, while at the same time reducing dilution by providing
    existing shareholders with 'call options' that give them the right to purchase a
    large proportion of this new equity at the same price for which it was originally
    provided by the government. My business school web pages, www.cass.city.
    ac.uk/cbs/activities/bankingcrisis.html, contain my discussion of this and other
    schemes for addressing the crisis.

funding to insure the senior tranches of newly issued mortgage-backed securities, a policy proposed in the November report on the financing of the UK housing market by Sir James Crosbie. Other countries may well introduce similar insurance against disastrous losses, exactly the policy measure that this book proposes in order to break the feedback loops shown in Figure 1.1.

Altogether, governments and central banks worldwide have committed around $7 trillion in support of their banks and financial systems. Much of this is in the form of guarantees or purchases of relatively good-quality assets that will not default. Nonetheless, this is a vast commitment of resources and should certainly be large enough to address the $3 trillion overhang of mortgage-backed and structured credit assets that triggered the crisis in the first place. In the United States, and possibly in the United Kingdom and the rest of Europe eventually, much of this support is in the form of purchases or guarantees of mortgage-backed and structured credit securities. Through these particular measures the governments and central banks are accepting, on behalf of taxpayers, responsibility for the extreme tail of credit risk, in a similar manner to the disaster insurance proposed in this book.

Why, then, are these efforts not already stimulating a recovery of bank lending? In part this may be because the scale of response is even now not yet large enough to reverse the feedback loops illustrated in Figure 1.1 and so turn around expectations and lead to recovery. The impact on expectations of investors and bankers has not been as powerful as the authorities would have hoped. This is partly due to the fragmented nature of these schemes, with a number of different facilities and approaches. It is also because countries other than the United States have not committed themselves to a similar approach. It seems unlikely, even by the time of the 2 April 2009 meeting of the G20 countries, that we will have a more consistent global approach, helping to persuade markets and practitioners that government policy is putting a cap on the amount of losses to which banks are exposed and hence lead to the reopening of bank funding markets and the restarting of bank lending.

Another reason why these initiatives have so far had only a limited impact is that they have been focused on supporting the balance sheets of individual institutions – such as money market mutuals or AIG and Citigroup – and not on directly addressing the illiquidity of senior structured credit markets or supporting the lending of other

institutions. In short, the support needs to be both comprehensive –
offered on a wide range of bank loan assets and structured securities
– and global – available for all banks in the developed world. This is
rather like jumping a stream. Half-hearted support, let's do a little bit
and see if it works, is not enough; the scale of disaster insurance must
be such that the industry can leap to the other side, allowing a strong
recovery in bank lending and economic output and employment. Once
this is done recovery can begin.

Further reading

Brunnermeier's paper, referred to in the notes on further reading in
Chapter 1, is the best short account of the entire crisis of which I am
aware, and like my own work emphasizes the key role of credit market
illiquidity.

Martin Wolf's recent book, *Fixing Global Finance* (Yale University
Press, 2009), has already been referred to in the introduction. It is a
magisterial discussion of the challenge of dealing with the world's
current-account imbalances, covering a huge amount of the relevant
economics literature. He documents how large current-account deficits
have typically resulted in financial crises rather being resolved through
a smooth adjustment, and considers the very considerable challenges
that must be met in order to deal with these global imbalances in an
orderly way, both by domestic policy adjustment and through reform
of the architecture of international financial relations.

The IMF Global Financial Stability Reports of March and October
2008 (www.imf.org/external/pubs/ft/GFSR/index.htm) present a quan-
tification of the losses similar to my own, quantifications that will no
doubt be updated in subsequent reports after this book is published.
There are two critical differences between my calculations and theirs.
My estimates are for Europe and the United States. The IMF estimates
are for US exposures only. Also they do not emphasize, as I do, the
distinction between temporary mark to market write-downs due to
illiquidity and the actual underlying credit impairments.

In order to make this a sharp distinction I use a slightly different
approach from theirs. I base my credit impairment calculations on
the total stock of *all* lending, whether on balance sheet or packaged
in structured vehicles. The IMF calculations of impairment are based
only on lending retained on balance sheet. My estimates of mark to

market write-downs refer *only* to changes in the accounting valuation of AAA vanilla securities that can be assumed not to default and to avoid double counting. I ignore any mark to market write-downs on any tranches rated at less than AAA or any restructured securities. Their calculations allow for write-downs on all forms of securitized paper. My calculations probably understate illiquidity losses, but avoid mixing together credit impairment and reversible illiquidity write-downs. Their calculations mix these two sources of loss but provide a better estimate of total loss.

Nouriel Roubini has recently (21 January 2009) produced an estimate of \$3.6 trillion of total credit crisis loss, very close to my own analysis of total severe case losses. This is in a Roubini Global Economics Monitor working paper, so is available for subscribers only. As far as I am aware (I have been unable to access his detailed report), the principal difference between the Roubini calculations and my own is that he makes no distinction between fundamental credit impairment and illiquidity write-downs.

Table 2.4 *part 1. Principal responses by financial authorities to the financial crisis – before the Lehman failure*

Date	Action	Amount
22 August 2007	ECB Supplementary Long-Term Reserve Auctions.	€40 bn
August–December 2007	Additional lending to US mortgage banks by System of Federal Home Loan Banks.	$250 bn
14 September 2007	Bank of England emergency loan to Northern Rock.	£30 bn
12 December 2007	Fed introduces Term Auction Facility (TAF), offering 28-day loans of reserves to a broad range of counterparties against a wide range of collateral. Actively used throughout the crisis.	Amount increased during the crisis, at end-2008 $300 bn outstanding
12 December 2007	Fed offers swaps of US dollars with ECB and Swiss National Bank for their domestic currencies for lending to domestic banks.	$24 bn
12 December 2007	Bank of England announces increase in scale and broadening of collateral for its term repo auctions.	Extended to £10 bn
11 March 2008	Fed Term Securities Lending Program (TSLP) offering swaps of Treasury securities for illiquid structured credit for periods of up to 28 days.	Up to $200 bn
12 March 2008	Fed offers further swaps of US dollars with ECB and Swiss National Bank for their domestic currencies for lending to domestic banks.	A further $12 bn to supplement the existing $24 bn
16 March 2008	Fed provides guarantees to support JP Morgan acquisition of Bear Sterns.	$30 bn
17 March 2008	Fed announces creation of Primary Dealers Credit Facility (PDCF), giving broker dealers access to discount window borrowing.	$30 bn
21 April 2008	Bank of England Special Liquidity Scheme, offering swaps of liquid UK government securities for illiquid structured credit securities for up to three years.	Up to £50 bn, extended in October to £200 bn
13 July 2008	US Treasury announces increase in line of credit to government-sponsored enterprises Fannie Mae and Freddie Mac.	Amount at discretion of the Secretary to the Treasury
30 July 2008	Fed extends PDCF until January 2009.	
6 September 2008	US Federal Housing Agency with US Treasury support takes Fannie and Freddie into 'conservatorship', with open-ended support of their capital.	Unlimited

Table 2.4 *part 2. Principal responses by financial authorities to the financial crisis – after the Lehman failure*

Date	Action	Amount
16 September 2008	US Treasury/Fed line of credit to prevent AIG failure in return for US taxpayer taking an 80 per cent share of AIG equity.	$85 bn, extended in November to $150 bn
18 September 2008	Fed offers swaps of US dollars with other central banks for their domestic currencies for lending to domestic banks.	$180 bn
19 September 2008	US Treasury announces Troubled Asset Relief Programme (TARP)	$750 bn
19 September 2008	Fed announces AMLF scheme to purchase asset-backed commercial paper from money market mutual funds.	$57 bn as at end-November 2008
22 September 2008	Fed approves applications of Goldman Sachs and Morgan Stanley to become bank holding companies, eligible to access Fed liquidity like other commercial banks.	
29 September 2008	Rescue of Fortis group by governments of France, Belgium and Netherlands.	€11.1 bn
29 September 2008	German government guarantee on funding provided by consortium of private banks to Hypo Real Estate.	€35 bn, extended to €50 bn one week later
29 September 2008	US House of Representatives rejects TARP legislation.	
30 September 2008	Irish government announces blanket guarantees on retail deposits.	
1 October 2008	Rescue of Dexia by governments of France, Belgium and Luxembourg.	€6.1 bn
3 October 2008	US Congress finally passes TARP legislation.	
7 October 2008	Fed announces commercial paper funding facility (CPFF), providing three-month finance for commercial paper and so support to the commercial paper market.	$282 bn as at end-November 2008
8 October 2008	UK government announces recapitalization (up to £50 bn) and wholesale funding guarantees (up to £250 bn) for UK banks.	Up to £300 bn
12 October 2008	European governments announce recapitalization and wholesale funding guarantees.	€2 trillion eventually pledged
14 October 2008	US Treasury announces bank recapitalization scheme.	$250 bn of TARP funds

Table 2.4 (*cont.*)

Date	Action	Amount
21 October 2008	Fed announces Money Market Investor Funding Facility (MMIFF), senior secured funding (90 per cent of total) to privately established special purpose vehicles purchasing commercial paper/certificates of deposit from money market mutuals.	Up to $540 bn
23 November 2008	US Treasury rescue of Citigroup: $40 bn equity plus $306 bn asset guarantees.	$346 bn
25 November 2008	Fed announces Term Asset Backed Securities Lending Facility (TALF), providing collateralized lending against AAA-rated ABS securities.	Initially $200bn, backed by $20 bn of TARP funds
25 November 2008	Fed announces programme of purchase of agency (Fannie and Freddie) mortgage-backed securities.	$600 bn

3 | *We have been here before, haven't we?*

This chapter takes a look at some previous banking crises during the past century, comparing them with the situation today. It examines the US banking panic of 1907, the problems of bank lending to Latin America in the early 1980s and two crises that emerged at about the same time in the early 1990s – the deep and protracted problems of Japanese banking and the banking crises in Scandinavia. It then looks at the widespread banking and financial market problems during the Asian crisis of 1997 and finally at the collapse of the Long-Term Capital Management (LTCM) hedge fund that followed in 1998.

This is a selective and highly condensed analysis of these episodes. A full survey of previous banking crises would go well beyond the compass of a single book chapter, but it is possible to pull out some common themes. It can be seen that there is 'no smoke without fire'. All these banking crises had their origins, like those of 2007–8, in a macroeconomic and credit boom and bust, accompanied by inadequate controls and risk management by at least some banks. Also all these crises arose following a period of financial innovation and deregulation, encouraging weaknesses of control and supervision.

It is also clear that in these crises panic and withdrawal of short-term funding played a significant role. This is most apparent in the panic of 1907 and in the Asian crisis of 1997 and the collapse of LTCM, but it is also present in other cases, for example Finland and Sweden, where the threat of withdrawal of short-term wholesale borrowing also worsened the situation. Since banks rely on short-term funding, crisis resolution requires that this funding is stabilized. This has typically required large-scale public-sector guarantees in order to maintain confidence in bank liabilities.

Was there a standard approach to resolving these banking crises? There seem to be two main lessons to be learned from them. First, as is widely accepted, it is much better to recognize bank-loan problems promptly and take firm action to maintain bank solvency. This is why 'recognize' and 'recapitalize' are two of the most important watch-words when dealing with a banking crisis. This approach was taken successfully both in Scandinavia and in the Asian banking crisis. Both bank lending and economic output then recovered quite quickly, in the context of a substantial exchange-rate depreciation and consequent strong export-driven economic recovery.

The admonition to recognize and recapitalize does not fully deal, however, with situation of 2007–8. What we have today is a global, not a national, crisis. The option of increasing competitiveness and accelerating recovery through a depreciating exchange rate cannot be taken by all countries at a global level, and so freeing banks to undertake more lending does not guarantee that they will lend. Still, 'recognize and recapitalize' is, as the logicians would say, a necessary if not a sufficient condition for recovery. Japan provides an object lesson in the difficulties that arise if problems are not recognized, and this is one reason why Japan has never fully recovered from the bubble of the late 1980s, although the causes of the long Japanese economic stagnation go well beyond the banking sector alone.

Another reason why 'recognize and recapitalize' cannot be so easily put into practice in this current crisis is the great difficulty of recognizing loan or credit problems when, as now, banks have got into difficulties at the very beginning of an economic downturn. This is particularly so when they are holding credit assets that are 'marked to market' and can fall very much further in value because of anticipation of yet worse news to come. The situation is even worse if there is no liquid market on which they can be bought or sold. In this circumstance it is virtually impossible to get consensus on an appropriate current valuation.

The second lesson, one most pertinent today, is perhaps not as widely accepted as it should be. Because of the instability of short-term bank funding relatively small initial shocks (the San Francisco earthquake, losses of Thai finance houses, poorly controlled sub-prime lending) can have large cumulative impacts. To deal with funding problems and restore confidence it is essential to provide resolute support on whatever scale is necessary to stabilize the situation. As 1907 illustrates, voluntary private-sector co-ordination of such support is problematic. The United States was fortunate then to have the powerful and dominating figure of J. P. Morgan to help persuade others to do what was necessary. In the modern context the responsibility for providing this support lies with the agencies of the state – both the central bank and the government itself. In the face of a systemic crisis this state responsibility goes well beyond central bank liquidity provision, requiring government guarantees and purchase of bad assets. Moreover, as the case of LTCM illustrates vividly, such support need not encourage 'moral hazard', because it is aimed at restoring liquidity and confidence, not at bailing out fundamental losses.

Much ink is spilled on the creation of asset management companies, or, as they are sometimes grandly named, 'aggregator banks' to take bad loans off the books of banks that are recovering from overwhelming bad loan problems. This is a useful practical device when a bank has been nationalized (in this case there is no need to value the bad loans to determine the claims of private shareholders). This approach was applied successfully at a late stage of the Finnish crisis, in Sweden, in Thailand and in South Korea. But there are other techniques for cleaning up bank balance sheets. Here the case of Latin American debt is most instructive. The Brady bonds are an object lesson in how this can be done in the absence of necessary consensus on valuation, through imaginative use of government guarantees.

The panic of 1907

There are many similarities between the banking panic that gripped the United States in 1907 and the global banking crisis 101 years later. Just like today, that panic came at the end of a period of strong economic growth. Industrial output in the United States had more than doubled in a little over a decade. These were some of the peak years of immigration from Europe into the United States and they were accompanied by a major boom in investment and the rapid growth of money and credit.

There was then a major shock, the San Francisco earthquake of April 1906 that caused damage of close to 1½ per cent of US national income and triggered correspondingly large insurance losses. Rather like the shock from losses on US sub-prime lending – which was of a very similar size relative to the US economy – this had an increasing and cumulative economic impact, ushering in a period of credit shortage and slowing economic growth. Stock price movements were also eerily similar to those of 101 years later, with US stock price indices peaking in September 1906 and then falling sharply over subsequent months.

This economic slowdown would not on its own have been enough to trigger a full-blown banking panic, but, again like today, the fuel for a crisis was laid down by period of rapid financial innovation, in which a new form of lightly regulated banks known as trust companies – the 'parallel' banking of their day – increased their balance sheets by close to 200 per cent. The original purpose of these New York institutions was providing clients with basic custody services such as registration and holding of securities, but as private banks they escaped many of the restrictive regulations applied to state and national chartered banks. For example, they were until 1906 exempt from reserve requirements and could hold equities as investments. This gave them a competitive advantage, allowing them to offer relatively high rates of interest on their deposits, and underpinned rapid balance sheet expansion. The trust companies were not, however, members of the New York Clearing House – the body that handled payments between banks – and so relied on a member of the Clearing House to act as their 'clearing agent' in order to offer their customers a full range of banking services.

The week before the panic saw the downfall of three rather disreputable New York financiers, Charles Morse and the brothers Otto and Augustus Heinze. On Tuesday 15 October 1907, Otto Heinze was ruined by a failed attempted to manipulate the price of the relatively small United Copper Company. This created doubts about the viability of a web of smaller banks owned by either Otto's brother Augustus or his associate Morse. By Sunday 20 October the New York Clearing House had forced Augustus Heinze and Charles Morse to give up all their banking interests.

These events were worrying but what triggered panic was the revelation on Monday 21 October 1907 that Charles T. Barney, the respected president of the Knickerbocker Trust Company, had an association with the Heinzes and Morse (the full extent of this association has never been clarified, although it is known that he was present at a meeting discussing the financing of the Otto Heinze stock manipulation). Barney had run the Knickerbocker on a personal basis, with few board meetings and little direct oversight from the board. When the association became public the board of the Knickerbocker asked Barney to resign (less than a month later Barney committed suicide). The same day the clearing agent for the Knickerbocker, the National Bank of Commerce, announced that it would no longer provide it with clearing services.

These actions and the lack of information about its activities destroyed confidence in the Knickerbocker. The following day, Tuesday 22 October, queues formed outside its two main offices – on Fifth Avenue and on Broadway – and at its two smaller branches in Harlem and in the Bronx, and some $8 million of its total deposit base of $69 million was withdrawn in just three and half hours; this was ended only by suspension of withdrawals and a closure of the teller windows. These events in turn undermined confidence in other institutions, leading over the following ten days to repeated and substantial runs, including on the much larger Trust Company of America, where Barney was a board member, and on the Lincoln Trust, as well as on many smaller banks, and also to a collapse of stock prices and a shortage of credit that threatened the insolvency of more than fifty members of the New York Stock Exchange. The panic spread from New York across the country, with large numbers of banks suspending deposit withdrawals. However, compared with earlier banking panics, there were few actual bank failures, only six of 6,412 national banks failing.

One reason for the spread of problems was that in 1907 there was no US central bank acting as a lender of last resort to provide banks with funds to meet deposit withdrawals or to co-ordinate support for institutions in difficulties (Congress established the US Federal Reserve in 1913, following two years of deliberations and a 24-volume report by the National Monetary Commission on the 1907 crisis). The response to the crisis relied on voluntary collective action, and this was, at least initially, slow and halting and hampered by the fact that the trust companies had no equivalent of the New York Clearing House to provide each other with support.

The seventy-year-old John Pierpoint Morgan, the dominant financier and banker of his day, played a key role in co-ordinating responses to the crisis in the days that followed (much as he had in the earlier banking crisis of 1893–5, when he arranged a massive loan of gold from the US Treasury). There was no single measure that killed off the panic, but after two weeks it did eventually subside, following loans by the largest national banks to the Trust Company of America and to the Lincoln Trust, the rather reluctant agreement of other trust companies to provide these two trusts with a longer-term $25 million facility, the provision of a US Treasury loan of $25 million to the strongest national banks in order to finance a loan pool offered to stock exchange brokers, and the issue by the New York Clearing

House of 'clearing house certificates', a form of temporary money that could be used by members to settle their obligations to each other. Also, most importantly for restoring confidence, there was the announcement and shipping of large sums of gold from London and other financial centres, with over $21 million having arrived in New York by mid-November.

The panic was accompanied by one of the most severe economic downturns in US history. This began *before* the panic, with industrial output falling by 11 per cent from May 1907 to June 1908 and unemployment increasing from under 2.8 to 8 per cent. But the widespread suspensions of deposit withdrawals were ended by January 1908 and the economy began to recover in the summer, expanding strongly and achieving pre-crisis levels of employment and output by late 1909.

Despite the marked parallels between 1907 and the current crisis 101 years later, a similarly quick economic recovery seems unlikely today. This time the crisis is global, not national, so that demand worldwide will remain weak for a long time, and the United States cannot rely on strong export growth to pull it out of recession. Also the United States was in 1908 the China of its day, harnessing both human and natural resources to meeting substantial and growing world demand for its agricultural and manufacturing output. The United States in 2009 does not have the same strong competitive advantage over other countries that it had then, so that it will be much more difficult to restore US output and employment.

The Latin American debt crisis of the 1980s

On 12 August 1982, the Mexican Finance Minister, Jesus Silva Herzog, telephoned the US Secretary to the Treasury Donald Regan, the US Federal Reserve Chairman Paul Volcker and the Managing Director of the IMF Jacques de Larosière, to let them know that Mexico had almost run out of foreign currency reserves and could no longer make payments on around $80 billion of foreign currency loans it had taken out from US and European banks. By November Brazil, similarly, had given up on repaying its own $90 billion of debt, and other debtor states, including Argentina, the third biggest Latin American borrower, and the Philippines soon followed suit. This was a global banking crisis. Many large Western banks were threatened with insolvency if their loans to emerging markets were written off.

How did this crisis arise and how was it resolved? Just as today's banking and credit crisis has its roots in global current-account balances, the problem of Latin American debt was rooted in the 'recycling' of the surpluses of oil-exporting countries of the Middle East, such as Saudi Arabia. In 1973, following restrictions on output agreed by the Organization of the Petroleum Exporting Countries (OPEC) – an alliance of most of the major oil exporting countries – the world price of oil jumped, and in the following years exporting countries deposited much of the proceeds of their oil sales with US and European banks.

The banks were then keen to find profitable opportunities for lending this money. At that time domestic lending markets were still fairly tightly regulated, so that a large part of these 'petrodollars' were lent on to governments and state enterprises in emerging markets, especially in Latin America. In his valuable account of the Latin American debt crisis, Pedro-Pablo Kucynski estimates that the ratio of external debt to national income across Latin America rose from 24 per cent in 1973 to 51 per cent in 1981, and the ratio of debt to exports from around 200 per cent to 300 per cent.

Much of this lending was at short-term 'floating' rates of interest, set at a fixed margin about the London money-market dollar Libor (London Interbank Offered Rate) rate. Then in 1980 and 1981 the indebted countries of Latin America were hit by a double shock – a big increase in dollar rates of interest as then Federal Reserve chairman Paul Volcker tightened US monetary policy to combat inflation, and a substantial decline in exports as the US and world economies moved into recession. The ratio of interest payments to exports jumped from 23 per cent in 1980 to 49 per cent in 1982. Moreover, viewing these problems as temporary, most Latin American countries responded by substantially increasing their borrowing from the international banks, especially at short maturities of less than two years.

The crisis was managed, during the years 1982 to 1985, through large-scale and much criticized programmes of assistance from the IMF. The fund provided sufficient funds for the indebted countries to keep current with their borrowing. The exposed banks were required to provide additional short-term loans and to reschedule existing borrowing to much longer maturities. The borrowing countries had to cut back their bloated programmes of public expenditure and their unsustainable government borrowing and also devalue their currencies to help reduce their large current-account deficits running in excess of 6 per cent of gross national product (GNP).

This response was successful in avoiding default and reducing current-account deficits to around 1 per cent of GNP, but it was not a permanent solution. Economic growth remained low, hampered by a broad range of structural and institutional problems that hindered industry and enterprise in the indebted economies. The fierce reductions in government spending were politically unpopular and hit more vulnerable citizens especially hard (causing them to associate the IMF unfairly but indelibly with 'anti-poor' economic policies). The reality was that austerity measures were unavoidable (when the money runs out spending has to be reduced, with or without IMF borrowing) but could not restore economic growth as long as the world economy remained weak. As Kucynski puts the matter, 'The lesson to be drawn from these contrasting cases is that economic recovery depends upon a combination of a favorable world environment and the economic measures taken by individual governments; neither side of the equation can work by itself' (p. 98).

These efforts, ensuring that the debtor countries remained current with their international borrowing even if the underlying problems remained unresolved, were accompanied by a fierce public and political debate in the United States and Europe about how best to deal with the crisis. These debates raised almost exactly the same issues and questions as the debate over the present banking and credit crisis, a full quarter of a century later. A strong vein of opinion vehemently opposed using public money, through the IMF, to 'bail out' profligate bankers. There were repeated claims that banks should 'come clean' and write down their lending to market values (although this was controversial because, just as in the case of structured credits today, the secondary markets for these loans were extremely thin, and it was unclear that pricing reflected a reasonable view of prospective defaults). Until 1987 banks remained extremely reluctant to write down their Latin American debts, if for no other reason than to have done so rapidly would have wiped out one or two years of profits and could have raised doubts about their own solvency.

This balance of opinion against 'bail-out', and the unwillingness or inability of banks themselves to make provisions against loan losses, led policymakers to pursue the ill-fated Baker plan, drawn up in 1985 by US Secretary to the Treasury James Baker. Initially lauded as a solution to the Latin American debt problem, this envisaged a programme of renewed public- and private-sector lending, accompanied by fundamental structural reforms to promote growth. But this initiative foundered in the face of resistance from both banks, that would not lend more, and governments of the indebted countries who did not have stomach for more austerity.

Gradually the reality dawned that banks could not get back all that they had lent to Latin America. In 1987 Citibank made dramatically large loss provisions of some $3 billion against its Latin American lending, a move welcomed by financial markets and copied by several other banks. Total provisions by US banks against Latin American lending increased from $9 billion to $21 billion (although secondary market pricing suggested even greater losses, of some $49 billion, in 1988).

This recognition paved the way for a much more successful 1989 initiative introduced by the US Treasury Secretary under President George H. W. Bush, Nicholas F. Brady. This marked a major shift in policy towards the debt crisis, using a combination of public guarantees and private-sector debt write-downs to persuade the debtor countries to introduce the necessary structural and financial reforms that would support a return to economic growth. This plan created new instruments, the so-called 'Brady bonds', to replace the illiquid bank debt. Crucially these were designed so that they could be traded in liquid markets, making it much easier for banks to manage their exposure and, because they were liquid, achieving an immediate increase in market valuation of remaining debt.

The issue of Brady bonds was negotiated on a country-by-country basis and differed slightly from case to case. The key arrangement was the exchange of dollar loans for thirty-year bonds, with their principal value guaranteed by the issue of zero-coupon US government securities. If the debtors did not repay on maturity, then the US government securities would repay investors. There was also a write-down either of interest payments alone (so-called par Brady bonds) or of both interest and principal (so-called discount Brady bonds).

The Brady plan was the catalyst for a return to more normal financing arrangements, providing the indebted countries with renewed access to international capital markets and shifting the burden and risks off the balance sheets of banks and sharing it more widely among long-term investors such as pension funds and insurance companies.

Eventually most countries paid down their Brady bonds ahead of schedule. Between 1994 and 2006 the value of outstanding Brady bonds fell from over 60 per cent to around 2 per cent of total emerging market debt.

The protracted Japanese financial crisis

Japan enjoyed an extraordinary period of rapid growth from 1950 until 1990. During this time it established itself as the world's leading manufacturer and exporter of products ranging from motor vehicles to electronics. Japanese products gained an enviable reputation for quality of engineering, design and reliability. The leading Japanese manufacturing firms pioneered highly efficient production systems, making them by some margin the most cost-efficient manufacturing companies in the world.

By 1985 Japan was the world's second-largest economy, after the United States. Also, with its substantial surplus of exports over imports and the very high level of household savings, it was the world's largest 'creditor' state (i.e. held more foreign assets than any other country).

The development of most other areas of the Japanese economy lagged well behind their world-leading manufacturing export sector. Services and agriculture remained very inefficient. In particular, Japanese banks developed practices which made them very unlike their counterparts in the United States, the United Kingdom or most other industrialized countries.

- Banks retained close ties with firms through the so-called 'Keiretsu' system, in which groups of companies are linked through cross-holdings of equity, shared directorships and other arrangements. Each Keiretsu has its own bank, which holds substantial equity stakes in the Keiretsu companies and is closely involved in both their short- and long-term financing.
- Japanese banks, unlike those in the United Kingdom or the United States, have always made very low levels of profits, compared with the size of their balance sheets. Their typical 'return on assets' has been about 0.5%, compared with around 1% or 1.5% in the West, and interest margins only around 1% instead of 2 or 2.5%. Instead of focusing on margins and profits, their principal objective has been providing low-cost finance to corporate customers. Their

business strategies emphasized balance sheet growth and market share, not profitability.

- Retail lending markets, such as mortgages and credit cards, remained relatively undeveloped in Japan.
- Until the early 1980s Japanese banks operated under a range of restrictive controls on interest rates and amounts of credit. These controls were then relaxed, allowing the subsequent rapid increase in lending of the late 1980s.

Japan thus had major structural problems that limited the growth of its domestic economy. Further problems built up for the Japanese banks during the late 1980s. During this period, known as the 'bubble economy', prices of financial assets rose to extraordinary levels. The Nikkei index of equity prices peaked at 39,000 (even today it trades at less than 10,000). Land prices, especially in Tokyo, rose even more (the grounds of the imperial palace in Tokyo were said to be worth more as real estate than all of California).

The bubble was created by a combination of easy monetary policy and rapid growth of bank lending, with very weak standards of credit assessment. Typical practice was to lend generously, secured on land and equity prices, with little regard to business plans or the ability to repay. Bank loans were used to purchase more land and equity, pushing up prices even higher. In a single year, 1989, at the peak of the bubble, Japanese bank lending grew by an extraordinary 25 per cent, this in a period of low inflation.

At the same time some of the Japanese banks grew, on the basis of total assets although not profitability, to be the largest banks in the world. They expanded their activities into the United States, the United Kingdom, and elsewhere, acting as the main intermediary for Japanese investment overseas. This competition from Japanese banks, which operated with low levels of capital and very narrow interest rate margins and so were able to undercut UK and US banks, was one of the main drivers behind the introduction of the first 1988 Basel accord (Basel I) on international bank capital adequacy.

The bubble inevitably burst (the initial prick was a tightening of monetary policy in May 1989). First equity prices and then land prices slowed and then collapsed, followed by a sharp fall in domestic investment expenditure. The growth in manufacturing exports also declined, as Japanese companies – while still world leaders in many areas of manufacturing – faced increasing competition from both emerging markets and firms in the industrial world. Most responded by making their activities much more international, locating substantial amounts of their manufacturing capacity outside Japan. There followed a deep recession followed by a long-drawn-out economic stagnation that at the time of writing – nearly twenty years later – still continues. Monetary policy was gradually loosened, with interest rates held close to zero from 1995 onwards but this did not revive Japanese growth.

The post-bubble recession revealed the very poor quality of Japanese bank lending. Something like 20 per cent of Japanese bank loans were non-performing in the early 1990s. Until 1998 there was little action to resolve these bad loans. Japanese regulators and accounting rules allowed the greater part of non-performing loans to be carried on bank books without being written off. Japanese banks were throwing good money after bad, hoping for some economic resurgence that would magically turn non-performing loans into performing loans, but instead increasing the level of ultimate losses. By the mid 1990s a large part of the Japanese banking system was insolvent.

High household and corporate saving meant that Japanese banks continued to attract inflows of deposits, and could use these inflows to fill the gap in their cash-flow caused by non-service of existing loans. This practice of course made the problem worse; interest payments due on loans was being added to the existing stock and increasing the problem of non-performing loans. Only the fact that interest rates themselves fell to the lowest possible level (market interest rates falling to less than 25 basis points or 0.25 per cent), and Japanese depositors were protected by both explicit deposit insurance and the 'implicit' promise of support from the Japanese government, which prevented an immediate crisis (in 1995 this implicit promise was made explicit by the announcement of a blanket guarantee on all bank deposits).

By late 1997 real output was once again falling, leading in November 1997 to the failure of a large regional bank and then of the giant securities firms Sanyo and Yamaichi. This prompted the Japanese parliament to introduce in 1998 a number of more radical measures to deal with the financial crisis, including large-scale commitment of public funds to recapitalize 'solvent' financial institutions and the creation of new institutions to take over the assets of failed banks. Two of the long-term credit banks were also nationalized. Subsequently many of the major Japanese banks have merged.

Although the 1998 measures dealt with some of the worst of the non-performing bank loans, the practice of lending good money to prop up bad borrowers has continued. Banks have continued the practice of lending to existing corporate customers, regardless of their ability to repay loans. As a result there is a continuing problem of non-performing loans that could yet get much worse if the economy slows. Loans to households, such as mortgages, credit cards or personal loans, constitute only a small share of total bank lending. With weak domestic demand consumer price inflation has fallen below zero, prices falling by about 1 per cent per year from 1999 onwards.

Other parts of the Japanese financial system are also very weak. The large life insurance sector had a practice of offering high levels of guaranteed returns to policyholders, returns that may have seemed realistic during the 1980s but could not be sustained in the 1990s. Many insurance companies have failed and the solvency of many of those surviving is still doubtful. There has also been a large, inefficient, network of government agencies lending funds collected through the Japanese postal saving system – the largest collector of retail savings in the world – lent on to a variety of public-sector agencies with poor controls on the use of these funds. The post office savings system was privatized in 2007, but the various government agencies remain and continue to distort the allocation of savings.

Because of the problems in the financial sector and the weakness of the domestic economy, the Japanese economy has grown only slowly since the end of the bubble. It has also fallen repeatedly into recession, in 1997, then again in 2001 and, most recently, in late 2008. Only very high levels of government spending on construction and other public works projects have prevented much larger falls of output, but these major fiscal stimulus packages, resulting in fiscal deficits averaging around 5 per cent of national income for more than a decade, have been only a temporary palliative and have pushed up government debt to as much as 180 per cent of national income (compared, for example, with only around 40 per cent in the United States or 50 per cent in the United Kingdom).

This is a problem of domestic, not external, finance. Savings rates remain extremely high (partly because of a rapidly aging population and the expectation that with such a large stock of government borrowing there will be little money to spare for social security and health expenditure). Japan is still a wealthy country. Japan has some of the highest standards of education in the world. Recorded unemployment remains low, at around 4 per cent of the workforce.

A number of commentators refer to the 'lost decade' in Japan, arguing that had problems of bad loans been addressed quickly and forcefully in the very early 1990s, when they first emerged, then Japan need not have endured the subsequent humiliating years of slow growth of incomes and output or be faced with its present daunting burden of government debt.

While Japan might have confronted its banking problems at an earlier stage, this interpretation is too simplistic. It is clear that the challenges faced by Japan go far beyond the bank losses arising from the credit boom and bust of the late 1980s and early 1990s. Calculations by Fukao (reported in 2003) reveal that cumulative loan loss provisions by Japanese banks have amounted to some 18 per cent of 2002 Japanese GNP, more than enough to deal with the losses incurred during the bubble.[1] Japan faces much deeper institutional and structural problems that prevent savings being allocated efficiently, restricting consumption and other private expenditure and discouraging innovation and productivity improvements in its domestic economy and service sectors.

How this will ultimately be played out is far from clear. There does not yet seem to be either the political will or a broad public consensus for major structural changes in the Japanese economy or for an orderly resolution of the problem of Japanese government debt. Continued stagnation and an eventual government debt default is a possible outcome, or Japan may yet muddle along as it has done to date for many years yet. Avoiding these outcomes is not just a matter of economics and finance. It is a broad social and political challenge. The rest of the world can only hope that Japan meets this challenge, because a resurgent and confident Japan, with strong growth of private-sector household and corporate spending, could play an extremely valuable role in easing the global current-account imbalances and restoring growth to the world economy.

---

[1] Reported in Misuhiro Fukao, 'Financial sector profitability and double gearing', in Magnus Blomstrom, Jenny Corbett, Fumio Hayashi and Anil Kashyap (eds.), *Structural Impediments to Growth in Japan* (University of Chicago Press, 2003), pp. 9–35.

The emergence of the Scandinavian banking crises

Three Scandinavian countries – Sweden, Norway and Finland – suffered severe banking crises in the early 1990s; the crisis was especially severe in Finland, which suffered a cumulative decline of output of around 10 per cent and where unemployment rose to 17 per cent, the most severe recession at that time of any industrial country since the Second World War (only South Korea in 1998 comes close).

These crises are of particular interest because – in contrast to Japan or also the United States when dealing with the problems of the savings and loans in the 1980s – the authorities of the Scandinavian countries dealt with the problems of their banks promptly and determinedly. While the three crises differed in important respects, the ways in which they were handled are regarded as examples of good practice from which other countries can learn.

There were a number of common structural and macroeconomic features in all three countries. Financial deregulation in the early 1980s freed up banks to engage in many areas of business that had been hitherto barred, removed all controls on interest rates and lending volumes, and gave banks access to foreign sources of funding. Banking supervision was lax. Generous tax subsidies encouraged both corporate and household borrowing. Larger banks lost market share to smaller banks or non-bank finance companies. Norway's banks were especially exposed because of their relatively low levels of capitalization .

An external demand stimulus, with improving terms of trade, triggered an investment and, latterly, a consumption boom. The timing differed. Norway's boom was in 1984–7, following a rise of world oil prices. Sweden and Finland's were in 1987–9, following the subsequent oil price fall, a rise in the prices of timber/paper products, which were major exports for both countries, and general global expansion as monetary policy was eased after the 1987 global equity market crash.

The consequence was a rapid expansion of bank lending and, in Sweden and most markedly in Finland, an increased current-account deficit, peaking at around 3 per cent of gross domestic product (GDP) in Sweden and 5 per cent of GDP in Finland. Bank lending in Finland grew by around 150 per cent in just six years between 1985 and 1991, with a rise of 47 per cent in 1989 alone. In Sweden bank lending grew from 90 per cent of GDP in 1986 to 140 per cent of GDP in 1991, with a rise of 30 per cent in 1989. Norway experienced similar but more modest credit expansion.

Monetary policy was tightened, but too little and too late. In Finland, when interest rates were raised in 1989, a number of banks turned to lower-interest-rate foreign-currency borrowing, a strategy that resulted in substantial exchange-rate losses when the Finnish markka depreciated in 1991 and 1992. Swedish banks also borrowed in foreign currency and so suffered large exchange-rate losses in November of 1992.

A further consequence of the credit boom was a jump in real estate prices. In Finland the price of housing doubled in real terms between 1980 and 1990 (i.e. after correcting for the increase in the consumer price index, Norwegian house prices rose by around 75 per cent in real terms. In Sweden there was a somewhat smaller real house price appreciation in the late 1980s.

All three countries were then hit by a negative macroeconomic shock. For Norway this was the 1986 decline in oil prices. For Sweden and Finland it was the slowing of the global economy and the decline in world paper prices in 1991 and 1992. In addition monetary policy in 1990–2 was deflationary, setting interest rates at high levels in order to maintain a peg of their exchange rate against a basket of other European currencies (the ECU). Finland devalued in September 1991 and then all three countries abandoned their exchange rate pegs in late 1992 (just as the United Kingdom had been forced to abandon its peg in September 1992). Interest rates were then substantially reduced.

The shock in Finland was exacerbated by the 1991 collapse of the Soviet Union – the destination of around 15 per cent of Finnish exports, which then declined by some 70 per cent in a single year. By late 1992 the debt service burden of Finnish households had risen from 4 to 10 per cent of disposable income, and for the Finnish paper industry jumped to 150 per cent of pre-interest earnings.

The consequence was a cessation of growth in Norway in 1989 and a major fall in output in the other two countries in 1991, with a decline in GDP of 1 per cent in Sweden and of no less than 6.5 per cent in Finland. Unemployment rose to 17 per cent in Finland, 9 per cent in Sweden and 6 per cent in Norway. Output fell further in 1992, by 1 per cent in Sweden and by 3 per cent in Finland, before a fairly strong recovery.

The resolution of the Scandinavian banking crises

In all three countries the most serious banking problems appeared towards the end of the recession, *not* at the beginning of the downturn (in contrast to some other banking crises, including the global banking crisis of 2007 and the Asian crisis of 1997). All three countries benefited from exchange-rate depreciation which helped to lead them to relatively rapid economic recovery, with the export sectors reviving in 1993. As the banking crisis worsened, both Sweden and Finland introduced explicit state guarantees on *all* bank liabilities that played an important role in reducing the costs of wholesale funding, especially that provided by foreign investors.

The details of the resolution of the three crises varied. In Finland most of the loan losses emerged in the savings bank sector (the savings banks were small mutual banks providing mortgages and business loans), and in Skopbank, the 'central bank' for the system of Finnish savings banks. Skopbank provided the savings banks with payments and liquidity services and was also a commercial lender. During the 1980s Skopbank aggressively expanded its loan book, for example financing Tampella (a Finnish heavy industry manufacturer that went bankrupt in 1990), and funding itself from short-term money markets. Its losses mounted quickly in the downturn and it failed in September 1991 and was acquired by Bank of Finland.

In 1992 the Finnish government began taking additional measures. In early 1992 parliament agreed funding for a resolution fund with broad powers. One use of the fund was to recapitalize the entire banking system through an offer to purchase preference shares taken up by virtually all Finnish banks.

Also in 1992 the government forced forty-two savings banks to merge into a single institution, the Savings Bank of Finland (SBF), recapitalized out of the resolution fund. The fund also acquired Skopbank from the Bank of Finland. The crisis was still not over, and the fund gave further support in the form of guarantees to the two largest commercial banks, Kansallispankki (KOP) and Suomen Yhdyspankki (SYP), which were later merged to form Merita (now part of the Nordea group). It also assisted the co-operative banking sector and acquired the worst assets of the failed commercial bank Suomen Työväen Säästöpankki (STS). By end-1992 some 17 per cent of Finnish loans were non-performing and total loan loss provisions had mounted to 5.5 per cent of total bank lending. In 1993 the SBF was broken up, with its non-performing loans transferred to a special asset management company, Arsenal.

In Sweden the losses were spread among all categories of banks. Problems first emerged in 1990 in some smaller finance companies that specialized in real estate lending. Then, in 1991, the largest commercial bank, Nordbanken, which was majority state-owned, and the largest savings bank Första Sparbanken reported substantial loan losses. They were both recapitalized with state support, Nordbanken receiving 5 billion kronor in new equity capital (about 1½ per cent of its balance sheet) mostly from government. In the autumn of 1992 it was given a further 10 billion kronor and a minority of private-sector shares were bought out for 2 billion kronor. In 1991 Första Sparbanken was recapitalized by the savings bank movement, backed by 7 billion kronor of state guarantees and subsidized loans.

Loan losses continued to mount across the entire banking industry, and in September 1992 the Swedish authorities announced comprehensive action, establishing a resolution agency to deal with the crisis, with the necessary legislation passed by the Swedish parliament that December. This response had three main elements. First was an announcement of blanket guarantees on all liabilities of the Swedish banking system. The second element was an insistence on full disclosure of loan losses and asset values. The third element was recapitalization of all banks on a sufficient scale that they could operate as viable institutions. The process was facilitated by a bipartisan political approach (with full disclosure of the various steps taken to resolve the banking problems and a member of the political opposition on the board of the resolution agency).

The seven largest banks, accounting for some 90 per cent of the industry, provided full information on all loan losses and agreed a realistic assessment of the value of their assets. Four of the seven were able to manage without any government support (among these SE Banken raised additional capital from private shareholders). One, Föreningsbanken, was classified as viable in the long term and supported through a state guarantee allowing it to raise private capital. Two banks, Nordbanken and Gota Bank, had much higher loan losses than any of the others, and were no longer viable even in the long term. Nordbanken was already by this stage state-owned. Gota Bank was nationalized, its private shareholder equity fully written down to zero. To clean up the balance sheets of these nationalized banks, two asset management companies were set up: Securum, which took assets of Nordbanken (about 20 per cent of its entire loan book), and Retriva, which took assets of Gota Bank (nearly a half of all loans).

In Norway, bank losses first emerged in 1988. Until 1990 it appeared these could be managed without any government intervention. Some fifteen smaller banks failed, but these were handled by the savings bank and commercial banks deposit guarantee funds.

In 1991 the crisis intensified. The previous losses had exhausted the two bank deposit guarantee funds. High interest rates, slow growth and continuing declines in real estate prices were leading to mounting loan losses across the Norwegian banking system. The overall level of losses was less than in Finland or Sweden, but the banks' low profitability and capitalization meant that many were now on the brink of failure. The government responded in early 1991 by creating a Government Bank Insurance Fund (GBIF).

At first the GBIF simply loaned money to the two bank deposit guarantee funds, but by late 1991 these funds had borrowed all they could without themselves failing. So the GBIF then began taking shareholdings in Norwegian banks. It did so under strict conditions, insisting that all losses were first absorbed by writing down the original private shareholder equity before any government funds were exposed to loss. By 1992 the GBIF was the owner of three of the four largest Norwegian banks (Den Norske, Christiana and Fokus), accounting for 54 per cent of banking assets. The private shareholder equity of all three banks was completely wiped out. In contrast to Finland and Sweden, an asset management company was not used to take non-performing loans off the banks, and, while there was an informal political promise to guarantee all bank liabilities, there was no formal legislative guarantee of the kind provided in Finland and Sweden.

An important feature of the resolution of the Scandinavian crises (see Table 3.1) is that the net costs to taxpayers of their resolution were substantially less than the gross costs. The Norwegian taxpayers actually made quite a decent profit once the nationalized banks were reprivatized, and the sale of government stakes in Swedish and Finnish banks also greatly reduced the overall fiscal costs.

While all three countries acted promptly and determinedly to deal with their banking problems, they did so in different ways. The

Table 3.1. *Fiscal costs of bank support (% of 1997 GDP)*

	Gross cost	Net cost
Finland	9.0	5.3
Norway (present value % of 2001 GDP)	3.4	−0.4
Sweden	3.6	0.2

Source: Table 4.1 of Seppo Honkapoija, 'The 1990s Financial Crises in Nordic Countries', Bank of Finland Discussion Paper, 2009, 5.

Swedish authorities applied a comprehensive due diligence procedure to its largest banks, involving international experts and ensuring full disclosure of loan losses and agreement about asset valuations. The authorities of both Finland and Norway, in contrast, continued to rely on standard accounting statements, leaving more room for dispute about the extent of losses.

The Norwegian authorities were much stricter than those of either Sweden or Finland, avoiding the use of public funds to support the interests of private shareholders. They insisted that all losses were absorbed first by equity holders and then by the privately owned deposit guarantee funds. The only public subsidy provided by the Norwegian government was a relatively small programme of subsidized loans to banks introduced in late 1991. Because of the scale of losses and the low level of Norwegian bank capitalization, the outcome was the nationalization of three of the four largest Norwegian commercial banks, with private shareholder equity written down to zero.

Sweden adopted a similar principle of no subsidy to private shareholders in autumn 1992, but by this time it had already used state funds to buy out the minority private shareholding in Nordbanken and to provide guarantees and subsidized loans to the largest Swedish savings bank. So in practice it applied this approach only to Gota Bank, which was resolved in a similar manner to the failed Norwegian banks, through nationalization, with its private shareholder interest written down to zero.

The Finnish authorities took the most pragmatic approach, rather than one based on any announced principles. Their bank losses were concentrated among their mutually owned savings banks. Absorbing these losses required very large sums of public money, provided first from the Bank of Finland and then from the resolution fund, and resulted in a major restructuring contraction of the savings bank sector. The two largest commercial banks also benefited from state guarantees, allowing them to raise fresh capital without a further write-down of shareholder interests.

The build-up to the Asian banking and exchange-rate crisis

In July 1997 a dramatic and almost entirely unexpected banking and financial crisis struck Thailand, Indonesia, Malaysia, the Philippines and South Korea, forcing them into substantial exchange-rate devaluations, imposing major currency losses on many of their domestic banks and exposing large amounts of non-performing loans. Thailand, Indonesia and then South Korea turned to the IMF for financial support, accepting tough conditions on their monetary and fiscal policies until this lending was repaid. The Philippines expanded an IMF programme already in place before the crisis. Only Malaysia managed without IMF money, but could not avoid a painful economic slowdown. In all these countries investment collapsed and growth fell well below trend for the next two years. The crisis also affected other Asian economies, such as those of Hong Kong, Singapore, China and Taiwan, and weakened investor confidence in all emerging markets. Just like the Latin American debt crisis of the 1980s, this crisis also raised doubts about exposures of Western banks to emerging markets. Then, in 1998, as a kind of coda to the crisis, there was a new shock to global financial markets following the default by Russia on some of its domestic debt obligations which in turn led to the collapse of the world's largest hedge fund, Long Term Capital Management (LTCM).

These events are worth describing in some detail, because they echo many features of the current global banking crisis. The Asian crisis was also produced by a combination of fundamental problems – in this case the use of bank borrowing for too many uneconomic and unproductive investments – with unstable short-term financing arrangements. Banks and investors, placing a somewhat naive faith in the continuation of business as usual, were unaware of their exposure to a disturbance of the entire system. The speed of subsequent developments took them entirely by surprise. A relatively small initial shock – the emergence of losses in the smaller, lightly regulated Thai finance houses – cumulated in a major global financial disruption. There was contagion, the initial shock undermining investor confidence not just in Thailand but in all the countries that had absorbed large sums of short-term portfolio investment, exposing the fragility of banks and exchange-rate arrangements across the region. But the withdrawal of investor funds and crisis of confidence was greatly overdone; within a couple of years strong growth resumed in all these countries, exchange rates appreciated and the capital flight that undermined them was reversed.

The countries directly affected by the Asian crisis are very diverse. At one extreme is Indonesia, with a vast population of 221 million people and exceptionally rich natural resources, but with poor communications and transport and great ethnic and linguistic divisions. The Philippines is somewhat smaller, with 83 million people, and lacking natural resources, but with similar problems of transport and communications and frequently battered by tropical storms. The Philippines also has a large number of citizens working as migrants in other countries and remitting their earnings back home. Both Indonesia and the Philippines have average per capita annual incomes of less than $1,000. At the other extreme is South Korea, a rich manufacturing country and a member of the club of industrial nations, the Organization for Economic Co-operation and Development (OECD), with its population of 48 million enjoying an average per capita annual income of close to $20,000. Thailand and Malaysia fall in the middle, with populations of 64 and 25 million and average per capita annual incomes of around $2,000 and nearly $4,000 respectively, based on successful exports of light manufacturing, clothing, textiles, electronic assembly, agriculture and tourism.

What these five countries have in common is rapid economic growth (especially in Thailand, Malaysia and South Korea), high savings ratios of around 30 per cent of GNP (but a lot lower in the Philippines, at 18 per cent) and fixed investment close to 40 per cent of GNP (the Philippines again a lot lower, at just over 20 per cent). The increase in output and incomes has been mostly based on the exploitation of low labour costs through high levels of savings and physical capital investment. Productivity improvement was not the main source of growth, with much of the fixed capital investment yielding rather low rates of return.

In all these countries the financial sector had been relatively underdeveloped, with low levels of share ownership and equity trading. Most companies remained family-owned or, as in South Korea, part of the large family-controlled industrial conglomerates known as chaebol, and relying on bank debt rather than equity for external financing. Standards of bank credit assessment were weak, with little tradition of analysing business plans or using credit analysis to assess the ability of borrowers to repay. Lending decisions were instead usually based on personal connections, and credit protection relied largely on collateral, such as land or property.

The reliance on bank lending for financing these high rates of fixed capital investment resulted in a very large increase in the stock of bank loans, mainly to companies rather than to households. Between 1990 and 1997, bank loans to the private sector increased from 65 per cent to 116 per cent of GDP in Thailand, from 100 per cent to 145 per cent of GDP in South Korea and from 71 per cent to 108 per cent of GDP in Malaysia. The Philippines and Indonesia had more modest levels of bank lending, but there, too, total lending had expanded rapidly and problems of inadequate credit controls were especially severe in Indonesia, where much bank lending was politically directed to cronies of the Suharto regime.

The sustainability of bank lending and the quality of bank credit assessment did not seem to be an immediate concern in the highly successful export-orientated economies of Thailand, Malaysia and South Korea. They were all enjoying rapid and sustained economic growth with real incomes rising at between 6 and 8 per cent per annum – no need to worry too much about the business plans of customers when revenues and asset values were so buoyant. Current-account deficits, especially in Thailand and Malaysia, were uncomfortably large, and some of the South Korean chaebol had become unprofitable because of their rising labour costs. At some point, with prospects for growth slowing, bank lending would have to be allocated more efficiently. But there seemed to be no urgent need to starve customers of funds in the name of maintaining high standards of credit assessment, because the fundamentals supporting economic growth still appeared to be very strong.

Fundamentals alone do not explain the Asian crisis. The dramatic reversal of investment and growth would not have occurred without excessive reliance on short-term foreign currency borrowing exacerbated by mistakes in macroeconomic management. The macroeconomic mistake was the policy of capital account liberalization combined with the maintenance of a fixed exchange-rate peg against the US dollar and the subsequent misguided efforts to maintain these pegs against an overwhelming outflow of capital. The removal of capital controls in the 1980s was beneficial. It encouraged capital inflows and thus bridged the gap between high domestic savings rates and even higher rates of fixed capital investment. Since the countries of south-east Asia had an impressive record of growth, high domestic savings rates and generally modest fiscal deficits, there was little reason to believe that they could not maintain fixed exchange rates for a long time to come. The stability and apparent sustainability of their exchange rates encouraged large-scale inward portfolio investments from international investors looking for exposure to emerging markets. Fixed exchange rates also had another, much less desirable, effect. They encouraged local banks to use short-term foreign currency borrowing for financing their long-term domestic lending.

This was a yield play strikingly similar to the flawed short-term portfolio investment in senior structured credit tranches at the heart of the current global credit crisis. Domestic interest rates remained as much as 5 per cent above dollar rates of interest on global financial markets. Better to pay 5 per cent for foreign currency borrowing than 10 per cent for domestic currency deposits. If the money was lent out to domestic borrowers at, say, 14 per cent, then the interest margin – the profit on the lending provided that there is no default – would be 9 per cent rather than 4 per cent. This additional lucrative interest margin was an irresistible temptation.

How could domestic interest rates remain so much higher than dollar interest rates when the exchange rate was pegged and capital controls had been removed? The proximate reason was relatively high domestic inflation, with economic growth outrunning domestic productive capacity and consumer prices rising at around 5 per cent per annum compared with less than 3 per cent in the United States. This meant that domestic interest rates had to be kept relatively high to restrain domestic borrowing and help keep a lid on inflation. The more fundamental reason was a largely unappreciated devaluation 'risk premium'. However unlikely, there was always the possibility that the currency pegs might be abandoned. For this reason foreign and domestic investors alike demanded an additional higher rate of interest for keeping funds in Thai baht, Malaysian ringgit or South Korean won.

The temptation to use foreign-currency funding for domestic lending was irresistible and was carried to an extreme in Thailand and South Korea. The foreign-currency borrowing of the Thai banking sector reached some 25 per cent of GNP. Much of this was financed through the Bangkok International Banking Facility, which allowed foreign-currency borrowing and lending by Thai-based institutions. The thinking behind this facility was to make it possible for Bangkok to compete with Hong Kong and Singapore as a regional centre for international banking, but in practice it was primarily used by local banks to fund their domestic lending. South Korea was even more exposed, with short foreign-currency bank exposures of over $100 billion, close to one third of GNP.

The 1997 Asian crisis: the trigger and the policy response

This highly unstable arrangement, using substantial amounts of short-term foreign-currency borrowing to finance long-term domestic lending set the stage for the extreme financial crisis that followed. The trigger was the emergence in the first half of 1997 of problems among the relatively small Thai finance houses. These lightly regulated banks had financed a booming Thai real-estate market and were heavily involved in securities finance and other relatively risky exposures. The cooling of the Thai real-estate market in early 1997 resulted in the failure of the largest of these finance houses, Finance One, whose assets of $4 billion ranked it in about twelfth place among all Thai banks. Finance One was merged with a larger Thai bank, but the problems of the finance houses were not fully resolved, and increasing doubts emerged about the sustainability of the peg of the Thai baht against the US dollar.

At first it appeared that the Thai authorities could contain these problems and maintain the currency peg. The Bank of Thailand reported large foreign-currency reserves that could be deployed to maintain the fixed exchange rate. They successfully fended off an initial speculative attack on the currency on 14 and 15 May 1997. But the published statistics did not reveal the very large hidden commitments by the Bank of Thailand for purchase of the Thai baht using the currency forward market – in effect the large majority of foreign-currency reserves had already been deployed in defence of the currency. While the scale of these forward positions was not in the public domain, domestic and international investors were well aware that the currency was vulnerable and capital flight out of the baht into dollars continued. Then, on 2 July 1997, in the face of a renewed speculative attack, the Bank of Thailand ran out of ammunition, and the currency peg was abandoned.

What then followed was a financial whirlwind. Within days the currency pegs of Malaysia, Indonesia and the Philippines also collapsed. The Thai baht, the Malaysian ringgit and the Filipino peso all depreciated, falling by around 40 per cent against the dollar over the subsequent six months, and the Thai government arranged a large loan facility of $17 billion from the IMF. The Indonesian rupiah fell alongside the other currencies and Indonesia borrowed an even larger $40 billion from the IMF. But the Suharto regime's legacy of corruption, mismanagement and political uncertainty made it much more difficult to control the situation, and there followed a rapid monetary expansion, rising inflation and continued currency depreciation, with the rupiah eventually falling by an astonishing 80 per cent. South Korea held out for longer; its external deficits were clearly manageable and this allowed it to maintain the won peg for some months, but growing financial problems among many of the chaebol and the large amount of short-term foreign borrowing by South Korean banks led to a sharp depreciation in November 1997 of the South Korean won, which eventually also fell by around 40 per cent, and South Korea also turned to the IMF, receiving a huge loan package worth $57 billion.

Somewhat controversially, as a condition of its lending the IMF imposed the conventional remedies of higher interest rates and tight limits on government borrowing. In the first months of the crisis Thailand and South Korea raised their domestic interest rates to over 20 per cent and Indonesian rates, in the face of very high inflation, went much higher still. Government expenditure was redirected to dealing with the problems of bank balance sheets, offering banks funding (both loans to compensate for the withdrawal of foreign funds and guarantees of bank liabilities), closing a number of weaker institutions, acquiring and recapitalizing others, and setting up holding companies (the Indonesia Bank Restructuring Agency (IBRA), the Malaysian Danaharta, the Korean Asset Management Company (KAMCO), and at a later date the Thai Asset Management Company (TAMC)) to manage non-performing loans.

The direct government expenditures on bank recapitalization were relatively small, working out at around 2 per cent of GNP. The much bigger budget item were the loans and guarantees to banks, reaching 25 per cent of Indonesian GNP, 15 per cent of South Korean GNP and nearly 40 per cent of Thai GNP.

The loss of investor confidence and the withdrawal of capital by both domestic and foreign investors resulted in substantial falls in investment, output, expenditure and employment. In 1998 fixed capital investment fell by more than one third in Indonesia, by one quarter in Thailand and by a fifth in South Korea. Economic output was down 17 per cent in Indonesia, 8 per cent in Thailand, 7 per cent in Malaysia and 16 per cent in South Korea. Domestic expenditure fell even more, by as much as 21 per cent in Thailand and 22 per cent in South Korea, as economic activity was reoriented towards export markets. Recorded unemployment rates rose sharply across the region, from less than 2 per cent to over 6 per cent. The contraction was severe but the trough was reached after about a year and sustained growth then resumed; for example, South Korean output rose by 9 per cent in 1999, boosted by the exchange-rate depreciation and by strong global demand and growing regional trade.

These are the bare statistics. They do not communicate the panic and confusion of global investors during 1997 and 1998 and the huge uncertainties about the financial systems of the Asian economies, especially Thailand, Malaysia and South Korea. What was behind these astonishing exchange rate movements? These were driven both by the absence of reliable information and by an exceptionally powerful feedback loop, remarkably similar to those illustrated in Figure 1.1 in Chapter 1. The collapse of the exchange-rate pegs and subsequent currency depreciation undermined bank balance sheets. This in turn led to increasing doubts about the viability of local financial institutions and withdrawal of funds, provoking a capital flight that in turn exacerbated the exchange rate depreciations.

The result was a considerable overreaction, a withdrawal of funds and a consequent fall in investment and output far greater than was required to correct the growing imbalances of the south-east Asian economies. But this overreaction was unavoidable because of the underlying weaknesses of financial arrangements. Both banks and industrial companies were used to relying on leverage and short-term funding for growth, paying little attention to governance or transparency and avoiding external disciplines that might have restrained them during the rapid economic expansion. But the resulting absence of transparency of both banks and industrial companies made it next to impossible to identify investment opportunities in the midst of the crisis or to work out which institutions were solvent and viable and which were not. Good and bad companies alike paid the penalty when capital withdrew.

This is remarkably similar to what has taken place during the current global credit crisis, in which banks worldwide have preferred short-term financing to selling debt securities to long-term investors and have done little to communicate or explain their business models to shareholders or investors. As a result all banks, good and bad, have paid the penalty now that confidence has collapsed.

Dealing with this situation required large-scale government restructuring and support for the banking sector. The contrast with Japan is marked. Malaysia, Indonesia and South Korea moved quickly to deal with bank balance sheets. They provided large-scale guarantees to prevent rapid withdrawal of funds. They introduced improved bank accounting procedures to prevent banks hiding the extent of their difficulties and strengthened the legal arrangements for dealing with corporate bankruptcies.

Once loans had been written down to realistic values, the Indonesian and South Korean governments took a large proportion of non-performing loans off balance sheets, in exchange for government bonds, and transferred them to state-owned resolution companies. Banks were recapitalized, mostly using state funds. Malaysia had relatively small stock of non-performing loans, but these were also transferred into a state-owned asset management company.

Thailand also provided guarantees to stabilize its banking sector, and closed down almost all its finance houses. Bankruptcy laws in Thailand remained weak, however, and the Thai government was relatively slow in dealing with non-performing loans and the recapitalization of its banks, delaying until 2001 before establishing its own asset management company to transfer loans off bank balance sheets.

A combination of government support for their financial systems, substantial exchange-rate depreciation and strong growth in the world economy led to relatively rapid economic recovery across Asia. Output growth was restored and high levels of unemployment were reduced. One lasting consequence was that all the affected countries began using their export revenues to build up large reserves of foreign exchange. This protected them from exposure to another flight of short capital, but at the same time contributed to the growing number of global current-account imbalances. The risk of crisis from withdrawal of short-term funding was falling in Asia but increasing in the United States and other Western deficit economies.

A coda to the Asian crisis: Russian default and LTCM

LTCM was at the time of its failure the world's largest hedge fund. Hedge funds are private investment funds set up to make money from trading on financial markets. Each hedge fund usually pursues some specific trading strategies, in which it believes the knowledge and experience of its managing partners will allow it to make money. There are many potentially successful trading strategies and so many different kinds of hedge funds. Some of the best-known funds pursue macro-trading strategies, taking positions based on their expectations of the future path of exchange rates, interest rates and equity prices. Other hedge funds pursue so-called 'relative value' strategies, looking for firms that are undervalued, purchasing their equities and at the same time hedging these exposures by selling (going 'short') on the equity of other overvalued firms in the same industrial sectors. Yet another curiously named hedge fund strategy is 'risk arbitrage', a curious name because it has nothing to do with either risk or arbitrage. These funds identify prospective takeover targets and purchase their shares, hoping to make a large profit when there is an announcement of a proposed acquisition.

The principals of LTCM were renowned figures in the financial world, including the trader John Meriwether and the Nobel laureates Myron Scholes and Robert Merton. They founded LTCM in 1994 and had large equity stakes, so to an important extent they were trading with their own money. They also employed some of the most able staff in the industry, both for designing and implementing trading strategies and for risk management. Like almost all hedge funds, LTCM was highly leveraged, borrowing substantial sums to add to the wealth contributed by (rich) private investors and the LTCM principals.

The basic trading strategy adopted by LTCM was the bond liquidity or convergence play – they identified bonds that were underpriced, relative to other bonds, due to lack of market liquidity. The classic example of this trade was the 'on the run – off the run' Treasury trade pioneered by John Meriwether when he was in charge of bond trading for Salomon Brothers in the 1980s. This brilliant ploy was based on his observation that the newly issued 'on the run' 30-year US government bond was actively traded, whereas the very similar 'off the run' 29-year US government bond was largely ignored by traders and held only by institutional investors. The 29-year bond was not often traded, but when it did come up for sale the price was relatively low because there was so little secondary trading. So Merriweather adopted a policy of purchasing the 29-year bond whenever it was available and, at the same time, selling (going short of) the economically equivalent 30-year bond.

This position was almost risk-free, since any change in economic fundamentals (e.g. higher inflation, bigger government fiscal deficit, etc.) had the same impact on both sides of the trade; the position might lose, say, $1,000 if the price of the 29-year bond fell, but at the same time it would gain close to $1,000 as the price of the 30-year bond also fell. Even though it was risk-free the position could still make a profit, because as the 30-year bond came off the run it became illiquid and the price would fall. It could take some time and money to close this position (to buy the now illiquid 30-year bond and sell the illiquid 29-year bond) but Merriweather found that he could still make a consistent profit with this trade.

LTCM pursued essentially the same strategy all round the world, for example going long on Italian government bonds and short on German government bonds, anticipating that approaching monetary union would raise the prices of the Italian bonds so that they were closer to those of the German bonds. It had similar trades with Danish mortgage bonds (where it held an astonishing 80 per cent of the entire market) and in bonds of many other kinds. The positions were not greatly subject to market risks, because they were hedged against movements of interest rates and exchange rates, but they *were* exposed to a 'flight to quality' – that is, a sharp fall in prices on relatively illiquid securities.

LTCM's risk models suggested that they had more than enough equity capital, and they actually repaid a substantial amount of capital to investors in late 1997. But then, in 1998, the Russian government defaulted on short-term bonds known as GKOs. LTCM had some exposure to these bonds and its losses were larger than expected because of the default of its hedging counterparts in Russia. But that was not what brought down LTCM. The Russian default, coming as it did only a year after the Asian crisis, when many investors were already cautious about emerging markets, led to 'flight to liquidity'. Investors worldwide sought safety in the safest instruments, such as AAA corporate or government bonds. They shunned a wide range of illiquid instruments, including many held by LTCM.

The further problem for LTCM was that many other banks, such as UBS of Switzerland, Merrill Lynch, Dresdner and Credit Suisse, had been pursing very similar strategies (and were often explicitly copying LTCM trades). The situation was almost exactly analogous to that of the many banks holding senior AAA structured credits in 2007. While individually they could trade into and out of these positions, when all those holding similar positions wanted to sell out at the same time, they found it impossible to do so without suffering very large losses. The result was a feedback loop: sale of illiquid bonds → fall of price → mark to market losses → sale of illiquid bonds. This created huge mark to market losses even for those banks that tried to hold their positions and pushed LTCM into insolvency.

This was a *liquidity*, not a *solvency*, issue. LTCM's trades were fundamentally sound. They were providing liquidity to the market by holding illiquid instruments and, because of the scale of their trades, making substantial profits. But they were caught out by the flight to liquidity. After turning down an offer of takeover from a consortium of Goldman Sachs, AIG and Warren Buffet, LTCM was saved on 22 September by a Federal Reserve Bank of New York-organized life-boat. Eight banks were persuaded to injected new equity capital into LTCM. Eventually the participants in the lifeboat made a substantial profit, once markets returned to normal. The LTCM trading strategies were low-risk and profitable but LTCM lacked sufficient liquidity and capital to back them up, much as in 2007 the banks pursuing negative-basis and similar yield-based trades did not have enough capital to support their positions.

LTCM is relevant today because it illustrates how financial support, in this case a voluntary private-sector action co-ordinated by the Federal Reserve Bank of New York, can overcome such problems of illiquidity, essentially the same problem that is now undermining the global banking sector through its holdings of senior structured credits. There is no question of encouraging 'moral hazard' – that is, pro-moting excessive risk-taking in the future – through such a liquidity support operation. This action was not protecting LTCM from fundamental losses. In any case the shareholders lost their claims on what turned out, eventually, to be very profitable positions. The difference, of course, is that, in saving a single institution, there is no great problem in finding sufficient private-sector capital to effect a rescue. Saving the entire global banking sector from illiquidity will require a somewhat different approach, but still should not raise moral hazard concerns.

Other crises and a conclusion

This chapter has been a selective survey of banking crises, focusing on some of those of most relevance to the current global banking crisis that began in 2007. Much has been left out. The Spanish banking crisis of 1978–83 is regarded as one of the biggest of developed-country banking crises. There is no account given here of the many examples of stock market bubbles and crashes. The Asian crisis and the cases of Finland and of Sweden are both examples of 'twin crises' affecting both the exchange rate and the banking sector. There are many other such twin crises, for example Mexico in 1994 and Argentina in 2002. Including emerging markets and the eighteenth and nineteenth centuries, well over one hundred banking crises could have been mentioned here.

Perhaps the biggest omission is any account of the banking crises of the 1930s – both across Europe and in the United States in 1930 and 1931 and the even bigger US banking crisis in late 1932 and early 1933, before the newly inaugurated President Roosevelt declared a national bank holiday. There are still considerable differences of opinion about these banking crises, both over how they were resolved and over their contribution to the wider economic problems of the time. Without entering into the complex details, these episodes illustrate the importance of a supportive macroeconomic environment to maintaining financial stability. The problems of European banks, notably the failure of Credit Anstalt in 1931, were bound up with the efforts to re-establish the gold standard at pre-First World War exchange rates, an effort that was never entirely credible in the face of the disruptions to world trade caused by the weakening US economy and the resulting significant misalignments of exchange rates, and was undermined by bank failures.

Kindleberger, in his book *The World in Depression 1929–1939*, cogently argues that these bank failures and the wider global downturn could have been alleviated if there had been a stronger macroeconomic stabilizer. This argument very much aligns with the view set out in this book that the current banking crisis can be overcome through determined use of public-sector funds and the public-sector balance sheet to offset the destabilizing withdrawal of bank funding. US bank failures were largely consequential, a result of a weak agricultural sector, the falling prices of corporate bonds and rising loan losses in the Great Depression, although there is some evidence of reverse causation from bank failures onto the real economy. A determined monetary easing would have done a lot to help prevent bank failures.

The overall lesson is that, while there is much to be learned from the study of these other crises, they all differ in important ways and there are no neat solutions that can be transferred, directly, from one situation to another. At the same time there are general lessons. Resolution of a systemic banking crisis requires that the authorities both address problems of illiquidity and funding *and* at the same time clean up bank balance sheets and restore net worth as best they can. The best approach to both these tasks is to respond quickly and in an unstinting manner.

Further reading

There are several very readable books giving alternative accounts of these and other crises. For comprehensiveness it is impossible to match Charles Kindleberger and Robert Aliber, *Manias, Panics and Crashes* (5th edn, Wiley, 2005). The chapters on resolution of financial crises are especially good on the choice between letting financial crises burn themselves out or using public money to limit their impact. As they document, whatever the theoretical arguments in favour of laissez-faire, the choice in practice has almost always been for extensive intervention. Niall Ferguson's delightful and readable *The Ascent of Money* (Allen Lane, 2008) provides both a historical perspective and many vivid insights into more contemporaneous events. My interpretations are perhaps closest to those of Paul Krugman in his short book *The Return of Depression Economics and the Crisis of 2008* (Penguin, 2008), although his analysis does occasionally skate over some important details. There is also a considerable academic literature on a vast number of banking and financial crises, a comprehensive recent study with full references is Carmen Reinhart and Kenneth Rogoff, 'Banking crises: an equal opportunity menace', NBER working paper, 2008, dispelling the notion that major crises only happen in poor countries.

My account of the 1907 crisis is drawn largely from Robert F. Bruner and Sean D. Carr, *The Panic of 1907: Lessons Learned from the Market's Perfect Storm* (Wiley, 2007). For an account of the Latin American debt crisis I recommend Pedro-Pablo Kuczynski's *Latin American Debt* (Twentieth Century Fund, 1988), which remains perhaps the best analysis of the origins of the crisis. His book was published before the Brady bonds were issued, but this development is described in several web sources.

The financial and economic problems of Japan are a complex and involved story, and my own account hardly does justice to the social, cultural, political, economic and institutional issues involved. An insightful analysis is Takeo Hoshi and Anil K. Kashyap, 'Japan's economic and financial crisis: an overview', *Journal of Economic Perspectives* (winter 2004). Gillian Tett's *Saving the Sun: A Wall Street Gamble to Rescue Japan from Its Trillion-Dollar Meltdown* (HarperCollins Business, 2003), is a readable and illuminating history of the problems of one major Japanese financial institution, the Long Term Credit Bank, and the pressures to hide loan problems and avoid restructuring even when it had been purchased by Western investors.

A succinct comparison of the Scandinavian financial crises and their resolution is provided by Seppo Honkapoija, 'The 1990's financial crises in Nordic countries', Bank of Finland Discussion Paper, 2009-5. The central banks of the region, the Riksbank, the Norgesbank and the Bank of Finland, have all published more detailed accounts of their own crises which can be downloaded from the web. The collection of Thorvald G. Moe, Jon A. Solheim and Bent Vale (eds.), *The Norwegian Banking Crisis* (Norgesbank, 2004), is a particularly insightful comparison of Scandinavian experiences.

The Asian crisis is another complex story and even my extended treatment omits many aspects of what took place. Phillippe F. Delhaise's *Asia in Crisis: The Implosion of the Banking and Finance System* (Wiley, 1998), is one of the most detailed descriptions available of the build-up to the crisis, taking full account of the differences between the various Asian countries and the peculiarities of their banking systems. A wealth of economic data and analysis can be found on the web, notably in various analyses of the IMF and the Asian Development Bank.

Lively accounts of the rise and fall of LTCM are given by both Nicholas Dunbar, *Inventing Money* (Wiley, 2000), and Roger Lowenstein, *When Genius Failed: The Rise and Fall of Long Term Capital Management* (Fourth Estate, 2002).

4 | A basic funding tool – the tranched mortgage-backed security

This chapter and the two that follow look at the new arrangements for the funding of consumer and corporate credit that supported the recent global credit boom. As Figure 2.2 illustrates, these were rather complicated. But they are not impossible to understand. The right place to start is with the basic building block, the relatively simple financial product known as the tranched mortgage-backed security. This 'tranching', derived from the French word *tranche*, meaning 'slice', is used to protect the holders of so-called senior securities at the top of the structure, giving them the first claim on the interest and principal payments of the underlying loans. Most of the more complex and more dubious arrangements that broke down during the crisis were built upon this simple, secured financing instrument.

The mortgage-backed security (MBS) has become a very widely used financial instrument around the globe. Banks in different countries, not just in the United States, have used them to finance their lending. For example, in the United Kingdom, according to the interim report of Sir James Crosby commissioned by the Treasury (*Mortgage Finance* (HM Treasury, 2008) http://www.hm-treasury.gov.uk/fin_mort_crosby.htm), the issue of mortgage-backed securities provided some two thirds of the funds for new mortgage lending in 2006, the peak of the UK mortgage boom.

Mortgage-backed securities are similar to the bonds issued by larger companies. Like those bonds they offer a fixed regular 'coupon' payment and then, eventually, a repayment of the original investment, known as the 'principal'. Like corporate bonds they are assessed by rating agencies who give them letter grades such as Aaa, Aa or A (these form the Moody's scale of ratings; other rating agencies use a scale AAA, AA, A). There are also some differences with corporate bonds. By the end of this chapter readers of this book should understand these securities fairly well and how banks use them for raising funding and maintaining their liquidity.

Tranched mortgages are a simple and useful financial innovation. They allow banks to raise long-term finance at low cost. The problems in the global credit markets stem not from the use of these securities, but from the further, more complex financial arrangements based on the basic techniques for tranching of pooled credit risk described in the following two chapters. But we need to cover the basic instruments first.

The origins of tranching

The original mortgage-backed securities were the pass-through MBS issued by the giant US government-sponsored enterprises Fannie Mae and Freddie Mac. These so-called agency mortgage-backed securities, whose collateral is guaranteed by Fannie Mae, Freddie Mac and the other, smaller agencies, have been a major source of mortgage finance in the United States for many years and finance nearly half of all US mortgage lending. But it is important to emphasize that these agency MBS are fundamentally different from privately issued traded credit instruments. The credit risk is relatively small, because only the best-quality 'conforming' mortgages are included in these securitizations and it is the agencies, not the markets, that hold the credit risk by guaranteeing the underlying securitized loans.

Over time banks have found that they could sell their own 'private label' securities (so-called because US government agencies do provide a guarantee), allowing commercial banks to transfer loan assets off balance sheet and 'package' them as securities, without agency support. These techniques have allowed US banks and thrifts to securitize a much wider range of assets, including various forms of consumer loan such as credit cards and vehicle loans and also 'non-conforming' mortgages which do not comply with the strict standards on credit quality which qualify them for guarantees from the US government-sponsored agencies. These mortgage-backed securities are referred to as non-agency or 'private label' MBS. There are also very similar non-agency securities, backed by retail loan assets such as credit card receivables, vehicle loans and student loans, which are referred to as asset-backed securities or ABS (the convention is that the term 'ABS' does *not* cover mortgage-backed securities; note also that in the United States some ABS are backed by public-sector guarantees, rather like the agency MBS).

Banks in several other countries, notably the United Kingdom, the Netherlands and Spain, have used the same techniques to create securities backed by bank loan assets, even though there is no equivalent of Fannie Mae or Freddie Mac providing a guarantee on the underlying loan collateral. Thus the techniques of structuring have proved extremely important to banks in many different countries (and the current credit crisis now threatens their ability to continue doing their business in the way to which they have become accustomed).

Creating low risk assets that investors will buy

Banks needed to overcome a big challenge in creating these private label securities. The key problem is that there is strong investor demand for safe debt assets, but relatively weak demand for risky debt. Investors, such as pension funds or insurance companies or the treasurers of local municipalities who are responsible for managing the assets of schools and other local bodies, are required to be extremely careful when making investments. They usually prefer to put most of their portfolio in the best-quality debt securities, those known as 'investment grade' bonds with ratings of Baa or better. In some countries, including the United States, this preference for safety is backed up by regulations requiring pensions, life insurance and trustees managing investments on behalf of others to invest only in 'investment grade' debt.

This preference for safety and additional portfolio regulations means that the opinions of rating agencies on the quality of a corporate bond or a mortgage-backed or asset-backed security are extremely important to investors. Without a good-quality, investment-grade rating it can be very difficult for investors to buy a debt security, including a structured mortgage-backed credit. This is not a problem for the agency MBS. The guarantees provided by Fannie Mae and Freddie Mac, and the high quality of the loans they securitize, ensure that their mortgage-backed securities qualify for the very best AAA ratings. The challenge for investment banks was to find a way to create bonds backed by mortgage and consumer loan collateral to which rating agencies could award a similarly high investment-grade rating, even though the underlying collateral is of lower quality and there is no agency guarantee. This chapter explains the very simple tranching technique used to do this, a slicing of the securities so as to concentrate all the risk in a very small part of the structure, and hence make the remaining part very safe so that it easily qualifies for the highest, investment-grade ratings.

Preliminary: a corporate bond example

The tranching of a mortgage-backed security or of other structured credit instruments creates new securities intended to be similar, in terms of both risk and the promised returns, to the very highest-quality corporate bonds. Therefore, before describing even the simple tranched mortgage-backed security, it is useful to look first at an example of a corporate bond. This will also explain what is meant by the credit rating labels such as Aaa or BBB. If you happen to be completely comfortable with terms such as 'coupon', 'basis point', 'yield to maturity', 'credit spread' and 'credit rating' then you can skip this example; but if you have little previous experience of analysing financial instruments then read through this example. It is not so hard and with a little effort you will master the tools needed to understand the somewhat more complex world of structured financial products and the role played by these products in the current worldwide financial crisis.

The example I have chosen is the Pacific Bell 2026 bond, offering investors a coupon of 7.13 per cent and one of the very large number of corporate bonds traded worldwide. Pacific Bell 2026 is a widely traded security and any reader, with a few thousand dollars to spare, could easily instruct their bank or broker to buy some of this bond. You can look in the financial media to obtain current price information.

I am not making a buy or sell recommendation; I know little about Pacific Bell other than a bit of its history. It is one of the US telecommunications companies created from the 1984 regulatory break up of AT&T. Nowadays it is a subsidiary of AT&T Inc., the largest telecommunications group in the United States, formed in a 2005 merger that reconstituted much of the original AT&T business. Pacific Bell is doing business as AT&T California.

Let us suppose that you happen recently to have inherited some money and you use this inheritance to purchase $100,000 of the Pacific Bell 2026. What will you get in return? Provided AT&T Inc. does not default on its obligations, every year until 2026 you will receive 7.13 per cent of this par value – that is, each year you will get

$7,130 in interest payments. Finally, on the March 2026 redemption date, if you have not in the meantime sold the bond, you will get back the full par value of $100,000.

These payments before redemption are referred to as the bond's coupon. The term 'coupon' comes from the eighteenth-century practice of issuing bonds in paper form with a series of small dated detachable slips or coupons. On each coupon payment date the relevant coupon could be exchanged for cash. This system meant that there was no need to register bond ownership to establish entitlement to the bond, the bearer of the bond could simply detach the coupon and claim the payment.

Rating agencies play a key role in both corporate bond and structured security markets in the United States, Europe and other global financial marketplaces. Three companies – Moody's, Standard and Poor's, and Fitch – dominate this industry. Their core business is to provide 'opinions' on the ability of bond or other security issuers to make interest payments and return the original principal to investors. The rating agencies provide these opinions in the form of their widely used three-letter ratings on a wide range of bonds, issued by emerging market governments (so-called sovereign bonds) and by larger cities (the dollar-denominated bonds issued by US cities, known as municipal bonds or munis). A rating of AAA (or Aaa which is the equivalent rating issued by Moody's) indicates that the borrower has considerable financial strength and is not expected to have any difficulty in repaying the bond. The slightly lower ratings AA (Aa in the case of Moody's), A, and BBB (Baa in the case of Moody's) are also considered investment grade – that is, the borrower is considered very likely to have sufficient financial strength to make the promised payments on the security.

Pacific Bell 2026 is rated 'A' by all three leading rating agencies, which means that they regard it as a strong company which should be able to pay all the promised coupon payments and return the full par value of the bond at redemption. What does this rating tell us? It reveals that in the opinion of the rating agencies the issuer of Pacific Bell 2026, AT&T Inc., is a healthy company in a good position to make all the promised payments on this bond, but there is some small but appreciable risk of it getting into difficulties and not being able to repay (this small risk is why the rating is A not AA or AAA). This is still a good-quality 'investment grade' security.

On the day I am writing this paragraph it so happens that the market price for $100,000 of Pacific Bell 2026 is $102,630 – that is, it costs a little more than the redemption value of $100,000. In the jargon of the financial markets this bond is trading 'above par'. It trades above par because investors reckon that the relatively high coupon of 7.13 per cent is higher than the general level of market interest rates for this particular maturity and more than sufficient to compensate for the small risk of default. They are therefore willing to pay a little more than the 'par' value of $100,000.

The market price (the $102,630) you must pay for this purchase is slightly greater than the par value (the $100,000). This in turn means that Pacific Bell 2026 offers a 'yield to maturity' (an implied interest rate based on the market price) that is slightly less than the coupon rate. This yield to maturity, calculated using today's market price, works out at 6.87 per cent. The equivalent yield on a US government bond of the same 2026 maturity is about 4.37 per cent. Thus the corporate bond offers a yield which is 2.40 per cent or 240 basis points higher than that on the US government bond, a difference known as the corporate bond 'credit spread'. A very cautious investor, one who would not sleep easily at night because of the risk that AT&T Inc. might fail to pay back the coupon and par as promised, could instead purchase a 2026 US government bond for the same $102,630, but this would offer a much smaller regular coupon, roughly 4.37 per cent of the investment each year instead of 6.87 per cent (this calculation is only approximate because it does not allow for the differences between market values and par values). This difference in yield is the cost to this particular investor of their good night's sleep, knowing that their investment is backed by the full faith and credit of the US government. Whichever of these two bonds the investor chooses to purchase, they will get back (approximately) the same redemption value, but the lower yield on the government bond (assuming the US government bond is trading at par) would reduce their annual interest income from $7,130 to $4,370.

Safe senior tranches

This example of Pacific Bell 2026 has covered some of the essentials of bond analytics, including 'coupon', 'credit rating', 'yield to maturity', 'credit spread' and 'basis point'. With this background we can turn to look at a structured credit product for the first time.

These are in many ways very similar investments to corporate bonds. They also have a par value (an amount that must be repaid by their final maturity date) and a coupon payment. The main difference is that structured assets are backed by other financial assets, not by a business. This makes it a little bit more difficult for an investor to assess the risk of the underlying assets that support structured products, for example the mortgages that support the payments on an MBS or the retail loans that support an ABS. In the case of a corporate issuer such as AT&T Inc., the investor can visit the company website and can look at their accounting statements, which have been audited by a reputable accountancy firm and provide a great deal of information about their operating and financial performance. An investor can also get the opinion of various business commentators on the general prospects for the telecommunications industry and for various telephone companies including AT&T Inc. and its main competitors.

The purchaser of an MBS or an ABS faces some problems which do not arise when they purchase a corporate bond. Compared with the bond of a well-known corporate issuer, it is more difficult to obtain information on and understand the quality of the underlying borrowers. Behind a typical MBS there are several thousand mortgage borrowers whose payments of mortgage interest and principal provide the coupons and eventual redemption of the security. These borrowers may reside in many different places and there is a lot of variation in their individual situations. However, modern information technology helps here; the issuer of the structured security can nowadays report a host of detailed statistics about the underlying loan pool. Provided that this information is accurate, the investor can have access to a large amount of information on underlying credit quality.

The second and more fundamental problem is that in such a pool of mortgages it is almost certain that at least some borrowers will default and, moreover, the overall default rate could rise sharply if economic conditions deteriorate and a large number of borrowers lose their jobs or suffer a decline in their earnings. The consequence is that a single security collateralized on such a pool of borrowers, while it might offer a very attractive coupon, would always suffer some default, and there is a risk that the level of defaults could be fairly large. Placing all the mortgages, without any guarantee, as backing for a single security will make the security too risky to attract an investment-grade rating or be of interest to most long-term investors.

Investment banks have developed a simple and effective procedure that gets around this problem of default risk on pools of retail loans. Instead of creating a single security offering claims on the underlying pool, they instead create a *structured* security with several different tranches, each having a different priority over the interest and principal repayments on the underlying loans. The most senior tranches obtain the very best credit ratings (all tranches are rated by the rating agencies such as Standard and Poor's, Moody's or Fitch) because they have the first claim on borrower payments. The securities are structured so as to make these senior tranches almost free of default risk.

It is possible to create a surprisingly large amount of default-risk-free securities from relatively risky collateral. Senior tranches that are effectively free of default risk in practice amount to around 75 per cent by value of the total pool of a non-agency MBS or 70 per cent of an ABS or sub-prime MBS. These sounds like large percentages, but they are still very safe because the other 'subordinated' tranches provide the senior tranches with the necessary credit protection. If the structuring is effective it is not necessary to have so much detailed information about the underlying pool, in order to be confident that these senior tranches are very unlikely to default and thus have investment characteristics similar to the very safest securities such as US government bonds or AAA corporate bonds.

Safe senior tranches really are very safe

How does this work? Consider the structuring of a pool of 4,000 'Alt-A' mortgages (Alt-A borrowers are not as risky as sub-prime borrowers but there is a greater probability of default than for the 'conforming' mortgages purchased by Fannie Mae and Freddie Mac). Suppose also that each of the mortgages is for $250,000. These figures are convenient because together these make up a total asset pool of $1 billion. The claims on this pool might be structured along the lines shown in Figure 4.1.

How risky, then, is this senior AAA tranche which corresponds to $750 million of the total underlying mortgage pool of $1 billion? Some rough and ready calculations give some idea of this risk. Most Alt-A borrowers have fairly secure jobs, even if their incomes are a little uncertain, or they already have other debts or they are borrowing quite a lot compared with their incomes. Typically we might observe,

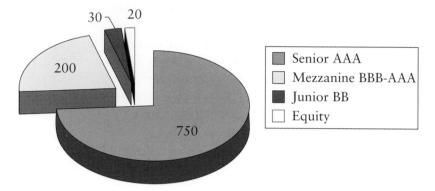

Figure 4.1. Tranching of a $1 billion pool of mortgages.

say, 2 per cent of them falling into arrears over five years and then eventually being subject to 'foreclosure'– the forced sale of the house in order to repay the mortgage. This means that on average there might be default on $20 million of the mortgages in this pool.

Actual losses from the mortgage pool will be smaller than the rate of default, since if a borrower falls into arrears on their payments and there is eventually a foreclosure a large part of the mortgage can still be repaid from the proceeds of selling the house. In some cases the sale of a house can fully repay the mortgage. In other cases there are some losses, because the value recovered is not enough to pay back everything owed: the amount borrowed, the arrears of payments, and the legal and other costs of foreclosure. Typical 'loan to value' ratios might be 80 or 85 per cent. In normal times overall losses following foreclosure (in the finance jargon 'loss given default') might average about 5 per cent of the amount loaned. This means that in normal business conditions overall portfolio losses over five years would be only 4 per cent of $40 million – that is, $1 million out of every $1 billion or only 0.1 per cent of the par value of the bonds.

This means that in normal economic circumstances – when there is no major global economic downturn – these securities are extremely safe. Because they are regarded as risky these mortgage borrowers pay fairly high rates of interest on their loans. Even after netting out all the administration costs borrower interest payments might be 2 per cent per year more than would be paid by risk-free borrowers such as the US government. This 2 per cent surplus, amounting to 10 per cent over the typical five years or so before mortgages are repaid (most mortgages are repaid early) generates more than enough surplus to cover prospective losses of 0.1 per cent. It is also usual practice to provide a further 2 per cent of protection through 'over collateralization' – that is, the mortgages in the pool are worth about 2 per cent more than the par value of the structured bonds. All this means that in normal times even the junior BB bonds are very safe.

Of course it is possible that the five years following the issue of the security are not normal and that there is a deep recession accompanied by a sharp fall in house prices. Safe investment-grade debt should still be safe, even in such difficult economic conditions. Let us suppose that in a deep recession the proportion of Alt-A mortgages that end up in foreclosure rises from 2 per cent to, say, 8 per cent of the pool, and that house prices fall by about one-third, which suggests that the eventual loss on each defaulted mortgage (after allowing for all the legal and other costs and the arrears of payments) works out at around half of the amount lent. Total losses on the pool would then be half of 8 per cent – that is, 4 per cent of the pool of $1 billion, or around $40 million. The remaining 92 per cent of the mortgages still pay the interest on their mortgages, so over five years the interest surplus still amounts to around 9 per cent of the pool.

This level of losses – the level experienced in a severe housing market recession – is still very far from triggering a default of payment on the senior tranches – the top 75 per cent of the structure. In order for senior tranche holders not to be fully paid, around 50 per cent – one in every two of these borrowers – would have to default and house prices would have to fall around 70 per cent so that losses on each loan were around one third of the amount lent. These losses would be enough to wipe out the interest surplus and expose the senior tranches to risk of loss.

If tranched mortgage-backed securities are so safe, why will no one buy them?

The above are exactly the kind of calculations that rating agencies conduct when they offer an opinion on the senior tranches of a mortgage-backed or asset-backed security. Their analysis is, of course, more detailed than this one just presented. They look more closely at the repayment ability of individual borrowers (for example at the credit ratings of the borrowers and their loan-to-income ratios) and take into account the ratio of the value of each underlying mortgage to the value of the house on which is secured. When the loans are 'seasoned' – that is, securitized some months after the original date of origination – they can get further information on underlying credit quality by taking account of the history of default in the underlying pool between when the loans are first made ('origination') and the subsequent issue of the security. Based on this information they can estimate the amount of default, the decline in house prices, and the consequent losses from the loan pool that might arise in a deep recession. They allow for the likely build-up of cash surplus in the pool occurring because the interest payments by mortgage borrowers exceed the payments due on the securities, since this provides extra security for the senior tranches. There is no exact science here, but agencies can reach a reasonable judgement on whether senior tranches are secure; indeed the structures themselves are constructed, with advice from the rating agencies, so that the senior tranches can be given an AAA rating.

The financial press and the general media have fiercely criticized the rating agencies for providing inappropriate ratings on sub-prime mortgage-backed securities. There have indeed been major mistakes by rating agencies in providing ratings for the more complex structured securities; but the opinions of the rating agencies on the basic structured credit product, the AAA-rated senior tranches of structured mortgage-backed securities, still seem sound. Despite the severity of the downturn in US housing markets, there has been virtually no default on the AAA tranche of any sub-prime MBS. Tranching has proved effective at providing credit protection for the holders of senior AAA liabilities. Barring a collapse of the US economy much more severe even than that which occurred in the 1930s, in which case many AAA-corporate bonds would also default, these AAA MBS will pretty much all be fully repaid.

There are some mortgage-backed securities that are not so safe. Investment banks created 'restructured' securities, known as ABS-CDOs and CDO^2, whose ratings have proved to be unsound (these restructured securities are described in the next chapter). Sub-prime mortgages are inherently riskier than this Alt-A example, and a minority of sub-prime MBS have proved to be based on very low-quality loan pools. The range of performance of different sub-prime securities is very wide, so although in aggregate arrears on sub-prime mortgage lending are around 20 per cent, there are individual securities where arrears have risen to 40 per cent or more – still not enough to result in failure of any payments on senior tranches, but large enough to make investors worry that there could eventually be some senior tranche default on some securities.

But the main reason why investors no longer trust and will not buy such vanilla mortgage-backed securities is fear. Market prices, even of the safest AAA tranches, have fallen by 20 per cent or more. Investment managers' main concern now is not to earn returns but to keep their jobs. If they purchase these tranches at 20 per cent below par and they fall further, to 25 per cent below par, then they could be made redundant. In today's investment environment no one will lose their job for refusing to buy risky assets and holding cash instead. Fear of volatility of structured asset prices means that no investor will purchase these assets.

A real world example: the issue of tranched mortgage-backed securities by Countrywide Financial

Mortgage-backed and other securitizations have been somewhat misleadingly described as 'shadow banking'. In fact there is a huge amount of information available on mortgage-backed securities. One good place to start is with the website www.absnet.net, a standard industry reference for information on mortgage-backed and other securitization deals. Registration is free and provides basic information on many deals (although full access to the site is a paid-for premium service). Further information on publicly issued securities, including the initial investor prospectus and regular reports on performance, can be found on the SEC website. There are also a large number of commercial information services giving investors all the information they need to assess these securities.

When I last looked, www.absnet.net contained information on some 19,000 US dollar deals going back to the early 1990s, including over 11,000 securitizations backed by mortgages and home equity (absnet also covers a smaller number of securitizations in other currencies, mostly UK pound sterling and euro deals).

An instructive exercise is to look at the mortgage-backed securitizations of Countrywide Financial, a pioneer in the use of tranched mortgage-backed securities as a source of funds for mortgage lending.

Countrywide, founded in 1969 by David Loeb and Angelo Mozillo, is a remarkable American rags to riches story. Starting from very small beginnings, operating out of David Loeb's kitchen, Countrywide rose to be the number one US mortgage lender. Countrywide initially operated as a traditional mortgage bank or 'thrift', taking retail deposits and making mortgage loans. But from the early 1980s it began using mortgage-backed securitization to finance its rapidly expanding loan portfolio with remarkable success. In the years 2003–7 Countrywide originated over $2.4 trillion of mortgage loans, more than 13 per cent of all US mortgage lending (this includes both customer loans and 'wholesale purchases' from other lenders). In these years $2 out of every $15 of US mortgage lending was provided by Countrywide.

Countrywide – unlike, for example, its more aggressive competitors Ameriquest, New Century Financial and Household Finance – took a relatively small share of the sub-prime mortgage lending market. It was a big sub-prime lender only because it was a big mortgage lender, not because it chased business in this market. Over the same period 2003–7 Countrywide loaned some $171 billion to sub-prime borrowers – around $1 of every $15 of US sub-prime mortgage lending.

Until the US housing market weakened Countrywide's strategy of rapid loan portfolio growth financed using securitizations was good for everyone. Borrowers benefited from the competitive lending rates offered by a large, low-cost lender. Stock owners enjoyed both substantial dividends and rapid growth in share prices (Countrywide's stock price rose from around $1 in the early 1980s to around $40 per share in early 2006, providing a better return than any other NYSE-quoted share over this period). Employees and management enjoyed the excitement and rewards of being part of one of the most rapidly growing companies in the United States.

Securitization and loans sales were key to the Countrywide business model. Although it originated some $2.4 trillion of mortgages from 2002 to 2007, it had retained only $98 billion of these mortgages on its balance sheet at end-2007. Around $1.3 trillion of Countrywide mortgage originations were prime conforming mortgages that could be sold on to either Fannie Mae or Freddie Mac. A further $100 billion were Department of Veterans Affairs loans qualifying for government-backed insurance from the FHA and so easily sold to third parties, for example to Ginnae Mae for packaging in their securitizations. But this leaves a further $900 billion of mortgage origination between

2002 and 2007 that had to be financed through securitizations. Thus Countrywide securitized nearly $150 billion per year of mortgages and home equity loans as 'private label' tranched mortgage-backed securitizations. To manage this flow Countrywide was conducting more than one hundred securitization transactions every year. One example – Countrywide ABS 2006-19 – is described in the text box.

Box 4.1.   The Countrywide ABS 2006-19 securitization

Here is one example of these hundreds of securitizations conducted by Countrywide, the Countrywide ABS 2006-19 securitization. This is a 'sub-prime' transaction – i.e. backed by mortgages taken out by borrowers with blemishes on their credit records, high borrowings relative to their incomes or irregular and sometimes undocumented incomes and hence classified as sub-prime rather than prime borrowers. Countrywide ABS 2006-19 sold a total of $892 million of securities to investors who applied to purchase the securities by the closing date of 26 September 2006. The issuing entity responsible for making payment of interest payments and principal to investors was a special purpose trust CWABS 2006-19. The mortgages were provided by the Countrywide subsidiary CWABS. All the details of the securitization are contained in a 170,000-word prospectus and 42,000-word free writing prospectus which can be downloaded from the SEC website. (Meaty documents, these two prospectuses for this one securitization issue are together about twice as long as this entire book!)

CWABS 2006-19 is backed by 4,794 mortgage loans with a total value of $900 million, i.e. the average mortgage size is nearly $188,000. Appendix A of the prospectus provides a statistical summary of these mortgages. The mortgages are divided into two 'pools', but their characteristics are fairly similar, so they can be summarized together. About three quarters of the mortgages, by dollar value, are adjustable rate mortgages, which pay an initial interest rate based on Libor dollar for the first two or three years of the mortgage before resetting to a fixed rate. The remaining one quarter are conventional fixed-rate mortgages. The average loan-to-value ratio is close to 80 per cent, i.e. the amount of the mortgage is about 80 per cent of the house value at the time the loan was initially made, and almost all the mortgages have loan-to-value ratios of less than 90 per cent. Close to 20 per cent of the mortgages are to borrowers in California and 14 per cent to borrowers in Florida. The remaining two thirds of borrowers are spread around the remaining forty-eight US states.

The main difference between the two loan pools is the borrower information. About two thirds of the loans in the first pool are 'full documentation'; the remaining one third are stated-income mortgages which rely on the borrower's own assessment of their income. In the case of the second pool about half of the loans are full documentation and half stated income. The second pool also has a slightly higher proportion of floating-rate mortgages.

The payment of interest and principal on these mortgages is what pays the interest and principal on the securities issued by Countrywide ABS 2006-19. Because these are risky mortgage borrowers they pay relatively high interest rates on their borrowing. At the time the deal was put together (October 2006) the average interest rates paid by the pool of mortgage borrowers was 8.8 per cent. Even after taking out the 0.5 per cent per annum paid to the 'mortgage servicer' who collects the borrower repayments (the mortgage servicer is in fact the servicing arm of Countrywide) and the cost of funding, this leaves an interest surplus in Countrywide ABS 2006-19 of about 2 per cent per annum.

Table 4.1 lists the securities sold to investors in this securitization. There are four AAA rated notes – 1-A, 2-A-1, 2-A-2 and 2-A-3 – which together account for just under $671 million or 74.5 per cent of the underlying mortgage pool. Recall that there are two separate pools of mortgages within this structure. The first, slightly smaller, pool, containing a total of $349 million of mortgage loans, is used to pay the interest and principal on the 1-A note. The second, slightly larger, pool, containing $551 million of mortgages, is used to pay the interest and principal on the 2-A-1, 2-A-2 and 2-A-3 notes. These notes are paid in numerical order – interest payments and principal are made first to the 2-A-1 notes. When these are fully paid, interest and principal payments are made to the 2-A-2 notes and after that to the 2-A-3 notes.

The 2-A-1 note is an example of what is called in the industry a 'super senior' note. Because of the extremely high degree of seniority, with protection from both the 2-A-2 and 2-A-3, it is much safer than AAA. In fact, since it has mostly been repaid and will likely be repaid in full in another year or so, it is now tantamount to cash. You still might be able to purchase it, however, because of the illiquidity of the mortgage-backed security market, for a lot less than its par value.

Table 4.1. *Securities sold to investors by Countrywide ABS 2006–19*

Notes	Par values $ mn	Outstanding, March 2008 %	Coupon Libor + basis points	Ratings by: Moody's	S&P
1-A	259.8	53	14	Aaa	AAA
2-A-1	186.5	12	6	Aaa	AAA
2-A-2	182.2	100	16	Aaa	AAA
2-A-3	42.4	100	25	Aaa	AAA
M-1	53.6	100	33	Aa1	AA+
M-2	44.6	100	34	Aa2	AA
M-3	17.1	100	35	Aa3	AA-
M-4	19.8	100	40	A1	A+
M-5	17.6	100	42	A2	A
M-6	12.6	100	50	A3	A-
M-7	13.5	100	90	Baa1	BBB+
M-8	8.6	100	120	Baa2	BBB
M-9	11.7	100	250	Baa3	BBB-

The remaining 'mezzanine' notes from M-1 down to M-9 are paid interest and principal only after the A notes have been paid. Again, these payments are made in order of seniority, the first payments made to the M-1 note and only when this is fully paid is there any payment to the M-2 note, and so on right down to the M-9 note. These mezzanine notes all still attracted investment-grade ratings from both Moody's and Standard and Poor's at the time of the October 2006 issue. Altogether their par value is $199 million, or just over 22 per cent of the total underlying mortgages. The remaining $30 million of claims on the pool are retained by Countrywide, in the form of a sub-investment grade B security with a par value of $13 million and an unvalued equity residual C security that eventually benefits from any surplus generated by the structure.

The third column of Table 4.1 reveals that in the two-and-a-bit years since this structure was put together there was a large amount of prepayment of the underlying mortgage pools. Around $137 million of the pool 1 mortgages have been repaid early ('prepayment') as borrowers have found better deals and refinanced their borrowings. This repayment of principal has been used to pay down 47 per cent of the capital of the 1-A notes. Similarly, there has been about $164 million of early repayment of the pool 2 mortgage loans and so, as the rules of the securitization require, this money has been used to pay down 88 per cent of the safest 2-A-1 notes.

The fourth column of Table 4.1 shows the coupon payments on these notes. Coupons are paid monthly. These are all 'floating rate' coupons, meaning that the investors are paid a rate of interest calculated as a margin above the current one-month Libor dollar rate. So, for example, the very safe 2-A-1 note is paid only 6 basis points above Libor, reflecting the fact that this is the safest note in the entire structure, benefiting from the protection not just of the equity and mezzanine M-1 to M-9 notes but also from seniority relative to the 2-A-2 and 2-A-3 notes. The 2-A-3 notes are somewhat riskier than the other AAA notes, so were given a coupon of 25 basis points. Coupon rates on each of the M1–M9 notes range from 33 to 250 basis points above Libor, reflecting the increasing risk further down the tranche structure.

Now we come to a crucial question: how much repayment can investors expect from these Countrywide ABS 2006–19 notes? This of course depends on the interest and principal repayments made by the 4,704 mortgage borrowers in the underlying pools. Arrears and foreclosures have risen substantially, rising to $215,000 in March 2009 (24% of the original $900,000). In addition there had already been some $59,000 of loan losses and $251,000 of voluntary or involuntary prepayment.

This is a serious arrears problem, but a closer look shows that the more senior securities, the M3, M2, M1 and various AAA senior securities are still extremely safe. Why? One reason is the high level of credit protection built into the original structure. Countrywide was directly exposed to the first loss, taking the first $30,000 of loan losses from its overcollateralization of the deal and its retention of the B equity tranche. In addition the high interest margin paid by these borrowers generated an interest rate surplus of around $36,000 during the two and a half years since its first issue. This was enough to absorb the $59,000 of losses, so that in March 2009 none of the issued securities were yet in default.

In addition, partly as a result of various US government initiatives to support troubled borrowers, the level of arrears and foreclosures in this pool has begun to decline, falling from a peak of 33% of original balance in December 2008 to only 23% in March 2009. Loss rates on foreclosed loans have been fairly high, running at around 20% of the mortgage principal, and are likely to grow higher still. But a conservative projection of a maximum possible default of a further $270,000 of mortgages and a loss rate of 30%, yields additional losses of only $81,000 (9% of the original balance). Even on this extremely cautious projection all of the A, M1, M2 and M3 securities will be fully repaid. If a sale is made they would probably go for a fraction of their par value, but in fact the prospects of their repayment are still extremely good. The A notes in particular are clearly entirely free of default risk and should, although they do not, trade freely at close to par.

Subordinated senior, mezzanine and junior equity tranches

The magic of the tranched mortgage-backed security has now been revealed – the banks that structure these securities use tranching to concentrate risk in the lower part of the structure hence create extremely safe senior tranches out of risky collateral. However, the risk does not disappear, it is transferred to the other mezzanine (i.e. investment grade and thus still fairly safe) and junior bonds and equity (extremely risky) tranches.

This job of assessing credit risk is a good deal more difficult for these remaining tranches – making up, say, the bottom 20 per cent of an MBS structure – than for the senior tranches. The remaining subordinated senior tranches – the 'best of the rest' in the claims on the underlying payments – accounting for perhaps around 20 per cent of the structure, can still achieve an investment-grade rating (BBB or better) and thus can still appeal to investors, albeit at a lower price and higher yield than the highest-ranked senior AAA tranches. Remaining tranches, the 'junior' and 'equity tranches' – those that do not qualify for an investment-grade rating and account for perhaps 3 per cent of the structure – are at a fairly high risk of default and much more difficult to sell.

A further difference between the best senior AAA tranches and the remaining riskier tranches is that it is relatively difficult to quantify the exposure of these other tranches to underlying credit risk. The position of a holder of a BBB subordinated mezzanine or a B junior tranche is a bit like that of a child on a seaside beach, standing a little distance from the water's edge and assuming that as the tide comes in the waves will not be strong enough to reach them. An unexpectedly large wave can still take them by surprise and soak their shoes and socks. The credit ratings and the payments on these junior and subordinated tranches of a structured MBS are sensitive to economic conditions, much more so than either AAA tranches of a structured MBS or equivalently rated corporate bonds.

Most investment-grade mezzanine MBS tranches are generally safe investments, but if the tide of default comes in unexpectedly far it is still possible that investors might find themselves exposed to some credit losses. More junior mezzanine MBS tranches are exposed to a high level of risk; even the normal range of variation in pool performance will affect these mezzanine tranches and investors should realize there is quite a high chance that they will not get all their money back.

The main motivation for commercial bank-sponsored MBS and ABS is to reduce funding costs, not to transfer credit risk

Mortgage-backed securities (MBS) and the similar asset-backed securities (ABS) are used principally as a bank funding tool, not for transferring risk out of the sponsoring bank. This should not be a surprise, since the main purpose of tranching is to concentrate risk and create senior MBS and ABS securities that are effectively default-risk-free. What happens to the remaining tranches that carry the risk is of lesser importance. If they can be sold at a good price, fine, but, if not, they can always be retained.

The overwhelming motive for commercial banks to securitize their assets is to reduce their long-term funding costs. This is possible because the senior tranches achieve an AAA rating which is better than that of the bank itself. A typical rating for a bank is AA or AA–. Thus, at least before the credit crisis broke in summer 2007, it was always cheaper for a mortgage bank to issue MBS than to issue a long-term bond. At the market rates of interest prevalent in 2005–6, before the crisis, the most senior AAA mortgage-backed security might require a yield of only 15 basis points above the reference Libor (London inter-bank offered rate) floating rate – that is, would offer a yield of 5.15 per cent when Libor is 5 per cent. A long-term floating rate AA bond might have to offer 50 basis points above Libor – that is, a rate of 5.50 per cent. For a bank, whose overall pre-tax earnings are only perhaps 1 per cent of total assets, this is a very big difference in funding costs.

Consider a large bank with a $500 billion portfolio recording pre-tax profits of $5 billion per year. If they securitize, say, 20 per cent of their entire balance sheet, by issuing MBS of $100 billion, this can increase their profits by 20 basis points on $100 billion or $200 million every year. A simple security market transaction and they have raised profits from $5 billion to $5.2 billion for, say, the next five years. As the commercial bank sponsor of such an MBS deal, they would be happy to pay an investment bank perhaps $50 million to conduct this deal on their behalf. A 1 per cent fee of this kind is in fact pretty much the usual fee paid by a sponsoring bank for such a securitization.

A second important motive for asset- and mortgage-backed securitizations is liquidity management. Securitizations create assets (the senior notes) which can be retained on balance sheet and used as collateral for short-term borrowing. This can be done through conducting a repo – the form of secured borrowing described in Chapter 1 – from the central bank. (As discussed further in Chapter 9, central banks do not always accept MBS as collateral for lending; while this has been done on a regular basis by the European Central Bank (ECB), the US Federal Reserve and the Bank of England have only recently begun accepting MBS as collateral.) Alternatively the MBS could be used as repo collateral for repo borrowing from another bank or for raising finance through an 'asset-backed commercial paper' conduit. All these techniques are explained more fully in Chapter 6.

As a result of these funding and liquidity benefits there is a large demand from commercial banks to sponsor MBS, ABS and other so-called 'balance sheet' securitizations. There are some other benefits to issuing these securities; for example, securitizing the traditional 30-year mortgage reduces exposure to interest-rate risk. However, securitization is a relatively expensive way of reducing interest-rate risk. If the only objective is to reduce exposures to interest-rate risk, it is far cheaper to use another, more standardized, contract, the interest-rate swap. A securitization can also reduce exposure to pre-payment risks. However, investors need to be compensated for this prepayment risk, so mortgage-backed securities must pay a relatively higher yield reducing the funding cost benefits. If funding is the over-riding goal, it may be better to issue relatively short-term mortgage-backed securities and refinance as necessary by issuing more. Finally, as already described, at least under the old Basel I rules there could be a regulatory capital motive for conducting a securitization, since the capital requirement could be a lot lower when loans were securitized rather than held on balance sheet.

It is incorrect to think of mortgage-backed securitization as a tool for transferring credit risk to the acquirers of the securities. This misunderstanding is most commonly found in the use of the phrase 'originate and distribute' to describe the practice of securitizing commercial bank assets. This labelling is misleading, since most of the time much of the credit risk is retained by the sponsor through its holding of junior and equity tranches and the implicit support provided when these tranches are sold. A sponsoring bank can obtain some protection from the extreme tail of credit risk if it sells the mez-zanine tranches to investors. In this case, if there is a very deep reces-sion the riskier mezzanine tranches can lose money, hence protecting the bank shareholders. But equally often banks will retain mezzanine tranches so that there is no credit risk transfer, only a reduction of funding costs.

What is implicit support? A large bank that regularly conducts securitizations in order to lower its funding costs cannot easily stand by while a securitization that it sponsors experiences a shortfall of returns. In this situation, which has occurred fairly often in consumer

ABSs, it is extremely usual for the sponsor voluntarily to put additional funds into the securitization vehicle in order to protect the holders of the riskier notes and maintain confidence and liquidity in the higher-rated senior notes. The reason they do this, of course, is to ensure that they will still obtain an attractive pricing for their securitizations in future.

In almost every deal commercial bank sponsors retain all, or at least a very large part, of the equity tranche and junior bonds, and sometimes also several of the mezzanine tranches. Acquisition of the equity tranche is not always obvious. Typically, commercial bank sponsors may 'overcollateralize' by putting a relatively large amount of mortgages into an MBS, compared with the value of senior and mezzanine notes sold. This is economically equivalent to the purchase of the large part of the equity tranche, since the same outcome can be achieved by not overcollateralizing but creating and then holding a lower tranche below the equity. Banks also sometimes provide an explicit guarantee of financial support, at least up to some level of losses, on the mortgages in the structure; or make a commitment to purchasing underperforming mortgages back at prices which do not fully reflect the amount of credit impairment that has taken place.

Beyond the basic tranched mortgage-backed security

This chapter has described the most basic of structured products, the tranched mortgage-backed security, and its use for reducing bank funding costs. We have not covered everything that an industry professional would need to work with these instruments. We have not discussed the legal and practical issues involved in creating the special purpose entities that hold the mortgages and issue the tranched notes. We have not looked at the servicing of mortgages. We have not examined the problem of pre-payment risk, a big concern whenever a securitization holds a large proportion of fixed-interest mortgages. Finally, we have not considered the treatment of mortgage-backed securities or other securitizations by bank regulators, especially in the calculations of minimum regulatory capital. These are all important practical concerns, but not central to the credit crisis, so they have been put to one side.

The tranched mortgage-backed security matters because this simple instrument has been used extensively by banks around the world to fund their lending. The industry statistics presented in Table 2.2 of Chapter 2 reveal some $2.3 trillion of tranched mortgage-backed securities issued worldwide, almost all of which were sold to investors during the credit boom of 2002–7. The related asset-backed security market is worth $2 trillion worldwide. Together these securities funded lending equivalent to about 30 per cent of US national income.

These basic instruments are central to the argument of this book that illiquidity in the structured credit markets is the principal reason for the current squeeze on bank lending. Without the ability to issue mortgage-backed securities and the closely related asset-backed securities, banks can no longer use their main tools for raising either short- or long-term wholesale funding. Once raised, these funds are not necessarily used for mortgage or retail lending; funding is 'fungible' – it can be applied for any purpose. This means that if liquidity is not restored to the markets for mortgage-backed and asset-backed securities, lending by any bank that relies to a large extent on wholesale markets for funding will, almost inevitably, fall well below the levels reached during the credit boom.

But *why* have investors responded by shunning even safe senior mortgage-backed security tranches, when underlying loans began performing poorly? One of the main conclusions to be drawn from this chapter is that the top 70 or 75 per cent of senior tranches of the basic mortgage-backed securities, even most of those secured on sub-prime loans, remain, even now, extremely safe. There is no real reason at all for investors not to purchase these securities, since they will continue to repay even in very poor economic circumstances.

One problem is that banks, instead of keeping these securities as simple as possible and selling them to long-term investors, adopted excessively complex business strategies that were much too reliant on short-term funding. Mortgage-backed and asset-backed securities were not the only new credit instruments; many other, much more complex, instruments were developed. Banks also adopted a widespread portfolio strategy of holding mortgage-backed and other structured securities themselves, financed almost entirely from short-term funding. The problems of these more complex business strategies have destroyed confidence in the entire structured credit asset class. The task of the next two chapters is to look at these other business strategies. With this background we will then be in a good position to follow what happened during the credit crisis and to look at what authorities can do to fix the problems of banking.

Further reading

There is little published material providing a sound introductory description of the way in which mortgage-backed securities work and are used in practice. The Wikipedia entry on the subject is worth looking at, providing a sound description of the various uses made of mortgage-backed securities (a list which quite correctly does *not* include risk transfer), but Wikipedia did not, when I checked, make the distinction between agency and private label MBS clear.

The lack of introductory materials is not entirely surprising. Most professionals learn about these products on the job. There are a number of technical reference manuals, but these jump very quickly to product details and so are difficult to read for those not already familiar with these instruments. Otherwise my advice is to ignore almost every industry description of mortgage-backed and other structured credit securities, because these are almost all some form of sales brochure, not accurate statements of how the securities work and how they are used.

One other researcher who has looked closely at these instruments is Professor Gary Gorton of Yale. His 2008 Jackson Hole paper, 'The panic of 2007', available at www.kc.frb.org/home/subwebnav.cfm?level=3&theID=10697&SubWeb–10660, explains in detail how subprime mortgage-backed securities worked and, like my chapters, looks at real world examples, but his paper focuses on transaction deals undertaken to finance sub-prime mortgage lending. Other papers by Gorton (linked via his homepage www.som.yale.edu/faculty/gbg24/html.html) discuss other aspects of securitization.

A good way to understand individual products is to look up SEC filings on performance subsequent to initial issue. Names of individual structures can be identified from www.abs.net. Professionals in the industry have ready access to a very large amount of statistical and other information about these securities through data services such as Bloomberg.

A number of academic papers study implicit recourse – the widespread practice of banks making up losses on securitized loan vehicles even though they have no legal obligation to do so. See for example

Todd A. Vermilyea, Elizabeth R. Webb and Andrew A. Kish, 'Implicit recourse and credit card securitizations: what do fraud losses reveal?', *Journal of Banking and Finance* (2008), and Eric J. Higgins and Joseph R. Mason, 'What is the value of recourse to asset-backed securities? A clinical study of credit card banks', *Journal of Banking and Finance* (2004).

5 | Using tranching to make short-term transaction profits

The previous chapter described the tranched mortgage-backed security or MBS, like its close cousin the asset-backed security or ABS, a simple and effective product. The purpose of tranching these structures is to create a hierarchy of securities, from most senior to most junior tranches, whose repayment is based on the underlying loans. This concentrates risk in the lower junior and mezzanine tranches, thus allowing the senior AAA tranches to be for all intents and purposes free of the possibility of default. Tranched MBS and ABS deals do this job very well, creating as much as $70 or $80 of default-risk-free debt from $100 of underlying loans.

In this respect the AAA tranches of MBSs and ABSs are very similar to covered bonds, the bank-issued bonds such as the *Pfandebriefe* widely issued and held in Germany, which are secured or 'covered' by bank loans, but MBSs and ABSs have been preferred by banks in many other countries because of their simplicity and flexibility.

Simple tranched securities of this kind have been around since the 1980s. They were really rather boring, a basic tool for commercial banks to raise low-cost funds. But as traders and investors became familiar with these products, investment banks saw an opportunity to do something more exciting and more profitable. Their innovation was to use the same tranching techniques to make a short-term trans-action profit. These profits depended on selling the tranched securities. They found that they could make more profit by creating much more complex products and by extending the range of credit exposures that could be securitized (the so-called 'hunt for yield'). This chapter explains how this was done.

What is different about transaction deals?

A traditional mortgage-backed securitization does not make a profit. It is what is known as a 'balance sheet' deal. The loans backing the securities are transferred off the balance sheet of a sponsoring commercial bank. The purpose is to provide low-cost funding and liquidity to the sponsoring bank. The commercial bank pays a fee to the investment bank doing the deal on its behalf.

A radical new application of tranching occurred when investment banks sought to by-pass the commercial banks altogether. The idea was for investment banks to buy loans or other credit-risky assets in the market, packaging them inside a special-purpose entity and then issuing and selling tranched securities secured on these purchased loans. If the securities could be sold for more than the costs of purchase of the underlying loans, the deal makes an immediate transaction profit.

These deals are known in the industry as 'arbitrage deals' to distinguish them from the balance sheet deals conducted in order to earn a fee. This term 'arbitrage', though, is a bit misleading, suggesting as it does that there is no risk to the issuer. A better term is 'transaction deal', to emphasize the point that the profits from such deals are made from conducting the transaction, not from earning a fee.

Transaction deals extended substantially the range of assets that can be 'structured' or 'securitized'. To give one example, it is possible to purchase a pool of traded corporate bonds and use these as the collateral supporting the payments on a group of tranched securities. This kind of deal is called a 'collateralized bond obligation' or CBO, an appropriate name indicating that the underlying collateral are bonds. The terms 'CDO' or 'collateralized debt obligation' are also use to describe deals which use either debt securities or credit derivatives as collateral – that is, any tranched structured product except the MBS and ABS is a CDO. A CBO is one particular type of CDO.

Transaction deals are typically applied to riskier credits than traditional balance sheet deals. In a balance sheet deal the sponsoring bank retains much of the risk, the goal being to make the senior AAA securities as safe and secure as possible and so obtain the lowest cost of funding. This goal is best achieved with relatively low-risk and low-yield loan assets. In contrast an arbitrage deal needs high-risk high-yield assets, in order to offer an attractive return on the more risky subordinated senior, mezzanine and junior equity tranches. For this reason transaction deals rather than balance sheet deals were widely used for creating securities out of sub-prime mortgage loans and became a major source of finance for the US sub-prime mortgage boom.

A further innovation in many transaction deals, one which helped to reassure investors when the underlying assets were relatively risky, was to have another financial intermediary, known as the collateral manager, responsible for buying and selling assets in order to maintain the credit quality of the collateral pool and hence make it more likely that there would be a pay-off to the junior equity tranche holders. This sounds a good idea, but collateral management, while it works fairly well in normal credit conditions, fails in periods of market stress when many credit assets are impaired and the underlying markets are no longer liquid. The price of lower-quality assets then collapses because there are few buyers and many sellers and selling into such a stressed market creates large losses.

Transaction deals are very attractive during a credit boom

In order to understand the recent credit boom, it is important to realize that the balance of risk and return in these transaction structures is very dependent on the credit cycle. When the economy is performing strongly and loan losses are low, transaction deals can be very attractive to investors, offering high returns in exchange for relatively low risk. The risky tranches sell for high prices and it is relatively easy to make a profit by selling the tranches for more than the cost of putting together the deal.

In contrast, when the economy is weak and loan losses are rising transaction deals are unattractive, the likelihood of high losses on riskier tranches is very great and it is extremely difficult to sell the tranches for more than the cost of purchasing the assets. Transaction deals are inherently cyclical business propositions that succeed in providing credit to borrowers that are not otherwise 'bankable' but work effectively only in business expansions, the arbitrage supply of credit automatically cutting off in business cycle downturns.

Transaction deals turned out to be remarkably adaptable; they were extended to a very wide range of different securitizations, not just corporate bonds or sub-prime mortgage loans. Another common application was the so-called collateralized loan obligation, or CLO, where the collateral was tradable syndicated loans. Syndicated loans are very large loans to corporations or sometimes governments, in which a number of different banks and other investment institutions participate. These participations can be bought and sold and so can be used as collateral in a CLO. The most common application of these deals – reflecting the fact that arbitrage securitizations are used for relatively high-risk credit – was to hold 'leveraged loans' used to provide the debt finance for a wide range of private equity transactions during the credit boom.

Another type of transaction deal, a bit more technical than the others, was based on the contract known as a credit default swap, or CDS. A credit default swap is a bit like an insurance contract; a protection buyer pays a protection seller a regular premium for protection against the default of a bond. If the bond defaults then the protection seller reimburses the protection buyer for the loss in value caused by the default (the actual reimbursement usually takes the form of a cash payment of the promised 'par' value in exchange for delivery of the defaulted bond or some other similar bond issued by the same company). By selling protection on a pool of CDS contracts it was possible to create another structure known as the synthetic collateralized debt obligation, or CDO.

Yet another application of the arbitrage deal was using tranching to create securities using other tranched securities as collateral. These deals were called ABS-CDO when they held ABS or MBS tranches and CDO^2 when they held other tranched securities. These restructured credit deals played a critical role in supporting the boom in structured credit. They were also misrated by credit rating agencies. Tranches issued by these structures experienced some of the largest of all price falls in the credit crisis.

Box 5.1. An example of a collateralized loan obligation: Grosvenor Place CLO III

This quick overview of structured credit products omits many details, some of which mattered a lot in the credit crisis. To understand better what went on it is helpful to look at another individual transaction. The example presented here is a recent issue of a recent collateralized loan obligation or CLO, i.e. a structured credit deal where the debt purchased and held as collateral is in the form of traded corporate loans, in this case high-yield leveraged loans used originally to finance private equity acquisitions and buyouts.

This particular structure – the Grosvenor Place CLO III – was brought to market on 1 August 2007 by Lehman Brothers.[1] It is listed with the Irish Stock Exchange in Dublin and sold globally. However it is not traded on the Irish Stock Exchange; like all other structured products it is traded privately between investors in so-called 'over the counter' markets. In the United States it is a 'rule 144a' security, meaning that it does not need to be registered with the SEC but can only be bought and sold by professional investors. Most of the notes issued by Grosvenor Place CLO III are denominated in euros, but it has also issued some senior notes denominated in US dollars and UK pounds sterling.

On 30 June 2008 the Grosvenor Place CLO III held some €333 million worth of leveraged loans, consisting of about two hundred different loan facilities to sixty different European companies, almost all these loans maturing between 2012 and 2016. The ten largest company exposures, together accounting for a little over a quarter of the entire portfolio, were to Wind, Italy's third largest mobile telephone operator, Amadeus, the global air reservations network, Iglo Birds Eye, the frozen foods business, Ferretti, the Italian luxury yacht maker, Avio, the aerospace engine maker formerly a division of Fiat, Doncasters, the UK engineering group, Capital Safety Group, a manufacturer of height safety and fall protection equipment, Orangina, the French beverage company, Prosienbensat.1 Media, Germany's largest commercial broadcaster, and Nycomed, the Danish pharmaceuticals company.

A key participant in Grosvenor Place CLO III is the 'collateral manager', an alternative investment management company named CQS Investment Management Limited, which has offices in Grosvenor Place, London (hence the name of the CLO). The responsibility of CQS as 'collateral manager' for the CLO is for buying and selling the underlying loans in order to maintain the asset quality and obtain as good a return for the CLO as possible. CQS is paid a small committed fee for this work and earns a much higher fee if the loan assets in Grosvenor Place CLO III achieve sufficiently good returns. CQS also holds some of the highest risk tranches (the subordinated notes) which are most exposed

---

[1] The details of the CLO are taken from the 265 page prospectus and the June, 2008 management report, both available via www.globalABS.net.

to loan performance. Thus CQS has strong incentives to achieve good portfolio returns.

The loans in this portfolio are all fairly high risk. They are mainly so-called 'bullet' or interest-only loans, meaning that the borrower pays only the contracted interest payments until the end of the loan and then repays in full. These loans are rated by both Moody's and Standard and Poor's as below investment grade (they mostly have a B1 or B2 rating from Moody's and B+ or B from Standard and Poor's) but in compensation for a relatively high default risk these loans offer investors a high yield, around 200 basis points (i.e. 2 per cent) per annum more than floating rates of interest on safe government or AAA bonds. On average this loan portfolio was paying interest rates of 7.15 per cent. This yield is what underpins the CLO arbitrage profits.

The structure taken as a whole is less risky than the individual loans. Since the loans are to a wide range of different industries and countries, investors enjoy the 'diversification' benefit of a large dispersed loan portfolio – i.e., it is unlikely that a very high proportion of all these borrowers from so many different industries and countries will default all at the same time. Looking through the list of the collateral of Grosvenor Place CLO III, investors can take comfort from the thought that if the borrowers from, say, Italy are struggling to repay, then there is a good chance that other borrowers from Germany are not doing so badly; or, again, if travel companies are falling into payments arrears, then media and TV companies may be much better. The collateral manager CQS will also provide some further protection to note holders by selling poorly performing loans while they still have some value. Thus – provided there is not an exceptionally deep worldwide economic recession between 2009 and 2014 (and this structure was created before the onset of the credit crisis, so that such a possibility would have then seemed very remote) – investors can be confident that a high proportion of these loans will end up being repaid.

Grosvenor Place CLO III has issued some €312.5 million of class 'A' senior notes, all awarded the highest AAA rating by Standard and Poor's and Moody's; some €85 million of notes in classes 'B', 'C' and 'D', which also achieved investment-grade ratings ranging from AA to BBB; and finally €14 million of notes in class 'E', achieving a BB rating. All these are sold to investors. As well as these €411.5 million of rated notes there is in addition a further €40.5 million of unrated 'subordinated' notes (€40.5 is the par value of these notes; their actual value may be lower). These subordinated notes are the 'equity' share of Grosvenor Place CLO III. If there is additional receipt of interest and principal from the loans over and above the payments due to the A–E note holders, then this additional 'profit' can eventually be paid out to the holders of the subordinated notes. All these notes have a legal maturity (date when investors must be repaid) in October 2023. The rules of this CLO are that following a five-and-a-half year 'reinvestment period', ending in October 2013, the notes will then be paid down as the underlying borrowers repay, so that in practice the actual maturity of the notes will be between 2013 and 2019 (the most senior notes are paid down first and thus have a relatively shorter maturity).

Risk and return in the Grosvenor Place CLO III

In order to assess the risk and return let's look at a few numbers. Table 5.1 shows the prospective return – the interest margin earned taking account of the coupon rates promised on all these different loans and notes. This interest margin is fairly large, a surplus of €8.93 million per year after subtracting the €22.58 annual interest payment to rated note holders from the €31.51 annual interest receipt from the loans. Why such a large interest surplus? This is because nearly 90 per cent of the notes are investment grade. As a result only the holders of the €14 million of speculative grade E notes, rated as BB, require a higher coupon rate than that paid on the underlying loans (9.78 per cent instead of 7.15per cent) and these notes account for only about 3 per cent of the entire structure. The substantial interest margin offers the prospect – provided underlying loan performance is good – of a large profit on the subordinated notes.

Analysis of the prospective returns on this CLO must also take account of both loan default and management costs. Loans in this portfolio have an average five-year maturity. Historical data for the past thirty years suggest that over a five-year holding period about 10 per cent of loans of this quality (B1/B2 or B+/B) will default – i.e., default will be about 2 per cent per year. Recoveries – i.e.

Table 5.1. *Interest margin on the Grosvenor Place CLO III*

Assets (collateral)	Amount (€mn)	Coupon %	Annual interest receipt (€mn)	Note classes (credit rating)	Amount (€mn)	Coupon %	Annual interest payment (€mn)
High-yield leveraged loans (at least 85% senior)	433	7.15	31.00	A1–A2 (AAA)	313	5.02	15.70
				B–D (AA–BBB)	85	6.48	5.51
				E (BB)	14	9.78	1.37
Cash	13	4.00	0.51	Subordinate	34	na	na
Total	446		31.51	Total	446		22.58
Margin			8.93				

Note: Subordinated notes are here valued on a 'net asset' basis, that is, value of assets less that of all rated notes, not at par.

the amount of money that is returned to lenders after a loan defaults – can be expected to be reasonably good, since historical experience has been that corporate bank loans default lenders still recover about 80 per cent of the amount loaned (again an average figure; there is a great deal of variation in recoveries from one corporate bankruptcy to another). Assuming a five-year loan holding period of underlying loans, this suggests that average annual loan losses on this portfolio will be about 20 per cent of 2 per cent applied to the €433 million of loans, i.e. €1.73 million per annum. There are in addition committed management fees of 0.15 per cent of loan assets paid to the collateral manager and 0.10 per cent of loan assets paid to the trustee (if the underlying loans perform well then the collateral manager also receives higher 'subordinate fees' and an incentive payment of 20 per cent of surplus margin).[2] These committed

[2] The CLO trustee (Deutsche Trustee Company Limited) monitors and reports on performance, takes payment from the borrowers and ensures that all note holders receive payments due to them. The trustee also checks that the CLO obeys a number of par value and interest payment coverage tests – these provide further protection to senior note holders – and instructs the collateral manager to take appropriate action when these tests are failed.

Table 5.2. *Adjusting the Grosvenor CLO III returns for*
expected losses and costs

Expected margin	Margin (€mn)	Margin (% total assets €446mn)	Margin (% equity €34mn)
Before costs (from Table 5.1)	8.93	2.00	25.8
Expected credit losses	1.73	0.39	5.00
Committed management costs	1.08	0.24	3.13
Promised subordinated coupon	3.09	0.69	8.91
After costs ('arbitrage spread')	3.14	0.70	9.07

fees amount to a further €1.10 million per annum. Finally, there
is a promised coupon on the subordinated notes (7.50 per cent
of their face value of €40,500 or €3.09 million per year).

Table 5.2 shows the impact on the CLO returns of adjusting
for both expected default losses and these other costs. The 'arbitrage spread' for the Grosvenor CLO III – i.e. net expected returns
as a proportion of total cash and loan assets – works out at 0.70
per cent or, in the more usual jargon, 70 basis points. Taking into
account the incentive payments to the collateral manager – about
one fifth of the arbitrage spread – implies that holders of subordinated note holders can expect an overall return on the equity they
provide (RoE) of about 16 per cent, provided that these investors
purchase these notes for their net asset value.

A 16 per cent prospective return sounds fairly good, but the
returns on the subordinated notes are far from being risk-free (the
use of the phrase 'arbitrage spread' is rather misleading because
it suggests that returns are a sure thing, whereas they clearly are
not). This CLO, like all other structured finance products, *concentrates* risk through leverage. The subordinated note holders
are carrying virtually the entire risk of this structure and the
actual outcome for them could be somewhat better or a great deal
worse than shown in Table 5.2.

Consider the potential downside. We now know that there
will be a serious recession in the global and European economies
during the life of this CLO. Actual defaults on this loan portfolio might be, say, 25 per cent of the portfolio or – spread over a

five-year period – 5 per cent per year. Recoveries might also turn out to be lower than expected: let's say 60 per cent of principal. The overall loan losses (equivalent to €8.4 million per annum spread over five years) would then eliminate the interest margin of the CLO for the first five years of its life. Taking into account the committed management costs, this would mean that little or no coupon was paid on the subordinated notes and they would lose about 10 per cent of their nominal value.

This comparison, between the performance of the subordinated notes in boom and in recession, makes it clear quite how sensitive are the returns of a transaction deal of this kind to investors' perceptions of future economic conditions. If they believe that economic performance will be strong for the next few years, then the subordinated notes and the speculative-grade mezzanine securities above them in the hierarchy can yield very good returns. Investors then will pay well for these securities, and the arbitrage profit can be very high (the arbitrage spread is large). If, on the other hand, investors are concerned about future economic prospects they will think that there is a high chance of a recession in which subordinated equity notes and mezzanine do very badly. In this case they will pay little for these securities and the arbitrage profit will vanish altogether.

How could the issuer Lehman Brothers and the collateral manager CQS Investment Management Limited make money out of this CLO? For CQS the incentive was the fee structure. They could make a substantial profit if the loan portfolio performed well and still make something even if the loan portfolio performed poorly. For Lehman Brothers the opportunity was the 'arbitrage' profit from the marketing of the CLO: if they succeeded in selling the investment-grade and subordinated notes for more than the value of the cash and collateral in the CDO, they make an instant profit from the issue, regardless of subsequent performance. As we have just discussed, this arbitrage profit opportunity is very dependent on investor confidence; if investors are very concerned about high prospective loan losses then it is possible that no arbitrage profit will be achieved.

The actual selling prices of the notes in Grosvenor Place CLO III are not public information, but the prospectus established a par value for the subordinated notes of €40.5 million. This indicates that Lehman were looking to make something like a €6.5 million gain on issue from this CLO (the difference between the €40.5 million par value of the subordinated notes and their €34 million 'net asset' value). This is an ambitious target. Lehman's gain from sale is the subordinated note holders' loss, and sold at this par value the expected return on equity to subordinated note holders would work out at only 12 per cent per annum, rather than 16 per cent, and investors could lose as much as 15 per cent rather than 10 per cent in the event of a major recession. Beauty is in the eye of the beholder, but sold at their par-value the risk-return trade-off offered by the Grosvenor Place CLO III subordinated notes does not look particularly attractive. It is likely that these notes were sold at somewhat below their par value, thus lowering Lehman Brothers' arbitrage profit on this deal. Lehman's gain from sale will also be reduced if they have to purchase loans for above their par value or sell the rated notes for less than par.

In practice it is difficult to sell all the high-risk subordinated notes in such a structure for par. The ownership of the Grosvenor Place CLO III subordinated notes are not publicly documented, but it is also likely that, in order to maintain their issue price, many of these subordinated notes were acquired by Lehman Brothers and by CQS. Purchasing these notes at a price close to par – or persuading the collateral manager to do so – allows the issuer Lehman Brothers both to book a higher level of profit from the structuring of the CLO and to enjoy the prospect of further additional returns from good performance. But this practice of holding rather than selling the highest risk tranche also exposes the issuer and the collateral manager to substantial post-issue risk.

Structured finance: fee income versus transaction profits

Time to recap. Why do investment banks create structured credits? They answer is, of course, in order to make money, but, as we have seen, they obtain these revenues from structuring credit in two quite different ways. The first source of revenue are fees from the balance sheet structures such as the MBS and ABS described in the previous chapter. In this case a customer, usually a commercial bank, pays a fee for the creation of the structure. They do this in order to 'securitize' some of their assets, transferring them off balance sheet into the structured financial vehicle, and so reduce their funding costs and increase the liquidity of their balance sheet and benefit, sometimes, from transfer of extreme credit risk.

The second source of revenue is the direct trading gain from the creation of a transaction structure of the kind described in this chapter, when the 'notes' – the various tranched securities issued by the structure – are sold for more than it costs to purchase the collateral and set up the structured vehicle. The Grosvenor Place CLO III described in Box 5.1 is an example of this kind of deal.

The profits of a transaction deal are typically a lot higher than the fee income from a balance sheet deal. A commercial bank is willing to pay perhaps $50 million for a five-year securitization of, say, $100 billion of mortgages or consumer or corporate loans. This is not huge money for the investment bank (one fifth of 1 per cent of the issue to cover the costs of creating the structure and marketing the loans) but it is very safe money; the investment bank is not directly exposed to any risk.

Lehman Brothers did not earn any fee for issuing the Grosvenor Place CLO III; its profit came instead from selling the tranched notes issued by the CLO. As we have seen, this structure obtained a reasonably high 'arbitrage spread' (interest margin net of costs) of 70 basis points – that is, on the $444 million of assets there is a prospective profit of €3.0 million per year. We do not know what sum Lehman Brothers was able to get from sale of the subordinated notes – the risky equity tranches – of this CLO or how much of the subordinated notes it ended up retaining. At a guess, they might have been able to make a gain on this transaction of perhaps €2 million or $3.5 million. This is a fairly good return – but despite the label 'arbitrage' that is often applied to such structures, this profit will not have been completely risk-free. In order to achieve this profit it is possible that Lehman were forced to retain a substantial share of the subordinated notes. If their exposure is substantial then an issuing bank could even now still lose all their profit on this type of deal, should the underlying loans perform especially poorly. This may not matter so much for the individuals involved in the deal; by the time these risks emerge they may well have moved on to other jobs, elsewhere in the bank or with other firms, or they may have left the industry.

For the staff working in structured credit departments the reward-to-effort ratio of such a CLO is pretty good. As I am writing these paragraphs, a natural yardstick for me to use is a comparison with my own reward-to-effort ratio in producing this book, which is taking about eight months of my life to write. I am in an optimistic mood. Suppose this book turns out to be very successful, exceeding my own and my publisher's expectations and sells, say, 100,000 copies. I might get about 50¢ per copy or a total of $50,000 or £35,000. Not so bad for eight months of mostly enjoyable work.

A structuring is a less solitary and also a somewhat quicker activity than writing a book. There are a variety of professionals involved; as well as a senior manager an experienced lawyer and a specialist in risk management and derivatives are needed. Also needed is a senior staff member responsible for writing the prospectus and eventually promoting and selling the notes. All these people need to be supported, so there might be another dozen in supporting roles, and in addition the issue requires a couple of days involvement from the Lehman Brothers global sales force, during the offer period when the notes are available for purchase. Two months of work from the supporting staff, plus all departmental overheads, might cost Lehmans $500,000. The global sales effort could cost another $500,000. But this still leaves around $2.5 million dollars to provide the remuneration of the senior team members and profits for Lehmans. Each senior team member could easily end up with $250,000 in salary and bonus, which is a pretty good reward for a project lasting a few weeks. Moreover, the payment prospects of the structuring professionals probably seemed a bit more reliable than my own prospects as an author. Sales of a book are very unpredictable, I may well end up with much less than $50,000, while only unanticipated economic circumstances could lead to the failure of a structured transaction.

This is not to say that the unanticipated never happens. Since summer 2007 investors have been reluctant to buy even the senior tranches of CDOs and MBSs at any price. As a result several deals have been 'warehoused' – that is, structured but not sold to investors. But few in the industry saw this coming. Deal volume remained high right up until the market collapse.

Transaction profits and the hunt for yield

Earning transaction profits from credit structuring has been a very attractive business opportunity, yielding much higher revenues than can be obtained from fee-based balance sheet transactions for commercial bank clients. Having learnt the trick of conducting transaction deals, investment bankers began to look around for relatively risky assets offering the high yields that would produce the required arbitrage profit. The hunt for yield had begun and it was this that drove down interest rates for risky borrowers to low levels and led to the boom in credit for a wide range of borrowers, both in the United States and elsewhere in the world.

The most popular raw material for these high-yield transaction structures was lending to US households, especially sub-prime mortgage and home-equity lending. Mortgage-backed securitization was previously mostly fee-based balance sheet structuring, allowing commercial bank clients to fund more mortgages than they could carry on their own balance sheet using deposit finance alone.

The investment banks involved knew that these loans were risky, but they believed that they were still an excellent investment opportunity. Sub-prime borrowers were willing to borrow at much higher rates than those of safe 'prime' borrowers with perfect credit records, but in the event of a default losses would be limited by the underlying loan collateral. The sub-prime mortgage contracts held by these transaction structures were also deliberately set up with a large jump in mortgage interest rates after three or four years (the so-called 'exploding' ARM deals). The reason for doing this was not intended to exploit the borrower, but simply to make sure that the borrower remortgaged with some other lender and paid back the loan relatively quickly. This early prepayment was designed to limit the exposure of the investors in the arbitrage vehicles. Again, this arrangement worked well during the boom, when sub-prime borrowers could easily remortgage. As long as the housing market seemed strong the resulting deals appealed strongly to investors, offering high returns and apparently low risk, even on the riskier lower equity and mezzanine tranches, and offered the structuring departments of investment banks substantial 'arbitrage' profits.

But this then posed a problem for the investment banks. Relying on commercial banks to bring pools of mortgages for securitization limited this profit opportunity. Commercial banks were still mostly comparatively cautious lenders and so did not bring as many potential high-yield mortgages for balance sheet securitization as they might have done. Investment banks therefore located new sources for sub-prime mortgage and home equity lending outside the traditional banking system, mortgage brokers that would sell them loans outright instead of retaining an interest in the securitization structure. This way investment banks were able both to increase their volumes dramatically and to take a much larger share of any resulting profits.

This is exactly what happened, with the total volume of sub-prime mortgage securitization doubling every two years, rising from $87 billion in 2001 to peak at $465 billion in 2005. It was this increased demand from Wall Street banks, seeking out high-yield mortgages for inclusion in their arbitrage structures, which led to the dramatic increase in sub-prime and other alternative originations through mortgage brokers. This competition for volumes led in turn to both the widespread decline in underwriting standards and a house price boom which led many commentators to discuss the possibility of a major housing recession.

Despite this decline in loan quality and increase in risk, volumes remained nearly as high during 2006 as they were in 2005, and it was only in the course of 2007, when it became clear that the US housing market was weakening nationwide, that volumes of sub-prime securitization slackened off. They then fell precipitously, from $89 billion in the first quarter to only $12 billion in the fourth, a rate of securitization only about half that in 2001 before the boom began.

The hunt for yield was not just in sub-prime

A similar story played out in other markets at the same time. Wherever high-yield credits could be found, investment bankers purchased and securitized them. We will look at some statistics at the end of this chapter. But first, here is a description of the three other main types of borrowing – commercial mortgage-backed securitization, leveraged finance and investment-grade bonds – that have benefited from the hunt for yield in structured finance.

One boom area has been in commercial mortgage-backed securitizations – used to finance condominiums, office buildings and shopping malls. Commercial mortgage-backed securitization (CMBS) peaked in 2006 at around $200 billion in the United States and $100 billion in the rest of the world. The total stock of US CMBS is close to $1 trillion. This has channelled a large volume of funds, used both for the development of shopping malls and office buildings and as a source of debt refinancing for the owners of existing commercial properties. However, on the whole, commercial mortgage-backed securitizations have been conducted in a relatively cautious manner. Commercial property lenders still have clear memories of the large sums they lost on loans to speculative office and retail projects in the late 1980s and early 1990s. As a result most CMBS are secured not on speculative projects but on completed buildings with tenants in place. Some US CMBS for purchase of condominiums – multiple-occupancy apartment blocks – have suffered substantial losses. But only in the event of a major global economic collapse will the revenues on most other deals be threatened.

Structured finance has also supported a huge increase in lending for private equity projects, the form of lending known as 'leveraged finance'. This form of finance requires a bit of explanation. Private equity itself is not new – the term simply means that the stock of a company is owned by outside investors but is not traded on public markets such as the New York Stock Exchange, NASDAQ, or the London Stock Exchange. Private equity investment also differs from public equity because there are only a small number of private equity investors (often only a single fund) and these investors are actively involved in running the firm. They need to be actively involved because the usual safeguards such as stock exchange reporting requirements do not apply to privately held companies.

Small firms are often held privately. But in the 1980s a new, more aggressive and ambitious form of private equity emerged, using debt finance to purchase and restructure a wide range of companies, sometimes of very large size. The firm Kohlberg Kravis Roberts & Co. pioneered this approach in the 1980s, which culminated in their 1989 takeover of the firm RJR Nabisco for $31.1 billion. These buyouts were not always successful, the economic downturn of 1990–1 pushing many of the private equity transactions of that time into bankruptcy, and for the next decade relatively few private equity buyouts took place. Now, since 2003 there has been a new boom in private equity transactions, this time financed by leveraged loans rather than junk bonds. The leveraged loans were in turn funded using the structured credit vehicle known as the collateralized debt obligation, of which Grosvenor Place CLO III was one among many.

The aim of the private equity funds that conduct these buyout transactions is to increase the market value of these newly acquired firms, by lowering costs and increasing revenues, and then to sell out at a profit. Debt finance is crucial. Private equity funds are like minnows swallowing perch – their buyout targets are often much bigger than they are. The private equity companies thus finance their deals using debt, secured on the buyout companies. This leverage not only finances the deal, it also ensures that the private equity companies can keep any gain in value to themselves and do not have to share it with other equity investors.

Private equity buyouts are controversial. The changes they impose are sometimes painful, with job losses and the negotiation of much tougher contract terms with suppliers and workforce. They are also sometimes accused of focusing excessively on short-term increase in profits, without paying sufficient attention to long-term sustainable growth. But private equity deals are not just about cost reductions and short-term performance; they can also create long-term value by introducing more effective management and providing funds for investment in equipment, business processes and in the development of products and services.

Today there are a number of very large globally active private equity funds looking for buyout opportunities around the world, for example the Carlyle Group, Kohlberg Kravis Roberts and Blackstones. These funds have undertaken many new private equity buyouts, some as large as the 1989 RJR Nabisco deal – for example the 2007 $31.6 billion dollar buyout of the Hospital Corporation of America, the world's largest private operator of health-care facilities. But the big difference from the 1980s has been the much greater number of active funds and the very much larger number of deals that they have completed. According to the *Washington Post*, in 2006, private equity firms bought 654 US companies for $375 billion, representing eighteen times the level of transactions closed in 2003.[3] There has also been an equally large boom in private equity transactions in Europe. The value of deals and quantity of debt finance make this recent private equity boom much bigger than its predecessor in the 1980s.

Just as with residential and commercial mortgages, structuring has made a huge volume of debt finance available to private equity funds, providing a ready market for the purchase of the 'leveraged loans'

---

[3] Robert J. Samuelson, 'The private equity boom', Washington Post, 15 March 2007.

granted to the buyout companies. These loans are provided, at the time of the initial buyout deal, by a loan 'syndicate' – that is, a number of different commercial banks share the initial loan. Commercial banks have been very willing to do these deals, despite their risk, because there is a ready market for selling on their shares in these loans, sometimes to long-term investors such as pension funds and insurance companies, more often to investment banks for structuring inside collateralized loan obligations.

Structuring has also increased the demand for the bonds of high-quality 'investment grade' companies, with CDOs built to hold the risk of bond default both directly, by buying and holding the bonds directly, and also indirectly, using a derivative contract known as the credit default swap. These bonds or the associated credit derivatives provided the yield enhancement that supported the returns on the CDO. The low cost and ready availability of this debt in turn encouraged many large companies, including a number of big banks, to 'leverage up', offering bonds to market (good news for the investment banks, since this gave them additional underwriting income when the bonds were sold). Companies then used this money to finance their own investment projects or, more often, simply to buy back some of their outstanding shares and operate with greater leverage, increasing prospective returns to shareholders but also exposing shareholders to greater risk of loss.

The decline in credit spreads and credit quality

This 'hunt for yield', that is, the search for high-yielding loans and securities to package inside structured transaction deals, in turn put downward pressure on credit spreads – the difference between interest rates paid by risky borrowers and those on totally safe lending such as US government debt. With such great competition to lend funds to high-yield borrowers, it is no surprise that the rates charged to relatively risky borrowers and hence their 'credit spreads' declined.

This decline in credit spreads occurred for a wide range of debt assets, but is most readily observed for leveraged loans and bonds. The spread – the extra yield relative to safe assets – on B-rated leveraged loans fell from over 3 per cent in 2003 to close to 2 per cent in 2005 onwards. Credit spreads for US BBB-rated corporate bonds declined to around 2.14 per cent basis points in 2005, well below their peak of

3.30 per cent in 2002, and fell further to around 1.75 per cent in 2006 and the first half of 2007.

These spread declines were large, but equally big declines in corporate bond and leveraged loan spreads have occurred before; for example, the strong growth in the US economy enjoyed at the time of the first Clinton administration in the mid-1990s saw US BBB rates spreads fall as low as 1.50 per cent. Perhaps an even more important consequence of the 'hunt for yield' was that the quality of loans bought into structured credit vehicles weakened at exactly the time that yields were also falling. There is clear evidence of declining underwriting standards for the US sub-prime mortgages that were purchased for transaction deals over the years 2002–7. There were also declines in underwriting standards for leveraged lending, where the ratios of loan amounts to earnings before interest, taxes, depreciation and amortization fell sharply (this is the equivalent in this market of the loan-to-income ratio offered to a personal borrower).

There has also been a trend in leveraged finance towards so-called 'covenant lite' deals, in which lenders have more limited rights to early repayment than is customary in bank lending. For example, standard corporate loans usually include so-called 'maintenance' covenants – requiring companies to maintain the ratio of pre-tax earnings to interest payments above a minimum level – but bond contracts typically do not include such covenants. Many leveraged finance deals followed practice in bond markets and also exclude such 'maintenance' covenants (but like most bond contracts still include other 'incurrence' covenants which restrict the ability of companies to take on additional lending).

The hunt for yield and the resulting downward pressure on credit spreads has in turn had a major impact on the profitability of structuring. The low yields of 2007 CLOs such as Grosvenor Place CLO III, while still generating enough surplus to pay salary expectations to the investment bankers involved, leave rather little profit on the table for issuing banks, perhaps not even enough to justify the risks involved. Back in 2002 an equivalent portfolio of high-yield leveraged loans to that used in Grosvenor Place CLO III might have been offering a yield as high as 350 basis points instead of the 200 basis points on offer in 2007 (i.e. the equivalent loan portfolio could have offered a coupon rate of 8.65 per cent instead of the 7.15 per cent achieved in 2007).

Box 5.2. Declining credit spreads and CDO profits

As an illustration of the impact of declining credit spreads on CDO profitability, we can look again at the Grosvenor Place CLO III example presented above in Box 5.1. We can make the same assumptions as before of a 2.5 per cent annual default rate and of 80 per cent recoveries, but assuming a 300 basis point credit spread such as might have been achieved in 2004, instead of the 200 basis point credit spread of the summer of 2007. The arbitrage spread more than doubles, from €3.0 million to €7.4 million per year or (as a percentage of total CDO assets) from 70 to 166 basis points. The prospective return on equity for sub-ordinated notes, assuming that they were sold at their net asset value, would be a very healthy 26 per cent per year, and even if the subordinated notes were sold at par would still be around 21 per cent. What this shows is that there can be large prospective profits in a CDO structure, exploiting differences between yield on B-rated high-risk credit exposures of, say, 8 per cent and AAA rates of say 5 per cent. With such credit spreads it is relatively easy both to create value and to sell the risky subordinated notes to outside investors such as hedge funds. While yields on credit-risky assets remained high, the volume of structuring grew, which in turn helped to sustain the credit boom.

The hunt for high-yield assets contained the seeds of its own destruction. As it squeezed credit spreads it reduced the interest margins underpinning CDO profitability. It is unclear yet how many of the deals undertaken at the peak of the boom, in 2006 and 2007, will ultimately be profitable. Most of the problems with deals secured on US mortgage assets have already emerged, but, even by the time this book is published, it will not yet be possible to determine the success or otherwise of deals secured on leveraged loans or other corporate credits. The outcome of these deals will depend on the performance of the US and global economies in 2009 and 2010. If this performance is as weak as some fear then it is likely that a large proportion of deals made in the final years of the boom, in 2006 and 2007, will result in losses for holders of many subordinated tranches and – to the extent they have retained these notes – for issuers.

Restructured credit products

One might have expected a slowing down of structured finance activity, as the hunt for yield and the growing risk of recession reduced arbitrage spreads. Regrettably, investment banks seem to have drawn quite the wrong strategic conclusion. They perhaps drew an analogy with the major product innovations in over the counter (OTC) trading markets, such as interest-rate swaps and credit derivatives, where the leading firms have been able to make up for declining margins by increasing volumes, especially in the most standard vanilla products. In these markets it has been the few leading firms with the largest market share that have continued to make decent returns. This experience seemed to suggest that the best returns go to the most aggressive players who pushed hard for market share.

Whatever the reason, the structuring departments of the major banks made every effort they could to increase rather than reduce the volume of structuring activity. One device, introduced in order to maintain business volumes and profit margins, was innovative 'restructured' CDOs. These were CDOs built using the tranches of other structured products as their raw material. About $400 billion of ABS-CDOs were created to hold the lower-rated tranches of mortgage-backed securities and consumer ABS and perhaps in addition another $200 billion of 'CDO^2', which hold the lower-rated tranches of collateralized loan obligations, of other CDOs secured on corporate credits, or even of ABS-CDOs.

Why did investment banks pursue this idea of building 'structures upon structures' in this way? The problem they faced, and which limited their ability to earn revenue from the more basic MBS and ABS securitizations or from CLOs, was that as yields declined it was increasingly difficult to find buyers for the lower junior and mezzanine-rated tranches of MBSs and of ABSs backed by consumer credit (for example, the €14 million of BB-rated notes in Grosvenor Place CLO III or the lower-rated M notes issued by Countrywide ABS 2006-19). There was a ready market for the safe senior tranches – those rated AA or better by the rating agencies – but investors would pay only relatively low prices for the riskier tranches, especially those attracting B ratings. The high coupons demanded by investors for absorbing this risk threatened to reduce the arbitrage spreads on CDOs and ABSs to unacceptably low levels.

The solution found by the structured finance professionals – a solution which was responsible for much of the excess of the credit boom – was to re-structure these sub-investment-grade tranched securities using exactly the same techniques they were already applying to sub-investment-grade leveraged loans. The Grosvenor Place CLO III structure illustrates how structuring can create some $90 of safe investment grade securities for every $100 of risky sub-investment-grade debt, created alongside some $3 of sub-investment-grade mezzanine notes and maybe $7 of unrated equity. Applying the same procedure a second time to the remaining $3 of mezzanine could create a further $2 of 'safe' investment-grade debt.

Other basic structured products, notably MBS and ABS, produce greater proportions of mezzanine B- and BB-rated paper (Grosvenor Place CLO III appears to have been rather conservative in this respect, issuing no B paper at all) and can therefore raise even more additional financing by recycling tranches into ABS-CDO or CDO^2.

There are two major problems with these kinds of restructured product – that is, the ABS-CDOs and CDO^2 built upon the higher risk tranches of the basic structured credit vehicles that held underlying credit assets. The first problem is that payments on the notes issued by restructured products are very much more sensitive to aggregate economic risk than a conventional single-structured MBS or CDO. In the event of an economic downturn which triggers default on the mezzanine tranches of the lower 'ground story' structure, then virtually all the tranches of the higher 'upper story' structure are then at risk of failure. The second problem is that the complexity of these products has proved to be too much for the rating and risk professionals responsible for assessing the risk exposures of the different tranches of structured credit products. The rating agencies agreed AAA or other investment-grade ratings for the higher-level tranches of these restructured products, even though there was no relevant history of the past performance for the underlying collateral on which ratings could be based (unlike bank loans or corporate bonds for which there were thirty or more years of performance data). They also do not seem to have properly allowed for the fact that the underlying collateral, when it defaults, may yield little or nothing in the way of recoveries. Risk professionals then accepted the assurance of safety offered by an investment-grade rating without thinking through the high level of underlying risk exposure.

With the benefit of hindsight it is difficult to understand how responsible finance professionals could have created quite so many 'restructured products' without examining more closely the risks involved. The closest business analogy seems to be the practice in factory farming of killing battery chickens which have grown too old for egg laying, and then recycling their carcasses for use as chicken feed. The prospect of maintaining margins and spreads in existing structured activities seems to have blinded those involved to the obviously high levels of risk and the questionable basis for both ratings and risk-modelling.

Given the complexity and lack of transparency of these restructured products, it should be no surprise that it is ABS-CDO and CDO^2 that have suffered some of the biggest losses in the credit crisis so far. The IMF (*Global Financial Stability Report*, October 2008) has estimated that the market value of ABS-CDO tranches fell by around 60 per cent between August 2007 and March 2008, a decline of $240 billion. One of the biggest single losses acknowledged since the onset of the credit crisis has been by Merrill-Lynch in July 2008, when it sold out of its portfolio of mezzanine ABS-CDOs at a reported value of $6.7 billion, writing down its interest by some $24 billion. More losses on ABS-CDOs and CDO^{2}s are in prospect, and eventually – in the event of a deep US and global recession – the entire asset class may need to be almost entirely written off, a spectacular and, for the rating agencies, extremely embarrassing fate for $600 billion of securities much of which had attained the safest possible AAA ratings.

Structured financial products: how much money was raised?

The objective of this chapter has been to introduce a number of the new structured products, especially the relatively high-risk 'transaction deals' created during the credit boom of 2003–7 by the structured credit departments of the major investment banks. These were very different from the simple and safe tranched mortgage-backed and asset-backed securities used by banks to lower their funding costs in the more standard balance sheet deals. Transaction deals were highly leveraged structures that could make a lot of money when economic conditions were good, but were always highly exposed to an economic downturn. They were used to supply credit to a very wide range of risky borrowers, including sub-prime mortgage borrowers and the leveraged loans supporting the major private equity boom of these years.

We can complete the chapter by looking at the size of the entire market for structured financial products, both CDOs and the other main group of structured financial products – tranched ABS and MBS. These figures have already been presented in Table 2.2 of Chapter 2. This section provides some more detailed support for those numbers.

Grosvenor Place CLO III is just one of a very large number of collateralized debt obligations issued in recent years by the structured credit departments of the major investment banks. The industry website, www.absnet.net, lists some 1,735 CDOs with an aggregate portfolio value of $829 billion issued over recent years. This list appears to cover only part of the market; statistics from the Securities Industry and Financial Markets Association (SIFMA) and the European Securitisation Forum (ESF) suggest that the total amount of CDOs outstanding across the world is around $1.5 trillion. Using what is perhaps by now a familiar yardstick, the outstanding value of CDOs is about 3 per cent of the national income of the rich industrialized countries or 3 cents for every dollar of pre-tax wages, rents and profits.

The global CDO market has grown rapidly. In 2004, $157 billion of CDOs were issued worldwide. In 2005 total issuance climbed to $272 billion and leapt higher still to reach $552 billion in 2006. In the first half of 2007 the rate of issuance grew even more, reaching $724 billion (at an annual rate). But after the start of the credit crisis, issue of CDOs collapsed, falling to only $281 billion (at an annual rate) in the second half of 2007 and falling further again to only $74 billion (again at an annual rate) in the first half of 2008 – that is, issuance has fallen by 90 per cent compared with what it was at the peak of the credit boom. A consequence of this rapid rise and even more rapid contraction is that most outstanding CDOs were issued between 2005 and 2007 and are thus at relatively high risk of a deterioration in the credit performance of underlying assets.

Unlike Grosvenor Place CLO III, nearly three-quarters of all outstanding CDOs have been dollar-denominated and secured on US assets, US securities and loans to US companies – that is, CDOs have played an especially important role in the US credit boom and bust.

Alongside this is a substantial stock of other tranched securities backed by lending – mostly commercial and residential mortgage-backed securities and asset-backed securities secured on consumer loans. The largest share of all of these are the $5.9 trillion of mortgage-backed securities issued by the government agencies Fannie Mae, Freddie Mac and Ginnie Mae. These are, however, a special case because the payments of both interest and principal on the underlying loans are guaranteed by the agencies, with the perceived backing of the US government. The boom in structured credit, far from supporting agency securitization, actually competed with the agencies, and their bonds continue to be actively issued and traded, even while other securitization and structured finance markets are almost completely frozen.

As we saw in the previous chapter, tranching played a key role in providing funding for so-called 'private label' MBS and ABS, loan-backed securities that do not have any form of implicit or explicit government backing. We can divide these into three groups:

- At end-2007 there was $2.3 trillion in these private-label mortgage-backed securities outstanding in the United States and Europe (of which $1.3 trillion were backed by US mortgages, including about $0.8 trillion of sub-prime MBS, and the remaining $1 trillion backed by mortgages in Europe, predominantly loans in the United Kingdom, the Netherlands, Spain and Italy).
- Alongside this was some $1.1 trillion of commercial mortgage-backed securities (CMBS) (with $0.9 trillion secured on US property and $0.2 trillion on European property, mostly in the United Kingdom, Germany, Italy and Spain).
- Finally, there seems to have been about $2.0 trillion of ABS backed by consumer lending (of which $1.3 trillion was to US consumers, $0.4 trillion for various government-supported lending schemes such as student loans, and $0.3 trillion to European consumers).

Altogether – adding together the CDO and other loan backed figures – there was some $7 trillion of structured financial securities in issue or, netting out the $0.6 trillion of restructured securities, some $6.4 trillion. Of this perhaps about $4.8 trillion are senior AAA-rated notes, $1.2 trillion other investment-grade-rated notes, $0.3 trillion sub-investment grade tranches (many of which are held in re-structured products) and $0.1 trillion subordinated equity.

Structured financial products: where did the money all go?

Around $3.4 trillion of these private label structured products financed residential and commercial mortgage lending (RMBS and CMBS). The remaining $3 trillion were ABS and CDOs. About $1.7 trillion of ABS financed consumer lending (with another $0.4 trillion used for a variety of purposes) and about $0.9 trillion of CDOs (i.e. excluding restructured products) financed corporate investment.

Where did all this money end up? About one third of CDO money – nearly $0.4 billion – was used to finance the boom in 'private equity' transactions in the United States and Europe, in which funds such as The Carlyle Group and Blackstone took control of a variety of companies using high-risk debt finance. CLO structures, of which Grosvenor Place CLO III described in Box 5.1 is typical, purchased many of the 'leveraged loans' that financed these deals.

CDOs have also been used to raise credit for a variety of other purposes. Another $200 billion, or around one in eight of all outstanding CDO issues, appear to have been so-called 'balance sheet' CDOs. These structures are more like traditional MBS or ABS. There is a sponsoring commercial bank that wishes to raise securitization funding in order to transfer assets off balance sheet. The difference is that the assets concerned are perhaps 150–200 loans to large corporates, each for several millions of dollars, rather than a pool of thousands of mortgages or several thousands of personal loans. Investment banks conduct balance-sheet CDOs for the fees they earn from the sponsoring bank, not in order to earn 'arbitrage' profits.

A further $350 billion or so of outstanding CDOs hold investment-grade corporate assets. Of these around $200 billion are 'synthetics' – so called because they do not hold cash assets such as bonds or loans. The high yields that support these synthetic structures are obtained by writing contracts – similar to insurance contracts – in which the CDO receives a regular premium income (the yield uplift) in return for a promise to reimburse investment losses whenever a named corporate bond defaults. These contracts, known as 'credit default swaps', trade in highly liquid credit derivatives markets. As Chapter 8 describes, they were also used to provide insurance on better-quality structured credit securities. The remaining $150 billion is backed directly by corporate bonds. Both structures – cash or synthetic – help to provide additional funding to corporates.

More than 95 per cent by value of outstanding CDOs can be allocated to one of these five categories – collateralized loan obligations or CLOs; restructured products such as ABS-CDO and CDO^2; balance sheet CDOs; synthetic CDOs; and finally bond CDOs. The small amount of remaining CDOs are invested in other kinds of credit derivative or a mixture of credit assets.

To sum up, the increased supply of credit mostly ended up in three different places – in residential mortgage lending, especially US sub-prime, in leveraged lending to private equity companies both in the United States and Europe, and in commercial mortgage-backed securities, predominantly in the United States.

But the biggest issue of all turns out to be not 'where did the money go' but 'where did the money come from?' Only a relatively small proportion of these structured securities were sold to long-term investors. Most was retained on bank balance sheets and financed out of short-term borrowing. This risky and unstable practice of borrowing short in order to hold long-term structured securities is the subject of the next chapter.

Further reading

Again, just as with the basic tranched mortgage-backed security, it is difficult to find accurate introductory-level material on the products described in this chapter. The *Financial Times* is a useful resource for descriptions of many of the more complex products; see especially a number of articles by Gillian Tett. It is also well worth searching the *Financial Times* AlphaVille website for insiders' views on some of these products. The Wikipedia entry 'Collateralised debt obligations', unlike that on mortgage-backed securitizations, cannot be recommended, since it contains a great deal of inaccurate and misleading information.

There are some good recent books by experienced risk managers providing insight into the problems of some of these new financial innovations, for example Richard Bookstaber's A Demon of Our Own Design: Markets, Hedge Funds, and the Perils of Financial Innovation (Wiley, 2008) and Ricardo Rebonato's The Plight of the Fortune Tellers: Why We Need to Manage Financial Risk Differently (Princeton University Press, 2008). Even though they do not focus on the new credit products, the books of Nicholas Taleb on trading risk, for example The Black Swan: The Impact of the Highly Improbable (Penguin, 2008), are also relevant, explaining how short-term monitoring of trading performance encourages inappropriate behaviour because it rewards traders that make small profits every quarter, while still being exposed to a small risk of very large losses.

6 | *Borrowing short and lending long: the illusion of liquidity in structured credit*

The investment banking activity known as 'structured credit' created a zoo of new tranched products. The last chapter looked closely at one particular example, a collateralized loan obligation (CLO) deal, and briefly reviewed other types of transaction, including the very dubious restructured deals employing as collateral the riskier tranches of other structured credit deals. These transaction deals made an immediate profit and also provided credit to many types of risky borrower who found it difficult to access normal bank credit.

Investment banks in effect began to compete directly with commercial banks in the provision of credit, at the lower end of the credit quality spectrum. They engaged in a 'hunt for yield' – that is, a search for high-yield credit assets that could be bought, packed in these arbitrage structures and yield an immediate accounting gain. This hunt for yield resulted in a massive credit creation, especially in three areas: sub-prime mortgages and home-equity loans, commercial property and the 'leveraged loans' used for private equity buyouts.

A common feature of all these transaction structures was their employment of leverage. Leverage was the reason for using similar tranching to that of the more established MBS and ABS. By creating a large proportion of safe AAA tranches (in retrospect not always so safe, especially in the case of the dubious restructured deals), the returns to the remaining higher risk tranches were enhanced. In an environment of strong economic growth and rising prices for property and other assets, these higher-risk tranches offered high returns and so appealed to some investors. By selling even a small proportion of high-risk tranches, banks could declare an immediate gain on sale profit, based on the assumption that unsold tranches had a 'market value' the same as those sold.

These highly leveraged transactions worked in an environment of strong growth and rising asset prices. Once economic growth slowed and asset prices fell from their peaks, these same higher-risk tranches become very unattractive, offering poor prospective returns in relation to their high level of risk. Worse still, underlying markets became illiquid and the collateral management also used to provide some additional protection to investors no longer worked. The words of a song made famous by the empress of the blues, Bessie Smith, spring to mind. Leverage is your friend on the way up. Returns are good and everyone wants to know you on the way up, when you can 'afford to buy them champagne, whisky and wine'. But leverage is no longer your friend on the way down and making losses. 'Nobody wants to know you when you're down and out.' Such has been the fate of the transaction deals.

None of this would have mattered too much if investment and commercial banks had not compounded this mistake by acting as highly leveraged investment funds, relying on short-term funding to hold portfolios of long-term structured securities. This further layer of short-term leverage has been by far the greatest source of losses to the industry and created the wholesale funding feedback loop shown on the top right of Figure 1.1.

Short-term leveraged funding

What caused this feedback loop? Across the industry, the trading desks of investment banks used short-term funding to hold, and make a profit out of holding, senior AAA tranches of structured credit securities such as MBS, ABS and the various types of CDO. These short-term leveraged positions held by investment banking trading desks were paralleled by similar short-term maturity transformation by commercial banks and in a number of off-balance sheet vehicles known as 'conduits' and 'SIVs' (these vehicles are explained later in this chapter). These were all yield-based trades, the profit coming not from a capital gain earned when the price of the securities rose but from the difference between the relatively high yield offered by these safe senior structured securities and the relatively low interest rate paid on short-term secured funding.

This new business has to be seen as a 'mission creep', the pejorative term applied to military campaigns that end up pursuing objectives quite different from those that they were originally set up to achieve. The proper objective of investment bank trading desks is to make a return out of *short-term* trading. This role is well established in foreign exchange and equity trading, and in the government bond markets, as well as in many established various derivative markets such as interest-rate swaps and futures, commodity futures and equity options. Profits are made in such activities over a relatively short time – weeks, days, sometimes just minutes. Short-term trading by investment banks and by some other trading intermediaries such as hedge funds in turn provides markets with liquidity (allowing long-term investors to buy and sell with low transaction costs) and ensures that prices better reflect the views of market participants about future economic and financial conditions. But investment trading desks were now wandering away from their proper position on the sell side of security and derivative markets, and starting to compete with other financial institutions, with both commercial banks and investment funds operating on the buy side of the securities markets. Not only were they moving into inappropriate areas of business that they did not properly understand, they also failed to heed the lessons of other highly leveraged investment funds. Profitability of such an investment strategy depends on market liquidity, and it is the job of investment banks as short-term traders to provide this liquidity, not to make money relying on the provision of liquidity by others.

The position of the investment banks was very similar to that of LTCM in 1998 described in Chapter 3, only on a larger scale. They were holding (together with commercial banks and other vehicles pursuing a similar investment strategy) more than $3 trillion of structured securities which were now illiquid and no longer suitable as collateral for short-term funding. This was a market with few committed long-term investors, investors who understood these products and would be prepared to buy them at a good price. The problem was exacerbated by excessive leverage; banks did not have sufficient capital committed to short-term trading of these structured credit tranches to be able to maintain market liquidity. This inappropriate business strategy could not have been designed to create greater liquidity risk.

The vicious circle of falling prices

Investment bank trading desks had in effect, without even recognizing it themselves, adopted a risky commercial banking business model, borrowing cheap short-term funds in order to hold higher-yielding longer-term assets. Some banks such as Bear Stearns, Merrill Lynch and UBS, did this on a truly massive scale, expanding their entire balance sheets aggressively in order to hold structured credit assets.

This strategy was based on the mistaken assumption that the market for AAA structured credit securities would always be liquid and that these securities would continue to be accepted as security for short-term repo borrowing.

The problem for the industry was then that, with little long-term investor interest in holding these structured credits, deteriorating confidence in these products turned into a vicious circle of falling prices, increasing price volatility and withdrawal of short-term funding – that is, the feedback loop on the top right of Figure 1.1.

Even nineteen months after the credit crisis broke, this process still has a lot further to go. Continuing deterioration in the underlying economic conditions threatens to lead to yet further deterioration in these markets and further losses on bank holdings of structured securities.

With total exposures of $3 trillion or more to high-quality but illiquid AAA securities, these liquidity losses are already around $600 million and could well, in the context of a deep global economic slump, rise to $1 trillion or more, all market pricing losses on senior AAA default-free structured credit tranches and hence additional to the impairment of underlying loans.

One mistake was to assume that maturity transformation and the associated liquidity risk would be removed along with the hedging of interest-rate risk. Typically, trading desks hedged out any interest-rate risk and sometimes also (in the so-called negative basis trade) credit risk. They thought that holding long-term structured assets, financed with short-term borrowing, was an entirely risk-free transaction. The sophisticated risk models of the banks, which measured credit and interest-rate risk but not liquidity risk, agreed – these positions were both profitable and entirely risk-free.

In fact, as Chapter 8 describes, the credit risk insurance, arranged by purchasing credit default swap protection on the senior bonds from insurance companies such as AIG, proved unreliable. The illiquidity and fall in prices of the structured securities undermined the solvency of the insurance companies selling the protection. They were unable to fulfil their promise of protection in the face of a global systemic liquidity shock.

As the great fictional detective Sherlock Holmes said to his long-suffering assistant Dr Watson, it is a great mistake to confuse the unlikely with the impossible. In fact the events that transpired can be seen with benefit of hindsight as not even unlikely, but as an inevitable consequence of the massive maturity mismatch of the industry. They were piling into this trade on such a scale that eventually it was bound to fall over.

How the maturity transformation or 'yield-based trade' was conducted

Is risk-free profit really possible in competitive markets? The answer is no, but most of the world's largest commercial and investment banks were ignoring one of the most basic of finance lessons, that there really is no such thing as a free lunch in financial markets. This lesson can be illustrated by the much-repeated story of the Chicago finance professor walking in the streets outside the faculty with his Ph.D. student. The identity of the professor changes from one version of this story to another but let us suppose it is the deservedly renowned Merton Miller. Suddenly the student stops, turns around pointing, and exclaims 'Look, Professor Miller, there's a $100 bill lying on the sidewalk!' Professor Miller, whose understanding of finance was second to none, does not even bother to look in the direction indicated. 'That is unusual, but you realize of course that the bill is an obvious forgery. No genuine $100 bill would be left lying on the sidewalk without someone having already picked it up.'

During the credit boom both commercial and investment banks used short-term funding to hold AAA structured credits, in order to pick up not just a few $100 bills off the sidewalk, but around one hundred million $100 dollar bills every year. This practice in turn channelled many tens of billions of dollars into the credit boom. The banks were so busy enjoying the additional accounting profits they made from yield-based trading that they never paused to question what lay behind these profits and whether there was some unappreciated risk in this trade.

This yield-based trade worked as follows. Borrow money at, for example, 4.85 per cent, using it to hold an entirely risk-free bond offering a return of 5.15 per cent (structuring could produce a massive supply of effectively risk-free AAA bonds offering such returns for use in this trade). This means that if you buy $400 million of these bonds with a five-year life, you appear to have made a guaranteed profit of

0.30 per cent (30 basis points) on $400 million, or $1.2 million per year for five years. After five years the bond matures, you use the principal that you get back to repay the original borrowing, and the 'trade' is complete. You have picked up not one but 60,000 $100 bills that happen to be lying on the sidewalk. As we will have seen, the total stock of bonds held by banks in such yield-based trades rose from almost nothing in 2002 to around $3 trillion dollars by summer 2007, contributing more than $100 billion per year to global banking sector profits and providing the bulk of funding for the global credit boom.

How these trades were carried out

This was an attractive business proposition that appeared to offer a decent profit with no associated risk. Who actually carried out these trades? They were conducted by employees of the trading desks of a major bank that could borrow at these low rates of interest. They were also carried out by the so-called treasury departments of both commercial and investment banks, whose job it is to hold portfolios of liquid securities that can be sold whenever a bank has temporary need of funds. Many bank treasuries were treated as profit centres, giving them a strong incentive to hold high-yielding apparently liquid AAA structured credit securities as a way of making some additional yield profit. Box 6.1 examines how this trade took place.

Box 6.1.   How yield-based trading was carried out

Let's look a little more closely at how this yield-based trading was carried out. The trick is to ensure that you use the lowest-cost form of short-term secured borrowing and hence maximize the profit. It is standard market practice to quote short-term and floating rates of interest relative to a standard market reference rate known as Libor. Libor is the interest rate paid by banks, as reported by participants in the London interbank market for borrowing. So we can compare all interest rates to this reference.

Suppose that the Libor three-month dollar interest rate is, say, 5 per cent. The risk-free bond you purchase might be five-year AAA senior notes from a sub-prime MBS offering a yield that is 15 basis points above Libor – that is, 5.15 per cent. But you can finance this at less than Libor using secured borrowing.

If you purchase $400 million of notes you can pledge these notes in order to borrow perhaps $380 million in a sale and repurchase or repo contract. This is rather like a mortgage; you are taking a loan against collateral, the collateral is not a house but the senior sub-prime notes. Just like a mortgage you cannot borrow 100 per cent of the value of the collateral, in this case only 95 per cent. This difference – the remaining 5 per cent – is known as the repo haircut.

Using repo you might be able to borrow at 16 basis points less than Libor – that is, at 4.84 per cent instead of 5 per cent. You have to borrow the remaining $20 million at the unsecured Libor rate, so your overall average borrowing rate works out at very close to 4.85 per cent.

Second, you may want to 'hedge' (i.e. remove) some risk. Ideally the structured securities you have purchased, for example senior AAA sub-prime MBS notes, are 'floating rate'. This means that the contracted interest rate moves up and down along with a short-term money market interest rate such as the three-month dollar Libor rate. So if Libor rises from 5 per cent to 6 per cent, then the interest rate on the notes rises from 5.15 per cent to 6.15 per cent while your repo rate rises from 4.84 to 5.84. The profits on the trade are unaffected. Such floating-rate contracts are widespread, not just found in structured finance. For example, larger well-known companies often issue long-term bonds paying interest at a floating rate set at, say, 20 basis points over Libor. A floating rate is better for yield-based trading, because you are not exposed to interest-rate risk – the trade makes the same profit whether interest rates go up or down. But you can still do exactly the same thing holding a structured bond paying a fixed interest rate. In this case you just have to take out a further contract called an interest-rate swap, which eliminates interest risk by doing exactly what it says, swapping the fixed interest for a floating Libor rate.

There is still some remaining credit spread (or 'mark to market') risk on the bond. Remember, as already discussed in Chapter 4, the AAA tranches of mortgage-backed securities, even sub-prime MBS, are pretty much default-risk-free. Even if losses on the underlying pool of mortgage loans run as high as 25 per cent, which would be an extremely high level of loss corresponding to a default or foreclosure rate of 50 per cent or more, the AAA tranche is fully repaid. This is why they are rated AAA in the first place. But there is still a problem because, even when they are regarded as free of default risk, the market values of AAA notes fluctuate somewhat from one trading day to the next; the original $400 million could easily move up or down by, say, around $1 million. This is known as credit spread risk because when the market value falls the credit spread on the structured notes rises and when the market value rises the credit spread falls. This credit spread risk is a problem, because if the market value of the bonds falls to, say, $398 million, then the trading position would show a loss on a 'mark to market' (i.e. current market value) basis. Even though the profit is risk-free provided you keep the position for five years, this mark to market loss could force you to close out early, and then you would not make the expected risk-free profit.

Trading desks sometimes 'hedged' – that is, removed this 'mark to market' credit spread risk. The contract often used for this purpose was a credit default swap (CDS), usually purchased from one of the so called 'monoline' insurance companies, companies specializing in the business of insuring bonds such as municipals or senior structured credit notes, or from AIG, the largest seller of CDS protection. With this contract you pay a regular premium to the insurance company and in return you are compensated for the loss of value of the AAA structured notes in the unlikely event that it defaults. This also means that you are protected against changes in market value of the $400 million of AAA sub-prime MBS notes, since the hedge has a market value that moves in the opposite direction to the value of the bonds.

Before the credit crisis broke in summer 2007, such protection on AAA sub-prime MBS notes might be purchased for as little as 10 basis points per annum, which comes to $400,000 per annum on the $400 million.[1] Provided the insurance company does not go bankrupt, your trade is now entirely safe. Indeed, this insurance had been regarded as so effective that 'fair value' accountancy rules allowed such hedged trades to be taken completely off balance sheet, in which case there is no 'mark to market' risk at all.

---

[1] Such a hedged yield-based trade is often described as a 'negative basis trade', because, in this example, the cost of CDS insurance at 10 basis points is much less than the 36 basis points credit spread on the AAA MBS.

More often yield-based trading was carried out without hedging the credit spread risk at all, or using a partial hedge such as purchasing protection using the ABX credit index.

This trade was not just carried out by investment bank trading desks. Bank treasuries often included the senior notes of structured credit products in their pool of securities held for liquidity reasons – that is, as a reserve of liquid assets which there was no definite plan to sell but which could still be sold at short notice if the bank needed cash. Bank treasurers worked out that they could make a nice additional interest income if they used senior structured notes from an MBS or a CDO for this purpose instead of conventional securities such as government bonds. They could also increase their holdings beyond their immediate liquidity needs by financing additional holdings of high-grade structured credit products using repo borrowing – that is, leveraging up their returns. Commercial bank treasurers would not usually need to hedge out the credit spread risk, since their securities portfolios were expected to fluctuate in value, and, anyway, they could achieve a larger interest-rate margin without hedging.

Why were structured credit products so important to this trade? It was necessary to hold some form of credit-risky asset in order to get a yield that was higher than market rates of interest such as Libor. The only possible alternative source of high-yield assets for this trade was corporate bonds instead of structured paper. This trade is a far less attractive proposition. Corporate bonds are neither as safe (on average) or as homogenous as AAA structured credit notes. The risks of individual companies depend on many specific factors, such as the industry and country in which they operate and the quality of their management, so that (even before the credit crisis) there was a large degree of credit spread risk even on the best-quality corporate bonds. It requires sound financial understanding and excellent trading skills to trade corporate bonds profitably on an unhedged basis. To make money it is necessary to spot and purchase underpriced bonds while selling overpriced bonds. Also the trades have to be well timed, since you can still lose on an underpriced bond if the price falls still further below the purchase price. All this means that there are few $100 bills lying on the sidewalk to be picked up by holding corporate bonds for yield on an unhedged basis. If you don't have the knowledge and trading skills you can lose plenty of money from such positions. What about conducting a hedged trade instead? The problem then is that the cost of a credit spread hedge for a corporate bond – the premium paid on a credit default swap – is so large that it entirely wipes out the profit of a yield-based trade.

Yield-based trading by both commercial and investment banks using AAA structured credit notes increased at an extraordinary rate in the years 2003 -7, both for themselves and on behalf of clients. Banks from all over the world – from Asia, Europe and South America as well as from the United States – joined in the party. There are no precise statistics, but the total amount of money tied up in such trades appears to have risen to over $3 trillion (details of this estimate are provided in Chapter 5 above), mostly financed using short-term borrowing and contributing around $10 billion per annum to worldwide bank profits.

Surprisingly, this yield-based trading opportunity stayed around for some time, contrary to what Merton Miller would have predicted. For some years until the credit crisis broke in summer 2007, AAA tranches of structured credit yields continued to offer yields substantially better than Libor. This is confirmed by a variety of market data sources (many of these are now collected and published in various post-crisis reports by public authorities such as the Federal Reserve, the Bank of England, the European Central Bank and the IMF). Thus until the credit crisis broke AAA investment-grade private RMBS offered spreads of 15–20 basis points above Libor. AAA investment-grade CMBS (secured on commercial property) were more attractive still, offering spreads of around 50 basis points above Libor. There were big profits also on the double-structured ABS-CDOs, which also offered spreads well above Libor for their AAA tranches. This is not so surprising, since no one really trusted these securities, despite their approval by the rating agencies.

Given these attractive spreads and the apparent safety of these instruments (remember that they are AAA; underlying credit losses would have to be unimaginably bad for many of them ever to experience default), it is no wonder that so many banks jumped on this particular bandwagon. But yield-based trading has also eventually turned out to be a recipe for losing huge sums of money. By now something like 20 per cent of this $3 trillion has been written off as 'mark to market' losses: losses which are *additional* to the hundreds of billions of dollars lost because of the poor underlying performance of some loans made during the credit boom.

A puzzle about the economics of yield-based trading

There are a couple of big puzzles about this once lucrative but now disastrous yield-based trade. The first puzzle is why long-term investors such as pension funds, life insurance companies and sovereign wealth funds did not capture the profit of these trades from banks for themselves, by purchasing the safe high-return AAA tranches of structured bonds. If yield-based trading worked, then these long-term investors were getting an extremely bad deal. They were letting the trading desks of banks walk away with huge pay-offs in the form of bonuses for a trade that required little special insight, skill or ability. As shareholders and holders of investment funds, these long-term investors were getting the profits of yield-based trading, but only after paying out huge and unnecessary overheads in the form of management fees, salaries and performance bonuses to investment banks. They could have done the same trade for themselves at far less cost – simply by buying the low-priced high-yield safe AAA assets and holding them to maturity.

Long-term investors – both individuals and institutions such as pension funds, insurance companies and sovereign wealth funds – are always interested in secure yield (held either directly or for additional diversification as part of a mutual fund). In the United States individuals hold a large proportion of AAA municipal bonds (this is because the interest they pay is exempt from federal and state income tax). US Treasuries, like other bonds issued by the governments of developed countries, are sold in a much more international market, with more than half of US Treasuries held by international investors. These foreign investors in US Treasuries include both pension funds and life insurance companies and also sovereign wealth funds and governments of major resource and manufacturing exporters – for example Saudi Arabia and China.

Given the mushrooming of credit structuring between 2002 and 2007, it is not surprising that it proved difficult to persuade these natural purchasers of safe AAA paper to pay full price for the best-quality structured credit assets. These tranches would have competed in their portfolios with either government bonds such as US Treasury notes or with AAA municipals (a bond issued by a US public body below state level, such as a city or county with the high rating achieved through insurance from one of the major monoline bond insurers). But the high-quality tranches of structured credit are clearly quite different from these public-sector bonds.

First and most obviously there was little history of these securities. Corporate and municipal bonds have been around for more than half a century, while tranched MBS and ABS have been around only since the 1980s and CDOs only for a decade or so. With many structured products having been created so quickly, it was always going to be difficult to persuade final investors to hold them. Most importantly from the perspective of the investor, as well as there being an absence of any historical record of the performance of structured credits, these structured securities differed from other safe bonds because there is no single entity responsible for repayment. The promise of repayment relied on the accuracy of the default models used to rate these securities, not on the efforts of a corporate body or government to avoid the costs of default.

Life insurers, pension funds and other long-term investors may well have suspected that there were hidden legal or other risks in these trades, despite the fact that ratings suggested very low risk of default. This is a reasonable concern, especially with such new and untested securities. As we are now aware, it is possible, for example, that there might be a class action brought by borrowers who were aggressively sold an unaffordable level of credit relative to their income, such a high level of debt that they would never have the ability to repay. Such an action might find all the holders of structured notes, regardless of seniority, responsible for such mis-selling and they could then be forced to recompense these borrowers.

So, despite the seal of rating agency approval, these investors were far from comfortable with the new structured products. Of course they might have been prepared to buy at some sufficiently low price; the combination of low price and apparent safety would have soothed any concerns. But selling at such a low price undermined the original gain on sale profits in arbitrage structures and reduced the funding benefits of balance sheet structures.

Hindsight always gives 20:20 vision, but it is now clear that it would have been much better for investment banks to engage in an active and sustained marketing campaign to persuade long-term investors, and the asset managers that work for them, to purchase these structured notes for what they were really worth. But, given the natural doubts long-term investors had about structured credit, however remote the possibility of default, such marketing would have cost a lot of money and effort. It was going to take some years and considerable effort by issuers to educate the buy side of the market to acquire these notes for their fundamental value. It was cheaper and easier to forget about the cost and effort of marketing and book building needed to sell all the structured notes for full value of, say, $404 million and settle for the lower, but still profitable, price of $400 million, a price that could easily be obtained, often from a sale to a bank's own trading desks.

A second puzzle

A second puzzle is why the great demand from bank trading desks and the funds they operated for the safe AAA structured notes did not push up their prices, lower their yields and narrow the apparently fat profit margins in yield-based trading. This is the reason why Merton Miller asserted that the $100 lying on the sidewalk could not be genuine, because if markets operated freely any such 'arbitrage' opportunities had quickly to disappear as traders took profitable positions and as a result prices moved to close the gap between purchase and sale. Even without sales to long-term investors, competition to acquire structured assets by yield-based traders would still be expected to push their prices up (close to fundamental levels) and their yields down (close to the cost of holding a hedged position). The opportunity for risk-free profit should have been transient, not long-lasting.

One explanation of this is the sheer volume of structuring and the massive amount of paper created during the credit boom, with more than $400 billion a year of paper created by the structured credit departments of the investment banks. As a result structuring created very large volumes of the most highly rated possible AAA paper, nearly $5 trillion dollars worldwide by the middle of 2007 (see Chapter 5). This is far more than the amount of equivalent-quality AAA corporate bonds available to investors. (There are about $8 trillion of outstanding corporate bonds worldwide, but most of these are BBB to AA investment-grade issues and sub-investment grade; a relatively small proportion are AAA.) The issue of AAA structured credit has also far outstripped that of AAA municipal bonds (there are now maybe $3 of

AAA structured credit for every $1 of AAA municipals) and has grown to about the same size as the entire US government bond market.

So the supply of structured credit securities was growing rapidly with the demand. There was some decline in spreads and rise in price on senior structured notes over the period 2003–7, although not enough to eliminate yield-based trading profits. If this trend had continued, yield-based trading would have become less profitable, an expected outcome once senior structured credit was fully established as an asset class. But this was not a problem that especially concerned traders. If their positions were unhedged they would then make a profit from the capital gain on the securities they held. The profit opportunity might disappear, but in the meantime the obvious course of action was to 'make hay while the sun shines' – that is, while the opportunity was out there, purchase and hold as many of these highly-rated structured notes as possible, financing them at relatively lower borrowing costs.

As already mentioned in Chapter 5, this massive volume of structuring activity was in turn supported by rather misleading accounting rules, which allowed structuring desks to book 'arbitrage' profits at the time of the deal, profits that were in fact far from certain but relied on good performance of underlying collateral. This misvaluation was probably always fairly small, even at its most prevalent at the peak of the credit boom, adding perhaps 20 or 30 basis points on the total value of structured notes; but, even so, such a small valuation difference could often be enough to turn a marginal deal that would have been turned down into a profit-making deal that was pursued. Again, the industry was too busy taking profit to question whether the underlying positions made sound business sense.

Different ways to yield-based trade: conduits and SIVs

Yield-based trading does not require any great talent or unusual ability. Before the credit crisis broke, any bank with an AA credit standing was able to conduct this kind of trade, and once the opportunity became widely known most of them did. Yield-based trading then appeared in a variety of different guises (although the underlying trade was always essentially the same). The simplest and most widely used trade was the one already described – keeping the senior structured notes on balance sheet and financing them using repo (and sometimes making them disappear from the balance sheet altogether by hedging out all market and credit risks.)

A more sophisticated approach to conducting these trades was to use one of two different types of off balance sheet vehicles, known as conduits and structured investment vehicles.

- Conduits are off balance sheet vehicles owned by commercial banks. They are set up in order to purchase and hold investment-grade structured credit tranches, typically AAA-rated and issued by their parent 'sponsoring' bank, and finance these using short-term paper.
- 'Structured investment vehicles', or SIVs, are a form of leveraged investment fund, again holding high-yield assets and financing these by issuing short-term paper. There has been a wide range of ownership arrangements for SIVs; in some cases they were entirely owned by their sponsoring bank operating them as a pure trading vehicle. In other cases the sponsoring bank had no ownership stake at all, outside investors (usually customers of the sponsoring bank) owning the entire fund and claiming all profits. Very often the sponsoring bank and outside investors shared ownership of the SIV.

Conduits and SIVs sound rather complicated, but a pretty good handle on these vehicles can be obtained by looking at a number of points of similarity and difference between them.

(i)   Both conduits and SIVs issued asset-backed commercial paper (usually referred to by the acronym ABCP). This is short-term 'commercial' paper (i.e. issued by a company, not a bank or a government) secured on the assets of the conduit or SIV and issued with maturities typically of between one week and three months. ABCP (like its close cousin commercial paper or CP) is a popular short-term 'money market' investment, an alternative to holding a three-month Treasury bill (the T-Bill) or a bank certificate of deposit (the CD). Holders of ABCP include major companies, institutional investors and so-called 'money market mutuals' that offer investors a diversified portfolio of short-term investments.

(ii)   The assets held by conduits and SIVs were not limited to AAA tranches of structured products. They also held lower-quality investment-grade assets, rated perhaps AA or A, allowing them to achieve a greater yield uplift and profit than an on balance sheet yield-based trade.

(iii)   While ABCP provided the large majority of conduit funding, around two thirds of SIV funding came from medium-term asset-backed notes with maturities of over three months.

(iv)   Both conduits and SIVs (just like CDOs and mortgage-backed securities) relied on obtaining a best-quality AAA or AA investment-grade rating of their paper from the major rating agencies. Without such a rating they were unable to finance themselves and had to wind down. In both conduits and SIVs the achievement of AAA ratings for the ABCP paper relied on guarantees of liquidity support from the sponsoring bank.

(v)   Asset-backed commercial paper conduits have been used on a smaller scale for some years, since well before the emergence of yield-based trading. Their original application was as a low-cost method of financing bank loan assets such as credit card receivables or vehicle loans. By obtaining a high investment-grade rating on the issued paper (AAA or AA), the sponsoring banks could use a conduit to obtain relatively cheap funding.

(vi)   Conduits are directly controlled by their sponsoring commercial bank and are mainly used by them as a source of low-cost short-term funding and liquidity.[2] The arrangement is more flexible than an asset-backed securitization because assets can be moved in and out of the structure according to the bank's liquidity needs. Whenever a bank needed low-cost funding it could move mortgage-backed securities or other assets into the conduit. When the need for such funding diminished it could transfer assets back onto its balance sheet.

(vii)   SIVs were run under an investment mandate (a statement of investment policy and procedures) with rules for winding down of the fund and the returning of investors' investment capital should the SIV breach certain investment covenants. For example, one common covenant is to wind down the fund if net asset value (the value of assets minus the value of ABCP liabilities) fall below a stated trigger level.

(viii)   SIVs held a wider range of assets than conduits – for example bonds and CDOs, as well as MBS and ABS – all of which were

---

[2]   Conduits were used for other purposes as well, for example the 'credit arbitrage' conduit used to hold purchased credit assets, just like an SIV. See *Bank of England Quarterly Bulletin*, Q3, 2007, p. 348 for a more detailed review of their different applications.

purchased in open market, not transferred from the sponsoring bank. Also unlike conduits, SIVs actively bought and sold the assets in their portfolio to maintain portfolio quality.

(ix) As investment funds, SIVs were often given impressive names that would indicate to investors the kinds of exposure they were taking on. This aspect of SIVs was the subject of a memorable spoof by the UK television comedians John Bird and John Fortune.[3] Conduits had less ambitious names, reflecting their more limited role in tapping relatively low-cost ABCP funding.

The business rationale for setting up both conduits and SIVs was also similar; they were both created because of the difficulty of selling investment-grade structured credit products for full fundamental value and thus the correspondingly high yields on these structured credits when valued on a 'mark to market' basis – that is, MBS and other structured credit tranches achieved relatively low prices but offered relatively high-interest yields given their credit quality. Our CLO example, the Grosvenor Place III CLO from the previous chapter, provides a good illustration. It suggests that a price of $400 million or lower might be achieved when their real underlying fundamental value was $404 million. Price discounts on higher risk AA and A RMBS and on CMBS and CDO tranches could be even larger. But as a result they offered attractively high yields, with AAA tranches offering anything from 20 to 100 basis points above unsecured Libor borrowing rates.

---

[3] The clip on structured credit from their ITV show *The Long Johns* enjoyed a lot of viewing on YouTube until it was removed at the request of the copyright holder. The relevant excerpt from the transcript runs as follows (George is a spoof investment banker): 'JOHN: In view of the fact that in these packages is a lot of dodgy debt, what is it about it that attracts the financial risk takers? GEORGE: Well, because these . . . funds . . ., which specialize in these debts, they all have very good names. JOHN: You mean they are responsible companies. GEORGE: No, no. It has nothing to do with their reputation. They have actually very, very *good* names. The names they think up are very good. I'll give you an example. There is a very well known American Wall Street firm called Bear Stearns who have two of these hedge funds which specialize in these mortgage debts. And they lost so much money – well, lost so much of its value – that Bear Stearns announced that they would have to put in $3.2 billion into one of the funds to try and keep it afloat. JOHN: 3.2 billion! GEORGE: 3.2 billion. Yes. Yes. And even then they said the investors couldn't get anything out of it and they were going to let the other fund go. But one of these funds was called High Grade Structured Credit Strategies Fund and the other was called the High Grade Structured Credit Enhanced Leverage Fund. Well, that sounds very good. JOHN: It sounds very trustworthy.'

Conduits were set up because for banks conducting a 'balance sheet' transaction in order to obtain low-cost funding of their loan assets, it made better business sense to 'rent out' the tranches of a MBS as the collateral for short-term borrowing through an ABCP conduit, rather than sell them outright. This way the bank could fund itself at ABCP rates of interest that were considerably lower than the yields on senior tranches of mortgage-backed securities. This is not really a yield-based trade in the same way as the on balance sheet trading described in the previous section. The pay-off is obtained not as a trading profit but as a reduction in the cost of wholesale funding of the bank; but the business rationale is the same: exploiting the mispricing of structured notes. An ABCP conduit also has the advantage of being more flexible than an outright securitization. This is because assets can be moved in or out of the vehicle according to the liquidity requirements of the sponsoring bank.

SIVs were a more direct arbitrage exploitation of the pricing misalignment between senior structured credit products and secured short-term lending markets. The idea here was exactly the same as when pursuing an arbitrage opportunity in on balance sheet yield-based trading – that is, buying a range of high-yielding assets and financing them at the relatively lower interest rates on ABCP and secured medium-term notes. A bank would often use an SIV rather than hold the position on balance sheet in order to allow customers to participate in the investment opportunity; thus SIVs were typically operated by the asset management divisions of the investment banks rather than by their trading desks.

Conduits and SIVs have attracted much media attention during the credit crisis. This has conveyed the misleading impression that the credit crisis is like Enron writ large (Enron was the energy trading company that collapsed in 2001 after the emergence of financial problems hidden in off balance sheet vehicles), with unmonitored off balance sheet activities the principal source of the current credit problems. In fact the magnitude of off balance sheet asset holdings and the issue of short-term paper and their contribution to overall credit losses are much smaller than those of on balance sheet yield-based portfolios.

The available statistics back up this view that conduits and SIVs were not quite as important as the media spotlight would suggest. Even at the peak of the credit boom in summer 2007, SIVs only ever accounted for 6 per cent – that is, around $75 billion of the total

$1,200 billion dollar global asset-backed commercial paper market.[4] Even allowing for their issue of medium-term notes, the total assets held by SIVs were still only around $400 billion, of which around $100 billion were not structured paper at all, but bonds issued directly by financial institutions.[5] There were around $1,400 billion of assets held in the asset-backed commercial paper conduits used by banks for funding their own balance sheets.[6] However, about half of these assets were held in conduits owning loans, notably trade receivables, taken directly off commercial bank balance sheets. And only about two thirds of the remaining $700 billion of RMBS and ABS held by conduits were AAA, the remaining one third being lower-quality (BBB–AA) investment-grade structured notes, and not all SIV structured assets were AAA. Taking this into account it seems that, overall, these vehicles were holding around $1 trillion of structured credit products, of which about $650 billion was AAA-rated.

ABCP conduits have mostly continued to operate on a similar scale as before, but they have been forced to accept both a dramatic shortening in the maturity of the paper they issue, typically relying now on one week rather than one- or three-month funding, and accepting a sharp rise of funding costs. The rates of interest on three-month ABCP has fluctuated wildly since summer 2007, but has often jumped to around 150 basis points above secured lending rates – that is, well above even unsecured Libor lending rates. These spreads are a symptom of the underlying liquidity problems. Unsecured bank borrowing, while much more expensive relative to safe rates of interest than before summer 2007, can now be less costly than bank borrowing through ABCP secured on MBS and ABS. This sharp jump in ABCP rates has in turn substantially increasing the funding costs and reduced the net interest income of those banks most dependent on wholesale rather than retail deposit funding.

---

[4]   According to a JP Morgan analysis, reported by Reuters on 10 September 2007, SIVs accounted for 6 per cent of total ABCP issuance.

[5]   Based on the International Monetary Fund (2008) estimated breakdown of SIV and conduit assets and liabilities.

[6]   I am here relying on international Monetary Fund (2008) estimates that the total portfolios in these two types of vehicles were $1,400 billion in conduits and $400 billion in SIVs. The relatively large amount of conduit portfolios compared with their issue of ABCP seems to be explained by overcollateralization – in order to ensure AAA rating they held a lot more assets than they issued paper.

In contrast, mark to market losses on structured investment vehicles have been large, relative to the small scale of the credit portfolios they held. Since summer 2007 most SIVs have unwound. In many cases sponsoring banks have compensated customers who participated in these vehicles and thus had to take all the resulting losses on their bottom line. There appears to be no comprehensive documentation of SIV losses; they have been perhaps around $100 billion–$150 billion worldwide, and thus a significant contribution to the overall financial sector losses which had climbed to over $1 trillion by December 2008. But a line can be drawn under these particular losses, since most SIV positions have now been unwound. Overall, the attention paid to off balance sheet vehicles is perhaps rather greater than their importance in the current overall problems of credit markets.

The experience of individual banks is discussed in Chapter 8. The extent of on balance sheet losses varies considerably between banks. Some, for example Goldman Sachs and Deutsche Bank, did very little of this yield-based trading. They lost relatively little. Others, notably CitiGroup, Merrill Lynch and UBS engaged in this yield-based trade to a huge extent and have lost large sums.

Box 6.2.   How large were yield-based trading positions at the peak of the credit boom?

Chapter 5 discussed the aggregate statistics presented in Table 2.2 of Chapter 2 and looked at where the money was used. Using a range of sources and aggregating some flow data, it appears that some $6.4 trillion of net money was raised in Europe and the United States from the issue of asset-backed and structured securities (net because we are excluding restructured securities such as ABS-CDO). Altogether these instruments financed about $2.3 trillion of residential mortgage lending and more than $1.7 trillion of other household and personal lending. They also raised some $1.1 trillion for commercial mortgage lending and $0.9 trillion for corporate and business finance, including some $400 million of 'leveraged loans' for private equity deals.

This box looks at the other side of the picture, at where these securities were held, especially the $4.8 trillion of senior vanilla securities rated AAA, such as those issued by the Countrywide ABS-2006-19 and the Grosvenor Place CLO III, the examples of structured products explored in Chapters 5 and 6. These senior securities, still even now at very low risk of default, have been the main instruments held for yield-based trading positions and also, because of the practice of financing them short term with ABCP or repo, at the heart of the market illiquidity and collapse of 'mark to market' valuations.

How much of this $4.8 trillion was retained by banks in order to earn yield-based income, either in trading books or as part of bank Treasury portfolios? A reasonable guess is that banks kept about $3 trillion of this exposure. It is not possible to be precise because there are almost no statistics on who was holding the various structured securities. Still, a little bit of detective work suggests a figure of this magnitude. This 'guesstimate' can be supported by scattered statistics on global repo markets and by an examination of the losses that have affected the banking sector since summer 2007.

We can start with some estimates by the International Monetary Fund on the total size of bank-sponsored ABCP conduits and SIVs, suggesting that they held about $0.8 trillion of AAA paper (after netting out the restructured ABS-CDO). This leaves about $4 trillion of senior AAA paper either sold to non-banks investors or retained for on balance sheet yield-based trading. How much of this paper remained on bank balance sheets (either retained from their own structuring activities or purchased from other banks)? Here there is only anecdotal evidence, but it seems that more than half of the remaining $4 trillion of senior structures securities were held by banks, either in their trading books or as part of their Treasury portfolios of liquid financial assets. In total, through off balance sheet vehicles or on balance sheets, banks kept about $3 trillion of exposure to the safest AAA tranches of the vanilla MBS, ABS and CDOs.

This estimate is broadly consistent with available data on the size of US and European repo markets and the magnitude of their contraction during autumn 2008. The December 2008 ICMA-University of Reading survey of the European repo market (www. icma-group.org/market_info/surveys/repo/latest.aspx) reveals a sharp decline in repo lending in Europe, from its June 2007 peak of €6.8 trillion to €6.5 trillion in June 2008 and then, as the crisis intensified, falling by more than a quarter to €4.6 trillion in December 2008, i.e. a €2 trillion contraction, of which much was due to the inability of banks to continue using structured securities as repo collateral. There is no regular survey of the larger US repo market (the only publicly available statistical estimate is of $7.8 trillion in June 2004), but this also contracted sharply at the same time. An estimate of $3 trillion is also broadly consistent with the overall magnitude of write-downs and trading losses reported by the world's largest banks (see Table 8.1). Banks recorded about $230 billion in write-downs of available for sale bonds in 2007 and 2008, almost all attributable to the decline in the mark to market values of senior AAA tranches, suggesting that they were holding something close to $1 trillion of these securities in their Treasury portfolios.

What about the remaining $1.6 trillion of lower-rated tranches, those below the highest AAA rating? Again, there are no standard statistics. Around 10 to 15% of the securitized paper will have achieved lower investment-grade ratings – that is, around $0.7–0.9 trillion. Conduit and SIV holdings of around $400 billion account for around half of these notes, and the double structured products such as the mezzanine ABS-CDOs held a further $200 billion or so. This only leaves $100 billion–$300 billion, and some of this will have been retained by the issuers. Another 5 per cent or so of paper, perhaps $300–$400 billion, was sub-investment grade junior tranches. Again, only a relatively small amount of this lower quality speculative grade structured paper had to be sold to final investors or funds, those willing to gamble on credit losses remaining low, in which case these tranches would be highly profitable.

Finally, there were at least $300 billion of lowest-grade subordinated equity notes.[1] The majority of these high-risk

---

[1] The practice of 'overcollateralization' of balance sheet structures reduces the notional balance sheet value of liabilities relative to the asset portfolio, and this is reflected in a relatively low proportion of subordinated notes; but this is simply an accounting convention: the overcollateralization is economically equivalent to the holding of additional subordinated equity by the sponsoring bank. The estimate of at least $300 billion excludes this additional exposure.

notes, those carrying most of the risk of the underlying credit portfolios, were retained by issuing banks or sponsoring banks or were acquired by asset managers responsible for CDO portfolio decisions. In the case of balance sheet transactions, where the purpose of the structuring was to obtain low-cost funding of loan assets, there was no business reason to sell these notes at all. In the case of an arbitrage transaction, as we have seen in Chapter 5, it was common practice to sell only a proportion of notes to establish a profit for the deal and to retain the remainder. This way it was easier for the issuing bank to book an immediate 'arbitrage' profit.

What about the profitability of yield-based trades? The best profit margins could be achieved by holding the senior AAA tranches of the 'double structured' ABS-CDO and CDO^2, especially those mezzanine double structures which purchased primarily sub-investment-grade structured notes. There appear to have been a little more than $100 billion of such mezzanine double structured AAA notes created by the structuring departments of investment banks during the boom. These are especially complex structured products and as such are very difficult to sell to non-bank investors. There is no public information on the credit spreads available on these AAA tranches, but they may have amounted to 100 basis points above Libor and thus in aggregate will have offered yield-based trading profits to the world's banks of as much as $1 billion per annum.

The next-highest spreads were those on commercial mortgage-backed securities, where profits of 50 basis points were achievable. Combining the European and US data suggests that there was around $900 billion of AAA-rated CMBS paper, so if banks held on to $500 billion of this they would have earned further yield-based profits of another $2.5 billion per annum (reported either as trading profits or, in the case of balance sheet deals, as reduced interest rate costs). Similarly, there were around $600 billion of AAA-rated CDO tranches, and assuming banks held half of these, around $1.2 billion per annum of yield-based trading profits. Finally, banks may have retained around $1.5 trillion of AAA, ABS and residential MBS tranches, earning a further $5 billion per annum of yield-based trading profit. Altogether, yield-based trading profits will have been around $9–10 billion each year; in other words, each year the world's banks were picking up nearly one hundred million $100 bills lying on the sidewalk. This is about one $100 bill for every three citizens of the United States and Canada.

But, to date, banks conducting these trades have experienced 'mark to market' valuation losses of somewhere around 20 per cent of their total holdings of these securities worldwide – that is, around $600 billion dollars – that is, far more than their antici-pated revenues. But the last thing they want to do is to sell these positions and crystallize a loss; instead they prefer to hold on and hopefully make a reasonable profit.

Further reading

A number of other writers have identified the problem of maturity mismatch in bank's holdings of senior tranched structured credits. A very clear statement is that of Thomas Palley in his 'Why Federal Reserve policy is failing', at http://blogs.ft.com/wolfforum/2008/10/why-federal-reserve-policy-is-failing/#more-201. Like me, Palley uses the term 'parallel banking system' rather than the more misleading 'shadow banking system', since the problem was not opaqueness or lack of transparency of the instruments but the unstable funding structure.

A detailed account of this trading strategy and how it went wrong is revealed in the UBS report to shareholders on their sub-prime losses. It can be found at www.ubs.com/1/e/investors/shareholderreport/remediation.html.

A useful complement to this report is the short paper by Hugo Banziger, 'Setting the right framework for modern financial markets – lessons learned from the recent crisis', in the Banque De France, *Financial Stability Review*, October 2008, at www.banque-france.fr/gb/publications/rsf/rsf_102008.htm, stressing the point that many banks like UBS were holding structured products on their balance sheet instead of selling them and were thus exposed to risk. He claims that his institution, Deutsche Bank, avoided such exposures because of their higher standards of risk control, something that is borne out by their relatively low levels of write-downs on structured credits.

Adrian and Shin's Jackson Hole paper (www.kc.frb.org/home/sub-webnav.cfm?level=3&theID=10697&SubWeb=10660) is a valuable quantitative study of the rapid expansion of investment banks balance sheets during the bubble and their growing importance in credit intermediation, with a discussion of the implications for monetary policy.

There is an insightful literature on so called 'liquidity black holes' – situations in which market liquidity can suddenly evaporate. This is summarized by Adrian and Shin (2008) in their Banque de France article 'Liquidity and financial contagion', at www.banque-france.fr/gb/publications/telechar/rsf/2008/etud1_0208.pdf, that itself draws on the academic paper, Morris and Shin (2003), 'Liquidity black holes', at http://papers.ssrn.com/sol3/papers.cfm?abstract_id=446600. The first use of the phrase 'liquidity black holes' seems to be by Avinash Persaud; see www.g24.org/pers0403.pdf. An important related point made by Jon Danielsson, Hyun Song Shin and Jean-Pierre Zigrand in their paper 'Asset price dynamics with value-at-risk constrained traders', at http://papers.ssrn.com/sol3/papers.cfm?abstract_id=302307, is that both risk models (so called 'value at risk' models) and capital regulation (such as the new Basel accord) can worsen liquidity black holes by telling traders to reduce their exposure just when an asset market is illiquid. The Jackson Hole paper by Allen and Carletti (www.kc.frb.org/home/subwebnav.cfm?level=3&theID=10697&SubWeb= 10660) provides a wider and admirably clear review of the modelling of liquidity risk and how it is determined by 'money in the market'.

7 | *The levees break*

In the first half of 2007 loan losses emerged in one loan market segment – the US sub-prime mortgage market. This was not such a surprise. There had been warnings about unsustainable growth of house prices in the United States and other countries for some years. Sub-prime was the riskiest category of mortgage lending. Lenders knew well enough that losses were bound to emerge at some point.

They thought they were prepared. There was a lot of money committed to sub-prime mortgage lending – around $1.3 trillion dollars, or 10 cents for every dollar of US national income. But prospective losses in this market, even on pessimistic projections, looked to be perfectly containable. As I complete this book, taking a cautious view of losses on this sub-prime lending, it looks as though they might climb to around $300 billion dollars (the justification for this figure was given above in Chapter 1). This sounds like the sort of credit problem that banks can put behind them – recognize the losses and move on.

The huge surprise has been the wider impact of emerging losses on US sub-prime mortgage lending, first triggering bank failures in Germany and the United Kingdom, raising the cost of funding bank loan portfolios across the globe, and eventually triggering the run on the global banking system in September and October 2008. Why did the sub-prime losses have such a big impact? What were the links that transmitted this shock around the globe? This chapter tells part of the story, from the first emergence of problems in early summer 2007 to the failure of the UK bank Northern Rock in September of that year.

Background: the new global linkages

Before going through these events, we first need a reminder of how banks worldwide had become much more closely linked, through new securitized and structured credit products. The detail relating to all of this is found in the previous three chapters, but a brief review is appropriate to keep the main points fresh in the mind. Figure 2.2 in Chapter 2 provides a visual illustration.

The most basic of these new products, the tranched mortgage-backed security, is a modest and sensible instrument. It has proved of great value both as a tool for lowering bank funding costs and providing banks with liquidity, and is used on a large scale by banks in many countries worldwide with strong demand for mortgage borrowing, for example the United Kingdom, Ireland, Australia and Spain, not just in United States.

The key idea of tranching is to *concentrate* credit risk in the lower equity and mezzanine tranches. This means that the senior investment grade tranches, those with first claim on the payments of interest and principal of the underlying loans, are protected from all but the most extreme losses and therefore can find a ready market, either with other banks or with long-term investors.

The same kind of tranching is used in the same way to create marketable senior securities, in many other types of balance sheet structures, for example financing portfolios of credit cards, student loans and vehicle loans. These securitizations allow banks to escape the restriction of their own balance sheet. They no longer have to rely on their own customer deposit base to fund their loan book. Where they have excess deposits they can hold safe senior loan-backed securities. When they have insufficient deposits they can create loan-backed securities in order to raise funds and do more lending. This opportunity to securitize and then lend more is hard to turn down. Provided the lending was sufficiently profitable – that is, that the returns are high enough to compensate for the risks of default – the additional lending will increase both total lending and the returns on their balance sheet.

More serious problems arose with a further development of 'transaction' deals, cutting out the role of commercial banks in credit intermediation altogether. Investment banks created a large volume of these 'transaction' structures during the years 2002–7. These had similar tranching to the standard balance sheet securitizations used by commercial banks for many years to raise additional funds for lending. The difference was that the underlying assets did not come off a bank balance sheet. They could, for example, be mortgages collected by brokers (the standard arrangement in sub-prime mortgage securitization), the traded leveraged loans issued to finance private equity deals (with the private equity fund aiming to repay the debt by improving the operating performance of the company it acquires), or corporate bonds or credit insurance written on corporate bonds.

This new practice of 'transaction' securitizations released hundreds of billions of dollars of credit for lending to risky borrowers who could not access bank finance. These deals were often beneficial for both borrower and lender. They supported new business ventures in a wide range of consumer and business goods and services. They offered mortgages to many individuals who would not have dreamed of owning their own homes. The interest rates charged to these borrowers were high, but they could be paid as long as the economy remained strong, backed by rising house prices and growing business revenues. But these were fair-weather financial arrangements, only viable during a period of strong economic growth. Once the economy slowed, house prices first stalled and then began to fall, and this source of new credit halted, turning credit boom to credit bust.

But the single greatest weakness was that much of the new structured paper – both the conventional balance sheet securitizations, such as tranched securitizations of prime mortgages or credit cards, and the arbitrage securitizations including relatively high risk sub-prime mortgages and leveraged mortgage-backed securities – was retained by banks and financed short term. Investment banks seemed not to have made much effort to persuade, and certainly never succeeded in persuading, the institutions such as pension funds, life insurance companies or international sovereign wealth funds to invest much long-term money in structured credit products. Instead, commercial and investment banks alike turned to 'borrowing short – lending long'.

The financial storm: first signs of rain

Having looked at the complex chain of transactions used during the credit boom from 2002 to 2007, it is now time to trace the first stages of the credit crisis, from its early stirrings in late 2006 and the first half of 2007 to its eruption in July and its subsequent global impact in August and September of that year. Most links of the chain of credit broke down. Problems with mortgage repayment in faraway sunny California and Florida led to the failure of banks in Europe with no direct exposure to US sub-prime borrowers, and subsequently to a massive and still continuing amount of credit-related write-downs by the world's major banks.

What took place was a financial storm with devastating effects on the world's banks, with many parallels to the impact of a hurricane such as that of 'Katrina' on the city of New Orleans in August 2005. This account will distinguish four phases of this financial storm: (i) first signs of rain; (ii) rain turns to deluge; (iii) the levees burst; and (iv) the flooding of the banking system. This chapter describes the first three phases, ending with the run on the UK mortgage bank Northern Rock on 14 September 2007.

There were many early warnings about US sub-prime losses, well before they became headline news around the world in July and August 2007. A number of observers – notably the business and economics weekly *The Economist*, which began publishing a regular comparison of house prices in all the industrial countries – were concerned about the unprecedented increases in residential property prices, and warned about the danger of a house-price bubble, not just in the United States but also in the United Kingdom, Spain, the Netherlands and elsewhere. Central banks and financial regulators warned that the credit spreads had declined to unsustainably low levels. But spotting a financial bubble is one thing, predicting when it will burst is quite another. Most lenders remained optimistic, seeing that mortgage loan arrears remained almost everywhere at historically low levels. Yield-based trades continued to be safe and profitable, so the 'hunt for yield' continued.

Difficulties in mortgage lending markets first came to my own attention in March 2007, when I was invited by BBC-24, the UK digital television news channel, to comment on the 2006 results of the London headquartered global commercial bank HSBC. I have long been an admirer of HSBC.[1] They, more effectively than their biggest rival Citigroup, have succeeded in imposing a consistent and conservative banking culture on a geographically diverse business. HSBC's greatest strengths lie in traditional banking areas – deposit services and corporate banking – where a combination of global presence, especially in Asia, and disciplined credit analysis and controls give it access to a huge and profitable customer base.

---

[1] I am not unbiased, since I am indebted to HSBC for the sponsorship of one of my Ph.D. students.

The main concern about the 2006 HSBC results was with a rise in provisions for losses on loans made by their subsidiary Household Finance Corporation (HFC), the largest provider of credit in the United States to higher-risk sub-prime borrowers, through mortgages, home equity loans, credit cards and other personal loan products. As house price growth in the 'hottest' US states such as California and Florida first slowed and then began to fall, arrears on their loan repayments rose. As a result the 2006 provisions for losses on HFC loans increased by about $3 billion dollars compared with those made the previous year. This was only the beginning; the next eighteen months turned out to be very much worse. By December 2008 total HSBC loan loss provisions for HFC and other lending operations were some $25 billion dollars greater than might have been expected before the sub-prime lending difficulties began. Fortunately, other HSBC activities continued to be very profitable, so that even after absorbing all these loan loss provisions the bank still recorded pre-tax profits of $24 billion in 2007 and $9 billion in 2008.

This HSBC subsidiary was just one among many US lenders experiencing problems with their sub-prime loans in 2006 and early 2007. Ameriquest, once the leading supplier of sub-prime and Alt-A loans for mortgage securitizations in the country, was brought down by a major legal case alleging abusive lending practices. Following an out-of-court settlement, Ameriquest closed all its retail branches in May 2006. Then, in early 2007, Ameriquest loan servicing operations and its sister company Argent, a mortgage wholesaler, were sold by their parent, the privately owned holding company ACC, to Citigroup for an undisclosed sum.

Another major early casualty was New Century Financial, which filed for Chapter 11 bankruptcy protection with a Delaware court on 2 April 2007.[2] New Century had expanded its lending rapidly at the height of the house price boom and thus very quickly got into difficulties when loan performance deteriorated. By the end of 2006 loan impairments were increasing in many other large sub-prime lenders, such as Washington Mutual and IndyMac, with a rapidly rising proportion of borrowers in arrears and many more entering the foreclosure process.

The markets were taking note. The increasing perception of mortgage risk can be seen in the quoted prices for the specialized traded

---

[2] See the report by Paul Murphy posted on 2 April 2007 in www.ft.com.

credit derivative index, the ABX index, which offers a price for insuring against the default of a bundle of mortgage backed securities. Figure 7.1 shows the movements in the BBB and AA versions of this index, which reflects the cost of purchasing insurance on these different investment-grade tranches of twenty major residential mortgage-backed security deals. All purchasers of ABX protection pay a fixed contractual quarterly premium to the protection seller. The ABX index prices are additional upfront payment made on top of this fixed quarterly premium. The index is quoted relative to 100. When the ABX-BBB index is, say, 90, this means that you will pay an additional 10¢ upfront to insure $1 of these BBB-rated RMBS tranches for their remaining life. Figure 7.1 reveals the sharp fall in the value of this index beginning in early 2007, reflecting a greatly increased cost of insuring these MBS tranches.

The Case Schiller index – the most widely quoted index of US house prices – also shown in this chart, reveals that property prices in the main US cities peaked in about August 2006 and had fallen by about 5 per cent from this peak by end-year (the left-hand scale of the chart). The cost of insuring MBS tranches did not respond until February 2007, but then increased by around 5¢ in the dollar over the next couple of months (the right-hand scale of the chart). Later, as mortgage and financial market problems increased, the ABX index shows that the additional cost of insuring these relatively risky tranches rose to 40¢ in the dollar by mid-year and to over 95¢ in the dollar by late 2008.

As Figure 7.1 also reveals, the ABX-AA index, referencing higher-quality MBS tranches, eventually subsequently fell sharply, suggesting insurance costs of 80¢ in the dollar by early 2009. The corresponding insurance cost for the ABX-AAA 2006 H1 index (not shown in the figure) climbed to 30¢ in the dollar, far higher than underlying loan impairment and a clear indication of undervaluation due to market illiquidity.

The ABX index was a great opportunity for alert speculators to make money out of the increase in mortgage credit risk. For example, the small California-based hedge fund Lahde Capital Management, run by Andrew Lahde, made an 83.5 per cent return in just the first two months of 2007, taking on bets that the ABX indices would fall in value now that the housing market had turned (profits can be very large because traders can buy and sell the ABX index without having

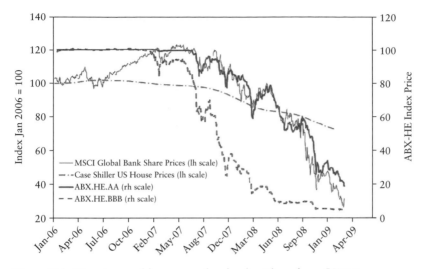

Figure 7.1. Housing problems spread to banks. Bloomberg, HSBC.

to pay very much money upfront; for example, buying protection on $100 in December 2006 at a price of 99.00 would cost only $1, and if this position is sold again later in April at a price of 96.00 it would return $4, making a profit of $4 on $1 down – i.e. a 300 per cent return in just three months). By September 2007 the trading strategy of Lahde's $60 million-dollar fund (basically following this strategy of 'shorting', i.e. selling and later buying back the ABX index at a lower price) was showing a profit of 410 per cent from the beginning of the year.[3] Lahde was the biggest winner in percentage terms, but he was far from being alone. According to press reports other hedge funds achieving big returns from taking short positions on the ABX index were the Pursuit Opportunity Fund, the SCSF hedge fund, Prudential Investment Management's Alpha Fund and MKP Capital Management. Other examples are Brigadier Capital, which report-edly rose 8 per cent, passport Capital – 13.8 per cent, and the Paulson and Company fund – 30%, all in the month of June alone.

With any such speculation there are always losers as well as winners. The losers in this case included a number of other funds heavily invested in mortgage-related assets. One early casualty was the $3.5 billion Dillon Read Capital Management fund, which had

[3] According to the *Financial Times* and a Reuters report of 13 September 2007.

been set up by its parent, the investment bank UBS, in 2005 to serve wealthy UBS clients as a high-yield investment vehicle. UBS decided to close Dillon Read Capital Management at the beginning of May 2007 because of a $123 million first-quarter 2007 loss on US sub-prime mortgage investments and a failure to attract sufficient inves-tor funds.[4] Several other funds pursuing an investment strategy of purchasing mortgage-related assets for yield were also performing poorly. To give three more examples from the pages of the *Financial Times*, Braddock Investments of the United States closed its $300 million Galena Fund, the London fund Caliber Global Investment was also closed and United Capital Asset Management 'suspended investor redemptions', following a decline in the fund's value of 32.9 per cent in June 2007 alone.

The biggest investment fund casualties at this stage were two Bear Stearns funds, which had a reported $20 billion invested in a variety of sub-prime mortgage assets. On 21 June Bear announced that it was providing additional liquidity to one of the funds with a line of credit of up to $1.5 billion, but this also prompted creditors providing the repo finance to the fund, including Merrill Lynch, to seize assets with the threat of selling them.[5] These Bear Stearns funds – the High Grade Structured Credit Strategies Fund and the High Grade Structured Credit Enhanced Leverage Fund, whose names were lampooned by John Bird and John Fortune – were heavily invested in the 'double structured' ABS-CDOs described in Chapter 7. As we saw, these are CDOs in which the underlying collateral is tranches of structured sub-prime mortgage-backed securities. The senior AAA tranches of these double-structured CDOs offered especially high yields and thus especially attractive returns from yield-based trading. At the same time these double structured CDOs were also doubly sensitive to under-lying collateral performance, and so their value had rapidly fallen alongside the underlying deterioration in sub-prime mortgage arrears and foreclosures.

As an aside it is worth noting that these examples call into question one of the most widely used techniques for hedge fund investing, that of investing a little bit of money in every available hedge fund (a so-called 'fund of funds') in the hope that this portfolio will make very high and

---

[4] Details taken from a *Financial Times* article by Peter Thai Larsen, 3 May 2007.
[5] Details taken from the Hedge Fund Implode-o-meter, at http://hf-implode.com.

also very safe returns. These examples suggest just the opposite. Those hedge fund strategies that make most money do so at the expense of other poorly performing hedge fund strategies. The only thing guaranteed by spreading your money among a large number of such funds is that some of the managers, those either skilful or just lucky, will earn a great deal from their management and performance fees.

This was not the only impact of the perceived increase in mortgage risk. By the early summer there was increasing nervousness among investors about how long the environment of low credit spreads and the associated strong demand for high-yield assets would continue. A number of more aggressive leveraged finance deals were pulled, for example the $350 million Magnum Coal leveraged financing deal, and the private equity buyouts of Catalyst Paper of Vancouver, Canada, or Thomson Learning the publisher. Confidence was ebbing in European markets, culminating in the Tuesday 17 July cancellation of the large leverage loan deal for Maxeda, the Dutch home improvements retailer, on behalf of Kohlberg Kravis Roberts.

High-yield 'speculative' bond issues were also affected. The Dutch supermarket Ahold shelved its $650 million bond offering by its US subsidiary US Foodservice, Arcelor Finance withdrew its much larger $1.5 billion bond sale because of volatile market conditions and Service Master, the lawn and home maintenance cleaning group, postponed its $1.15 billion high-yield bond issue. At the same time some 'initial public offerings' (IPOs) – in which a company's equity is brought to the stock market for the first time – fell well below price targets, for example the UK IPO of the Man brokerage in July 2007.

The financial storm: rain becomes a deluge

At this stage, the middle of July 2007, the global banking industry and the wider economy were not yet much affected. As Figure 7.1 indicates, bank shares worldwide continued to be very strong, supported by generally low levels of loan arrears outside sub-prime mortgages and continued growth in balance sheets, fees income and trading profits. While some banking deals had been postponed or cancelled, the flow of residential and commercial MBS, CDOs and other structured products continued to be strong. There was still a very healthy pipeline of leveraged loan deals.

Nor was anyone in financial markets much surprised by developments so far. Everyone knew that the credit boom would eventually slow and that when it did some of the more aggressive deals would no longer be viable. The widening of credit spreads was perceived by many as a buying opportunity rather than as a threat. The prices of leveraged loans were falling, increasing the profit margins on collateralized loan obligations. Mortgage-related assets had fallen sharply in price and now could be bought relatively cheaply. Concerns over sub-prime were discouraging the more aggressively priced and under-collateralized mortgage structures and allowed room for other, more conservatively structured, deals to go to market.

There were also as yet few investor concerns about other parts of the US or the global economy. There were no signs of consumer spending being reined in as a result of weakening US house prices. Corporate balance sheets and profits, as well as investment and employment, remained extremely strong. General confidence was such that on 17 July the Dow Jones industrial index closed above 14,000 points for the first time in its history.

Perceptions were to change radically over the next three weeks. On the evening of Tuesday 17 July the US investment bank Bear Stearns gave up the fight to save its two hedge funds, despite having already injected $1.5 billion into one of them when their trading difficulties were first acknowledged in June. These moved into Chapter 15 bankruptcy proceedings, and this decision was followed by the sacking of the managers responsible for these funds. There has also been a slew of court cases surrounding these two funds, accusing Bear Stearns of misleading investors and including claims (reminiscent of the Eliot Spitzer investigations of the IPO scandals of the dot.com boom) that the fund managers had left an email trail in which they acknowledged that the asset quality of the funds was lousy at the same time as they invited new investment in the funds. On the same day, 17 July, Federal Reserve chairman Ben Bernanke made a rather gloomy speech indicating that losses on sub-prime mortgage lending could rise to $100 billion and that this could affect other credit markets.

This combination of bad news and background worries triggered a much larger collapse of confidence. During the next twenty-four hours equity prices worldwide fell sharply by around 1 per cent, a fairly large one-day fall, while government bond prices jumped as investors fled for the safety of government bonds. Corporate credit markets – for bonds and syndicated and leverage loans – also saw further substantial price falls and thus increases in credit spreads. This one-day decline in equity prices was not especially unusual, and nothing like the scale of the 1987 stock market crash, but it marked the beginning of a see-saw of market volatility that continued for months. Every new piece of news, especially relating to credit markets, was to send share prices either soaring (if better than investors expected) or plunging (when investors were disappointed). In the first few months following 17 July the average level of stock prices was not too much affected. A bad day for equity prices was often followed by a good day, and the Dow Jones industrial index hovered close to its high; in fact it actually moved slightly higher, to reach its historic peak of 14,164 on 9 October 2007. But around the turn of the year equity markets were to follow credit markets downwards, and twelve months later on, in July 2008, the Dow Jones industrial average had fallen so much that it was 30 per cent below this recent peak.

One of the bigger concerns of credit market participants, which surfaced in late July 2007, was the possibility that the leading banks might face difficulties in selling the large 'pipeline' of leveraged loan deals agreed for various private equity transactions but not yet packaged into collateralized debt obligations. This deal pipeline was said in newspaper reports to amount to some $300 billion in the United States alone, with a correspondingly large volume of deals in Europe. What had previously been seen as good news – the continuing flow of new credit business – was now interpreted as very bad. This potential overhang of corporate loans had a particularly depressing impact on loan prices – why buy today when you might get something very similar in three months' time for a much lower price?

Another new concern was that liquidation of trading positions could lead to the forced sale of many types of asset – not just credit exposures – and thus all the global financial markets would become increasingly volatile and hence it would be more difficult to trade. A quotation in a *Financial Times* article of 18 July, immediately after the Bear Stearns announcements, nicely expresses traders' fears: "'Leveraged hedge funds are subject to leveraged losses and [could suffer] the same fate as the Bear Stearns funds, while real money investors can be forced by their investment mandate to sell non-investment grade paper," said T. J. Marta, strategist at RBC Capital Markets. "A vicious downward spiral could result, leading to the liquidation of other assets and positions, including the FX carry trade."' The FX carry trade was an exceptionally risky version of the yield-based trading described in Chapter 6, obtaining funding from a low-interest currency such as the Japanese yen or Swiss franc and investing in a high-yield currency such as the Australian or New Zealand dollar. As a result, the volatility of equity and credit markets was transmitted into foreign-exchange markets, with these currencies experiencing exceptionally large changes of value, both upwards and downwards, over the following months.

This fear of losses from forced liquidation played a central role in precipitating the subsequent massive collapse in demand for structured credit. Some reduction in demand was, of course, to be expected, simply because investors were now more concerned than before about potential default on credit-related assets. Investor concerns would affect both balance sheet and arbitrage deals. For a commercial bank seeking the lowest-cost funding of its assets (the motive for conducting a balance sheet deal), securitization was now rather less advantageous than before. For an investment bank seeking to make a one-time return from buying high-yield credit assets and packaging them for sale (the motive for conducting an arbitrage deal such as most CLOs and some sub-prime MBSs), the fall in price of structured credit tranches narrowed the 'arbitrage spread'.

But the increase in perceived credit risks in the first half of 2007 was far too small to explain the extraordinary collapse in demand for structured credit that took place in July 2007. At that point, despite the weakening US housing market, the underlying economic situation still seemed very strong. A revealing insight into the credit crisis appears in an ft.com/alphaville market insight story posted by Gwen Robinson on Friday 6 July 2007, a story which is well worth quoting at some length (a search engine will easily find the complete article): 'The "haircut", or margin requirement, on financing for the purchase of CDOs backed by subprime mortgage bonds has been increasing sharply, in many cases doubling, according to industry sources . . . Bear's crisis [this is a reference to the June crisis when Bear Sterns put $1.6 billion to support their funds, not to the closure of these funds later in July] was triggered when its funds failed to meet margin calls . . . however, prime brokers and others involved in financing hedge funds said there had been little change in margin requirements for products other than CDOs of asset-backed securities [i.e. what I describe as ABS-CDOs] . . . [A] London-based credit specialist . . . told the FT there were unlikely to be other big funds brought down by the margin hikes.'

What is a margin call, and why did this seemingly technical matter play a central role in the collapse of global credit markets? Why did the requirements for higher margins eventually affect all forms of structured credit, not just the high-risk ABS-CDOs? As has been described in Chapter 6, investors pursuing the more leveraged yield-based trading strategies would finance their positions using 'sale and repurchase' more usually known as repo. For example, $100 million of an A-rated ABS-CDO security might be used as collateral to borrow $95 million. In this case there is a haircut or margin requirement of 5 per cent. This ft.com story explains that such haircuts were increasing, to give lenders of money greater protection now that credit prices had become more volatile. A fund using such repo leverage is then hit by a 'double whammy', *not only* the loss of money because the $100 million asset falls in value from, say, $100 to $96, *but also* an additional margin call because the haircut is increased from $5 to $10. The fund must now come up with an additional $9 ($4 to cover the decline in market value of the security and a further $5 of additional margin).

At this point in the story, in early July 2007, these margin increases were still modest and applied only to the riskiest types of structured credit tranches. But this opinion of a London-based credit specialist, that margin changes would have only a limited impact on other instruments, could not have been wider of the mark.

Financial storm: the levees burst

This combination of margin calls and outright losses was seriously affecting, and in some cases overwhelming, banks pursuing yield-based trading strategies. The impact was akin to the bursting of the levees responsible for most of the devastation following Hurricane Katrina and that caused by the earlier great Mississippi floods of 1854, 1951 and 1993. All manner of investors who thought they were protected from credit and liquidity risks were suddenly affected.

The next prominent victim of the credit crisis was IKB – a relatively small (€60 billion in assets) Dusseldorf-based German industrial bank created from the 1974 merger of IndustrieKreditBank and DeutscheIndustriebank. IKB has an unusual ownership structure; only 39 per cent of its shares are publicly traded, while 50 per cent are held by state-owned financial institutions and the rest by a major private

investor. On 27 July IKB admitted major liquidity problems stemming
from a portfolio of more than €14 billion of structured credits held in
its off balance sheet vehicles 'Rhineland Funding Capital Corporation'
and 'Rhinebridge', together with another €7 billion of on balance
sheet structured credit assets.[6] Its exposure to structured credit was
thus very large, about one third of its total consolidated balance sheet,
and, moreover, it relied heavily on short-term asset-backed commercial paper for funding Rhineland and Rhinebridge. These entities
were no longer able to issue commercial paper without an explicit
commitment of 'liquidity support' from IKB – that is, a legally binding
commitment to purchase the asset-backed commercial paper when it
matured. This commitment was so large that it would have exhausted
IKB's own capital base and pushed it into insolvency.

This immediate liquidity problem for IKB was resolved over the
weekend of 4/5 August with the provision of €8.1 billion in liquidity
support for its ABCP funding from a banking pool consisting of IKB's
major shareholder, the state-owned KfW banking group, together
with other German banks. Eventually a total of four senior managers – the chief executive officer Stefan Ortseifen, the chief financial
officer, the head of risk management, and the managing director of the
IKB capital assets management division responsible for the structured
credit exposures – and two members of the management board were
removed from office. A team headed by new chief executive officer,
Dr Günther Bräunig, took on the task of recapitalizing IKB and refo-
cusing the bank on its core business of lending to mid-sized German
companies.

As in most yield-based trading portfolios, the structured credit
held by IKB was all investment-grade. Moreover, unlike the two
Bear Stearn's funds, it held mostly sub-prime MBS tranches and very
little of the highly risky ABS-CDOs.[7] But the market for all of this
structured paper had become almost totally illiquid, a sale of these
assets being possible only at very low 'fire sale' prices that would

---

[6] These vehicles were 'credit arbitrage' conduits controlled by the bank and set
up in order to enhance its income. The consequent credit market problems
are documented in an October 2007 press release and the conference call pdf
following the PWC special audit of IKB's structured credit losses, and on pp.
15–24 of their February 2008 restatement of their 2006/2007 annual report.
Both documents can be downloaded from www.ikb.de.

[7] The revised IKB financial accounts for 2006–7 provide a detailed breakdown of
its structured credit portfolio.

have greatly magnified losses. IKB has thus continued holding most of this structured credit. Its results for the year ending 31 March 2008 reveal a mark to market value loss of €4 billion on this structured credit portfolio, offset by a €2.4 billion accounting gain from the provision of liquidity support by the 'banking pool'. This was not the end of IKB's problems. IKB has since raised over €2 billion of additional capital from a rights issue and other capital instruments to shore up their balance sheet. In August 2008, its parent KfW sold off its shareholding in IKB to the distressed asset fund LoneStar. In December 2008 the German government provided a €5 billion guarantee on IKB borrowing to enable it to raise further funds to cover its liquidity problems. According to Bloomberg total write-downs of IKB credit exposures amounted to €15 billion by August 2008.

Although the funding technique was different (ABCP instead of repo), the problem that nearly brought down IKB was in fact very similar to that which triggered the closure of the two Bear Stearns funds: a combination of poor asset quality, falling portfolio valuations and tightening credit limits meant that they could not finance their structured credit portfolios. A profitable and apparently safe trading position had created a huge financing problem. Where IKB and the Bear Stearns fund differ is in their response. The Bear Stearns funds ended up in Chapter 15 bankruptcy, with assets disputed in the Cayman Islands courts. With various accompanying legal cases accusing Bear Stearns of misleading investors, the legal saga looks set to continue for years. IKB instead found a state-owned rescuer who was prepared to bridge their financing gap.

During late July and early August 2007 further credit-related problems continued to emerge, with more US sub-prime mortgage lenders under threat of bankruptcy and private equity deals cancelled, including the large $8 billion sale of the UK cable and mobile telecommunications group Virgin Media to the Private Equity group Carlyle. More structured credit funds and investors revealing losses, including the West LB Mellon Compass Fund, a US–German bank joint venture, funds in Australia and banks in Japan (Shinshei, Mitsubishi Financial and Sumitomo Mitsui Financial Group admitting some tens of billions of dollars of sub-prime-related ABSs). Investor concerns about structured credit products exposed to the US sub-prime lending continued to grow, with a number of structures being placed under ratings review, and an indication that their credit ratings may well eventually be downgraded.

On Thursday 9 August several more levees burst and the flood waters rose a good deal higher. The major French bank BNP Paribas announced suspension of three investment funds due to 'complete evaporation of liquidity' in some structured security markets, citing a collapse in demand that made these funds impossible to value. According to a *Financial Times* report the combined value of these three funds had fallen from about €2 billion to €1.6 billion, a decline of 20 per cent in less than two weeks. On the same day one of the largest hedge funds in the world, Renaissance Technologies, and the leading investment bank Goldman Sachs both acknowledged major losses in equity funds utilizing automated computer-based algorithmic trading, their fancy computer programs having been badly wrong-footed by the major jump in equity volatilities. Goldmans arranged a $3 billion additional injection of funds into its Global Equity Opportunity Fund.

The real significance of 9 August is not these particular events, but the accompanying market response. There was a major jump in inter-bank borrowing rates, with the Libor overnight dollar rate suddenly increasing from about 5.3 to 6 per cent and the Libor three-month rate increasing from 5.30 to 5.50 per cent. Interest rates and haircuts on secured repo borrowing also increased sharply.

What is the Libor rate and why does it matter? Libor stands for the London Interbank Offered Rate. It is the rate of interest at which banks borrow funds from each other and from other 'money market' lenders in the London interbank market. The quoted Libor rate is a 'composite' (i.e. an average of interest rates reported by a panel of dealers), computed and published on a daily basis by the British Bankers Association. There are in fact Libor rates for borrowing in ten different currencies, for borrowing rates including dollar, sterling, euro and yen (see Chapter 9 for further discussion).

Libor matters for two reasons. First, the Libor rates play a central role in global financial markets, with the published BBA-Libor the standard market reference rate for a huge number of traded financial contracts. For example, virtually all the contracts in the $120 trillion interest-rate swap market (in notional terms the biggest global financial market of all) use Libor rates to calculate the floating rate payments made by one side of an interest-rate swap agreement to the other. Libor interest rates, in all the different currencies, are also used as the basis for calculating the interest payment on most floating rate bonds for the settlement of the interest-rate options and futures traded on the major options exchanges such as the Chicago Mercantile. When Libor rates move as much as they did on 9 August 2007, the financial world takes notice.

The other reason why Libor matters is because these short-term money market rates reflect the demand for bank liquidity. When banks lend money, even overnight, they have to be compensated for the loss of access to that money. The alternative for a bank is to hold the money as a central bank deposit, where it can still earn some lower rate of interest. The difference is that a central bank deposit, unlike an interbank deposit, can always be used for making a payment – for a bank, keeping money in the central bank is just like carrying a $50 bill around in your wallet. Money in your wallet may not earn you any interest but you know it is always there if you suddenly need to buy something urgently, even if for some reason the credit card is not approved or the shop's card reader is not working.

On or around 9 August, banks around the world suddenly realized that it might be better to have a little bit more cash in the central bank and a little less on deposit or tied up in repo deals. Such liquidity now appeared very precious; any bank at any time could face a sudden urgent need – perhaps with only an hour or two of notice given – for example, to top up an MBS conduit, to bail out a structured invest- ment vehicle, or simply to cover an increased haircut on a portfolio of credit assets. But banks are pretty sophisticated about their cash management: provided there is no question regarding their ultimate solvency there is always a price at which they can borrow from other institutions, and there is also a backstop of expensive liquidity from the standing facilities of the central banks. What this meant was that banks, despite their growing concerns over having sufficient liquidity, were still willing to lend money as long as they were compensated with a slightly higher rate of return. This is why interbank Libor and secured repo rates soared.

Thursday 9 August also saw an across-the-board shift in the pricing of asset-backed and structured securities. Prices did not just fall, they also decoupled, with asset-backed securities that had previously traded at almost the same price suddenly diverging by as much as 10 or 20 per cent in value. Before early August the tranches of these various structures all traded at prices that were largely determined by credit rating – that is, market participants were not drawing any great distinction between one sub-prime mortgage-backed structure and another, or one CLO and another. The securities were treated as if each class (sub-prime MBS, consumer ABS, CLO, etc.) was homogenous and all an investor needed to know was the type of security and the rating, with not much need to look inside the structure at the performance of the underlying collateral.

This belief in the homogeneity of each class of structured assets was fragile. It depended on the general belief that when the asset was eventually sold on, the new buyer would not look too closely at the underlying collateral either, that credit rating and asset class would largely determine price. Now, as credit performance of all kinds but especially in sub-prime mortgage lending deteriorated, it became clear that pricing could no longer be based on credit rating and asset class alone. In order to decide whether a security should be bought or sold and at what price, it was now necessary to look very closely at the underlying collateral performance of each and every issue, a performance which differed markedly from one security to another. This fundamental change of perception led to an immediate and substantial divergence in reported prices. This divergence also created huge valuation uncertainty. Now every tranche of every structured security had to be valued individually, and if the tranche itself had not recently traded, it could be extremely difficult to find an appropriate reference price which could be used to 'mark to market'. As a result, valuation of the same tranche could vary considerably from one day to the next.

As a result of this valuation uncertainty there was also a major increase in repo haircuts for asset-backed and structured securities. As we have seen, these margins on the riskier tranches of structured securities had already shifted up from 5 to 10 per cent (committing $100 billion of single A structured securities to support borrowing of only $90 billion instead of $95 billion). Beginning on 9 August and over subsequent months these margins jumped very much further, in order to protect lenders as credit pricing became less stable and less reliable, and large margins became necessary on even the safest tranches with no real default risk. Over the following months it become impossible to repo some riskier structured credits at all, while repo margins on even the safest AAA structured securities – the form of borrowing most commonly used to support yield based trading – rose by a factor of 20 or more. For example, the haircut on AAA ABS rose from 3 or 4 per cent to as much as 50 or 60 per cent, an astonishing decline in market liquidity.[8] This, together with the increase in both secured repo and unsecured Libor rates, took much of the profit margin out of yield-based trading.

Central banks were quick to respond to this dramatic decline in market liquidity. That same day, 9 August, the European Central Bank announced that it was injecting extra emergency funding into eurozone money markets, and the US Federal Reserve took similar action only a few hours later. These were just the first of many central bank interventions in money markets over subsequent months. Chapter 9 examines these liquidity problems in the world's money markets and the responses of the major central banks. For now it is better to stick with the main story, of how growing concerns about credit risk overwhelmed the yield-based trading positions adopted by banks worldwide and resulted in such a large level of reported losses.

Unsurprisingly, given this evaporation of liquidity, by August 2007 many more banks and investment vehicles were reporting losses on their yield-based trades and mortgage-related exposures. One striking announcement in late August was the decision by Lehman Brothers – one of the leading issuers of mortgage-backed securities on Wall Street – to close its sub-prime mortgage securitization unit BNC Mortgage. Even more dramatically, on 17 August, another German bank, Sachsen LB, admitted a liquidity crisis remarkably similar to that of IKB but on an even bigger scale.[9]

The Leipzig-based Sachsen LB was a German public-law bank owned by the former East German Land of Saxony. Sachsen LB was another relatively small institution, similar in size to IKB with around €68 billion of assets on its balance sheet. However, it faced difficulties in growing its business and revenues and so turned to a new source of revenue, yield-based trading of exactly the kind described

[8] See Bank of England, *Financial Stability Review* (October 2008), p. 36, Table 5.B.
[9] The events leading to the collapse of Sachsen LB are well documented in a *Financial Times* article of 23 November 2007 by Gerrit Wiesmann and Ivar Simensen. Figures on the final portfolio are taken from the European Commission's March 2008 press release announcing the decision that the support complied with EU rules on state aid.

in Chapter 8. It did this through a Dublin-based division, Sachsen LB Europe, which in 2002 established a special investment fund, Ormond Quay, which, just like the IKB Rhineland Funding Capital Corporation, issued short-term asset-backed commercial paper and invested in longer-term structured credit instruments.

By the time of their collapse, in August 2007, Ormond Quay and another later-established conduit had expanded to hold more than €30 billion of structured paper (more than twice the size of the collapsed Bear funds and nearly half the entire balance sheet of the parent).[10] In the most recent 2006–7 financial year these conduit activities contributed 90 per cent of the entire pre-tax profits of Sachsen LB. Taking on a risk exposure of this kind was a major failure of governance. Management in Leipzig appears to have known little and asked even less about what was going on in Dublin. According to the *Financial Times* the 'hotshot' financiers who had established Ormond Quay, but by 2006 had departed for jobs in London, had been paid salaries of €500,000 per year each, which seems quite excessive for conducting the essentially trivial job of yield-based trading. Regulators had warned the management of potential problems as early as 2005, but because there was no formal breach of regulatory rules they were powerless to intervene.

Now Sachsen LB was faced with a liquidity call of €17 billion – one quarter of its entire balance sheet – in order to refinance its conduits' commercial paper. Insolvency was prevented only when financial authorities persuaded a larger *landesbank* from south-west Germany, the LB Baden-Württemberg of Stuttgart with end-2007 assets of €443 billion, to acquire Sachsen LB. This acquisition was further supported by a guarantee against losses on the structured credit exposures from Sachsen LB's owner, the Land of Saxony, and a liquidity facility to cover the needed €17 billion from the German savings bank association, the Sparkassen-Finanzgruppe. The financial details were settled by December, with a takeover price of €328 million and the loss guarantee set at €2.75 billion on a €17.5 billion portfolio of the riskier structured credits. In March 2008 the European Commission agreed

---

[10] The exact size of their portfolios is unclear. Press quotation of an unpublished Ernst and Young report on the Sachsen LB losses suggests a much larger €46 billion exposure by Ormond Quay alone. The smaller number in the text is taken from the European Commission and represents the size of the portfolio in December 2007 when it was purchased by the new parent LBBW.

that this support operation complied with European rules on state aid and the deal was then finalized.

In August and September many other funds collapsed or were closed; for example, on Wednesday 29 August the London-based hedge fund Cheyne Capital announced that it was winding down Cheyne Finance, a $6.6 billion structured investment vehicle. This was not the only fund failure. The website the Hedge Fund Implode-o-Meter lists (at the time of writing) some sixty-seven funds that have stopped operating since summer 2007, most collapses a result of deteriorating structured credit valuations. There were three main waves of failures, the first accounting for about twenty of these funds in the period July–September 2007, the second of more than twenty funds when credit markets deteriorated even further in February and March 2008 and the third in late 2008. But that takes us ahead of the story.

On the morning of Friday 14 September there took place the single event that more than any other has come to epitomize the first year of the credit crisis. Following a somewhat alarmist BBC television news item the previous night, queues of depositors began to form outside the branches of Northern Rock, the specialized UK mortgage lender. Television pictures of the first substantial depositor run on a UK bank since the reign of Queen Victoria were then broadcast around the world.

Northern Rock's situation was quite different from that of the two German banks IKB and Sachsen LB.[11] Its problems were not triggered by an excessively leveraged yield-based trading position. Its difficulties were much the same as those of Countrywide, and other wholesale financed US mortgage lenders, already described in Chapter 5. Like them, Northern Rock was a specialized mortgage lender (one which had grown fast and by September 2007 held 8 per cent of all UK mortgages), and also like them it had a very small retail deposit base, financing only a quarter of its total lending. No less than 40 per cent of its assets were funded by its Granite mortgage-backed securitizations and a further 24 per cent by wholesale unsecured borrowing. Moreover, its funding model required it to issue mortgage-backed

---

[11] These paragraphs are based on a detailed description and analysis of the failure of Northern Rock, Alistair Milne and Geoffrey Wood, 'Shattered on the Rock? British financial stability from 1866 to 2007', Bank of Finland discussion paper series, 2008.

securities amounting to around 15 per cent of its balance sheet every year.

Both the bank's management and their regulator, the UK Financial Services Authority (FSA), realized immediately that because of this reliance on securitization, the dislocation to securitization markets of 9 August created a major liquidity problem for Northern Rock. Beginning on Monday 13 August, management and the FSA were in contact at least twice a day, so that the FSA could monitor their liquidity position and discuss the resolution of the situation. They had only five weeks to save the bank. This is because Northern Rock had scheduled its next major Granite securitization issue, for a total of £5.8 billion, on Monday 17 September and while it had liquidity arrangements in place to fund its balance sheet until this date, without an alternative source of liquidity it would quickly default on its obligations thereafter.

However, it was not at all clear how to resolve the liquidity problem at Northern Rock. The UK authorities were in a much more difficult situation than their counterparts in the United States or Germany. In the United Kingdom, unlike in many other countries, there is no legal framework for the orderly resolution of a bank in financial difficulties. The only option is a court insolvency which requires deposits to be frozen for a lengthy period.[12] The main tool used by the US authorities to support its wholesale funded mortgage banks – emergency lending against mortgage collateral from the system of Federal Home Loan Banks – did not exist in the United Kingdom. Nor could the United Kingdom follow the German approach to dealing with the trading exposures of IKB and Sachsen LB, since there were no state-owned banks in the United Kingdom that could be encouraged to provide immediate liquidity and solvency support. The UK authorities were also unable to persuade any private-sector buyer to take over Northern Rock, without this being accompanied by unacceptably high (and possibly under EU law on state aid illegal) commitment of public financial support.

Eventually, on 10 September, for this seemed to be the only option to prevent a socially, economically and politically costly insolvency, the UK authorities agreed that the Bank of England would provide a

---

[12] The UK authorities have now introduced a new legislative regime providing them with more tools for resolving future bank failures.

loan to Northern Rock against mortgage collateral. This special loan to Northern Rock was *not* a standard central bank 'lender of last resort' operation. That phrase dates back to the nineteenth century and describes the activities of the central bank in providing short-term loans – that is, overnight or at most for a few days – against good collateral in order to ensure that there is no loss in confidence in the banking system as a whole. This was instead a medium- to long-term loan provided to an individual bank.

So far the financial authorities – the Bank of England and the FSA in consultation with the UK finance minister (the Chancellor of the Exchequer Alistair Darling) – had handled the situation well enough. They then managed to make an extraordinarily bad job of announcing and explaining their decision. Because of persistent market rumours the announcement of support, originally planned for the morning of Monday 17 September, was brought forward to Friday 14 September. Even then the story broke prematurely, with a dramatic leak on BBC television and radio news channels on the evening of Thursday 13 September. Moreover, the authorities had no clearly thought-out plan for explaining the situation to depositors and reassuring them that their money in Northern Rock was safe.

The BBC, despite being government-funded (through a licence fee), is not subject to political control, nor does it feel any obligation to be polite about the government of the day. The newscasts of that Thursday evening made it clear to all that if Northern Rock became insolvent, then depositors would have to wait many months for their money and even then might not get it all back.[13] The newscasts stated that the Bank of England loan was intended to prevent such an insolvency occurring but, understandably, long queues formed outside the Northern Rock branches the next morning and grew longer during the day, since the branches were not equipped to handle large amounts of withdrawals.

Government protestations that Northern Rock was safe from insolvency were doing little to quell the panic. Long delays getting through to the Northern Rock telephone call centre and the crashing of the Northern Rock website made matters worse. The run was only

[13] The UK deposit insurance scheme at that time provided a 100 per cent deposit guarantee up to only £2,000 and a 95 per cent guarantee for remaining deposits up to a maximum of £35,000.

stemmed on the afternoon of Monday 17 September, when Alistair Darling announced a guarantee of all retail deposits with Northern Rock. The collapse of confidence among retail depositors greatly increased the necessary scale of support, since that weekend and in the following weeks about half of Northern Rock retail deposits were withdrawn and the only replacement funding was the Bank of England loan.

Northern Rock's problems are far from over. On 17 February 2008, after some months of seeking to find a private-sector buyer, the government announced that it was taking the bank into public ownership, and the necessary legislation was rushed through both houses of parliament the next day. Northern Rock is now run as a state-owned bank, having reduced the size of its loan book and its dependence on wholesale funding, with the eventual aim of returning it to private ownership. This task is being made more difficult by both an increase in its funding costs and rising loan loss provisions as the UK economy and housing market deteriorate.

Further reading

There are several good books documenting the US sub-prime lending crisis. My own favourite is Paul Muolo and Mathew Padilla's *Chain of Blame: How Wall Street Caused the Mortgage and Credit Crisis* (Wiley, 2008). Muolo and Padilla are financial journalists with many years' experience of the mortgage finance industry, and this well-informed account makes it clear that while there were many problems with sub-prime lending, especially when this lending was securitized, the idea of providing mortgages to high-credit risk customers did originally make some business sense.

Robert Shiller's short and impassioned analysis of the sub-prime problems, *The Subprime Solution: How Today's Global Financial Crisis Happened, and What to Do about It* (Princeton University Press, 2008), has been mentioned already in the notes on further reading in the introduction.

There is relatively little on the spread of the sub-prime problems to other markets. Laurent Clerc, 'Valuation and crises', Banque De France, *Financial Stability Review* (October 2008), at www.banque-france.fr/gb/publications/telechar/rsf/2008/etud4_1008.pdf, offers a very clear description of how difficulties in the valuation of structured securities led to the breakdown of market liquidity. He reproduces a very insightful chart (his Chart 1) from an unpublished working paper by W. Perraudin and S. Wu, 'Determinants of asset-back security prices in crisis periods', Imperial College London, June 2008, that reveals how markedly the valuation of securities changed in August 2007.

For my own more detailed discussion of Northern Rock see Alistair Milne and Geoffrey Wood, 'Shattered on the Rock? British financial stability from 1866 to 2007', at www.bof.fi/en/julkaisut/tutkimukset/keskustelualoitteet/2008/dp2008_30.htm.

8 | *The flood of losses*

The bursting of the levees in August 2007 was followed by a flood of credit-related losses and write-downs, continuing throughout the rest of 2007 and during 2008. Banks and other financial institutions reported lower earnings for the third quarter of 2007, but this was only a taste of what was to come. There were much larger losses and write-downs in the following four quarters. By December 2008 total credit-related losses and write-downs by the world's largest banks and insurance companies rose to well over $900 billion, or around 2 per cent of their total assets.

The biggest bank credit losses and write-downs by far were in four major institutions – the Swiss investment bank and asset manager UBS, the US investment bank Merrill Lynch, the US banking conglomerate Citigroup and the internationally active UK bank HSBC. The biggest of all those was reported by Citigroup, once the world's largest bank by market value, which by the end of 2008 had acknowledged some $104 billion of loan losses and credit-related write-downs. With losses and write-downs of $63 billion, $56 billion and $54 billion respectively, Merrill Lynch, UBS and HSBC were not so far behind in this race to the bottom. There were some even redder faces outside the banking industry. The insurance giant AIG and the two US government-sponsored mortgage intermediaries Fannie Mae and Freddie Mac also posted huge losses – of $146 billion, $64 billion and $65 billion respectively. By the end of 2008 the total losses and write-downs recorded by these seven institutions climbed to an astounding $550 billion, close to half the credit losses and write-downs announced by the financial services industry worldwide.

Other banks and insurance companies recorded substantial losses and write-downs over the same period, but attempting to review and summarize the experience of all of them would be more confusing than insightful. To obtain a clearer picture, this chapter looks first at the experience of some individual institutions, at the six institutions that recorded the largest losses, and also at specialized US mortgage lenders and at Bear Stearns. It then looks at the related problems of the monoline insurance industry and the market for auction rated securities. The final sections of this chapter then review the losses of the entire banking industry in the United States and Europe. The overall picture is not quite as bad as for the worst institutions. All institutions have made losses, but to a large degree this is due to the unanticipated illiquidity in structured credit markets. The same problems of poor risk management and control are not found in all firms.

UBS comes clean

UBS was the first bank to acknowledge substantial losses and has been most candid about the reasons it got into difficulties. On 1 October 2007 UBS shocked markets by announcing that it would make a group loss for the third quarter – a huge surprise for an institution best known as the world's largest wealth manager, a low-risk business investing client's rather than the bank's own money, and a particular embarrassment in its home country, Switzerland, renowned for its conservative banking culture. The reason for this $712 million loss was a $3.4 billion fall in the market value of its trading portfolio of supposedly low-risk US mortgage-backed securities.

UBS losses mounted alarmingly over the ensuing months. A December trading announcement acknowledged a further $10 billion of these write-downs. This was supposed to mark a line under the bank's problems and was accompanied by the announcement that the bank was raising $11.1 billion of new capital from the Government of Singapore Investment Corporation and unnamed Middle Eastern investors. But only four months later, in early April, UBS recognized a further $19 billion of write-downs, prompting the resignation of its chairman Marcel Ospel.

The surprising scale of these losses prompted an investigation by the bank and Swiss banking regulators and the April 2008 publication of a revealing report to shareholders. This report is a detailed account of how a respected bank came to lose such large sums on supposedly safe holdings of senior tranches of US sub-prime mortgage-backed securities. Two things stand out from this report. Off balance sheet exposures played a relatively small role in its losses. Around two thirds of these losses were from its on balance sheet trading portfolio of mortgage-backed securities – where it had aggressively expanded its portfolio of US sub-prime mortgage-backed securities. Around half the remaining losses were from its holdings of similar securities in its treasury portfolio, the reserve of tradable securities held by any bank to meet unexpected cash needs. Almost all these losses came from pursuing the flawed trading strategy of borrowing short and investing in long-term senior mortgage-backed securities.

The second stand-out is the headlong growth and weak governance and risk controls in the fixed income trading division that recorded most of these losses. Like all banks, UBS was caught out by the surprising collapse in the values of senior tranches of sub-prime mortgage-backed securities, but its position was relatively worse than other banks because in its pursuit of yield and asset growth it had paid little attention to the quality of these assets. Many of its investments were in the senior tranches of the extremely dubious 'restructured' CDOs of the riskier tranches of mortgage-backed securities (the so called mezzanine ABS-CDOs). These offered attractively high yields but their AAA ratings proved to be completely unsound. Unlike standard senior sub-prime MBS the senior tranches of these mezzanine ABS-CDOs experienced substantial shortfalls in payments of both interest and principal. As the UBS report to shareholders points out, this high level of risk exposure was made possible by the very weak controls on its activities, with senior management failing to challenge internal reviews of trading exposure and the risk models themselves flawed by assumptions that allowed many exposures to be classified as zero-risk.

A line has been drawn under at least the worst of the UBS exposure, through an imaginative loss-sharing scheme with the Swiss government, first announced in October 2008. Under this scheme UBS is selling some $38 billion of MBS and structured credit exposure into a separate investment fund, backed by a Swiss government loan and a Swiss government equity injection (some of these assests were sold in January 2009 and the rest were expected to be sold in March or April). These assets are being valued conservatively at slightly below their mark to market valuation in the UBS balance sheet. Their original par values are very much higher.

This fund will most likely make a profit, since the mark to market valuations understate the prospective cash flows, in which case the Swiss government as the equity holder will make money. But there is an additional option clause, so that if the profits turn out to be large enough UBS will share 50:50 in any further returns (UBS needed to have some prospective return or it would not have sold these assets). If instead the fund makes a loss because of a further very substantial weakening of the US economy, the Swiss government is compensated by its own option to purchase UBS shares at a low price. This arrangement has many merits and as discussed further in Chapter 9 could be a blueprint for the way in which other troubled banks are dealt with.

More failures of control

The story of losses at the US investment bank Merrill Lynch has many parallels with UBS. Merrill also plunged into a surprising third quarter 2007 loss of $2.3 billion, after a record profit of $2.1 billion only the previous quarter. This prompted the resignation of Stan O'Neill, its chief executive, the first senior head to roll because of the credit crisis. Merrill had suffered a serious dent to its reputation – and a $100 million fine levied by the New York attorney general Elliot Spitzer – during the dot.com bubble of 1995–2001, because it failed to control conflicts of interest in its promotion of new share issues, especially by its star equity researcher Henry Blodgett. Since then O'Neill had achieved much at Merrill, cutting costs substantially and diversifying its business away from its traditional dependence on broking revenues.

O'Neill's failure, just like that of Marcel Ospel at UBS, is that he did not properly question the activities and reported profits of the rapidly growing fixed-income trading division at Merrill Lynch. Just as at UBS, Merrill Lynch traders had expanded aggressively into the high-yielding mezzanine ABS-CDOs of mortgage-backed securities. This portfolio, with a nominal face value of some $30.6 billion, had fallen in value to only $11.1 billion by the end of the second quarter of 2008.

In late July 2008 Merrill Lynch stemmed some of these losses by selling the entire mezzanine ABS-CDO portfolio to a private equity company for $6.7 billion. The loss of $24 billion on this portfolio accounted for nearly half of its 2007 and first-half 2008 credit-related losses. This deal was accompanied by the announcement of an $8.5 billion public stock offering, with a $3.5 billion commitment to purchase shares by a second Singapore government sovereign wealth fund, Temasek Holdings.

But the problems at Merrill Lynch were far from over, and it continued to be threatened by problems of confidence. These mounted to the point where a withdrawal of short-term funding could easily have triggered a rapid collapse, such as took place at Bear Stearns the previous March. But then, on Monday 15 September (the same day that its smallest competitor Lehman Brothers failed), its liquidity problems were ended through an acquisition by the leading US commercial bank, Bank of America.

This rushed meal, following the earlier acquisition by Bank of America of Countrywide Financial, has been followed by something of a bout of indigestion. There are concerns whether Bank of America has a strong enough and sufficiently well capitalized balance sheet to cope with continuing uncertainty about the value of the newly purchased MBS and structured credit assets. The increasing prospect of a long and deep economic downturn means that it will be a long time before either Countrywide's or Merrill's businesses generate enough profit to justify these deals. This has led Bank of America to use the US Treasury 'Asset Protection Programme' to insure some $118 billion of assets acquired from Merrill and also to tap the US Treasury's $195 billion programme for bank recapitalization, the 'Capital Assistance Program', to issue some $15 billion of preference shares.

Is this is a sign of deeper problems? These were all stock purchases and Bank of America has been least affected by the crisis of all the large US banks. Perhaps it could have snapped up Countrywide and Merrill for less had it waited longer, but it should still avoid falling into serious problems itself. US Treasury funds should be very safe.

The largest bank losses of all

The largest losses and write-downs of any bank were recorded by Citigroup, a sprawling financial empire with more than 350,000 employees, a balance sheet of over $2 trillion, and something of a history of inadequate controls. Banking specialists too often trot out a hackneyed line about big being better in banking because large mega-institutions benefit from diversification and economies of scale. If they lose money in one area of business they still always make money somewhere else and so are immune from major crises. The experience of Citigroup exposes the fallacy of this argument. Big too often means badly managed rather than diversified (as Mark Twain put it, better to 'put all your eggs in the one basket, and *watch that basket!*'). Citigroup or its predecessors have been exposed to virtually every major banking problem of the past thirty years, whether Latin America lending, property losses in the 1990s, or dot.com at the close of the century. During the recent credit boom it was no less foolhardy, and therefore it is not entirely a surprise that it was Citigroup that reported the biggest losses of all.

A major source of this loss was their portfolio of around $300 billion of corporate bonds and mortgage-backed and structured securities – more than one-eighth of the entire Citigroup balance sheet. The motive for building up this portfolio was once again the attractions of yield and the especially high margins that could be earned when financing these exposures using short-term borrowing. Unlike at UBS and Merrill Lynch, a large amount of these assets, some $87 billion, were held off balance sheet in structured investment vehicles financed by the issue of asset-backed commercial paper. The losses on these holdings jumped in the fourth quarter of 2007, with a quarterly write-down of some $19 billion (described by the *Economist* magazine as 'the mother of all write-downs') pushing Citigroup into a quarterly loss of nearly $10 billion. Further substantial write-downs and losses followed in subsequent quarters.

But unlike at Merrill Lynch and UBS the problems at Citigroup went far beyond its investments in sub-prime mortgage-backed and other structured securities. It held a large portfolio of leveraged loans (tradable loans to private equity buyouts such as those included in the Grosvenor Place CLO described in Chapter 5) which fell sharply in value. It is also a major loan originator, in the United States and other countries, in credit cards, mortgages and corporate lending, with a total loan portfolio of over $750 billion. As the US economy deteriorated Citigroup recorded substantial increases in its loss provisions on this lending. Before the crisis these loss provisions averaged around 1.3 per cent of its loan portfolio each year. In the five quarters following the crisis it recorded loan loss provisions on these traditional loans of $33 billion – nearly 5 per cent of its total lending. True to past form, in every business area where banks were making losses or write-downs, Citigroup was heavily involved.

In just two years, from November 2006 until November 2008, the market value of Citigroup fell by over 90 per cent, from $244 billion to less than $21 billion. A remark of Citigroup chief executive Chuck Prince to the *Financial Times* in July 2007 about Citigroup's exposure to leveraged buyout loans will long be remembered: 'When the music stops, in terms of liquidity, things will be complicated. But as long as the music is playing, you've got to get up and dance. We're still dancing.' This statement is a testament to poor governance. No financial institution should be doing business just because others are doing the same.

At the beginning of November 2007, as the full extent of Citigroup's exposure to the new credit markets emerged, Prince resigned, to be replaced by Vikram Pandit. Pandit made considerable reductions in costs, balance sheet and headcount, and by the end of 2008 was facing up to the need to break up the bank and sell large parts of it.

Like UBS and Merrill, Citigroup raised new capital from sovereign wealth funds and other investors – a total of some $50 billion of new private-sector investment including $7.5 billion investment in December 2007 from the Abu Dhabi investment authority and $6.9 billion in January 2008 from the Government of Singapore Investment Corporation. But all this was not enough to get Citigroup out of trouble; eventually it had to turn to the US federal government for support, which on 23 November 2008 provided a further $40 billion of capital and also insurance guarantees on some $301 billion of Citigroup securities and loans. At that date this was the biggest package of public support ever provided to a private company in any country, but was only part of the much larger programme of Treasury and federal support for the financial system in autumn 2008.

Losses at Citigroup have risen still further for the full year 2008, resulting in some further increases in the capital raised from the US Treasury. Unlike most other US banks where the US Treasury has purchased preference shares, much of this new capital has been in the form of ordinary equity shares, so the US government now owns some 36 per cent of Citigroup. The situation remains uncertain because of the parlous state of the US and global economies. Citigroup have provided against the possibility of a long and deep recession, but if the global economy continues to weaken then even these provisions may not be enough. The possibility of further recapitalization and of Citigroup ending up in majority or even complete government ownership cannot be ruled out.

US mortgage banks

Among the other victims of the credit crisis were US banks that had lent heavily from their own balance sheets to sub-prime, Alt-A and other riskier 'non-conforming' mortgage borrowers. Some of these lenders were mortgage subsidiaries of such major banks as Citigroup, HSBC, Wells Fargo, JP Morgan Chase, and Bank of America. These could absorb the losses and wind down the lending activities of their loss-making subsidiaries. But much of the non-conforming mortgage loans came from specialized mortgage banks, including Countrywide Financial, IndyMac, Washington Mutual, Ameriquest and New Century Financial, all of which appeared regularly in lists of the top ten non-conforming US mortgage originators during the sub-prime boom. What happened to these institutions?

Chapter 7 has already described the departure from the scene of the most aggressive of these sub-prime lenders, with the winding down and sale to Citigroup of Ameriquest and the bankruptcy filing of New Century Financial. A key support for the remaining independent mortgage banks has been loans from the system of Federal Home Loan Banks. In the second half of 2007 these independent mortgage companies all faced serious problems with financing themselves in wholesale markets, similar to the problems which brought down Northern Rock in the United Kingdom. Washington Mutual, for example, took $64 billion of loans from the various Federal Home Loan Banks, about three fifths of its total wholesale borrowing (although this did not prevent its eventual failure).

Countrywide was acquired by Bank of America for $4.1 billion, a deal first announced in January 2008 and completed by 1 July. This deal was not without risk; Countrywide has a $95 billion mortgage portfolio (from a total balance sheet of $170 billion) which includes a large proportion of sub-prime, home equity and other loans. It may also yet have to take back some loans sold for inclusion in mortgage-backed securitizations that have not passed subsequent performance tests. By 30 June 2008 Countrywide had already made loan loss provisions in excess of $3 billion, with possibly more to come as the US housing market continues to deteriorate. But Countrywide has a valuable mortgage-servicing business and industry-leading systems for mortgage origination. When the US mortgage market finally recovers, Bank of America will be well placed to increase its share of the market.

IndyMac was a somewhat smaller specialized mortgage lender, based in Pasadena, California, with a $30 billion balance sheet and a $16 billion portfolio of mortgages concentrated in sub-prime and Alt-A borrowers in California, one of the states which suffered the largest falls in house prices since 2006. It was also a major originator of loans which were then sold into mortgage-backed securities structured by Wall Street investment banks. IndyMac had been struggling since the onset of the credit crisis. But for some $11 billion of Federal Home Loan Bank lending, it would already have failed, and on 11 July 2008 it was closed by bank regulators, with its assets and deposits transferred into a 'bridge bank' now trading under the name IndyMac Federal Bank. Shareholders received nothing. The US Federal Deposit Insurance Corporation estimates that the IndyMac resolution will cost its deposit insurance fund somewhere in the range of $4–8 billion, a pretty big hole since the total fund amounts only to $53 billion. At the time this was the second biggest US bank closure in dollar terms; only the closure of the Continental Illinois with $105 billion of assets in 1984 was larger.

This record was eclipsed with the 25 September 2008 closure of the Seattle-based mortgage lender Washington Mutual, one of the largest mortgage lenders in the United States, with $244 billion of mortgages on its balance sheet at end-2007. An indication of the weaknesses of its loan portfolio is that in the first six months of 2008 Washington Mutual made $9 billion of loan loss provisions against these loans, an unusually high 3.5 per cent of the outstanding portfolio. The US deposit insurer the FDIC took control of Washington Mutual, selling its loans, deposits and branches to JP Morgan Chase for $1.1 billion. This sounds like a good deal for JP Morgan, the book value of loans and the branch network being a great deal more than the deposit liabilities, but again there are risks; the continuing deterioration in housing markets nationwide could lead to large declines in the value of the loan portfolio.

Surprisingly, one of the biggest recorded losses among sub-prime lenders is among the least remarked-on in the financial and business press. These are the massive loan loss provisions made by the UK bank HSBC on its specialized US sub-prime subsidiary Household Finance Corporation (HFC). At the height of the credit boom HFC was the largest sub-prime lender of all, providing some $122 billion in B and C loans from the first quarter of 2005 until the third quarter of 2007.

It has now had to write off more than $25 billion of this lending, and there could be more loan losses yet to come if the US housing market does not stabilize.

The reason why the HFC losses have not caused more concern is the strength of its parent, HSBC. As I have mentioned in Chapter 7, I have considerable admiration for HSBC and its cautious but highly effective banking culture. HSBC is the most profitable and best capitalized bank in the world. The acquisition of HFC was uncharacteristic; HSBC does not engage in lending to higher risk borrowers on anything like a similar scale anywhere else in its business. As the HSBC chairman Stephen Green has acknowledged, in retrospect the acquisition appears to have been a big mistake. But this also demonstrates that being well capitalized and enjoying healthy profits is the key to bank stability. There is a clear lesson for other banks and for policymakers: other profitable institutions that are being damaged by the crisis can easily be turned around simply by recapitalizing them. If this requires more public money, so be it, since the taxpayer will certainly make a profit from investing in fundamentally strong but temporarily weakened banks.

The liquidity crisis at Bear Stearns

In the middle of March 2008, in the most dramatic development of the credit crisis until that date, the US investment bank Bear Stearns was saved from insolvency through its acquisition for $10 per share by its larger commercial and investment banking rival JP Morgan, a takeover assisted by $30 billion short-term funding support from the US Federal Reserve.

Bear Stearns was smaller than many of its investment banking rivals. For example, it had only 14,000 employees and a balance sheet of about $0.4 trillion, compared with the 78,000 employees and $1 trillion balance sheet of Merrill Lynch. Bear was, however, a central player in the sub-prime mortgage-backed securities markets, acting as an issuer, a market maker, a fund manager and a major investor in its own right. Because of this close involvement it thought it understood rather better than many other banks the credit risks of these instruments and had taken good care not to take on large exposures to the lower-quality securities, such as the restructured CDOs of mortgage-backed securities in which UBS and Merrill were so heavily invested.

At the beginning of 2008 Bear Stearns management could be cautiously optimistic about their prospects. Revenues from the issue of structured products were sharply lower because of the effective closure of these markets and they had experienced losses on their portfolios of mortgage-backed securities, but the rest of their business remained very profitable. Write-downs on their own mortgage-backed and related securities made by Bear Stearns were a relatively small $3 billion, a much better outcome than that at Merrill, especially considering that these exposures were a relatively high proportion of the Bear Stearns overall balance sheet.

But Bear Stearns was, none the less, in serious difficulties. Their two main business activities required a lot of short-term funding. They were leading traders of corporate bonds, of the derivatives on bonds known as 'credit default swaps' and of structured securities. They were also a leading prime broker, providing the hedge funds – the privately financed institutions that take speculative risks in financial markets – with financing, with access to markets and with other services. To raise the funding for these activities, believing that they had rather low-risk exposures compared with other banks, Bear Stearns was also highly leveraged, operating with a lot of short-term debt and rather little capital. In what seems in retrospect a rather foolish decision, they had spurned the opportunity to raise more capital in late 2007, when other banks such as Citigroup were raising funds from sovereign wealth funds and other outside investors.

A fundamental underlying problem was their relatively undiversified business model when compared with other major Wall Street firms. There had been opportunities to acquire or to merge with other firms, but during the preceding 15 years, the period when Jimmy Cayne was chief executive officer from 1993 until he stepped down on 8 January 2008, these opportunities had been passed by.

The illiquidity of credit markets posed huge problems for both their core businesses. Bear Stearns held about $150 billion of illiquid securities, such as private label MBSs, ABSs, corporate bonds and CDOs. These were mostly of good credit quality but they still had to be financed, and Bear Stearns only had around $100 billion of equity capital and other long-term funding. It had to borrow the additional $50 billion to finance these positions using repo and other forms of short-term funding. As haircuts on these securities increased, rising to 30 or 40 per cent or more, this became increasingly difficult.

There were also mounting liquidity problems in their prime broker-age operations. One of their main sources of revenue was from lending both cash and securities to hedge fund clients. There were growing rumours in early March 2008 that Bear Stearns was short of cash. This in turn led many hedge fund clients to return illiquid securities to Bear Stearns in order to get cash out before it might be too late, and hence increase the cash drain on the firm.

The one serious recent attempt of Bear Stearns to diversify their business had been a disaster. This was the rapid growth of Bear Stearns Asset Management (BSAM), the division responsible for oper-ating their two client hedge funds with exposure to mortgage-backed securities, the High Grade Structured Credit Strategies Fund and the High Grade Structured Credit Enhanced Leverage Fund. In theory Bear Stearns was not itself directly exposed to these funds since they were run on behalf of clients with only a limited amount of direct firm exposure. As described already in Chapter 7, Bear had moved fairly quickly in July 2007 to close these two underperforming funds.

But these had been mismanaged, the correct procedures for record-ing and reporting trades having not been followed; they had much greater holdings of sub-prime mortgage-backed securities than had been acknowledged in their regular performance reports. In order to avoid legal action Bear Stearns had been forced to take over the funds and compensate investors, resulting in losses of more than $1 billion. The damage this caused was much more than just financial. Bear Stearns was big enough to absorb a loss of this size. But this mishap created doubts about the quality of its entire balance sheet.

The declining values of their portfolios of senior MBS tranches after August 2007 created mounting liquidity problems for Bear Stearns. Even the safest tranches of mortgage-backed securities, securities that would be expected to fully repay in almost any imaginable circum-stances, had fallen around 10 to 20 per cent below their par values. This pushed Bear Stearns closer and closer to negative net worth and even more crucially reduced the amount of funding that could be bor-rowed on such a collateralized basis.

Increasingly blogs and other internet sites were reporting alarm-ing rumours about Bear Stearns liquidity problems. Matters came to a head in the week beginning 10 March 2008, with a rush of cash withdrawals by prime brokerage customers. $18 billion of cash assets at the beginning of the week had dwindled to only $2 billion by the evening of Thursday 13 March. Since it held a broker dealer rather than a commercial banking licence, Bear Stearns had no direct access to short-term borrowing from the Federal Reserve discount window. Without help it could not survive even the next business day.

That evening Bear Stearns turned to JP Morgan – the much larger commercial and investment banking group with a market leading position in various over-the-counter trading markets and with a head office just across the street from Bear Stearns – and a deal was hammered out overnight with the help of the Federal Reserve Bank of New York. This was announced on the morning of Friday 14 March. JP Morgan agreed to provide Bear Stearns with twenty-eight days of collateralized credit, financing this by borrowing themselves from the Federal Reserve collateralized against Bear Stearns assets. The market reaction, however, was negative. Key terms of the deal such as the interest rate charged on this lending and other mechanics of the loan had not been agreed, and the decision to use Federal Reserve funding was seen as an indication of undisclosed problems in the Bear Stearns balance sheet. That day the major rating agencies downgraded Bear Stearns from AA to BBB and its share price dived. The outflow of cash continued, even with support from JP Morgan, and Bear Stearns barely survived until the Friday afternoon close of markets. The Federal Reserve was keen to find a resolution that avoided bankruptcy. Bear Stearns was heavily involved in the new credit markets, holding positions against many other major banks. For Bear to fail might have caused great disruption (as the failure of Lehman Brothers eventually did later, in September). But the Federal Reserve had room to manoeuvre because, unlike Lehman Brothers, the fundamentals of Bear's business were mostly sound.

The natural resolution was to find a buyer, and there followed forty-eight hours of frantic negotiations over the weekend of 15 and 16 March with two potential suitors, JP Morgan and the private equity group J C Flowers & Co. These talks eventually resulted in a deal. JP Morgan agreed to buy Bear Stearns, at a price of only $2 per share or $236 million (as some remarked at the time, this was less than the value of Bear Stearns New York headquarters). This was a huge loss for Bear Stearns shareholders, since it was trading as high as $170 per share in the first half of 2007 and at more than $60 dollars at the start of the previous week. The Federal Reserve supported this deal with some $30 billion of funding for an off balance sheet vehicle

'Maiden Lane' to absorb Bear Stearns's portfolio of senior tranches of mortgage-backed and structured securities.

This was something of a steal for JP Morgan. While there were major weaknesses in Bear Stearns, its credit-structuring business being unlikely to generate much revenue for the foreseeable future, other parts of the business were well worth having. JP Morgan was already the leading credit default swap dealer so there could be considerable cost reductions in combining these activities. The deal gave JP Morgan a much stronger position in the profitable prime brokerage market. Finally, the portfolio of senior structured credit assets could be held for an eventual profit. Unsurprisingly Bear Stearns shareholders threatened to block the deal, arguing that the price was too low. This led JP Morgan, once it had looked more closely at the Bear Stearns books, to revise up its offer to $10 per share, but it was still getting a great bargain. Taking advantage of another's misfortune is a long-established road to business success.

A further concern for the Federal Reserve was the possibility that other broker dealers – the US investment banks such as Goldman Sachs, Morgan Stanley and Lehman Brothers – could face liquidity problems similar to those at Bear Stearns, problems which would be difficult to address because in the US system of bank regulation the broker dealers are not commercial banks and so do not qualify for loans from the Federal Reserve. To head off this possibility the Federal Reserve announced at the same time as the Bear Stearns rescue the creation of a new temporary facility, the Primary Dealers Credit Facility, which allowed the Federal Reserve to provide up to $30 billion of collateralized lending to other broker dealers.

Monoline insurers and credit default swaps

It is time to taste a veritable alphabet soup of acronyms. In late 2007 and the early months of 2008 some unfamiliar names hit the headlines in the business pages – MBIA, AMBAC, FGIC, and other 'monoline' insurance companies because of their involvement in writing CDS (credit default swaps, a form of tradable insurance) on senior structured credits. What are monolines and how did they come to be dragged into the credit crisis? What were the wider impacts of their troubles?

The monolines are bond insurance companies. The core of their business is providing guarantees on US municipal debts – bonds issued by cities, universities and other public bodies below state level. They only offer this insurance when the underlying finances of the issuer – for example Los Angeles or New York – are sound. The monoline business is usually operated separately from other insurance activities because of the critical importance of maintaining a strong credit rating. As long as the monoline retains the best possible AAA rating from the rating agencies, their insurance allows municipal bonds also to be rated AAA. The monolines are thus a key support for the large 'muni' bond market that finances schools, universities, hospitals, road building and other projects across the United States.

Monoline insurance is a simple and profitable business. Like all insurance the key is diversification of exposures, a municipal bond always having an element of 'specific' risk. Political problems or a natural disaster might, for example, undermine the finances of a single city and lead to its defaulting on its bonds. But such municipal defaults are rare and will never occur in all cities across the United States at the same time. By offering insurance on a large portfolio of muni-bonds issued across the entire country, the monoline insurer can diversify this risk, taking a small premium perhaps 0.2 per cent per annum on all the bonds and obtaining more than enough revenue to cover the losses on individual bonds on the occasions when they do default.

The feature of this business that in the past has generated excellent profits for monolines is that they only ever insure remote risks. It is rather like being a house insurer who only insures against burglary in houses with high walls topped by barbed wire, searchlights in the yard, bars on the window and extremely nasty dogs ready to pounce on any would-be intruder. The premium rates are low but claims on the policies are even lower. The business is simple, safe and profitable. This cautious approach is what underpinned the AAA ratings of the monolines, ratings which in turn enabled them to support municipal bonds.

Had monolines restricted themselves to the insuring of municipal bonds they would not have been sucked into the credit crisis. But as the boom in issuing mortgage-backed and structured credit products developed, investors including banks wanted to have some additional protection against the possibility of default and changes in market prices on the senior AAA and better tranches of these structured products. This seemed like a lucrative business opportunity for the monolines. These senior tranches were not unlike muni-bonds. Although they did not offer US investors any tax advantages (interest on muni bonds is exempt from federal taxes), they also had very low risk of default. By offering insurance on these bonds at a premium of, say, 10 or 15 basis points, a new revenue stream could be established, once again in the expectation that very few bonds would default and that revenues would comfortably exceed payouts.

But there was a key difference between the monoline muni-bond and structured finance businesses. Because of their federal income tax exemptions municipal bonds were mostly sold to individuals. Most individual purchasers were only interested in the very safest AAA-rated bonds. So the cities and counties issuing the bonds purchase traditional insurance from a monoline in order to achieve these high ratings.

Monoline protection on senior tranches of mortgage-backed and structured securities works differently. These securities are already AAA-rated (they are regarded as more complex but safer than municipal bonds) and held mostly by banks, some wanting additional protection, others not. So monolines wrote contracts with investors instead of with issuers.

These contracts could not be traditional insurance contracts. Traditional insurance is not transferable to new owners when the security is sold and does not protect against fluctuations in market price. So, instead, the monolines wrote protection using the financial derivatives known as 'credit default swaps' or CDS. These contracts have been appropriately described by the US investor Warren Buffett as 'weapons of financial mass destruction'. The reason they are so potentially destructive is that they are re-priced on a daily basis against financial market prices. This exposes the provider of protection to huge cash flow risks. They must make continual 'margin' payments to CDS dealers (the middlemen in the CDS market between the protection buyers and protection sellers) to reflect any deterioration in the market's view of the value of these contracts. The consequence is to create a further feedback loop that can and did undermine the solvency of the insurance companies: falling market prices leading to substantial margin payments leading to doubts about the solvency of the credit insurers leading to yet further falls in market prices.

CDS are written on all kinds of bonds, not just structured securities, and have grown to be one of the largest financial markets in the world, with notional protection in excess of $65 trillion (this is the headline figure, but many of these contracts are offsetting, so that the net protection is much smaller). While they operate like insurance contracts – the protection buyer pays a premium to the protection seller in return for a promise of payments in the event that the bond defaults – they are not subject to insurance regulations.

The leading dealers are major banks such as JP Morgan, Goldman Sachs, and Deutsche Bank. Instead of deals being struck bilaterally between protection buyer and seller, both buyer and seller each agree their own contracts with a dealing desk. The terms of the contracts are standardized, so that protection buyers do not have to worry too much about the 'small print'. But the major attraction of using CDS is the resale market. Protection can be bought and sold along with the underlying bond, or can be cancelled. This also meant that protection sellers believed that they could control their own risks by selling their side of the CDS contracts and so limiting their losses.

This seemed very attractive business. Monolines could earn a healthy premium selling protection using credit default swaps, the risks of ultimate loss was small and, if perceived risks did rise, there was a resale market, so that the monolines could simply sell out of their position and so limit their losses.

This is not how matters worked out in practice. Standard and Poor's estimate that the monolines have provided $125 billion of insurance on senior AAA tranches of the restructured ABS-CDOs and CDO^2, tranches whose ratings have collapsed to B ratings or below and whose market value has fallen to perhaps 20 per cent of par. The monolines thus faced losses on these contracts alone of the order of $100 billion. There were also further monoline losses on other CDS contracts, written on the senior tranches of the simpler vanilla mortgage-backed securities and other structured products. While few if any defaults are in prospect, the market prices of these CDS contracts has also fallen, by between 10 and 30 per cent or more. Worse still, since liquidity had evaporated the monolines could only sell their positions at low fire-sale prices, crystallizing these losses.

By July 2008 monoline write-downs were approaching $200 billion, leading the rating agencies to downgrade almost all of them to well below their cherished AAA rating. For example, Standard and Poor's down-rated the second largest monoline AMBIA to AA and the largest of all, MBIA, to A. Some smaller monolines were re-rated as far down as BB – below even investment-grade status.

Many had feared that such monoline downgrading, when it eventually came, or, worse still, monoline insolvencies would be a severe systemic shock, creating further problems in credit markets. These fears were overstated. In fact the credibility of monoline insurance, even prior to the downward ratings, had already been largely lost. The knock-on effects of the monoline problems had largely been felt even before July.

Knock-on effects

What were these knock-on effects? The problems of the monolines hit banks by further lowering the market value of many structured credit portfolios, since the monoline insurance purchased to hedge the risk on these portfolios was no longer credible. These problems also raised the cost of borrowing in the municipal bond market, creating a major squeeze on US city and county finances large enough to offset the much-touted 'fiscal stimulus' in the form of rebate cheques mailed to US citizens in summer 2008. Finally, they led to the very public collapse of a specialized corner of the municipal financing market known as 'auction rate securities', or ARS.

ARS were developed by major investment banks, offering cities and counties an alternative fund-raising instrument to the traditional muni bonds, one that appealed to short-term investors. In order to set interest rates and provide liquidity, the banks organized weekly re-auctions of these securities, in which short-term investors would put in bids and the highest accepted bids would determine the interest rate paid. As long as there was confidence in the market the auction rate securities offered similar but slightly better returns to other money market instruments such as certificates of deposit.

This was another example of 'borrowing short and lending long', and like all such investment arrangements it depended on confidence. The market grew rapidly, peaking at around $330 billion in summer 2007. But by February 2008, with growing doubts about municipal finances, confidence evaporated and the ARS market disappeared. The securities no longer reached minimum reserve prices in auction and the investors were effectively left holding long-term municipal bonds.

Most of the major Wall Street firms had been selling ARS. By summer 2008, in order to protect their reputation and to settle legal actions mounted by the New York attorney general Adrian Cuomo and other state attorneys general, they had paid fines and bought back most of the ARS from investors (there were embarrassing echoes of the Elliot Spitzer actions over dot.com IPOs, with a number of internal emails indicating that banks had not been entirely open with investors about the risks of these securities). The losses to the banks were not themselves large, but the banks were encumbered with a large amount of illiquid securities, putting further strain on their already stretched balance sheets.

The collapse of AIG

American International Group International (AIG) is one of the world's largest insurance companies, with over 100,000 employees and marketing insurance products in 130 countries (the name of AIG is also familiar to many millions across the world as the shirt sponsor of the leading English football club and 2008 winner of the European Champions League Manchester United).

AIG has a $1 trillion balance sheet, and before the crisis broke was making profits of some $22 billion of pre-tax income on revenues of around $110 billion per year. It is one of the two largest insurance companies in the United States (the other is Berkshire Hathaway). Worldwide, only AXA of France and Allianz of Germany are much bigger. It was ranked by Forbes as the eighth largest of all US corporations and was one of the select group of thirty companies included in the Dow Jones share index until its removal in September 2008.

AIG started high and fell a very long way, recording one of the most spectacular share price collapses of any company in the credit crisis. In early 2007 it was trading at about $70 per share, giving it a stock market valuation of around $175 billion. By September 2008 its share price had fallen to only $20 per share and the subsequent crisis at the firm reduced this to around $2 per share and its market valuation to only $6 billion. Shareholders had lost 97 per cent of their investment.

What caused this collapse? Why should one of the world's largest insurance companies be so affected by the credit crisis when others have been little touched or have even prospered? The root cause was similar to that underlying the losses at UBS, Citigroup and Merrill Lynch – a failure of senior management to exercise effective control. AIG was betting its own solvency and AAA rating in return for a steady stream of credit-related premiums and yield – additional profits of perhaps around $400 million per annum – on exposures it did not properly understand.

There were two big risks lurking in the AIG balance sheet. First, it had been suckered into the same business as the monolines, writing CDS protection on seemingly safe senior tranches of mortgage-backed and structured securities. Critically, as it turned out, it chose to do so not through a separately capitalized subsidiary, as was the case with almost all its other insurance activities, but through a special 'financial services division' whose assets and liabilities were part of the AIG holding company balance sheet. This division competed heavily with the monolines, eventually writing CDS contracts on an astonishing $562 billion of senior structured credit products.[1]

The second risk was the massive exposure of the investment portfolio of AIG life insurance and retirement service divisions to credit risk of many kinds. AIG is one the world's largest providers of life insurance and pension products, taking premiums and pension contributions and investing them long term in order to pay insurance and retirement plans when due. Most of this money was invested in bonds – at end-2007 the total bond portfolio in the AIG life insurance and retirement services division was $309 billion – but very little – only around $2 billion – was invested in low-risk US government bonds. Most was invested in corporate bonds, municipal bonds, mortgage-backed securities and structured products, in all of which there is risk of default. For example, AIG held some $94 billion of mortgage-backed securities, including about $30 billion of home equity, sub-prime and Alt-A MBS, and not just the senior AAA tranches but many lower-rated senior and mezzanine tranches as well.

AIG's problems first became public in September 2007, when it reported write-downs in the market value of the credit default swaps it had written on senior mortgage-backed securities. By end-year these write-downs had risen to $11.5 billion, reducing 2007 group profits by around two-thirds. But the full extent of its losses took much longer to emerge; by December 2008 the cumulative write-downs on these credit default swaps had risen to $90.4 billion (all financial figures are taken from AIG SEC 10-K disclosures).

To this must be added its own investment losses. By end-December 2008 AIG also recorded an astonishing further $55.5 billion of

---

[1] 2008 10-K, p. 263.

impairment loss on its own securities portfolios, mostly losses on its holdings of MBS, structured products and corporate bonds. Its overall losses and write-downs taken onto its income statement were $104 billion, around seven times its pre-tax income, and its capital was eroded yet further by falls in the value of other securities that were recorded in its balance sheet but not its income statement.

A further problem for AIG was that although it was initially well capitalized, the book value of its equity – that is, the difference between the value of assets and liabilities at end-2007 – was about $95 billion, insurance regulations requiring it to hold much of this capital on the balance sheets of its many insurance subsidiaries. So not only was equity declining rapidly, but the holding company AIG International had far more liabilities than assets. This created severe cash flow problems, it could no longer borrow short term and it was struggling to meet the margin payments due on the credit default swaps it had sold.

Matters came to a head on Monday 15 September 2008, when a ratings downgrade triggered substantial cash calls from AIG creditors and on the very same day Lehman Brothers filed for bankruptcy protection. The US Treasury then surprised markets. Although it had refused to provide government funding to Lehman over the previous weekend, on 16 September it did come to the rescue of AIG, providing a two-year $85 billion dollar collateralized loan facility through the Federal Reserve Bank of New York, but the conditions were fairly tough, AIG paying both a high interest rate – 8½ per cent *above* market rates of interest on both drawn and undrawn funds – and giving the US Treasury an 80 per cent share of AIG equity and the right to veto dividend payments. This was a rushed and not entirely satisfactory response to the situation, because the high rates of interest on the Fed loan worsened rather than alleviated AIG's cash flow problems. AIG was still heading for bankruptcy as economic conditions worsened.

To prevent this the support package was radically revised less than four weeks later, on 10 November, when the US Treasury provided a further $40 billion of cash to AIG from the $850 billion dollar Troubled Assets Resolution Program fund now approved by Congress, in exchange for preference shares. Also the $85 billion Federal Reserve loan was restructured, with the direct loan reduced to $60 billion but extended from two to five years at a lower rate of interest and $52.5 billion of Fed money being used instead to finance two separate vehicles that would purchase both CDS and mortgage-backed securities from AIG at market prices (AIG was also required to put some debt and subordinated equity into these two). Altogether, with the $40 billion cash for preference shares, the $60 billion loan and the $52.5 billion of funds for these vehicles the authorities were putting in $152.5 billion; at its announcement this was the world's biggest ever corporate rescue, but this record was to stand for less than a fortnight, being surpassed by the $341 billion rescue of Citigroup on 23 November.

Even this support package for AIG has not proved enough. In March 2009 the US Treasury provided AIG with a further $30 billion of cash for preference shares. This additional funding has been politically very unpopular. The problems at AIG and its subsequent rescue have come to symbolize the excesses of the credit boom and been a lightning rod for resentment and criticism. AIG executives have poured oil on the fire by continuing to pay themselves and senior staff bonuses that, while small in the context of the entire rescue package, stick in the craw of the American public and create considerable jealousy among politicians and media commentators.

But the reaction to this bonus scandal has been overemotional. It is necessary to stand back and disentangle two quite separate issues. How do we deal with the financial and economic crisis, and how big are the underlying losses? What should senior executives be paid and how should their pay be related to performance?

Major questions have rightly been raised about the practice of awarding large bonuses, especially to senior staff and management, in banks and other big companies. Industry insiders are quick to justify these bonuses, remarking for example on the need to attract and retain key management staff and the importance of providing incentives for good management.

These justifications do not ring entirely true. If large bonuses were never paid by any firms in the industry, then staff would not be lost to other institutions. Satisfaction with a job well done rather than money should be the most important incentive to manage a business well. But whether bonuses are useful or, as I believe, rather damaging, it is essential to realize that fixing bonus arrangements has almost nothing to do with fixing the financial system and the economy.

We need to strengthen bank balance sheets, making them all secure, and this will stabilise the economy and the financial system. We can deal with the question of bonuses later on. We can control bonuses and yet, if we do nothing more fundamental to deal with the banking problems, then the economic and financial crisis will likely deepen and get even worse.

Public outrage has risen to such a pitch that many now believe not only that the system of large-scale bonuses should now end, but that in additional senior management of institutions like AIG should be punished for all the losses they have created, through clawing back past bonuses or even through criminal trial and prison sentences. In the meantime they and their firms should not get further public support.

Again, this is a muddled and overemotional response. Yes, there were major mistakes in many institutions, not least at AIG, but the underlying losses are much less than what is required to shore these institutions up. The US Treasury is investing in AIG in order to prevent a further calamitous decline in confidence in banks and the financial system. With the return of confidence much of the losses on AIGs credit default swap contracts and structured credit investments will be recovered. It is even possible that the US taxpayer could yet make a profit on this intervention. In the course of time there can be a full assessment of rights and wrongs, but this must not get in the way of fixing the US and global economic and financial system. This means continuing to support the business, if not necessarily the shareholders, of AIG and other major firms.

Conflicts of interest at Fannie Mae and Freddie Mac

Two other large financial institutions, the 'government sponsored enterprises' or GSEs Fannie Mae and Freddie Mac, also enjoyed the revenues from leveraged exposure to mortgage credit risk. On the surface they may look rather different, but scratch a little deeper and it turns out that their business activities were remarkably similar to those of Bear Stearns, the monolines and AIG.

Fannie and Freddie are large mortgage finance institutions, but they do not provide retail customers with mortgages for house purchase. They are the major players in the 'secondary' market for US mortgages, buying mortgages from banks, thrifts and other mortgage borrowers and then either holding these mortgages themselves or more often repackaging them as part of so-called agency mortgage-backed securities, which can then be sold on to investors. The GSEs are *not* supposed to take much risk. Most of the mortgages they purchase are so called 'conforming' mortgages, satisfying fairly strict regulatory standards for the credit quality of the borrower and limits on the amount borrowed, both in absolute dollars and also relative to the borrower's income and to the value of the house purchased.

There is nothing quite like Fannie and Freddie in the mortgage markets of any other country. Yet their activities did make some sense in the somewhat unusual institutional arrangements for banking in the United States in place from the 1950s until the early 1990s. Unlike in most other countries, nationwide commercial banking did not emerge in the United States before the 1990s (this was because of the regulatory restrictions that remained in place until the Riegle-Neal Interstate Banking and Branching Efficiency Act of 1994 and the Gramm-Leach-Bliley Financial Services Modernization Act of 1999, abolishing restrictions on interstate banking and on commercial banks offering investment banking and insurance services). As a result, most banks and the thrifts specializing in mortgage lending remained small or regional. There were substantial imbalances, with some banks having considerable surpluses of deposits over loans and others much greater lending opportunities, especially mortgage lending opportunities, than they had retail deposits.

A national institution purchasing good-quality mortgages could bridge these imbalances. This was the role of Fannie and Freddie, standing ready to buy surplus conforming mortgages and issue their own debt, which could be held by banks with a surplus of retail deposits or by other investors. The key to doing this successfully was diversification. Much as monolines took advantage of diversification of risk across different cities and counties, so the GSEs took advantage of the diversification of mortgage credit risk across different states and regions. Provided there was no nationwide collapse in the housing market the debt of Fannie and Freddie remained extremely safe, in fact in great demand, since it was perceived as benefiting from the support of government even though there was no legal obligation for the US government to protect Fannie and Freddie from bankruptcy.

In the 1980s Fannie and Freddie pioneered mortgage-backed securitization. These were not the tranched mortgage-backed securities later used to finance sub-prime and other mortgage lending not eligible for purchase by Fannie and Freddie. The agency securitizations are mostly relatively simple 'pass-through' structures in which all holders have the same claim on the underlying mortgage pool. But the key feature – which meant that purchasers did not hesitate to buy these mortgage-backed securities – was that Fannie and Freddie guaranteed the credit risk on the underlying pool. There had been no nationwide mortgage market crisis since the 1930s and the GSEs enjoyed at least implicit government support, so for both these reasons the Fannie and Freddie agency MBS were regarded as free of credit risk and sold for a high price and a correspondingly low yield.

All this meant that Fannie and Freddie enjoyed a virtual licence to print money, at least as long as there was no nationwide housing and mortgage market crisis. Year after year they were in effect collecting substantial 'premiums' for underwriting credit risk on good-quality conforming mortgages, generating revenues that were more than enough to cover any defaults on their portfolio. In practice these premiums appeared in their accounts in various different forms, as interest margins, the spread between the interest rates on the mortgages they owned and the cost of their debt finance and fee income from providing guarantees on their issued MBS.

The big problem was their limited capital. The GSEs, whether by purchasing mortgages and funding them either on balance sheet or through securitizations, supply the majority of financing for US residential mortgages. Together, on and off balance sheet, the two GSEs hold or guarantee $5.1 trillion of residential mortgages of the total $11.1 trillion of US mortgages outstanding. Their shareholder capital, at end-2007 before they were badly hit by the crisis, was $71 billion, not much more than 1 per cent of the mortgage stock they guaranteed. In addition, in pursuit of more income, they were taking on additional mortgage market and other related risks. Little wonder that a severe nationwide downturn in housing and mortgage markets threatens their solvency.

How did Fannie and Freddie end up taking on so much credit risk on so small a capital base? This was another example of poor governance, although these particular governance problems have long historical roots. Fannie Mae was originally created by the Roosevelt administration in 1938 as a government-owned corporation buying residential mortgages. In 1968, for budgetary reasons, the administration of Lyndon B. Johnson sold the equity of Fannie Mae to private stockholders. Freddie Mac was created in 1970 as a competitor and in 1989 was also listed.

This combination of private ownership with a public mission to provide funding and support the secondary market for US mortgages worked extraordinarily poorly. Properly fulfilling their public mission would have required Fannie and Freddie to remain very highly capitalized and to concentrate their resources on complementing the supply of private-sector funds to the mortgage market. Instead, they were subject to all the usual pressures from private shareholders to boost their revenues and to pay out income as dividends instead of retaining it as capital. This led Fannie and Freddie to compete directly with private-sector financial institutions and to push into a range of further profitable but risky housing-related exposures.

These conflicts of interest have been an obvious and growing cause of concern for some years as the scale of Fannie and Freddie's involvement in US mortgage markets grew. But political oversight was lacking, Fannie and Freddie instead running one of the most lavishly funded lobbying machines on Capitol Hill and successfully resisting all attempts to limit their activities, even when they were both hit by major (but quite separate) accounting scandals which required them to restate their earnings.

One consequence of this poor governance was that Fannie and Freddie became major purchasers of so-called 'private label' mortgage-backed securities – that is, the tranched mortgage-backed securities that were used to finance sub-prime mortgage lending and other 'non-conforming' mortgages that could not be automatically sold to Fannie or Freddie. Freddie in particular built up a vast portfolio, holding some $230 billion on its $800 billion balance sheet! Fannie was more circumspect, holding only $65 billion. Together the agencies were holding about one fifth of the entire market for sub-prime, Alt-A and other securitized non-conforming MBS. In addition they were also investing in commercial MBS, consumer and other ABS, and other structured securities. They were using their access to low-cost funding to pursue high-yield assets, with no concern about the risks this posed to their ability to conduct their principal task of supporting the secondary market for better-quality confirming mortgages.

Fannie and Freddie are taken into 'conservatorship'

Fannie and Freddie had risk exposures similar to those of Bear Stearns, the monoline insurers and AIG. They were all caught out by having too much exposure to illiquid senior structured credit tranches (either directly or through CDS contracts written on those tranches) with too little capital and too much short-term funding. AIG and Fannie and Freddie were also exposed directly to mortgage default risk, AIG because it held a number of lower-quality tranches of mortgage-backed securities without adequate risk controls, and Fannie and Freddie because it was their job to hold or guarantee residential mortgages. They all assumed, wrongly, that a nationwide housing market crash could never happen. They were all also so greatly leveraged that when this shock materialized they were overwhelmed.

In the case of Fannie and Freddie the critical developments occurred between July and September 2008. Further write-downs on their large portfolios of sub-prime and other structured securities revealed in their second-quarter results created serious doubts about their credit-worthiness, threatening to cut them off from the private funding markets on which their mortgage purchase programmes rely. To deal with this Treasury Secretary Hank Paulson announced on 13 July an unlimited extension of their borrowing lines from the US Treasury until the end of 2009 (the GSE charters allow the Treasury to lend each of them only $2.2 billion), a decision ratified by Congress in the end-July Housing Finance Reform Act. That act also merged the Office of Federal Housing Enterprise Oversight with the Federal Housing Finance Board, to form a single regulatory body, the Federal Housing Finance Agency, overseeing both the GSEs and the Federal System of Home Loan Banks.

These measures were not enough to ensure the GSEs' continued access to the debt markets. Losses and write-downs rose further. By the time of its third-quarter results Fannie had acknowledged credit-related losses and write-downs of about $40 billion, mostly in the third quarter and reducing net worth from $44 billion to only $9 billion. The situation at Freddie was still worse, with nine-month credit-related losses and write-downs of $53 billion, reducing its balance sheet net worth to a negative $14 billion (some $22 billion of these write-downs were temporary valuation falls in what were classified as 'available for sale securities' and so did not reduce profits, but these still reduce net worth).

Under the GSE charter, negative net worth would have required the new regulator, the Federal Housing Finance Agency, to put Freddie into receivership. Both GSEs would have lost access to private-sector funding, in turn cutting off their supply of finance to the already deeply depressed US housing market. The only other available course of action, taken on 6 September 2008, was for the Federal Housing Finance Agency, with the approval of the US Treasury, to take both Fannie and Freddie into 'conservatorship'. This means the regulator taking control from shareholders for an indefinite period. Fannie CEO Daniel Mudd and chairman of the board Stephen Ashley resigned, to be replaced by Herbert Allison (CEO) and Philip Laskawy (non-executive chairman of the board). Freddie CEO and chairman Richard Syron resigned, to be replaced by John Koskinen as non-executive chair and David M. Moffett as CEO. Other senior officers also resigned.

Two further measures accompanied this conservatorship. First, the US Treasury undertook to provide open capital support to Fannie and Freddie, providing sufficient cash as needed for the foreseeable future to maintain positive net worth. In return for this cash the US Treasury is taking preference shares paying a dividend of 10 per cent per year, for the amount of subscribed capital plus $1 billion. Second, the US Treasury is also given twenty-year 'warrants' to purchase 80 per cent of the shares of Fannie and Freddie for a nominal sum – the shareholders are effectively giving up to government 80 per cent of their shareholding. Finally, both Fannie and Freddie are being given access to a further permanent line of credit from the US Federal Reserve, enabling them to borrow directly against their mortgage-backed securities. If Fannie and Freddie are returned to profitability then shareholders would recover some value, and the 80 per cent government holding might then be sold to private investors. But this will certainly not happen at any time soon.

Accompanying this dramatic move – the US government seizing control of Fannie and Freddie from existing shareholders – are requirements on them first to increase and then later reduce their issue and holdings of mortgage-backed securities. In the near future they are expected to increase their purchases of mortgages to support the US housing market and then, from 2010 onwards, to reduce them by 10 per cent per annum, with the intention that this should occur through natural run-off as mortgages are repaid.

Both Fannie and Freddie remain on life support. The 2008 fourth quarter results were no better, with an additional $36 billion of losses and write-downs in the two institutions. Freddie Mac in particular continues to be squeezed by falls in the market value of its very large portfolios of private label MBSs. Its balance sheet reveals an additional $24 billion of write-downs that were not taken through the income statement (because they do not reflect underlying credit impairment) but which still require an injection of US government funding to maintain their minimum balance sheet capital.

But the same conclusion can be drawn for Fannie and Freddie as for AIG, Citigroup and all the other recipients of US taxpayer funds. This money is an essential investment to ensure the stabilization and eventual recovery of the US financial and economic system. In all likelihood yet more public money will be required. But somewhat paradoxically, it would be a terrible waste of taxpayer funds to provide this support stintingly and grudgingly. Why? Because failing now to maintain their balance sheets will lead to much deeper economic downturn than is already taking place and very much higher ultimate costs to the taxpayer.

The wider picture – not quite so bad

The headlines during 2008 were very bad. But the scale of losses reported by the institutions that dominated the headlines – UBS, Merrill Lynch, Citigroup, AIG and Fannie Mae and Freddie Mac – has been a good deal worse than for the banking industry as a whole, greater than the average by a factor of around three. The three banks – UBS, Merrill Lynch and Citigroup – hold less than 10 per cent of the assets of the world's top 50 banks but account for about 20 per cent of aggregate bank credit losses and write-downs since the summer of 2007. Non-bank losses are even more concentrated, in the monoline insurance industry and at AIG.

A simple and effective yardstick for comparing different banks is to look at the ratio of credit-related losses to annual pre-tax profit before the credit crisis. The outcome of this exercise is shown in Table 8.1. The comparison is restricted to the world's twenty-five largest banks; smaller banks such as IKB and Sachsen Landesbank, that lost several times their annual earnings, are not included. The table also incudes AIG, Fannie Mae, Freddie Mac and Lehman Brothers.

The entries in this table are ranked according to the ratio of total credit losses and write-downs to 2006 pre-tax earnings (the right-hand column). The first six institutions in this table form a 'list of shame' – institutions that managed their risk exposures so badly that losses

Table 8.1. *Major bank credit losses and write-downs compared with pre-tax earnings*

| Bank | Origin | Credit losses and write-downs, 2007–8 | | Ratio to 2006 pre-tax earnings |
| | | Taken in profit and loss | Total | |
		($ billion)		
Freddie Mac	US	64	88	22.2
Fannie Mae	US	65	71	15.3
AIG (insurance)	US	146	168	7.7
Merrill Lynch	US	63	73	7.5
UBS	Switzerland	56	56	5.5
Lehman Brothers	US	30	30	5.0
Fortis	Belgium/ Netherlands	13	34	4.3
HBOS	UK	29	42	4.0
Citigroup	US	104	114	4.0
HSBC	UK	42	61	2.9
JP Morgan	US	41	41	2.8
ING	Netherlands	7	38	2.6
Deutsche Bank	Germany	23	30	2.4
Barclays	UK	27	30	2.3
UniCredit	Italy	22	26	2.1
Morgan Stanley	US	19	19	2.1
Royal Bank of Scotland	UK	35	36	2.1
BNP Paribas	France	22	29	1.9
Bank of America	US	45	57	1.8
Credit Suisse	Switzerland	14	19	1.5
Credit Agricole	France	7	14	1.4
Mizuhuo Financial Group	Japan	9	9	1.4
Mitsubishi UFJ Financial Group Inc	Japan	10	13	1.3
ICBC	China	13	13	1.3
Sumitomo Mitsui Finance	Japan	8	9	1.2

Table 8.1. (*cont.*)

| | | Credit losses and write-downs, 2007–8 | | |
| | | Taken in profit and loss | Total | Ratio to 2006 pre-tax |
Bank	Origin	($ billion)		earnings
Santander	Spain	14	17	1.1
Société Générale	France	6	11	0.9
Goldman Sachs	US	10	10	0.7
Total		941	1,151	

Source: Annual reports, Bankscope, author's calculations. Includes the world's 25 largest banks by dollar assets (Bankscope global format) plus Fannie Mae, Freddie Mac, Lehman and AIG. Lehman and Fortis estimates only.

rose to more than five times their annual earnings in the first eighteen months of the credit crisis. Fannie and Freddie top this list, followed by AIG and Merrill Lynch and then UBS and Lehman. Citigroup and the UK bank HBOS follow a little way behind.

There are many lessons to be learned from this table. The first is that, although the financial crisis has been concentrated in the United States, it is far from just being a US crisis. Take for example HBOS, the UK bank with the largest credit losses relative to the size of its business. Its core activity is residential mortgage lending, in which it is the UK market leader. But during the recent UK property boom it rapidly expanded its corporate business, lending large sums to property developers, construction companies, hotel groups and other firms with exposure to residential and commercial property markets.

By 2008 it had built up a total corporate loan book of some £116 billion, nearly half as big as its mortgage portfolio. In the second half of 2008 there was a very high level of losses on this portfolio, of over £6 billion – half the impairment provisions of the entire group. This was the home-grown part of their problems. In addition HBOS also had substantial losses on holdings of US mortgage-backed and other structured credit securities. In September 2008 HBOS agreed to a merger with the much sounder UK bank Lloyds-TSB, but the scale of loss has been so large that the new merged group has still required substantial recapitalization from the UK government, which by March 2009 held a majority of the equity capital.

Other UK banks with relatively high levels of credit losses were HSBC, Barclays and Royal Bank of Scotland (RBS).

Perhaps surprisingly, of these three banks it is the one with the lowest exposure to credit problems, RBS, that is in the greatest difficulties and is now over 70 per cent owned by the British government. In fact the RBS credit exposures are very similar to those of its close competitors HSBC and Barclays. It was exposed to US mortgage-backed and structured securities through its global markets division. This exposure can be traced back to a US business, Greenwich Capital Management, inherited when RBS acquired another UK bank, NatWest. But the critical decision that undermined RBS was its 2007 cash acquisition of a part of the Netherlands bank ABN-AMRO, a deal in which it paid a very high price at the top of the market just before the credit crisis broke. Perhaps foolishly, it declared this deal to be a huge success before it was even integrated into the business, writing the excess it paid over book value into its own balance sheet as a notional asset, what accountants call 'goodwill'. But in the crisis most of this goodwill has had to be written off, creating the largest loss in UK corporate history and forcing RBS to turn to the UK government for new capital.

Other leading banks, even those focused on securities and new credit markets, fared rather better. Take for example Deutsche Bank, the German bank that has grown to become one of the largest investment banking operations in the world (the key to achieving this strategic goal was establishing itself in the United States through its acquisition of the US investment bank Bankers Trust). Deutsche Bank has also suffered substantial losses in the credit crisis, reporting write-downs of over \$23 billion. This is a large sum of money, equivalent to around two years of pre-tax earnings, but much smaller in relation to pre-tax earnings than those of banks at the head of this 'list of shame'.

The difference is not because Deutsche Bank was cautious and conservative, eschewing involvement in the new credit markets. Far from this being the case, Deutsche's policy was to embrace financial innovation. By 2005, new instruments including credit structuring accounted for around 50 per cent of group profits, a higher proportion than in any other major bank worldwide. Deutsche could not avoid some losses and write-downs when these markets turned bad.

But Deutsche, unlike, say, UBS, understood better and managed more effectively its exposures to these new credit instruments. While Deutsche manufactured and sold many mortgage-backed and structured credit securities, it held relatively few in its own trading and treasury portfolios. It realized that the ratings of the dubious 'restructured' products, such as the mezzanine ABS-CDOs on which Merrill and UBS lost so much money, were unreliable and so avoided these especially risky assets.

In the worst-performing banks increasing returns were rewarded without management questioning the risks taken in order to achieve those returns. In contrast, the senior staff of better-performing banks such as Deutsche took this responsibility much more seriously, ensuring they were well informed about portfolio credit quality and other risks and that individual exposure decisions were subject to detailed review, not simply assessed using the output of a 'black box' computer model. A major challenge for regulators and investors in future, in order to avoid a repeat of current problems, is ensuring that the management of all banks do likewise.

Another revealing case that can be highlighted from this table is that of the Netherlands-based bank ING. There are two measures of credit losses and write-downs in the table, in the third and fourth columns. In the case of ING these two measures are very different, the credit losses taken through profit and loss being only $7 billion – in relation to income among the smallest of any of these banks. But the total losses and write-downs, including also those taken on the balance sheet as a temporary reduction in market value, are $38 billion – among the highest in Europe.

What does this mean? ING is in fact a conservative institution that has not exposed itself much to risky categories of borrowing. But it has an internet banking subsidiary ING-Direct offering high-interest savings accounts in many European countries, including the United Kingdom.[2] The challenge for ING direct was that it had many depositors but no lending business, so it invested much of its surplus funds in the very safest MBS and structured credit securities.

These were not high-risk exposures. The senior AAA notes issued

---

[2] UK readers likely recall their lively and tuneful advertising, including, I believe, a toe tapping 1950s penny whistle jive by the South African kwela musician Spokes Mashiyane, a major figure in African popular music.

by Countrywide ABS 2006-19 and described in Chapter 4 are typical of the kinds of investment they were making and, as we have seen, there is little prospect of them defaulting. For this reason it has been quite justifiable for ING not to take any changes in mark to market values of these securities as a loss in their income statement. But the ING balance sheet was still being undermined by the collapse of liquidity and market prices for these and similar securities, because these declines were recognized as declines in their equity capital.

The government of the Netherlands, sensibly, dealt with this situation by using its own balance sheet to underwrite ING's exposure, offering ING insurance on terms similar to those provided by the US government to Citigroup. Where the crisis is undermining the values of safe and good-quality securities, then insurance is a sensible government response, and can make a small profit to boot. Does Table 8.1 reveal the complete picture about bank losses? The answer, unfortunately, is no. The underlying accounting statements are fallible. Just as risk controls can fail, so, too, can accounting and audit processes. The problems at some, less well-run banks, could eventually turn out to be worse than those revealed here.

But the main reason why this table does not give us the complete picture is not accounting error; it is simply that accounting statements are backward-looking, not forward-looking. There will be a deep global recession in 2009, very possibly continuing into 2010 and even beyond. As a result trading losses, provisions for loan losses and write-downs will get still worse in most banks before they get better. Banks are trying to anticipate this by making conservative provisions for loan losses, and when the economy does eventually recover their performance will quickly turn round. But in the meantime there could be much higher losses to come. Dealing with these future banking-sector problems is the greatest challenge now facing policymakers.

The losses are manageable

Since the credit crisis first broke in summer 2007 there has been a rising tide of credit-related losses and write-downs, by the end of 2008 totalling well over $1,000 billion worldwide (see Table 8.1) and set to rise a good deal further still in months to come (as projected in Table 2.3). The situation is difficult, but there are good reasons for believing that these losses are manageable.

The underlying fundamental credit losses (although these will rise much higher) are perhaps only half of total losses. Fundamental credit losses are the anticipated future loss (in the banker's jargon 'impairment') of mortgages and other loans, arising when a borrower falls behind with payments of interest or principal – whether these loans are held on balance sheet or are packaged within structured mortgage and asset-backed securities. Whenever a loan is impaired bankers have to make a judgement about the eventual recoveries and make a loan loss provision for the difference between money owed and money recovered.

Consider, for example, a borrower some months behind on the payments on a $200,000 mortgage. The lender will make an estimate of how much money will be recovered after foreclosing and then eventually selling the house. If this expected recovery is, say, $120,000, the impairment on this particular loan is $80,000 or 40 per cent. Of course, not all loans fall into arrears. If, say, one in ten loans is in arrears, and recovery is 40 per cent, then the impairment on the portfolio is only one tenth of 40 per cent – that is, 4 per cent.

Towards the end of 2008, around $500 billion or so of the loan losses and write-downs acknowledged so far can be attributed to fundamental credit impairment. Lenders with substantial exposure to the US sub-prime and other non-conforming mortgage markets – for example Countrywide – have made loan loss provisions of around 3 per cent of their loan portfolio. Underlying impairment in some US mortgage-backed securities has been somewhat higher. There have also been growing impairments on speculative-grade corporate exposures such as leveraged loans.

But impairment to date on other loan exposures – for example to conforming prime mortgage borrowers or better-quality corporate borrowers – remains less than 1 per cent. Although the world economy is weakening rapidly, outside the riskier US mortgage markets and speculative-grade corporate lending, fundamental loan losses rates still remain fairly low. Provided there is no global economic collapse on the scale of the 1930s, fundamental credit losses could easily rise to $800 billion or, if there is a deep downturn, even the $1,600 billion shown in Table 2.3. But losses on this scale are still manageable (remember, governments have already committed $7 trillion to address the financial crisis and this support should only be needed to cover the losses that cannot be absorbed by bank shareholders).

Fundamental impairment has not been the only source of credit loss. Around half of the losses and write-downs are illiquidity losses arising because market illiquidity has led to major falls in the 'mark to market' accounting value of financial instruments such as mortgage-backed and other structured securities and also in the value of the derivative contracts such as credit default swaps writing protection on these products. As discussed in Chapter 1, because there is no market on which to value them, these 'mark to market' valuations are usually based on hypothetical, not real, market prices.

Fundamental losses, driven by underlying default, are quite distinct from these additional illiquidity losses – that is, falls in the market value of traded credit instruments amplifying the underlying fundamental credit losses. Additional illiquidity losses have emerged because of the excessive short-term funding of and resulting overhang of illiquid senior tranches of structured credit described in Chapter 6. There are few willing buyers, so prices fall a long way below those suggested by underlying impairment. Because they are not caused by fundamental impairment they can be expected to reverse over time. So it is only necessary to give banks sufficient funding to hold these illiquid assets without being forced to sell them, and eventually the promised payments will be made and the losses recovered (again, of course, assuming that there is no global economic collapse on a scale even greater than the 1930s).

As the Bank of England, for example, has argued in the 2008 issues of its *Financial Stability Report*, the fall in the market value of senior tranches of mortgage-backed and structured products is much too large to be explained by expectations of fundamental losses alone. These illiquidity losses seem to have added several hundred billion dollars to 'write-downs' of trading and security portfolios. Not all of this has contributed to global credit losses, since accountancy rules sometimes allow banks to keep these losses out of their income statements if the fall in market price does not reflect fundamental impairment. But when these assets are held for trading purposes then the losses are an expense on the income statement, so much of these illiquidity losses go straight through on to the 'bottom line'.

So, in conclusion, banking-sector losses, while large, are manageable. The underlying credit problems are very serious in some institutions, but they are simply not large enough across the industry to explain the scale of credit contraction and the subsequent economic downturn. That has to be due, in large part, to other factors, especially the feedback loops illustrated in Figure 1.1 that have led to the breakdown of bank wholesale funding markets and the deteriorating prospects for bank lending.

Further reading

There are now many web and print articles and an increasing number of books on the problems of individual institutions described in this chapter. The standard of this material is very uneven. These notes mention two sources that I have found especially informative. The UBS report to shareholders (www.ubs.com/1/e/investors/shareholder-report/remediation.html) is essential reading on the UBS case. William D. Cohan's *House of Cards* (Doubleday, 2009) is a vivid account of the long history and sudden demise of Bear Stearns. He also has a useful epilogue on the collapse of Lehman Brothers. The further reading listed at the end of Chapter 6 is also relevant to this chapter. Many other accounts will be published, but I urge readers not to be too swayed by alarmism. The problems of the banks are serious. Many people will exaggerate them still further in order to try and attract more attention and sell their own accounts of what has gone on. But the best and most insightful accounts are those, like Cohan, that retain a sense of proportion.

9 | *Central banks and money markets*

Chapter 10 describes the global bank run that began in September 2008 and the subsequent government interventions that followed. But to understand those events, and the further actions that policymakers can still take to resolve the problems of the banks and the wider economy, we need first to take a close look at the central banks, at their operations in the markets for short-term money, and how they can respond to a financial crisis.

We look first at the money markets where banks borrow and lend short term and at how these markets have been dislocated by the crisis. We then examine monetary operations, contrasting the usual 'orthodox' approach to monetary policy where the central bank targets the short-term rate of interest with the possibility of employing an 'unorthodox' approach to monetary policy, where the central bank instead concentrates on expansion of its balance sheet and the purchase of financial assets.

Finally this chapter looks at the various actions that central banks can take in a financial crisis, namely liquidity provision (increasing balances in commercial bank reserve accounts with the central bank), extended maturity 'term lending' and, in the extreme situation of a systemic banking panic, acting as 'lender of last resort'. It examines the employment of these tools in the first year of the crisis, from August 2007 until early September 2008.

This chapter makes one key point that is not as widely understood as it should be. Central banks are a critical source of support to institutions that are having difficulty accessing funding in the money markets, but central banks cannot fund the entire banking sector on their own (or at least can do so only to a very limited degree by selling down their own securities portfolios). Their role in a crisis is the reallocation of funds between banks. Funds or guarantees of funding for the entire banking sector have to come from government, not the central bank.

Banks need access to short-term borrowing

Banks make payments every day to other banks. They need to do this in order to complete (or 'settle') customer payments to the customers at the other bank. The largest payments of millions of dollars or more are settled individually between banks. Other payments are bundled together and then settled using a single net interbank payment.

The usual method of making these interbank payments is as a transfer on the reserve accounts of the central bank – that is, just as customers need an account with a bank in order to make and receive payments, a bank itself needs an account with the central bank in order to make the payments owed to other banks and receive the payments due from other banks.

For the payment to go through, the bank must either have sufficient funds in the account it holds with the central bank or be able to borrow more. For the great bulk of smaller payments this is not an issue. Every hour and every day there are a very large number of routine transactions passing between banks, for example business payments by firms to their suppliers, salaries paid to employees, or consumer purchases made in shops or online. But while the overall flows of money of this kind are very large, roughly the same amount of money goes both in and out of each bank, and the net flow of these payments between banks largely cancels out.

But some access to liquidity (i.e. reserves with the central bank or the ability to borrow more) is still essential. While smaller routine payments mostly cancel out over time, there are still fairly substantial aggregate seasonal flows – for example around Christmas – and also some major large-value payments that are not cancelled out by other payments in the opposite direction. Many of these large payments originate in the financial markets, such as the stock exchange or the markets for trading of foreign currencies. For example, when a large firm issues securities such as stock or bonds, then one bank – where the firm issuing the securities deposits money – receives substantial payments from other banks – where the purchasers of the securities hold their bank accounts. Eventually this newly raised money is spent and ends up being spread around the banking system, but this takes time.

Other financial market transactions can also create large interbank payments flows, for example the issue of government bonds or the settlement of financial contracts such as futures (standardized contracts to buy or sell financial securities and commodities at specified future dates). Many financial market transactions of these kinds are fairly predictable, giving banks some prior notice of the resulting payment flows so that they can plan their liquidity needs ahead of time. Other large-value private transactions – for example the sale of a block of securities by a major investor, speculative transactions in foreign exchange markets or gains or losses and resulting margin payments by a trading institution such as a hedge fund – occur without prior notice and banks must have enough free funds or access to funds in order to cope with possibly large payments of this kind to other banks.

The consequence of such large, occasional, unanticipated payment flows is that banks face a liquidity problem similar to that faced by their own customers. They then need to borrow short term in order to make payments to other banks, in anticipation of payments that they will themselves receive later on in the following days and weeks.

Banks borrow and lend liquidity in the money markets

In normal times commercial banks raise short-term money from investors on what are known as the 'money markets'. The plural 'money markets' is required because these are several closely linked markets where money is borrowed and lent short term between large institutions. Before the crisis all money market interest rates moved closely together. After the crisis there were large and fluctuating differentials between the interest rates on different types of money market loan.

In normal times the money markets are efficient and competitive, providing participants with a low-cost source for borrowing money short term and a good return on lending money short term. Most banks use the money markets, either overnight or for a few days or weeks, for borrowing. Some banks do relatively little money market borrowing, those that are 'deposit rich' – attracting more money from customer deposits than they can profitably use for customer lending – but these liquid banks also use the money markets as a place for temporarily parking their surplus funds.

Money markets are not just for banks. There are many other lenders in these markets, including governments, central banks, large companies, institutional investors such as pension funds and insurance companies, and investment funds of many kinds – including hedge funds, short-term fixed income funds and 'money market mutuals' (these funds are a way for individuals and companies to access the money markets without directly holding money market instruments). Whenever a bank, a large financial institution, a large company or a major investor decides to hold cash – instead of long-term financial assets such as bonds or stocks – they do so by investing in the money markets. Whenever they want to borrow cash they also go to the money markets.

In the United States the main market for overnight unsecured inter-bank lending is the federal funds market (or Fed funds for short), an established market with specialized dealers in which banks either lend and borrow deposits with the Federal Reserve or with each other. It is common for smaller banks in the United States to deposit surplus funds with larger institutions through the Fed funds market, with these overnight deposits rolled over automatically every day. But they have a choice. Banks can also deposit money overnight in the New York money markets where both banks and non-banks supply short-term funds. In other financial centres there is no separate bank-to-bank market, there is instead a market for unsecured deposits of money with participation by both bank and non-bank lenders.

What return do banks or other investors get for placing cash in these money markets? A bank advertises the interest rate it offers on retail accounts, for example in newspapers, on the internet or in branches. Wholesale money market deposit rates have no such advertised rates. Every wholesale deposit has its own individual interest rate agreed between the investor making the deposit and the bank taking the money. These agreed rates change all the time, depending on conditions in money markets. This is an 'over the counter' market and there is no single market price such as is found on an exchange. But there is one measure of average returns more widely used than any other. This is the British Bankers Association London Interbank Offered Rate or, as it more usually called, Libor.

Libor is an index of average money market interest rates, compiled from returns by a small panel of banks estimating the interest rates they would have to pay each day for money offered for deposit by other banks in the London markets, the most liquid and competitive money markets in the world.[1] Libor rates are published daily by the

[1] Each contributing bank is asked to tell the British Bankers' Association 'the rate
    at which it could borrow funds, were it to do so by asking for and then accept-
    ing inter-bank offers in reasonable market size just prior to 11.00 am each day',
    at www.bba.org.uk/bba/jsp/polopoly.jsp?d=225&a=1413&artpage=3.

British Bankers Association for a range of maturities (from overnight to one year) and for several currencies, including the Japanese yen, the US dollar and the euro as well as the UK pound sterling. Another widely quoted index is Euribor, a different index of average euro inter-bank lending rates published by the European Banking Federation. Euribor is based on a much larger panel so arguably is more reliable, but Euribor and Libor euro interest rates are similar, the two indices usually tracking each other fairly closely.

The Libor indices are the most widely used measures of unsecured money market rates of interest, but they have to be interpreted care-fully. There is relatively little unsecured lending in the money markets at the longer money market maturities, such as three or six months. Moreover, they are somewhat crude measures, based on returns from a small sample of banks giving their opinion about what rate would be offered to them in the money market were they to seek deposits.

Banks borrow on a secured basis in the money markets using repo

Libor rates are *unsecured*. What does this mean? Suppose that a bank taking the money offered on deposit were to go bankrupt before the loan was due for repayment. The bank or other lender making the deposit would not get the money back as promised, instead becoming a general creditor in the bankruptcy, so that they have to wait until the assets of the bank are sold and the proceeds divided among all the different creditors of the bank.

The alternative for an investor placing money in the markets is a *secured* deposit. To avoid the risk of default, even if it is fairly small, banks and other money market participants often prefer where they can to lend in the money markets on a secured basis, typically using the 'sale and repurchase agreement' (repo).

As Chapter 1 explained, a repo is of form of secured loan in which the borrower purchases a safe financial security such as a short-term government bond, with a contractual agreement to buy it back later at a slightly higher price. If the borrower fails to honour this agreement then the lender can sell the bond and so recover their money.

Because it is secured against a financial asset, the rate of interest for money lent using a good collateral repo is less than for unsecured money market lending. Another widely used form of secured money

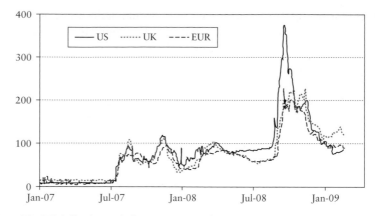

Note: The US dollar line only begins in November 2007 because Bloomberg does not provide a US dollar repo prior to that date.

Figure 9.1. Libor vs. good collateral repo rates (three-month).
Source: Bloomberg.

market lending is the asset-backed commercial paper described in Chapter 6, issued by off balance sheet conduits and structured investment vehicles. This is often secured on structured credit securities. The quality of the collateral makes a difference. When investors are concerned about the quality, then the interest rate on asset-backed commercial paper can be much higher than on the best collateral repo.

The spread between unsecured Libor and secured repo

Normally the return on unsecured lending has been only slightly above that on secured lending, but the credit crisis has fundamentally changed the relationship between the two (Figure 9.1).

Figure 9.1 compares three-month Libor rates with three-month repo rates secured against such good-quality collateral, from the end of October 2006 until the end of November 2008, in three of the major international currencies. This figure provides a vivid illustration of the dislocating impact of the credit crisis on money markets.

Before the crisis erupted in August 2007 the difference between these two money market rates – the relatively low secured repo lending rate and the somewhat higher unsecured Libor rate – remained very small, three-month Libor rates being no more than 0.2 per cent higher than the three-month good collateral repo rate. This meant that if unsecured money was being offered in the London money markets at, say, 5 per cent per annum over a three-month period, then by putting up good-quality collateral such as a Treasury bill a bank could borrow at a little over 4.8 per cent for the same length of time. A bank that had such good collateral to spare would of course prefer secured borrowing, since it is a little cheaper, but the difference in these interest rates is not so large as to make much difference to a bank's business decisions.

After the crisis erupted in August 2007 a large and fluctuating gap between unsecured Libor rates and secured repo lending rates emerged. For more than a year, until September 2008, this funding gap averaged around 0.75 per cent and also moved up and down substantially, sometimes falling a little below 0.5 per cent and sometimes rising to over 1 per cent.

Then, in September 2008, came the systemic run on the world's banks that followed the bankruptcy of Lehman Brothers. The gap between unsecured and secured lending rates rose very much higher, climbing to around 2 per cent for British sterling and the euro and even higher for the US dollar, where it peaked at over 3½ per cent before slowly falling back. All these spreads have remained around 100 basis points in the first months of 2009.

Lack of good collateral removed liquidity from the money markets

Many journalists attribute this dislocation of money markets and the jump of Libor spreads shown in Figure 9.1 to the reluctance of banks to lend to each other. This is a bit of an oversimplification. Many of the lenders in money markets are not banks but other institutions, such as money market mutuals, large companies and investment funds. The phrase also fails to explain why lenders are 'reluctant' to lend to each other. This has in part been because lenders demand a credit spread to compensate for the risk of default. But it has also been due to greater illiquidity in unsecured money markets, and a resulting shift in the balance of power from borrowers to lenders. When money markets were liquid there were very many lenders competing (making offers) to deposit funds at each bank, and borrowers could pick and choose from the crowd and so get very fine rates. Lenders in return had to put in a lot of sweat, making many offers, to find the best bargain.

When doubts emerged about the safety and security of banks the balance changed. Lenders suddenly had to exercise a lot more 'due diligence' – that is, checking that the banks to which they offered funds were sound – and as a result they would make fewer offers. But this was actually to the benefit of lenders, because banks had fewer offers from which to choose and with less competition would get less fine rates.

The 'reluctance to lend' story also masks another aspect of the market dislocation: the inability of banks to provide collateral to obtain secured borrowing. Reluctance to lend on an unsecured basis does not matter so much to borrowing banks if they have the alternative of borrowing on a secured basis. The 'liquidity' impact of reluctance to lend is short-circuited, and provided banks have plenty of collateral on which they can borrow they can then afford to be choosy about offers of unsecured funding. The unsecured market remains liquid even though lenders are concerned about credit risk.

But this alternative disappeared because of the maturity mismatch ('borrowing short and lending long') of many banks created by their strategy of holding relatively high-yield but safe senior structured credit tranches, financed using short-term money market borrowing.

This maturity mismatch and the resulting positive feedback loop illustrated in Figure 1.1 (fall of value → withdrawal of funding→ illiquidity → fall of value) caused the collapse of liquidity in structured credit markets. The resulting illiquidity of the markets for structured credit then spilled over into illiquidity in unsecured money markets because banks no longer had the alternative of using structured credit as money market repo collateral. This then led to increases of uncollateralized lending rates, because the bargaining power of borrowers (their ability to turn down offers) is weakened when they no longer have the alternative of secured borrowing, and led also – mostly at very short maturities – to increases in unsecured borrowing.

It is difficult to disentangle the impact of money market illiquidity and the risk of default on the Libor spreads shown in Figure 9.1. My own guess, for what it is worth, is that the most of the rise of spreads is due to illiquidity, mainly because spreads did not fall by very much in the week of 8 October, when the UK government and other governments across Europe (and later the US government) announced that they would provide capital to banks to prevent their insolvency. This support reduced concern about bank insolvency, but, as Figure

9.1 indicates, spreads, at least in the euro and sterling, did not come down by very much. US spreads did come down quite a lot during November, from very high levels, so this may have been a reduction of perceived default risk for banks borrowing dollars in London.

But whether or not the spreads reflect illiquidity or perceived default risk, it remains true that restoring liquidity to structured credit markets is absolutely critical to restoring liquidity to bank funding markets; only in this way will banks be able to borrow freely short term without paying substantial penalties or relying on uncomfortably short borrowing maturities.

Orthodox monetary policy

Before looking at how central banks responded to these dislocations of money markets, we can look first at how central banks conduct monetary policy. The usual 'orthodox' approach works as follows. Central banks set a target rate for short-term interest rates – such as the Federal Reserve's Federal funds target rate, the Bank of England bank rate or the European Central Bank main financing operations minimum bid rate. Then, as explained below, they provide banks with just enough central bank money in their reserve accounts to keep short-term market interest rates in line with this target. Finally, in order to guide market and investor expectations, central banks make a considerable effort to explain their views on the future course of the economy and of their target interest rate. Very often nowadays they also have an explicit target for inflation.

Orthodox monetary policy of this kind has been extraordinarily successful. It is how central banks finally tamed the tiger of inflation that so damaged the world economy in the 1970s and the 1980s. In particular, they learned how to guide and control effectively expectations of inflation. This was a major breakthrough. If rising inflation leads to expectations of even higher inflation yet to come, the only way to bring it under control – the approach famously pursued by the Thatcher government in the United Kingdom in the early 1980s – is deliberately to engineer a deep economic recession. Controlling inflation is very costly.

If, instead, investors, traders, businessmen and consumers expect the central bank to respond firmly with higher interest rates and for inflation to then fall quickly back to a moderate level, then it is much easier to control inflation. Quite small increases in interest rates can be enough to bring inflation back down towards the desired target. As it is expressed in the jargon of monetary policy, this means that inflation expectations do not become 'embedded'. Inflation then responds rapidly to monetary policy, interest rates may sometimes have to be increased sharply but they come back down quickly, and the costs of controlling inflation in terms of higher unemployment or lost output are low.

The implementation of orthodox monetary policy

How do central bank operations keep market interest rates close to the target set by the central bank? This is very simple. The reserves held by commercial banks with the central bank play a role in managing payments flows similar to the notes we keep in our own wallets or purses for managing small occasional expenditures. Living in London, I hold on average something like £30 in my wallet. When this reserve falls to £5 or £10 I go to a 'hole in the wall' and get out another £50 to top it up. The reason I hold this reserve is to meet unanticipated cash expenditures, perhaps the cost of a haircut or buying lunch or other occasional expenditures where a card is not always accepted or convenient. If I mismanage my reserves, and end up with no cash in my wallet, then I may have to delay my haircut or miss my lunch altogether.

The holding by a commercial bank of reserves with the central bank is much the same. A bank that has too low a level of reserves with the central bank runs the danger of being unable to settle its payments due to other banks, or instead paying a relatively high penalty cost for emergency borrowing in order to be able to settle its payments. A bank that holds too high a level of reserves is missing out on profitable lending and investment opportunities.

If a bank has insufficient reserves it obtains more by borrowing, from banks or non-bank lenders in the money markets or from the central bank. If a bank has excess reserves it lends to other banks in the money markets or reduces borrowing from the central bank. This means that the amount of reserves has a direct impact on market interest rates. If banks face a shortage of reserves they are keen to borrow more and this raises money market rates of interest. If banks have a surplus of reserves this pushes down the market rate of interest.

So the central bank can control market interest rates by supplying the appropriate amount of reserves. If the central bank wishes to lower interest rates then it can create more reserves, reducing the need of commercial banks to borrow from the market and therefore lowering very short-term money market rates of interest. If the central bank wishes to raise short-term market interest rates then it does the opposite, reducing reserves and forcing banks to borrow more from the market.

Thus the implementation of orthodox monetary policy requires only that the central banks supply exactly the amount of bank reserves to the market, through an auction process, demanded by banks at the policy rate of interest. Bank reserve demand can be affected by many factors (see Box 9.1 for some more details). But the central bank does not need to worry too much about why commercial banks demand reserves. All it needs to do is to be ready to supply reserves on demand to enforce its target policy rate.

Box 9.1. How central banks implement monetary policy in practice

Bank demand for holding reserves is also affected by 'reserve requirements' on commercial banks. These work as follows. Commercial banks are required to maintain the level of balances in their reserve accounts with the central bank, averaged over a period known as the 'maintenance period', close to a target level determined by the central bank (the Bank of England is slightly different, UK banks being able to choose their own target level at the outset of each maintenance period). These maintenance periods are fortnightly in the United States, and roughly four-weekly in the United Kingdom and the Eurozone. Central banks impose financial penalties if banks are above or below these averaged reserve requirement targets.

In past times, and in many less developed financial systems even today, reserve requirements were a tax on the banking system. Reserve requirements were set at high levels and no interest was paid on them. This was 'free money' on which the central bank could earn a substantial profit, profits which were then mostly turned over to government.

The central banks in the developed world no longer use reserve requirements as a tax; instead they pay interest on reserves at the target rate of interest (the US Federal Reserve has only recently made this switch, bringing it forward to October 2008 from its planned implementation in 2012 as a further measure to help support the US banking system).

The purpose of reserve requirements nowadays is to help maintain a more stable demand for bank reserves and thus make it easier for central banks to control market rates of interest. But (contrary to what many textbooks suggest) reserve requirements are not essential to monetary policy. If they were abandoned altogether – and they have already been greatly relaxed in response to the current crisis – commercial banks would still need reserves with the central banks. Thus the central banks can always control the overnight rate of interest by supplying sufficient reserves to meet this demand at their target interest rate.

There are further practical complications. For example, the supply of reserves is affected by variations in the circulating stock of notes issued by the central bank, since these notes are issued on demand and their issue reduces central bank reserves. Reserves must also be adjusted to offset the impact of payments flows from banks within the reserves scheme to financial institutions outside the reserves scheme holding accounts with the central bank (e.g. foreign central banks) and, most importantly, for drawdown in any government accounts held at the central bank (since such expenditure has the effect of increasing reserves held by the banking system). Bank demand for reserves also fluctuates, rising in periods of uncertainty when banks fear large payment outflows or are concerned about a possible breakdown in payments infrastructures.

In order to maintain the aggregate supply of reserves in line with demand, central banks conduct what are known as 'open market operations'. They are called this because the central bank makes the reserves available to all banks. If it provides a fixed amount then these are allocated to the highest bidders. If it offers reserves at a fixed price (something central banks only do at very short maturities to exert complete control over the interest rate), then they are offered to all banks.

There are two different types of open market operations: out-right transactions and reserve lending. Central banks conduct outright sales of reserves in exchange for securities, usually government bonds. Since these transactions are settled in central bank money, a sale of a bond reduces central bank reserves while a purchase of a bond increases central bank reserves.

To supply reserves on a temporary basis central banks use 'sale and repurchase agreements' or repo contracts – the same secured lending arrangement widely used in the money markets. These repos can be for several weeks or months (so called 'term' lending), for a short period such as a week or overnight. Most repos are offered to the market on a fixed quantity basis, with banks tendering in order to borrow reserves, and those willing to pay the highest interest rate being successful in their tender.

As well as conducting open market operations, the central bank also lends reserves to individual banks. In order to avoid grid-lock in the daily payments made between banks, central banks provide 'intraday' repo – loans that allow banks to pay other banks but must be repaid by the end of the day – to individual banks without any interest rate being charged. Central banks also offer access to so-called standing borrowing and deposit facili-ties. Individual banks can approach the central bank and ask to borrow reserves, usually overnight, against collateral at a penalty rate above the policy rate.

In the United States this standing facility where banks can borrow is the discount window of the Federal Reserve (www. frbdiscountwindow.org), where they obtain loans paying a little bit more than the current Federal Funds target rate. Suppose this rate is 1 per cent. Eligible banks can borrow for up to ninety days from the discount window paying 25 basis points more than this Federal Funds target rate, i.e. 1.25 per cent. Similarly banks in the United Kingdom borrowing from the standing facilities of the Bank of England pay 25 basis points more than the bank rate set by the Bank of England, and the European Central Bank has been offering a marginal lending facility at a rate 50 basis points above the current level of its monetary policy rate, the main refinancing operations minimum bid rate (although there is an intention to increase this to the more normal 100 basis points).

In practice, banks in the United States and the United Kingdom make little use of these standing facilities. This is for three reasons. First, these loans are usually more expensive than those obtainable on the open market. Second, there are limitations on the acceptability of collateral: where only best-quality collateral such as government bonds is accepted, then a bank may get a better deal offering other collateral to another market participant. Finally, because of 'stigma': in the United States and the United Kingdom use of the standing facilities is publicly disclosed, and as a result banks are reluctant to use them for fear of suggesting that they are no longer financially sound.

In contrast, banks in the euro area make substantial use of the standing facilities provided by the European Central Bank, because these three factors do not apply to the same extent. Money markets in some European countries are relatively thin, with rather few participants, making it more likely that a collateralized loan from the standing facility will be competitively priced. The ECB among all the major central banks has the broadest rules on the acceptability of collateral. It will lend routinely, for example, against senior tranches of mortgage-backed securities. Thus most euro-area banks have acceptable collateral available for borrowing from the standing facilities. Finally, the use of the ECB standing facilities are anonymous, so there is less concern about stigma.

On occasion, central banks have provided collateralized loans to individual banks outside the normal standing facility arrangements, for extended periods or against unusual collateral such as a pool of unsecuritized loans. Such loans, unlike those from the standing facility, are discretionary. The central bank is under no obligation to lend, but, in consultation with the finance ministry and banking regulators, may choose to do so. The emergency lending facility provided by the Bank of England to Northern Rock in September 2007 is an example.

Expectations and the shift to unorthodox monetary policy

This orthodox approach in which the central bank sets a target for interest rates is not the only way for a central bank to conduct monetary policy. In a deep financial crisis such as is now occurring, with expectations of a worsening economic slump, it may become impossible for the central bank to control the feedback loop on the left-hand side of Figure 1.1 just by lowering interest rates. This is particularly likely when, as now, bank access to wholesale funding is limited, with the consequence that banks cannot access the funding to increase lending in response to lower interest rates.

This has recently led to an almost unprecedented development. The Federal Reserve since December 2008 has, at least temporarily, abandoned orthodox monetary policy altogether. It no longer focuses on short-term interest rates (these are left to languish in the range from zero to 0.25 per cent). Instead it is now pursuing what chairman Ben Bernanke has described as a 'credit easing', with massive expansion of bank reserves and the acquisition, backed by US Treasury guarantees, of a wide range of credit risky assets.

This is one form of 'unorthodox' monetary policy, but the term refers to any form of monetary policy by which the central bank shifts from control of interest rates to management of its own balance sheets. Japan in the period 2001–6 also adopted an unorthodox approach to monetary policy, often referred to as 'quantitative easing', where it set targets for the growth of aggregate bank reserves and used the resulting expansion of its balance sheet to purchase government securities. This, they found, did not do much to increase bank lending, however. The Bank of England in the UK has, in March of 2009, announced a similar policy of quantitative easing to that pursued by the Bank of Japan, although it may also purchase corporate securities.

There is a substantial difference of opinion as to which form of unorthodox monetary policy is most effective, the 'quantitative easing' of the Bank of Japan and the Bank of England or the 'credit easing' of the Federal Reserve. Some believe that anything which increases central bank liabilities has an expansionary impact on the economy. According to this way of thinking, central bank liabilities are 'high-powered money' and an increase in high-powered money always leads to more spending and higher aggregate economic output. They believe that quantitative easing will have a powerful impact.

Others believe instead that it matters what the central bank purchases when it increases high-powered money. If it purchases government bonds or Treasury bills, this will not lead to much more spending because this is a substitute of one highly liquid asset for another. There may be some increase in spending, because the purchase of government bonds lowers long-term interest rates, but the impact is unlikely to be large. They argue that unorthodox monetary policy will be much more effective if the increase in high-powered money is used to purchase illiquid assets such as corporate bonds, or leveraged loans or mortgage-backed securities, or even bank shares.

There is little evidence to settle this debate, because quantitative easing has been tried only once before and the Federal Reserve is the first central bank ever to try credit easing. What evidence there is relates to the quantitative easing by the Bank of Japan between 2001 and 2005, and this does not appear to have had much impact on spending and economic activity.

Neither the Federal Reserve nor the Bank of England has yet made up its mind about this debate. Their attitude seems to be, let's try both of these policies and see if either of them works. The shift to 'credit easing' by the Federal Reserve has been followed by the announcement of government bond purchases. Short-term market interest rates in the United Kingdom are also close to zero, but the Bank of England is pursuing an unorthodox monetary policy, primarily through purchase of government bonds with some purchases of corporate bonds. The European Central Bank has continued with orthodox monetary policy implementation.

The world's central banks have little experience of unorthodox monetary policy implementation. There will be plenty of experimentation to find out what works best and it is far too early to say what the impact will be. But one point can be made even now: the shift from orthodox to unorthodox monetary policy does not raise any new funds for banks and so cannot directly offset the breakdown of wholesale funding markets. The total quantity of reserves is still fixed by the central bank and circulates among banks, so that these additional reserves cannot be used for lending. Once trust in banks returns and confidence in the illiquid structured credit securities is restored, banks will have ready access to funding and they can then easily expand their lending. But unorthodox monetary policy implementation only helps indirectly, if central banks purchase structured credit assets to reduce the overhang of illiquid securities on banks' balance sheets or if the central bank lends money directly to bank customers so releasing funds for banks to lend out.

Unorthodox monetary policy does not directly do anything to repair commercial bank balance sheets or help commercial banks with their lending. The only exception to this statement might be if the financial authorities required commercial banks to make a large one-off issue of new equity capital which was then purchased by the central bank, financed through the creation of high-powered money. Unorthodox monetary policy would then be directly recapitalizing bank balance sheets.

Central bank liquidity provision during a financial crisis

In a crisis central bank operations provide banks with a useful, sometimes critical, source of short-term borrowing. This central bank lending is often described by phrases such as 'liquidity provision' or 'liquidity injection'. I have lost count of the number of headlines that have appeared since summer 2007 saying that 'The Bank of England today injected £25 billion of extra liquidity into the banking system to reduce strain in money markets' or similar.

But phrases such as 'liquidity injection' are imprecise and don't explain very well what is going on. Virtually all central bank actions can be described as providing or taking away liquidity. They provide liquidity by increasing their lending to banks or purchasing assets so banks have more reserves. They take away liquidity by reducing their lending to banks or selling assets, so that banks have fewer reserves. This is what central banks do every day, as part of their routine monetary policy implementation as well as in response to a financial crisis.

More useful is to focus on the reasons for, and different mechanisms of, liquidity provision in a financial crisis. One reason has been to offset 'prudential' increases in the demand of commercial banks for holding reserves with the central bank at times of heightened uncertainty. This type of liquidity provision, while not routine, has happened on many occasions. A well-known example was at the end of 1999, when there were concerns about possible 'year 2-K' disruptions of bank computer systems because older programs did not distinguish 2000 from 1900. Because of this, banks wanted to hold unusually large reserves at end-December 1999 in case payment systems were affected.

Central banks responded then with a very public provision of additional reserves, so that the industry concerns about payments disruption were minimized and a spike in overnight interest rates was avoided.[2] Other examples of the many cases of liquidity provision to meet an increased prudential demand for reserves were during the 1987 stock market crash, at the time of the collapse of Long Term Capital Management and in the aftermath of the 9/11 2001 terrorist attacks on the United States.

There have been several similar increases in the 'prudential' demand for holding reserves with the central bank during the current crisis, for example on 9 August and on the following days when investors first lost confidence in structured security investments. On this occasion and again when Bear Stearns failed, central banks had to supply considerable amounts of overnight lending to hold down the level of overnight rates.

A second reason for central bank lending to commercial banks during the crisis has been to help banks cope with the substantial contraction of the maturities at which they have been able to borrow in money markets. With loan-backed securities no longer acceptable as collateral, the banks turned of necessity to unsecured borrowing, but this unsecured borrowing was usually only available overnight or at most at one-week maturity. If they could borrow for one or three months they paid the very high penalty spreads shown in Figure 9.1. As a result the maturity of bank money market liabilities contracted sharply, forcing banks to refinance a large proportion of their balance sheets on a daily or weekly basis. A bank that does end up in this situation will find it especially difficult to obtain good offer rates from private-sector lenders. Moving the central bank part of their lending to longer maturities at least made sure that they did not need to refinance that part of their liabilities.

Bank runs

This maturity contraction of unsecured lending in money markets was only a precursor of a much more damaging collapse of investor confidence, a loss of confidence that led to the large-scale withdrawal of money market bank deposits from many institutions during the global bank run of September and October 2008. This run required central

[2] For a nicely written review of this episode from the perspective of the Reserve Bank of New Zealand, see www.rbnz.govt.nz/research/bulletin/1997_2001/2000mar63_1Hampton.pdf.

banks to offer a third form of liquidity provision, acting as a 'lender of last resort' to stem the systemic banking panic.

Bank runs have a long history, almost as long as that of banking itself. They occurred many times in the eighteenth, nineteenth and early twentieth centuries. Among the largest and best known were those at the time of the failure of English bank Overend Gurney and Company in 1866 and the runs on the Knickerbocker Trust Company and many other US banks during the widespread 'banking panic' of 1907 (that episode was described in Chapter 3).

Banks are, of course, susceptible to runs because they borrow short term in order to hold illiquid assets, loans, which cannot easily be sold. This is the underlying reason for the global bank run of September and October 2008. As we have seen in earlier chapters, banks use many different arrangements for short-term borrowing, taking short-term wholesale loans from other banks, financial institutions and larger companies, as well as demand deposits from retail customers.

Once these providers of funds come to believe – for whatever reason – that their money is no longer safe with the bank, they will withdraw at the first opportunity and hold their funds in a safer form. Such a loss of confidence feeds on itself. The more that short-term funds are withdrawn the closer the bank is to being unable to meet its commitments. Once depositors are aware that a run is taking place they have a very strong incentive to join the run as soon as possible. If the bank fails the depositors at the back of the queue will not get back their money.

Bank loans are hard to sell, exposing banks to risk of a run, because it takes time and expense to assess the quality of bank loans and the prospects for repayment. This is one of the main functions of a bank, to assess the ability of borrowers to repay loans and charge an appropriate interest rate that compensates for the risk of loan default. It is difficult for other banks to assess loan quality, even when they have access to customer repayment histories. So loans must be sold at a deeply discounted price, if they can be sold at all, to overcome the suspicion that their quality is much worse and prospective repayments much lower than the history of past repayment would suggest.

Bank runs today differ from those of the nineteenth century in one critical respect. Then, paper money and gold both accounted for a large share of the total money supply. Investors withdrawing money from the banks were likely to ask either for central bank notes or for gold, thus taking money right out of the banking system. In the twenty-first century bank runs take place through a transfer of deposits from one bank to another. In the global bank run of September and October 2008 money was transferred from the very many banks regarded as unacceptably risky to the rather fewer banks regarded as safe.

Runs usually occur among wholesale, not retail, depositors

Runs are actually rather uncommon in purely retail funded banks. Retail depositors do not follow closely the business affairs of a bank, so that they are among the last to realize that a bank is in difficulties. A run usually starts – as it did in the case of Northern Rock – with the withdrawal of wholesale funds, because the professional money managers looking after these funds pay close attention to the safety of the banks to which they lend money. The bank regulator and the central bank try to deal with any wholesale run before retail investors take fright. The main reason for the depositor run on Northern Rock was the failure of UK authorities to reassure retail investors that their deposits were safe.

Most retail runs are on relatively small institutions with little or no wholesale borrowing. It is then possible for rumours or newspaper reports about substantial losses to trigger a retail run. A recent example with no close connection to the global credit crisis was the 27 September 2008 run on the Hong Kong Bank of East Asia because of rumours of trading losses.

Runs on larger institutions invariably start in wholesale markets. All large banks use wholesale funding and therefore have to maintain the confidence of other banks and the large non-bank lenders and fund managers that provide these funds. The slightest suspicion that a bank might face difficulties repaying these loans will result in its being shut out of the market.

Once wholesale investors lose confidence in a bank's ability to continue attracting new wholesale deposits to replace maturing deposits, a bank's balance sheet rapidly unravels (this is sometimes called a 'silent run' because wholesale depositors do not queue outside a bank branch, rather they simply fail to renew their short-term deposits as they mature). The bank is forced to borrow over shorter and shorter periods. When deposits come up for renewal and three-month money is not available, it must turn to one-month money. When one-month money is no longer available it must turn to one-week money. When one-week money is no longer available it must borrow one day at a time.

A bank in this situation is then teetering on the edge of a precipice. It might still be able to sell some remaining marketable assets – such as government bonds – to survive a few more days. But it will quickly exhaust all such remaining sources of short-term funds. The only remaining course of action is to begin selling off illiquid assets such as loans. These are difficult to value and impossible to sell quickly without having to accept low 'fire sale' prices. If this can be done at all it only brings insolvency closer. So a bank cannot survive a loss of investor confidence for long without an outside intervention – either its acquisition by another, stronger bank or by borrowing from the central bank or from government.

'Lender of last resort'

The notion of a 'lender of last resort' and its importance in preventing bank runs dates back to the second half of the eighteenth century. The original French legal phrase, 'dernier resort', was applied to banks by Francis Baring in the 1790s. Several writers, notably Henry Thornton in 1802 and Walter Bagehot in his 1873 book *Lombard Street*, stated the policy with clarity. In the event of a 'run' on the banking system a credible institution, usually this will be the central bank, needs to provide generous short-term funding on a collateralized basis in order to quell the panic.

The experience of banking crises in the nineteenth and early twentieth centuries demonstrated that a central bank freely providing credit can end a systemic liquidity crisis. In 1866 the failure of Overend Gurney and Company – at that time much the largest UK bank – threatened to spread into a much more general banking panic, with withdrawal of deposits in exchange for gold at many other banks. But by then the Bank of England knew what action was necessary and stopped the panic by lending gold to all those banks that required it. The Bank did not, however, need to save Overend Gurney and Company itself.

The run on US banks during the panic of 1907 had a much more serious impact on the banking system, because there was at that time no central bank to act as lender of last resort. It was eventually stopped with the help of the financier John Pierpoint Morgan, who organized loans from his own pocket and those of other bankers and from the US Treasury, together with the arrival of large-scale gold shipments from London to New York. The adverse economic impact of the panic of 1907 eventually led the US Congress to acknowledge the need for a lender of last resort and, in December 1913, after an enquiry and lengthy deliberation, to establish the Federal Reserve.

The phrase 'lender of last resort' has become dulled over the years, being extended to describe any central bank loan to a commercial bank unable to fund itself in private markets, with the justification that a central bank should be ready to support any bank that is 'illiquid but solvent' – an impractical suggestion, since it is impossible to distinguish illiquid from insolvent banks. It is far from clear whether and in what circumstances a central bank loan should be provided to an individual bank, instead of being offered to any bank able to provide collateral, and even if an individual bank is supported, the central bank is not then acting as a 'lender of last resort', at least in the classic sense of Thornton and Bagehot, because it is not offering to lend to all banks.

The term 'lender of last resort' has also been applied to 'lifeboats', where the central bank co-ordinates the private-sector rescue of failing institutions, either banks or non-banks; to international lending to governments that can no longer borrow from private sources (so called 'international lender of last resort'); and even to central bank actions to stem sharp falls in asset prices. Examples of lifeboats include the rescues of the failing 'secondary banks' in the United Kingdom in 1973 and of the US hedge fund LTCM in 1998.

Whether justified or not, referring to any of these actions as 'lender of last resort' confuses. The term is best limited to collateralized short-term lending by the central bank at relatively short maturities to any bank, solvent or otherwise, that wants to take this credit, when there is a panic withdrawal of deposits across the banking system. Having such a lender of last resort has proved critical to maintaining banking system stability in the nineteenth and early twentieth centuries. It has proved so again in the twenty-first century.

Central bank actions during the first year of the current credit crisis

No one can accuse the central banks of sitting on their hands during the current credit crisis. While a full account of these central bank actions would require a book of its own, it is worth reviewing some of the main responses. This description covers the period only up to early September 2008. Chapter 10 describes the response of central banks and their actions as lenders of last resort during the global bank run of September and October 2008.

A July 2008 study by the Committee for Global Financial Stability, a group of central bankers from several countries, lists in its Annex 2 some 190 separate special actions taken between August 2007 and June 2008 by central banks worldwide, as well as the Federal Reserve, the Bank of England and the European Central Bank, the Bank of Japan, the Swiss National Bank, the Bank of Australia and the Bank of Canada. Many more such measures were taken after this report, especially during and after the pronounced financial market tensions of September and October 2008. All these steps were additional to the routine weekly and monthly operations taken to match the supply and demand of reserves and so keep short-term money market interest rates in line with monetary policy targets.

There have been conscious efforts by central banks to work together, especially when dealing with cross-border liquidity problems. On several occasions – for example 11 December 2007 and 12 March and 18 September 2008 – the Federal Reserve provided substantial amounts of dollars to other central banks, in the form of foreign exchange swaps with the European Central Bank, the Bank of England and other central banks in Europe and, more recently, in Asia. This allowed the recipient central banks to provide dollar loans to banks struggling to obtain funding for their illiquid holdings of dollar-denominated mortgage-backed securities. Another example of co-operation came on 8 October 2008, at the point when confidence in banks reached a new low, with an unusual co-ordinated 50 basis point reduction of interest rates by the Federal Reserve and five other central banks worldwide.

A further challenging practical problem for the US Federal Reserve during the crisis has been the time-zone difficulties associated with strong demand from European banks for US dollar funding of their holdings of US mortgage-backed securities and other structured credit assets. European banks prefer to obtain this funding during their working day – late afternoon in London, Paris, Frankfurt and Milan, but before 11 a.m. in the morning in New York. This has periodically created massive demand for US dollar funds during the morning session in New York, resulting in spikes in US overnight lending rates, which have only been reduced later in the day by the additional supply of reserves by the New York Federal Reserve.

Another response made by central banks at a relatively early stage of the crisis was to raise reserve requirements and then supply additional reserves so that banks could meet these higher requirements. Imposing higher reserve requirements over a two- or four-week maintenance period gives individual banks more day-to-day flexibility. They can run down their reserves further before hitting the zero-bound that would required them to offer collateral and pay a standing facility lending rate for more reserves, and they are therefore somewhat less concerned about the uncertainties of payment flows. It is also a cost-less response because the central bank can buy in securities on the open market to supply the additional reserves and pay the necessary interest from the returns on those securities.

The Bank of England has been quite wrongly accused of lagging behind the Federal Reserve and the European Central Bank because it did not announce reserve increases of this kind; but this ignores differences in operational procedures. In the United Kingdom reserve targets are not announced by the Bank of England but are chosen by banks themselves at the beginning of each maintenance period. The reserve targets in fact increased by a similar extent at all three central banks (before being effectively abandoned in September and October 2008).

Another central bank response to the crisis has been to reduce the cost of borrowing using the standing facilities, lowering it closer to the policy rate of interest. The Federal Reserve lowered this cost of borrowing from the discount window from its usual 1 per cent above the Federal Funds target rate to only 0.5 per cent above, and then down to only 0.25 per cent basis points above the target. These moves were largely symbolic, since even at these lower rates there has not been much borrowing from the Fed discount window. More significant, because the facility is used to a much greater extent, was the similar reduction by the ECB of the cost of borrowing from its standing facility – the 'marginal lending facility' – to 0.5 per cent above its target monetary policy rate (although there is now a plan to raise this back to 1 per cent).

Central banks have taken further extraordinary actions to address strains in the money markets. They have offered banks much larger than routine amounts of medium-term – one- to six-month – repo financing. For example, as early as 22 August 2007 the European Central Bank announced a supplementary longer-term refinancing operation, auctioning some €40 billion of three-month open market repos. Similar term financing was subsequently provided by other central banks, notably the term auction facility, or TAF, introduced by the US Federal Reserve in December 2007, initially offering some $40 billion of medium-term secured credit, and the expanded three-month longer-term repo facility of the Bank of England, also first introduced in December 2007. All the central banks have provided medium-term repos of these kinds on an increasing scale as the credit crisis has progressed. The Bank of England and the Federal Reserve accepted a much broader range of collateral for these loans than they accept for routine monetary operations.

A second novel measure, conducted on a large scale by both the Bank of England and the Federal Reserve, has been to offer 'asset swaps'. Under these schemes the central bank for a fee takes assets that are no longer acceptable as money market collateral – including senior MBS tranches – in exchange for better-quality securities such as Treasury bills. During the period of the swap these better-quality assets can be then used by banks as collateral in order to access short-term borrowing from the money markets. The first such scheme was the Term Securities Lending Program announced by the Federal Reserve on 11 March 2008, providing up to $200 billion of swaps of Treasury securities for illiquid assets such as AAA MBS, for periods of up to twenty-eight days. The Bank of England has taken a slightly different approach, offering longer, three-year, asset swaps under its 'special liquidity scheme' announced on 21 April 2008. This originally had a take-up period of six months, but the closing date was put back to January 2009. During this period UK banks were expected to take up £50 billion or more of these swaps for periods of up to three years, giving them extended access to additional short-term funding.

An assessment: liquidity provision but no new funds for lending

Many of the measures taken by central banks during the credit crisis up to early September 2008 were the standard central bank responses during periods of financial stress. The main central banks lowered interest rates, reducing the burden on borrowers and providing an incentive to banks to maintain their lending. This is not everywhere and always the response. In emerging markets with weak under-developed financial systems central banks have almost always had to respond to financial crises by raising interest rates, in order to maintain the confidence of domestic and foreign investors and prevent a panic outflow of investment funds.

Central banks have also provided all the additional reserves that commercial banks wanted in order to meet their increased precautionary demand for reserves with the central bank. In order to give banks sufficient access to their borrowing both the Federal Reserve and the Bank of England considerably increased the range of collateral that they would accept for their repo lending, until their collateral rules, at least those for term lending of a month or more, were almost as broad as those of the ECB.

The central banks responded in more novel ways to the dislocations of the money markets and the sharp rise of money market spreads shown in Figure 9.1. They offered substantial increases in the amount of term lending offered to commercial banks, to offset the maturity contraction in unsecured money market deposits. The Federal Reserve and the Bank of England also introduced central bank asset swap schemes, offering banks loans of government-issued Treasury securities that could then be used as collateral for borrowing in money markets, in exchange for illiquid mortgage-backed and other structured securities that could not.

While these measures were helpful in reducing money market stresses, it should come as no surprise that they did not succeed in reversing the decline in bank lending. While the central bank can provide liquidity (higher balances in reserve accounts) and can use its lending to extend the maturity of short-term bank liabilities, it can do relatively little to provide banks with additional funding.

When there is an increased precautionary demand from commercial banks to hold reserves with the central bank, they use their additional central bank borrowing to hold more reserves, not to lend. When the central bank provides term lending to banks, this alters the maturity structure of bank borrowing, but the central bank has to offset the resulting reserve increase by lending less at short maturities. The reserve increase is, in other words, 'sterilized'.

Even the provision of liquidity when there is a systemic 'run' – a panic withdrawal of deposits from many banks – provides no new funds for lending. The central bank is simply replacing lost funding, lending to weaker banks in place of deposits lost from the money markets.

The different asset swap schemes constituted one measure that did to a limited extent help with bank funding. The Bank of England scheme involved quite a substantial fee and so was of use only to the most constrained institutions. The Federal Reserve scheme was less expensive but aimed at the broker dealers, providing them with assets that could be used for collateralized borrowing in money markets, to make up for the fact that they were not commercial banks and so could not directly borrow reserves from the Federal Reserve. This gave them some help with funding but did not help the entire banking system.

The bottom line is that the ability of central banks to plug directly the wholesale funding gap faced by commercial banks is limited. In fact, central bank 'liquidity' provision, whether responding to increased demand for reserves or to the withdrawal of funds from money markets, does not provide any additional funds for lending. It cannot offset the wholesale funding feedback loop shown at the top right of Figure 1.1.

The only way in which a central bank can provide net funding for commercial banks is by selling down its portfolio of securities (government bonds usually constitute a large proportion of the central bank balance sheet) or other assets and then lending this money to commercial banks. The impact on reserves is neutral (the fall in reserves from the sale of the securities is offset by the increase in reserves from the lending), but commercial banks now have to seek a smaller proportion of their funding in the market.

Even the shift from orthodox to unorthodox monetary policy, where the central bank no longer targets the short-term market rate of interest but instead creates bank reserves at will in order to purchase financial assets, does not directly help banks with their funding needs. The central bank can now increase its balance sheet and the reserves of commercial banks as much as it chooses and the corresponding securities purchases will increase deposits in the banking system, but the wholesale funding gaps will remain.

Further reading

Willem Buiter has written several insightful and provocative pieces on central bank operations. His lengthy Jackson Hole paper, 'Central banks and financial crises' (www.kc.frb.org/publicat/sympos/2008/Buiter.03.12.09.pdf), ranges over many of the issues, arguing that central banks should act as 'market makers of last resort' as well as 'lenders of last resort', although to me it is unclear how he envisages this working in practice. His Maverecon blog, http://blogs.ft.com/maverecon/, contains several further discussions, including insightful analyses of the recent expansion of central bank balance sheets and of unorthodox monetary policy.

A recent speech by Ben Bernanke, 'The crisis and the policy response' (www.federalreserve.gov/newsevents/speech/bernanke20090113a.htm), explains the Federal Reserve's shift to unorthodox monetary policy – what he calls 'credit easing'.

A debate worth following is the argument for so called 'helicopter drops' of money; see Eric Lonergan, http://blogs.ft.com/wolf-forum/2008/12/central-banks-need-a-helicopter/, and the sixteen comments found there (including from me; I maybe get slightly the worse of this exchange, but whatever its merits this particular approach to policy is not what the world's central banks are actually doing).

10 | *The run on the world's banks*

In the middle of September 2008 the crisis mutated from a loss of confidence in institutions pursuing aggressive and high-risk business models into a loss of confidence in all banks, with little regard to their actual exposure to potential credit losses. This was a run on the entire banking system of many countries. The resulting withdrawal of money from the world's banks was only stemmed by central banks acting as 'lender of last resort' to banks that could not otherwise obtain short-term funds, and only ended when governments committed large amounts of public money to strengthening bank balance sheets, providing banks with new capital and offering guarantees on a wide range of bank liabilities.

This chapter describes this run on the world's banks from the failure of Lehman Brothers on 15 September 2008 until the introduction of these massive packages of government support, and assesses the response of the authorities. These were an extraordinary four weeks, a period of great investor uncertainty with a huge impact on financial markets. Stock prices around the world swung wildly, with particularly large changes in the value of bank shares and equally astonishing movements of foreign exchange rates. The dislocation of money markets that had first emerged in summer 2007 worsened considerably. Wholesale funds were withdrawn from banks on a huge scale, and central banks vastly increased their balance sheets as they loaned banks money to replace these lost wholesale deposits.

Financial markets did eventually stabilize, but the economic impact will be longer lasting. Banks across the world, both those that have accepted substantial government and central bank support and those that did not, remain very reluctant to lend. This has increased the cost and greatly reduced the amount of credit offered to bank customers. The outcome is a sharp contraction in consumer and business expenditure and an accelerating decline of global output and employment, set to continue throughout 2009, which central banks seem to be powerless to prevent. Following the global banking crisis of September 2008, we are now entering the deepest global economic downturn for more than seventy years.

The failure of Lehman Brothers

This run on the global banking system occurred because of widespread loss of investor confidence in banks and bank liabilities. The single event that did most to trigger this loss of confidence was when the US investment bank Lehman Brothers filed for US Chapter 11 bankruptcy protection, on 15 September 2008.

Lehman, while a well-known institution in London and New York, was somewhat smaller than many of its rivals, with a total balance sheet at end-2007 of $700 billion compared with the $1–2 trillion of the biggest global investment banks, and around 29,000 employees, fewer than half the number in Merrill Lynch, UBS or Deutsche Bank.

Although it was a smaller competitor, much of Lehman Brothers business was successful. It had a broad mix of revenues in three main divisions: investment banking (mergers and acquisitions, equity issuance and trading), fixed income (the underwriting and trading of government and corporate bonds and trading of foreign exchange and over the counter derivatives such as interest rate swaps and credit default swaps) and a smaller asset management division.

But Lehman, led by chief executive Dick Fuld, wanted more; it wanted to grow its business and catch up with its larger rivals. To do so, just like Bear Stearns it expanded heavily into securitization and structured products. It was one of the leading sponsors of both mortgage-backed securitizations and other structured products such as collateralized loan obligations. It also held a substantial trading portfolio of mortgage-backed and structured products. As a result it had some of the largest exposures to residential mortgages of all the investment banks.

Also, and rather unusually for an investment bank, Lehman invested substantially in commercial property, a broad category of assets including offices, hotels, shops and residential apartment blocks. This portfolio increased to around $50 billion – 7 per cent of its entire balance sheet – by end-November 2007 (Lehman Brothers 10-Q, 2008 Q2, p. 69). It was made up of $13 billion of holdings of tranched commercial MBS (similar to the tranched residential MBS but backed by loans to commercial property companies), $26 billion of 'whole loans' to commercial real estate companies, plus nearly $8 billion of equity and $5 billion of debt issued by real estate investment funds.

In the early months of the crisis Lehman Brothers seemed sound. Its share price fell from around $85 in early 2007 to $65 dollars at the time of the Bear Stearns rescue, a share price fall similar to that experienced by other banks. But concerns about the viability of Lehman grew. Like Bear Stearns it had large holdings of mortgage-backed and other structured securities funded short term. It was a more diversified business, so that the revenues from investment banking and investment management prevented an immediate funding crisis. But there were clearly serious problems. By June 2008 Lehman had acknowledged losses of about $8 billion on its holdings of mortgage-backed and structured securities, and there were serious questions raised about the potential for further losses, especially on commercial property. The share price continued to fall, to around $18 in early September.

Lehman needed to raise more capital, either by finding an investor willing to put money into the firm or by selling assets. There were talks with the state owned Korean Development Bank (KDB), but the acquisition price offered by KDB together with a syndicate of Korean banks was turned down by Dick Fuld, and talks about KDB taking a minority 20 per cent stake on its own for $6 billion also came to nothing.

A big barrier to any deal was uncertainty about the scale of Lehman's losses. Lehman had been less than candid. It held $37 billion of mortgage-backed and asset-backed securities and $13 billion of CLOs and other non-mortgage structured securities. These included a relatively high proportion, around 15 per cent in the case of mortgage-backed securities, of speculative-grade and equity tranches, mostly retained from its own structuring activities. More conservative accounting would have written these investments down to zero, implying losses of around $8 billion in addition to the falls in the market value of its investment-grade mortgage and asset-backed securities.

Finally, critically, there had been far too little acknowledgement of loss on its $50 billion commercial property portfolio, including the $8 billion of risky equity stakes (one individual deal – a $2.2 billion equity stake in Archstone of Denver, Colorado, purchased at the height of the boom – seemed especially suspect). A conservative treatment of losses on these assets could have resulted in write-downs of perhaps a further $15 billion. Altogether, Lehman appeared to have underprovided against credit losses by at least $20 billion, unsurprisingly, since such an acknowledgement would have all but wiped out its shareholder equity and forced it to apply for Chapter 11 bankruptcy protection.

These problems would have been apparent to anyone who looked closely at Lehman's business in late summer 2008, but its results for the quarter ending 31 August, brought out ahead of schedule on 10 September, still shocked the markets, with a further $8 billion write-down on its portfolio of mortgage-backed and structured securities. Lehman was on the brink of failure. The US authorities sought to obtain a takeover deal similar to that which saved Bear Stearns, and there were detailed talks over the weekend of 13 and 14 September with Bank of America and with Barclays Bank of the United Kingdom. But, with the huge uncertainties surrounding the values of Lehman's assets, these potential suitors wanted very substantial guarantees against loss from the US Treasury. These were not provided and the deal was off. On the morning of Monday 15 September Lehman filed for Chapter 11 bankruptcy protection.

There followed a 'fire sale' of the Lehman business, with Barclays snapping up its US operations and the Japanese securities house Nomura, which had a long-cherished ambition to be a full-scale investment bank, acquiring its Asian business and European investment banking (the acquisitions were made for fairly small sums, e.g. $225 million for the Asian business, but both Barclays and Nomura had to pay much larger sums to integrate the back offices and retain key staff). The Lehman fixed-income trading portfolio and commercial property will have to be sold, but this will take a long time. There are also likely to be lawsuits against Lehman. It will be years before there is a final payout to creditors.

An indicator of the scale of problems at Lehman comes from settlement of credit default swaps, the tradable insurance contracts, written on Lehman bonds (contrary to gloomy prognostications the auction process to determine this price worked smoothly – at least one part of the new credit markets was working well). The final settlement price was only 8.625 per cent – that is, holders of CDS protection were expecting, post-default, that they would recover less than 9 cents in the dollar, implying huge losses of asset value, perhaps as much as $100 billion over and above what was acknowledged in the accounts.

Part of this can be explained by the fire sale of assets at low prices, but it also reflects the huge uncertainty about what was on Lehman's balance sheet and the very real threat of legal actions against Lehman Brothers.

The run on the banks: week 1

Lehman's failure was a huge shock for several reasons. If Lehman, a reputable and generally successful bank, could have hidden such large losses in just two business areas – commercial property and traded credit securities – what were other banks hiding? Who was exposed to Lehman and how much might they lose? If the US authorities were willing to let Lehman fail, then who else might go under? Investors were already nervous about bank liabilities, especially because of substantial losses experienced by a number of middle-sized regional US banks holding Fannie and Freddie preference shares after Fannie and Freddie were taken into conservatorship on 6 September. After Lehman, investors were looking to hold anything but bank liabilities. This in turn triggered a giddying series of events that even now are difficult to absorb.

On the same day as Lehman filed for bankruptcy protection there were further dramatic developments. The positive news was that Bank of America (their executives had a busy weekend!) had agreed to purchase Merrill Lynch in a $50 billion all stock deal, but investors focused more on the negative, the announcement of the ratings downgrade of AIG, further undermining the confidence of the non-bank lenders in mortgage-backed securities and short-term money markets, and triggering the withdrawal of funds from money market mutual funds – the intermediaries that place money on behalf of investors in the money markets. There was yet more loss of confidence only a day later (despite the decision of the US Treasury to then support AIG) when a money market mutual, Reserve Primary, froze withdrawals for a week. In the following days a number of money market mutuals 'broke the buck' – that is, the value of their money market assets fell below the value of money put into them by investors. Suddenly one of the safest of investment assets, money market mutual deposits, widely used especially in the United States, no longer seemed fully secure. This resulted in the further dislocation of money market interest rates illustrated by the jump in credit spreads shown in Figure 9.1.

The further dislocation of money markets increased the funding pressures on all banks reliant on wholesale funding. In the United Kingdom there were immediate doubts about the continued viability of a relatively small specialized mortgage lender (Bradford and Bingley) and the very large mortgage and savings and fifth largest UK bank, Halifax Bank of Scotland (HBOS). In the course of the week the share price of HBOS fell around 50 per cent, from 290p to less than 150p, and its ability to borrow even overnight was being questioned. It lacked ready collateral to borrow from the Bank of England (it was a major user of the Bank's 'special liquidity scheme' which allowed it to swap mortgage-backed securities for more acceptable collateral Treasury bills, but it had not anticipated funding pressures on this scale and had not conducted swaps on a sufficient scale to surmount the pressures). Rather than offer another emergency loan, such as that made almost a year to the day earlier to Northern Rock, the UK government agreed to waive the normal constraints of competition law, allowing the embattled HBOS to announce two days later an agreed takeover by the fourth largest UK bank, Lloyds-TSB.

Once such a feeding frenzy has driven one bank under then it can move on. There is always a further bank 'next in line' to be assaulted by similar doubts. In the United Kingdom, as soon as HBOS was rescued through an agreed and government-approved merger with its competitor Lloyds-TSB, doubts then arose about the funding of the Royal Bank of Scotland Group (RBS), the UK bank with the greatest reliance on wholesale funding after HBOS. This run on RBS was halted only by the 8 October 2008 announcement of the huge government funding package to support UK banks.

Similar 'next in line' logic drove liquidity runs and price falls affecting banks worldwide. For example, after Lehman and Merrill Lynch doubts among the US broker dealers began to mount about Morgan Stanley and Goldman Sachs, the two US investment banks that had suffered the smallest losses from their credit exposures. A problem for both these banks was that, although they had strictly controlled their credit exposures, they were highly leveraged, dependent on short-term repo funding for financing their large trading portfolios.

Also, unlike other banks active in the securities and derivatives markets such as JP Morgan Chase, Bank of America or Barclays, they were not part of a larger commercial banking group that was eligible for short-term central bank funding. Morgan Stanley and Goldman

Sachs were the very last of their breed, the stand-alone investment bank focused on major securities markets transactions, such as mergers and acquisitions or initial public share offerings, and on securities and derivatives trading. Investors were now sceptical about the viability of any business – even those that were well run – that depended on large-scale repo borrowing, and thus doubted the stability of stand-alone investment banks.

The US authorities were the first to respond to the situation. The Federal Reserve took dramatic steps to restore liquidity to money markets, with its $180 billion internationally co-ordinated programme of swap facilities to other central banks designed to ease the strains in dollar funding markets announced on 18 September, and then, the following day, the announcement of its asset-backed commercial paper money market liquidity fund (AMLF) facility, a scheme to provide loans to banks for the purchase of asset-backed commercial paper from money market mutual funds.

These liquidity initiatives were immediately followed by the announcement by US Treasury Secretary Hank Paulson of proposed legislation to create a $700 billion fund – the Troubled Asset Relief Program (TARP) – to address the financial crisis. This proposal was first revealed in an emergency meeting on the evening of Thursday 19 September with senior members of Congress, where Paulson was accompanied by Federal Reserve chairman Ben Bernanke. These two most senior US economic officials described the crisis, in words that shocked Congress members, as an 'imminent meltdown of the US financial system'.

Their announced intention was to use this fund to purchase troubled mortgage assets, taking them off the books of US banks so as to unclog the credit system. The purchase was supposed to be made where possible using market pricing, for example using a technique known as a 'reverse' auction (in a normal auction buyers make bids for purchasing an asset and the seller accepts the highest bid; in a reverse auction sellers submit offers for selling an asset and the purchaser accepts the lowest price). However, the proposed legislation was deliberately very flexible, with a great deal of discretion in the use of funds; they could be used to purchase any assets that might help to restore the health of the US banking system and could also be used for insuring the value of assets.

The TARP proposal drew comparisons with the Resolution Trust Corporation established by Congress in 1989 to hold the assets of savings and loans that failed in the 1980s. However, it was really a very different idea. The purpose of the Resolution Trust Corporation was to deal with the assets of failed institutions in an orderly fashion, to make sure that the loss of money was minimized. The purpose of TARP was to support banks as going concerns, and it was not at all clear that purchasing assets was a cost-effective way of doing this. What assets were to be purchased and at what price? Was the fund even big enough to achieve its goals?

Weeks 2 and 3

If week 1 of the global bank run was bad then the following two weeks, Monday 22 September to Friday 3 October, were worse. Further signs of a slowing global economy raised doubts about the capital adequacy of many banks: was their capital – the difference in value between their assets and their short- and long-term borrowing – sufficient to survive a steep recession? Banking analysts were assessing worst-case scenarios for banking losses and write-downs and finding that banks worldwide might need $400 billion or more of new capital (they would need this money to reduce their indebtedness and so survive losses and write-downs without being in danger of failure). At the same time there was a continuing withdrawal of funds from many banks as investors were more and more reluctant to provide repo finance against any form of credit-related assets, and less and less willing to place unsecured funds in bank deposits, pushing banks more and more into borrowing reserves from central banks.

Banks did what they could to allay these concerns about their solvency and liquidity. Both Morgan Stanley and Goldman Sachs accepted capital from outsiders on rather expensive terms (Mitsubishi Finance bought a 20 per cent stake in Morgan Stanley, and the veteran value investor Warren Buffet paid $5 billion for a combination of shares and warrants – these are contracts allowing him to buy further shares – in Goldman Sachs). Of even greater historical significance is the decision of these two banks to announce, within days, that they were converting to bank holding companies, with the intention of developing a commercial banking activity alongside their investment banking, and the expedited approval of this change by the US authorities.

This marked the end of an era. For seventy-five years, since the Glass-Steagall provisions of the 1933 US Banking Act had separated commercial and investment banking, the independent US broker dealers had been the key intermediaries in global security and derivative markets. Lightly regulated, at least from the perspective of risk taking and portfolio decisions, more than any other firms they are emblematic of free-market financial capitalism. Now, within six months, the five major independent investment banks – Bear Stearns, Lehman Brothers, Merrill Lynch, Morgan Stanley and Goldman Sachs – either had been acquired or had failed, or had adopted a mixed commercial–investment banking business model.

Further bank failures followed. The US FDIC shut down Washington Mutual after the closure of markets on Thursday 25 September. The UK government nationalized a small, troubled lender, Bradford and Bingley, on Monday 29 September, after failing to find a buyer in frantic talks over the weekend. Eventually the branches and deposits of Bradford and Bingley were sold to the Spanish bank Santander, already the owner of the UK banks Abbey and Alliance and Leicester. That same day Citigroup announced that it was acquiring the troubled US bank Wachovia, although this offer was eventually bettered by a rival bid from Wells Fargo.

It was not just in the United States and the United Kingdom that banks were in difficulties. There were escalating withdrawals of funds from banks in many European countries. The Danish government saved another small bank on Monday 22. By the end of that week the very much larger Fortis, a successful bank headquartered in Belgium and with large subsidiaries in the Netherlands and Luxembourg, was running short of funds. The Fortis balance sheet had been stretched by the cash acquisition of parts of ABN-AMRO earlier in the year (as was the balance sheet of its partner in this deal, Royal Bank of Scotland). Having overpaid for this acquisition Fortis now looked very under-capitalized. On Friday 26 September its share price fell 10 per cent amid speculation that it was unable to raise private-sector capital. On Monday 29 September it obtained government capital injections of €11.1 billion. Proponents of pan-European action were dismayed. The rescue was done on a piecemeal *host* country basis, with the three main countries in which it operated each recapitalizing its own national subsidiary in order to protect local depositors.

Two days later the governments of France, Belgium and Luxembourg provided another large capital injection of €6.4 billion, again with support divided along national lines, to the specialized public-sector lender Dexia, a bank whose business model had been undermined by the failure of the monolines on which it had relied for hedging of its public-sector bond exposures. Even more spectacular was the 29 September €35 billion loan from a consortium of German banks and guaranteed by the German government, to support the huge German bank Hypo Real Estate, a loan increased only a week later to €50 billion. Hypo Real Estate is one of Germany's largest financial institutions, a bank with a €400 billion balance sheet and on the DAX-30 index of the thirty major German companies trading on the Frankfurt Stock Exchange. Hypo Real Estate, like Dexia, posted large write-downs on fundamentally fairly safe but illiquid public-sector loans through its subsidiary DePfa, together with substantial further losses and write-downs on mortgage lending and portfolios of structured products. The losses were large, but it remained solvent. However, its business model was undermined because it relied entirely on relatively short-term wholesale funding.

Governments were responding to the situation, but in an ad hoc, uncertain and unco-ordinated fashion. A symbol of government uncertainty was the halting progress of the TARP through the US Congress. The plan was supported by all senior US politicians, including President George W. Bush, both presidential candidates (John McCain announcing suspension of his presidential campaign in order to return to Washington and lend his support) and the House and Senate leaders of both parties, but there were serious doubts among some Democrats and many more Republicans about its merits.

On Wednesday 24 September Treasury Secretary Hank Paulson and Federal Reserve chairman Ben Bernanke made another joint appearance before the Senate Banking Committee to explain the proposed TARP fund, but they were rather unsuccessful in explaining the thinking behind the idea. The Committee chairman, the Democratic senator for Connecticut, Christopher J. Dodd, assessed the proposal after these hearings as 'stunning and unprecedented in its scope and lack of detail' and complained that it would allow Paulson to act with 'absolute impunity . . . After reading this proposal, I can only conclude that it is not only our economy that is at risk, Mr Secretary, but our Constitution, as well.' It was not just the more independent-minded members of Congress who had doubts. Constituents were complaining about what appeared to be a bail-out of greedy bankers, and their concerns did not go unnoticed by the many members of Congress, including all the House of Representatives, facing re-election in only a few weeks' time.

Nonetheless, the seriousness of the financial crisis was evident and the main argument of the proponents of the bill – that something simply had to be done or there would be a disaster – seemed to have the upper hand. So it was a huge shock to markets when, late on Monday 29 September, the House of Representatives rejected the proposed TARP.

Eventually the sense of urgency prevailed. The Senate passed an amended version the next day and the TARP legislation, the Emergency Economic Recovery and Stabilization Act, was finally approved by the House of Representatives on Friday 3 October. By this time it included a wide range of additional clauses, including an increase in the level of deposit insurance from $100,000 to $250,000 per deposit and various measures to support homeowners struggling to repay mortgages, financed through an increased budget of $850 billion. Importantly, for later action the bill had also acquired an additional insurance clause (Clause 101 mandates the fund to purchase assets, Clause 102 mandates it to provide insurance guarantees), something that was to prove critical in subsequent months when the Fed gradually came to embrace its policy of purchasing credit-risky assets, backed by insurance from the TARP funds.

The responses of governments across Europe were equally uncoordinated. On Tuesday 30 September the Irish government announced, without consultation with other European governments, a blanket guarantee on deposits with Irish banks, raising accusations of poaching deposits from other EU banks, especially in the United Kingdom, where many Irish banks offer savings deposits. The Icelandic government was also out in the cold, grappling on its own with the overwhelming problem of being the home of three ambitious banks which had built up a large international portfolio of corporate and commercial property loans but, in an echo of Northern Rock in the United Kingdom, with balance sheets backed by only around 30 per cent of retail deposits.

When the Icelandic government announced that it was taking an equity stake in the weakest of these three, Glitnir, there followed panic and then an undignified scramble. These important pan-European institutions – Glitnir, Landsbanki and Kaupthing – died, simply because they were too big for their home country Iceland to save, and European governments seized assets where they could to protect their own local depositors, the UK government, for example, using anti-terrorist legislation to take control of Icelandic bank assets in the United Kingdom. In the weeks that followed a somewhat more co-operative approach emerged, the governments of Finland, Sweden, Norway and Denmark developing a joint programme to deal with the Icelandic bank assets and liabilities in Scandinavia and providing the beleaguered Icelandic government with much-needed credit. Iceland is not a full member of the European Union, only of the European Economic Area, but still, the entire episode is not the best illustration of European unity.

Week 4: the government rescue packages

By the following Monday and Tuesday, 6 and 7 October, strains in short-term money markets were getting even worse, with the important US markets for commercial paper coming close to complete closure. The Federal Reserve took further action, with more provision of term loans and the 7 October announcement of its Commercial Paper Lending Facility that would set up and provide support for special legal vehicles to provide underwriting guarantees on commercial paper.

The biggest development of that week came the following day. The UK financial authorities had botched the announcement of Northern Rock emergency loans the previous year. HM Treasury made up for that mistake on the morning of Wednesday 8 October, with a masterly piece of political theatre: unveiling a plan to save UK banks conceived on an astonishing scale.

The UK government, less restricted by constitutional checks and balances than the US government, was underwriting UK banks to the tune of £600 billion, through a combination of new equity, guarantees on liabilities and asset swaps. This bold move was a programme of support worth around 40 per cent of UK national income, proportionately around eight times larger than the US TARP fund, which was a mere 5 per cent of US national income. Opposition politicians were wrong-footed, unable to come up with any coherent response to this initiative. Prime Minister Gordon Brown basked in the media spotlight, as the man who came to save the UK banks from their own mistakes and enjoyed a notable bounce in his opinion poll ratings.

Under the UK scheme all major banks have to increase their capital substantially (the detailed calculations of these new capital requirements emerged later) and the government stood ready, if this capital could not be raised privately, to provide banks with up to £50 billion of new capital, in exchange for preference shares paying 12 per cent (in the event there were legal difficulties with this arrangement and the actual capital was provided through underwriting rights issues). The size of the Bank of England special liquidity scheme, the asset swap arrangement that allowed banks to exchange illiquid AAA mortgage-backed securities for liquid Treasury bills, doubled from £100 billion to £200 billion. Finally HM Treasury offered guarantees on up to £250 billion of medium-term bank wholesale liabilities, charging a premium cleverly calculated using past market spreads for private insurance of bank default.

Across continental Europe governments were also taking action. The Spanish government announced its own €50 billion fund that would be used to buy bank assets. France announced the setting up of a body to take stakes in failing banks. Germany and Denmark switched from fierce criticisms of Ireland only days earlier for its uni-lateral announcement of deposit guarantees to announcing their own sweeping unilateral guarantees of bank liabilities.

Then, following a meeting of heads of state and government over the weekend of 11 and 12 October, the countries using the euro announced a common approach to supporting their banks, modelled on the UK initiative. This had two main planks: the first was government purchase of bank preference shares and the second (in a move that went beyond what had been done in the United Kingdom) was providing guarantees on bank debt with maturities of up to five years. The guarantee funds, worth a reported €500 billion in Germany, €360 billion in France and €200 billion in the Netherlands, could still be in use in 2014, since requests for five-year guarantees will be considered until the end of 2009. Over subsequent weeks Eurozone governments committed over €2 trillion in support of their banking systems, in both purchase of preference shares and debt guarantees.

These actions by the United Kingdom and the rest of Europe left the US government looking rather leaden-footed. The original idea of the TARP legislation had been to purchase troubled mortgage assets, but there was now a consensus that banks needed not to have assets taken away from them, but to have more money to increase the total value of their asset portfolio and hence their capital (the difference between assets and liabilities). On 9 October Treasury Secretary Paulson said that they would consider using TARP for bank recapitalization, and on 14 October the US Treasury announced that one third of the original TARP funds would now be used for providing banks with more capital, through a $250 billion scheme for purchasing preference shares paying a fixed dividend of 5 per cent over five years (and then increasing to 9 per cent) and with attached 'warrants' to give the US taxpayer a share in any recovery in the value of bank shares. Nine of the largest US banks, including Bank of America, had agreed to participate in the scheme even before its announcement, taking $125 billion of the available funds. The remaining $125 billion was to be allocated among smaller banks and thrifts that applied before a 14 November application deadline.

Similar actions were announced in other countries. On 12 October the Australian government introduced both blanket guarantees on all deposits and a scheme for government insurance of term funding of more than one year, which would extend to Australian bank issues of Eurobonds (i.e. bonds sold outside Australia). The Canadian government announced plans to buy senior mortgage-backed securities and also introduced, on 23 October, its own scheme for insuring bank term funding. The Japanese government had done a lot of bank recapitalization in the late 1990s, providing funds for recapitalizing many of its own banks. Now its own banks were among the least affected by the global crisis, but it was the first contributor to a World Bank fund for recapitalizing banks in smaller emerging markets.

The response of central banks to the global bank run

The global bank run of September and October 2008 had a massive impact on central bank balance sheets. There was a huge withdrawal of funds from the money markets, and banks became increasingly reluctant to lend money to each other, preferring to hold reserves with the central bank instead. The outcome has been that banks now mostly lend and borrow via their central banks, rather than from each other through the money markets.

Another action has been to reduce the penalties for exceeding reserve requirements. From 6 October 2008, the US Federal Reserve began paying interest at the target Federal Funds rate on all banks reserves, even excess reserves that exceed the maintenance period average reserve requirement. The only remaining penalty is on reserves that fall below the required level. The Bank of England has come close to abandoning reserve requirements altogether. Its normal system has been to impose a penalty if reserves are more than 1 per cent away from the reserves requirements, but during the crisis it has widened this range enormously, to plus or minus 20 per cent or higher. During periods of extreme market stress UK banks have been allowed to miss their reserves requirement by as much as 60 per cent in either direction without penalty.

As the global bank run swept the world's banks in September and October 2008, the major central banks acted as lenders of last resort, pretty much exactly as Thornton and Bagehot would have recommended. They stood ready to lend to all banks who wanted to bid for reserves and thus replace lost money market funding.

These actions have produced some astonishing changes in central bank assets and liabilities. At the beginning of August 2007, before the crisis broke, the assets of the Federal Reserve system were about $900 billion, of which nearly $800 billion were securities such as Treasury bonds. The main liability was greenbacks – a little over $800 billion of notes in circulation. Deposits by commercial banks with the Federal Reserve were relatively small, fluctuating around $13 billion. Until early September 2008, despite the many liquidity measures undertaken by the Federal Reserve, the overall balance sheet had not changed much. As explained, in order to maintain control over interest rates they were taking away with one hand what they gave with the other.

But with the global bank run after September 15, there was an extraordinary expansion of the Fed balance sheet. As bank confidence in their money market counterparties collapsed, they took shelter in the safety of depositing with the central bank. By 5 November 2008 total currency in circulation remained about the same, but otherwise the balance sheet of the Federal Reserve was transformed. Total assets had more than doubled, to over $2,000 billion. The various liquidity facilities had expanded dramatically, including some $380 billion in short-term and term repo loans, and $350 billion in other credit of different kinds, including loans to broker dealers and the financing of the AMLF asset-backed commercial paper facility. The other big change in assets was a further $240 billion of funding provided to the Commercial Paper Funding Facility (CPFF).

How were all these facilities financed? Securities holdings had fallen by around $300 billion, to just under $500 billion – that is, the Fed had sold off about $300 billion of Treasury securities in order to finance liquidity loans. Even bigger was an entirely new item: a $560 billion US Treasury supplementary financing facility – the Federal Reserve borrowed much of this money directly from government. Finally, there was a very large increase of nearly $480 billion in bank deposits with the Federal Reserve – that is, the reserves with the central bank, now paying interest.

There has been a similar money market disintermediation and expansion of other central bank balances. The balance sheet of the system of European Central Bank has almost doubled, from around €1 trillion to €2 trillion. But the outright winner, in the competition for inflation of the central bank balance sheet, is the Bank of England, whose assets and liabilities have risen an astonishing threefold, from around £80 billion in early August 2007 to £240 billion in early November 2008, although regrettably the Bank of England weekly bank return gives rather little information about the composition of this expanded balance sheet.

While all the central banks provided extensive funding to replace that withdrawn because of the global bank run, the Federal Reserve went a lot further than the others. During the months of September and October 2008 the Federal Reserve announced an extraordinary set of measures. The first three were introduced to support money market liquidity, creating special funds to purchase money market assets. These were the Asset Backed Commercial Paper Money Market Mutual Fund Liquidity Facility (AMLF) of 19 September, the Commercial Paper Funding Facility (CPFF) of 7 October, and the Money Market Investor Funding Facility (MMIFF) of 21 October.

The smallest of these is the AMLF, established to counter the immediate stress of money market mutual funds by purchasing asset-backed commercial paper from them so that they could meet redemptions without a damaging loss of value. By end-November there had been some £57 billion of such purchases. The CPFF buys three-month unsecured commercial paper and secured asset-backed paper from issuers, alleviating their refinancing pressures as the maturity of what could be sold in the market contracted to as little as one day during the global bank run. The only limit on this programme is that it cannot be used by any issuer to expand its issuance beyond the average level between

January and August 2008, prior to the run. By end-November the CPFF held some £282 billion of paper.

Potentially the largest dollar commitment is to the MMIFF, which has authorization for using up to $540 billion of Federal Reserve funds. The idea is that the Federal Reserve will provide 90 per cent of most senior funding for private-sector special purpose vehicles, that will in turn purchase a variety of short-term money market assets from money market mutual funds, thus providing investors with greater assurance as to the liquidity of underlying instruments and money market mutuals themselves. But this is a more challenging programme to operate, because it requires the private sector to hold the remaining 10 per cent of riskiest junior funding in these vehicles. It is unclear how easy it will be to attract private sector investment into the MMIFF.

On 25 November 2008 Federal Reserve policy went even further, with the announcement of two further radical initiatives. The first was a massive programme to purchase some $600 billion for the purchase of conforming mortgage-backed securities issued by Fannie and Freddie. This programme appeared to have an immediate impact on the cost of borrowing, with a substantial fall in long-term interest rates on prime conforming mortgages, falling as low as 4.6 per cent in early January 2009, compared with over 6 per cent in October 2008.

The second programme was the Term Asset Backed Securities Lending Facility (TALF), in which the Federal Reserve is purchasing up to $200 billion of senior ABS-securities, backed by a $20 billion first loss support from TARP funds based on the critical Section 102 of the Economic Recovery and Stabilization Act. The programme has taken time to get going properly, with large-scale purchases only beginning in March 2009, so it is unclear whether enough is being done to have a major impact on these markets. But the Federal Reserve has made it clear that it is willing to consider expanding this programme, extending the amount of funding available and the coverage to include private label mortgage-backed securitizations.

On 16 December 2008 the Federal Open Market Committee that steers Federal Reserve monetary policy announced that it was adopting a target range for Federal Funds of 0–0.25 per cent, an historic moment marking the transition from orthodox to unorthodox monetary policy. The importance of this policy announcement is that the Federal Reserve no longer has any obligation to maintain the reserves in line with the demand from commercial banks and can use its powers to create reserves for unlimited expansion of its balance sheet. The implication is that there is no longer any limit on the funding available to purchase private-sector assets. This could herald an even bigger expansion of agency mortgage-backed securities than has already taken place. With further commitment of TARP funds the Federal Reserve could also greatly increase its holdings of commercial paper and ABS and start purchasing private label mortgage-backed securities.

The aftermath: banks are stabilized but equity markets weaken

The unprecedented scale of central bank lending to banks in order to replace the withdrawal of money market deposits prevented more widespread bank failures during the four weeks of the run from 15 September to 10 October. After the announcements of government support packages, first in the United Kingdom on 8 October and then in other countries, the extreme panic of the previous four weeks subsided.

Money markets remained very dislocated, with spreads between unsecured Libor interest rates and other secured rates of interest (Figure 9.1) remaining elevated since their peak of early October 2008. But at least funds were no longer being withdrawn from banks on a massive scale, and the large scale of Federal Reserve acquisition of money market assets in November and December has helped to produce some further reduction in the spreads between unsecured and secured lending rates.

What had changed were perceptions. There is now a clear commitment, by governments worldwide, that they will protect banks from insolvency. The capital provided by governments to support their banks may eventually prove to be insufficient; it will be no great surprise if they have to provide more, but a clear precedent has been set. Governments will support deposit-taking banks. Lehman's failure does not mean that many other banks will be allowed to fail.

This is clear from further government actions to support banks and other financial institutions. In the United States more public money was committed in November, with further support for AIG and the huge bail-out of Citigroup described in Chapter 8. But, despite some confidence in banks being restored, the economic and financial situation in the aftermath of the banking crisis remains very difficult.

While the banking sector stabilized, the wider economic outlook deteriorated in the last months of 2008. One indicator of poor future prospects has been a worldwide fall in share prices, driven not only by worsening economic fundamentals but also by distressed sales by over-leveraged hedge funds.

Outside the banking sector share prices showed no clear trend during the first couple of weeks of the global banking panic. There were big falls but also big increases. But share values worldwide then fell sharply. The S&P500 – a more representative index than the Dow Jones Industrial Average – was trading at around 1,200 from early summer to late September 2008. But there was then a brutal sell-off, with the S&P 500 declining by a quarter, from 1,213 on 26 September to 899 on 10 October. By 20 November, before the Citigroup rescue, it had fallen further, to 792, and although it recovered to its October levels it then remained close to 900 into mid-December. There were similar declines in share price indices in Asia and Europe at the same time.

Why was there such a steep decline in share prices? This has been due both to deteriorating fundamentals and to sales by distressed leveraged hedge funds. The fundamental reason has been the continuing weakening of the global economy and the growing realization that because of the shortage of bank credit we are entering not the more usual short recession, but instead a deep and prolonged economic contraction.

The impact of these economic concerns on share prices has been amplified by difficulties faced by many 'hedge funds', the specialized private investment funds accounting for a majority of the day-to-day trading of shares in the major financial centres such as London and New York. Hedge funds are high-risk but also usually highly profitable investment vehicles. Their managers participate in the fund and are paid largely according to their performance. They take funds from wealthy and knowledgeable investors (often themselves from the investment banking industry) and increasingly also from institutions such as pension funds, and use these funds to pursue a number of sophisticated trading strategies. Chapter 3 describes the liquidity problems of Long Term Capital Management in 1997, at that time the largest hedge fund in the world. While LTCM was wound down there are still hundreds of other hedge funds, with many more having been created in the past decade and a dramatic increase in assets managed by hedge funds over recent years. Among the best known are the Paulson and Co. fund run by John Paulson, which has made a lot of profit in the past two years taking positions in mortgage-backed credit, Renaissance Technologies of Jim Simons, the Tudor Investment Corporation of John Paul Tudor and Soros Fund Management, which includes the Quantum group of George Soros.

Hedge funds follow many different trading strategies. But what is common to all of them is that they depend on the short-term borrowing and lending of shares, bonds and other securities to control their risks and increase the return on each invested dollar. The failure of Lehman and the subsequent disruption of money markets interfered with many hedge fund trading strategies. This was exacerbated by the bans on the short selling of financial stocks. In early October 2008 there were increasing investor concerns about hedge fund performance, especially those focused on equity-trading, prompting investor withdrawals which in turn forced hedge funds to close positions and take losses. Bloomberg reports data from Hedge Fund Research Inc. of Chicago that indicates that the hedge fund industry lost $115 billion in October 2008 on net assets of $1.7 billion, with investor withdrawals of a further $40 billion, prompting several funds to put a temporary halt on withdrawals (something hedge funds can do that banks cannot). The trading desks of many investment banks have also recorded trading losses; for example in October 2008 both Goldman Sachs and Credit Suisse reported relatively large trading losses.

The underlying problem: continuing pressure on bank balance sheets

The underlying problem behind the deepening worldwide contraction is not hedge funds, or even share prices, but the continuing pressures on the banks. Despite government support, the situation of banks worldwide is much more difficult than at any time in the past seventy years, even those experienced during the stagflation of the 1970s or the Latin American debt problems of the 1980s. Japanese and Scandinavian banks faced problems on this scale during their banking crises of the 1990s that followed the equity and property booms of the late 1980s, but the banks of other developed countries have experienced nothing similar since the 1930s.

The worsening situation of banks can be explained with the help of Figure 1.1 in Chapter 1. While central bank actions, especially those of the Federal Reserve, have at least stabilized bank wholesale funding problems (the feedback loop on the right-hand side of Figure 1.1 is no longer sucking funds out of the banking system), the deterioration in both the economy and the availability of bank lending is creating a cumulative downwards spiral of falling bank credit, lower output and reduced global trade (the feedback loop on the left-hand side of Figure 1.1 is now having a considerably bigger impact than earlier in the crisis).

Banks also face additional funding problems because the financial situation of their customers is deteriorating along with the slump in the world economy. Companies' revenues are contracting much faster than costs. As a result many large companies are either reducing their bank deposits or 'drawing down' so-called committed lines of bank credit. These lines of credit are to companies what credit cards or overdrafts are to individuals, they are facilities that can be drawn down whenever funds are in short supply. In many cases banks have signed legal agreements, with no wriggle room, committing themselves to providing companies with such facilities for a period of years ahead. Many households are also drawing down bank deposits, in order to cope with a lower income or the shock of redundancy.

The provision of these committed lines of credit, which on some measures are as high as $5 trillion dollars worldwide, is another example of underwriting a 'systemic risk'. When the monolines and AIG provided insurance on the market value of the best quality mortgage-backed securities, or Fannie and Freddie guaranteed prime conforming mortgages, they were unprepared for a large deterioration in price or credit quality affecting their entire insured book. They assumed that credit risk would always be diversified in a large portfolio. Similarly, when banks signed these committed lines of credit they never imagined that a large proportion of corporate customers might want to draw down on them at the same time. The banks have signed a kind of insurance contract to provide money when money is in extremely short supply, an insurance contract that they now find very difficult to honour.

Another problem for some banks is increasing losses on corporate structured credits of the kind described in Chapter 5. Unsurprisingly, as the global economy goes into a steep downturn, a high proportion of leverage loans deals, such as those included in the Grosvenor Place CLO, are turning sour. Write-downs are also increasing on synthetic

CDOs and similar structures exposed to investment-grade credits. The exposure of these structures is, in one way, much greater even than in sub-prime mortgages, because there is little or no collateral behind much of this lending, no house that can be sold if the borrower does not pay.

For these reasons and others, the value of bank assets continued to deteriorate in late 2008 and early 2009, threatening to eat up all the government-provided capital and more. The lower lending → higher credit impairment → lower lending feedback loop is proving especially powerful. The situation at most banks continues to be extremely difficult and at some banks is deteriorating further.

'Scandinavian' solutions to the crisis

The biggest challenge facing economic policymakers in 2009 is how to break into this feedback loop, providing conditions under which banks and other providers of credit will begin to increase rather than reduce their lending.

But how is this to be done? The political criticism of banks – never especially popular at the best of times – is intensifying. Some politicians and economic commentators are urging banks to do their public duty and are also brandishing big sticks, such as the possibility of outright nationalization, in case they do not. The more moderate are simply pointing out that banks must do more to increase lending to avoid an economic slump.

Government and central bank policy is gradually being brought to bear on this problem. The initial policy response to the global banking run in October 2008 was modelled in some respects on the approach taken by the Norwegian, Swedish and Finnish governments during the Scandinavian banking crises of the early 1990s. While these three governments all dealt with their respective crises in slightly different ways, there were several common features. Government provided new capital to banks in exchange for shares or for 'warrants' (the opportunity to buy shares as a later date at a low price, thus ensuring that if the bank returns to profitability taxpayers share the benefits). A number of banks were taken into full public ownership. In Sweden and Finland non-performing loans were taken off bank balance sheets and transferred into 'bad banks', with the purpose of removing this source of further potential loss from the balance sheet of the banks and also of trying to recover as much value as possible from these loans. The emphasis was on fully and quickly recognizing the extent of losses and ensuring that neither bad assets nor inadequate capital prevented banks from continuing to meet their customers' demands for credit. Finally, the governments of Sweden and Finland provided blanket guarantees of bank liabilities to ensure that the crisis was not worsened by problems with bank funding or withdrawal of deposits.

The idea of adopting a similar approach to solving the current banking crisis is attractive. It is essential to avoid what took place in Japan in the same period, when, to far too great an extent, banks extended additional loans to struggling borrowers in order for them to appear 'current' with their loans; this approach only hides the full extent of loan losses and allows them eventually to mount very much higher than if they are dealt with promptly. Similar 'forbearance', when regulators allowed insolvent institutions to stay in business, greatly increased the scale of losses in the US savings and loans crisis in the 1980s.

Certainly it is essential, as discussed in Chapter 1, to provide banks with sufficient capital in order to avoid a damaging further contraction of bank credit after the emergence of bank losses. The Scandinavian solutions also achieved another desirable outcome by imposing heavy costs on shareholders, so penalizing them for the excessive risk-taking by the banks during the preceding credit boom.

But there are major differences between the situation of the Scandinavian banks in the early 1990s and of banks worldwide in early 2009, which means that taking exactly the same approach will not work. The first, and perhaps most critical difference, is that this current global banking crisis has emerged *before* the economic downturn, rather than *after*, as was the case in Scandinavia. This is because of the mechanism explained at length in this book. Unlike in Scandinavia, bank losses have in the main been generated not from a major increase in non-performing loans (with some exceptions such as US sub-prime mortgage lending) but because of the widespread maturity mismatch between long-term assets and short-term borrowing, generating the feedback loop – lower structured asset values → withdrawal of wholesale funding → lower structured asset values – that has cut banks off from their sources of wholesale funding. Even by the end of 2008 the level of loan losses in most banks remained reasonably low (again, there are of course exceptions, such as Citigroup, specialized US mortgage lenders and HBOS in the United Kingdom).

The major problem for banks today, unlike in Scandinavia in the early 1990s, are not losses already incurred but the losses yet to come, losses that could yet grow very large if there is a deep and long-lasting economic slump. This in turn is driving the second feedback loop – lower lending → higher credit impairment → lower lending – a feedback that is relatively more powerful than in previous crises because this banking crisis is global.

Because the losses have not yet been incurred, it is impossible to work out their eventual extent and how much capital banks might need. According to some bleak scenarios all banks are insolvent and should therefore be fully nationalized with very substantial capital injections or with open-ended capital support such as has already been given by the US government to Freddie and Fannie. But there are less bleak scenarios in which the global economy recovers and in which the banks are restored to profitability. This means that nationalization without compensation is fiercely resisted by bank shareholders. With some justification they regard this as an expropriation of shareholder property, depriving them of future income that they could expect to obtain once the economic situation recovers. Nationalization is not such a problem if shareholders are compensated for their losses, but this requires some way of valuing bank assets today. However, this can only be done when the worldwide slump has clearly hit bottom and there is a clearer picture of the extent of bank losses.

How about using 'mark to market' accounting to value bank assets? This way we can have a forward-looking market view of the value of bank assets, and this can form the basis of valuations used for the required bank resolutions. But this does not get around the problem because of the problem of illiquidity. Very few credit assets are tradable. There were some for which there used to be liquid markets, such as syndicated loans or the senior tranches of mortgage-backed and other structured securities. But now even these markets are extremely illiquid and the resulting hypothetical market prices (largely based on dealer opinions, not actual trades) grossly undervalue assets relative to their fundamentals.

Extreme loss insurance

The Scandinavian solution is not so easily applicable to the current situation and, as a result, policymakers are now exploring alternatives.

Instead of purchasing banks' bad assets (the original idea in the TARP proposals and something which is very difficult to do in any sensible way, because there is no means of valuing those assets) the authorities are now instead shifting towards insurance of banks' assets, hoping thereby to provide some limit on the bank losses and thus support bank balance sheets.

The US authorities have been taking the lead. They are now explicitly underwriting the losses on the assets of Fannie and Freddie, through the conservatorship and open capital support. They are underwriting AIG CDS obligations on senior structured credit, explicitly insuring extreme systemic credit risk.

The bail-out of Citigroup on 23 November 2008 is another prominent example. As described in Chapter 8, the US Treasury has offered guarantees on $306 billion of structured credits, leveraged loans and other relatively high-quality credit-related assets, in which Citigroup takes the first 10 per cent of loss and then a further 10 per cent of all remaining losses. In January 2009 a similar deal was announced for Bank of America, providing insurance on undervalued credit assets inherited from its acquisition of Merrill Lynch.

The Federal Reserve programme for purchase of the senior AAA tranches of ABS (backed by TARP funds) is another example of extreme loss insurance. Extreme loss insurance, in return for a premium, is exactly what is received from the sale of such senior tranches. The senior holders receive a small additional yield relative to Libor in return for absorbing the very extreme tail of loss on the underlying loan portfolios. Indeed, the entire policy of 'credit easing', to which the Federal Reserve is now committed, is a form of extreme loss insurance. The Federal Reserve, having moved to unorthodox monetary policy in which it no longer focuses on a target for interest rates, instead uses its balance sheet to purchase a range of credit-risky assets supported by US Treasury guarantees. Only the best-quality credit assets are being purchased so, while the US authorities are accepting credit risk, this is only at the extreme tail of the distribution.

In early 2009 the policies of the UK government have been moving in a similar direction. A large-scale programme of loan guarantees has been introduced, the 'asset protection scheme' with the agreement that the government will underwrite losses on some £325 billion of assets held by Royal Bank of Scotland and some £250 billion of assets of the Lloyds-TSB-HBOS group. In return the authorities are being given an increased shareholding in these banking groups which are now both majority state-owned and has received a promise that these banks will maintain lending in 2009 at the same level as in 2007.

The more serious charge against the insurance provided by the US and UK authorities is that it does not go far enough to restore full confidence in the safety and soundness of banks. Not all bank assets and liabilities are covered. Much risk still remains on bank balance sheets and, despite the insurance, banks still appear to be at serious risk of insolvency as the economic downturn continues. There are two ways to remedy this deficiency. Banks can be required to increase their capital much further, through the issue of equity or preference shares, to levels very much higher than at present; or insurance can be extended further, perhaps to cover the entire bank balance sheet. The strongest way of protecting banks against economic disaster would be to do both, on a sufficient scale to remove all insolvency risk.

Banks will resist further recapitalization, since this increases the exposure of shareholders to losses. In current circumstances any new shares will have to be purchased by government and, unless they are compensated, existing shareholders will suffer a financial penalty from the dissolution of their current shareholding. Compensation is, however, possible. It can easily be provided by giving shareholders a warrant or option to purchase the newly issued shares from the government at some appropriate strike price.

As an example, suppose Bank XYZ shares are trading at say 50 pence each with a total market capitalization of £10 million (so there are 20 million shares in total). The government decides that there must be a new issue of a further £10 million of ordinary shares underwritten by the government at a minimum issue price of 40 pence per share. Since this is lower than the current market price, this requires a further 25 million shares to be issued, and if private investors do not buy the shares at the issue price Bank XYZ ends up in majority ownership. Suppose that after issue the shares are trading at, say, 35 pence. This means that the original shareholding is now worth £7 million and the original shareholders have lost £3 million.

But the original shareholders can be compensated by being given a warrant to purchase the shares in government ownership for, say, 60 pence each, that is at twice the issue price. If there is economic recovery, and sufficient recapitalization of the entire banking system can ensure this, then these warrants are in fact potentially very valuable.

Suppose, indeed, that the entire banking system is recapitalized in this way, so removing all threat of bank insolvency and ending the financial crisis (this doubling of capital might not be enough to achieve this goal, but in this case all that is needed is to increase the scale of recapitalization even further). Then the value of Bank XYZ benefits from a recovery and rises substantially, to say 120 pence per share. The shareholders then exercise their warrants and end up paying the government £15 million for shares that originally cost the government £10 million to purchase. This is a win-win arrangement; everyone is better off.

How can this be so? The reason is the solvency and liquidity externalities illustrated in Figure 1.1. Bank share prices are currently substantially undervalued because of these feedback loops that are destroying bank liquidity and bank solvency. This is a co-ordination problem. Once all banks, worldwide, are sufficiently well capitalized (and the sufficient level of capitalization could easily be three or four times current levels of capitalization) then the negative externalities, caused by loan reductions and asset sales on credit quality and the price of traded credit securities, are removed.

Insurance of bank assets can be more acceptable to existing shareholders provided that the cost of this insurance, whether paid in cash or in newly issued shares, is low enough. Again, because the goal is to offset the negative externalities illustrated in Figure 1.1, there is a win-win outcome. By providing sufficient insurance and recapitalization across the entire banking system, at a global level, the authorities can break into the negative feedback loops and ensure that there is ultimately no call for payouts on the insurance they provide. The payment for this insurance, whether in the form of cash or shares, is pure profit for the taxpayer.

These efforts taken so far as insuring banks against extreme losses are as yet rather fragmented. They are not yet being conducted on a sufficiently global scale and are not imposed as they should be on all banks worldwide. Their rationale and likely impact are not being clearly explained or communicated, which is counterproductive, since guiding expectations is a critical aspect of limiting the worldwide economic downturn.

But these efforts to support our banks, using both insurance and recapitalization to restore bank balance sheets and hence ensure the safety and soundness of the world's banks, are exactly the right policies to pursue. The alternative, of standing back, compensating banks for losses only as they occur, on a reactive basis and on the minimum scale needed to protect depositors, is insufficient. It will not end the downward spiral of deteriorating liquidity and credit quality that is now undermining first our banks and now the global economy. The right way to protect taxpayers is to be unstinting in support as early as possible.

Further reading

The intensity of events during the four weeks following 15 October can be appreciated by looking through the many articles on the crisis published by the *Financial Times* during those four weeks (www. ft.com). Press releases describing all the key policy responses to the run on the banks can be found on the websites of the US Treasury (www.ustreas.gov/press/ – this is also the place to monitor what has since been happening to TARP funds) and the UK Treasury (www. hm-treasury.gov.uk/press_notices_index.htm – this is the place to follow announcements about the United Kingdom's asset protection scheme, the insurance scheme similar to that put forward in this book, and other UK initiatives). European Union statements on the crisis can be found on the Commission's website, http://ec.europa.eu/news/ economy/archives_en.htm?Page=1, but individual government initiatives can only be traced using national sources.

This chapter restricts attention to the United States and the United Kingdom and other parts of the European Union. Information on developments and policy response in other countries, for example Australia, Canada, Ireland or Japan, can most easily be found in press releases on the websites of their finance ministries and central banks.

Another omission from this chapter is the discussion of the impact on smaller economies and on emerging markets. For more on Iceland see Jon Danielsson, 'The first casualty of the crisis: Iceland', at www. voxeu.org/index.php?q=node/2549. Both the World Bank and the International Monetary Fund write extensively about the impact of the crisis on emerging markets.

Leading economists were quick to present their own views on how to respond to the crisis. Many of these can be found on the *Financial Times* Economists' Forum. Among the many articles that can be found in their archive, I would draw particular attention to the following:

Raghuram Rajan, 'Reshaping the banks: time to ask the IMF for help', at http://blogs.ft.com/wolfforum/2008/10/a-capital-crisis/#more-203, and 'Desperate times need the right measures', at www.ft.com/cms/s/0/13a60574-862b-11dd-959e-0000779fd18c.html, which is an articulate statement of 'mainstream' thinking as I describe it, emphasizing the need to recapitalize banks and discussing how this should be done, but downplaying the possibility of directly addressing the illiquidity in structured credit markets. There is valuable commentary on both these articles by other economists.

Luigi Zingales puts forward a useful 'debt for equity' proposal as a quick way to deal with uncertain asset valuations (and criticizes TARP because of the difficulty of valuing impaired assets), at http://blogs.ft.com/wolfforum/2008/09/why-paulson-is-wrong/#more-190.

Together with Gilad Livne, at http://blogs.ft.com/wolfforum/2008/09/liquidity-measures-will-help-restore-bank-capital/#more-191, I have argued for the importance of a centralized exchange for promoting liquidity in structured credits, but, while helpful, it is doubtful that such an initiative on its own would do the job.

Michael Bordo and Harold James, 'The Fund must be a global asset manager' (www.ft.com/cms/s/0/b8bc82a0-9eb2-11dd-98bd-000077b07658.html), advocate a stronger role for the International Monetary Fund in providing credit when the private sector is unable to do so, managing the reserve assets of the surplus countries and using these reserves to address problems of illiquidity.

Brandon Davies and Tim Congdon, 'How to restore liquidity to triple A securities' (www.ft.com/cms/s/0/c38293fc-8461-11dd-adc7-0000779fd18c.html), suggest that liquidity can be restored to structured credit markets through banks providing credit guarantees instead of monoline insurers or insurance companies such as AIG. They are addressing the key problem, but it is unclear to me that any private-sector institution can credibly protect against such systemic withdrawal of liquidity. Further views on how to respond to the crisis are noted at the end of the concluding chapter.

Conclusions: repairing the house of credit

This book argues against the widespread extreme pessimism about the world's banks and the quality of their assets. Yes, there was an unsustainable build-up of mortgage debt in the United States, the United Kingdom and other countries over recent years. Yes, many in the banking industry failed to anticipate the ending of this consumer credit boom and so exposed their firms excessively when the bubble eventually burst. There were many poor lending decisions. Banks have lost a great deal of money on US sub-prime mortgage lending and on the 'leveraged loans' to speculative-grade private equity buyouts. But the problems that are now causing such a widespread and severe contraction of credit are the panic responses to this situation, the lack of buyers for illiquid assets, the withdrawal of short-term funds, the lack of trust in banks and the fear of how deep the current downturn can yet become.

This is a key policy issue. Every financial crisis is unique, but every crisis raises much the same questions about how governments and financial authorities should respond. Should government and the financial authorities stand aside and let private businesses and individuals suffer the consequences of their own actions? Or should public funds be used to protect borrowers and investors from the consequences of their decisions? In the case of financial panic the answer is clear. The solution is long-term financial support and in an extreme crisis only the state is in a position to do this.

Behind this argument is the important role of both psychological and cultural factors in the current credit contraction. Excessive pessimism has replaced blithe optimism. Investors now shun the new credit structured assets, assuming that they are all unsound, when, as Chapters 4 and 5 have documented, senior tranches have considerable credit protections and even in a deep economic downturn will not default. Bankers who ignored risk and aggressively pursued market share and portfolio growth in loan and securitization markets during

314

the boom are now concerned only with reducing their exposure to credit as much as possible, selling all kinds of credit-related assets and cutting their lending to the bone.

The extent of this panic is partly a consequence of the specialized silos in which bankers, investors, journalists, civil servants and regulators work. There are many intelligent, hardworking, well-trained and skilful people working in and overseeing the financial services industry. But most of them only know one small part of the system very well, and their knowledge of the rest is often only sketchy. This does not matter when markets are working well, but it is a problem when the financial system is hit by a systemic shock.

How panic and illiquidity initiated the crisis . . .

This panic has given rise to a cumulative downward spiral created by the powerful feedback loops illustrated in Figure 1.1 of Chapter 1. Understandable doubts arose about the quality of sub-prime mortgage and other loan-backed securities. This, however, was not what undid the banks. What has brought many of them to their knees were large investment and trading portfolios of the *safest* tranches of these securities, financed using short-term borrowing (the maturity mismatch described in Chapter 6).

Banks did not appreciate the substantial liquidity risks to which this investment strategy exposed them. They assumed that the market for these securities would always be liquid and hence, in the event of a withdrawal of funding, these securities could be sold and losses would be limited.

This was a crucial misperception. While individual banks were not exposed to liquidity risks from this strategy, banks could not collectively sell these securities because there no ready buyers outside the industry. A small weakening in confidence in these securities then set in train a destabilizing series of events, with absence of buyers triggering a withdrawal of the short-term funding, resulting in a freezing of the market for all these structured securities.

These tranches will not default, but fear that they might and the resulting market freeze has led to insolvency, because 'mark to market' valuations have collapsed and these securities are no longer acceptable collateral.

Chapters 4 and 5 look closely at these structures. In most cases these are fairly simple and well documented. The accusation of lack of transparency simply does not stick. The AAA senior tranches of these simple vanilla structures, accounting for more than 60 per cent of the total outstanding of all loan-backed and other structured securities at the heart of the crisis, appear very sound. They are protected from default by their seniority in the structures that issued them, by the excess of assets relative to issued securities ('overcollateralization') and by the substantial excess of interest received on the underlying loans over interest due on the issued securities.

There were some serious problems with the transaction deals described in Chapter 5. These were the deals that supported the 'parallel' banking system in which the structuring departments of investment banks purchased all manner of high-yielding credit assets, packaged them within a tranched structure, and sold the resulting securities (sub-prime MBS, ABS-CDOs, CLOs and other types of CDO) to investors for a profit. Investment banks used these instruments to compete directly with commercial banks in providing household and corporate credit.

The attractiveness of these transaction deals, like many others that rely on a high level of borrowing, was based on the assumption of continued strong economic growth. As long as house prices were rising and consumer and corporate expenditures were growing, then leverage magnified the prospective profits and investor demand was strong. It was easy to structure and sell the securities at a profit. Investors in the riskier tranches did not look as closely as they perhaps should at the quality of the underlying assets. But when the market turned in the summer 2007, then leverage worked in the other direction, the deals appeared very suspect and it became almost impossible to sell them.

Parallel banking was thus very cyclical, contributing substantially to credit expansion in the upswing and then disappearing in the downturn. The focus on transaction profits also created the dubious restructured ABS-CDOs and CDO^2, excessively complex structures which were created as a way of disguising and selling riskier tranches of transaction deals, tranches that were otherwise difficult to sell. Not surprisingly these exceptionally highly leveraged transactions quickly fell apart when the housing and other credit markets turned, and account for a large part of recorded bank losses.

Despite this weakness, the most senior AAA-rated tranches of these products of almost all the basic deals, both the simple tranched structures used to raise funds for bank lending described in Chapter 4 and the transaction deals described in Chapter 5, will still be little affected by default, even in the event of a steep economic downturn. That is to say, $4.8 billion of the total of $7 billion of structured securities, shown in Table 2.2 of Chapter 2, should be regarded as extremely safe, even though their 'market prices' (something of a fiction, since there is no market for trading these securities any more) are 10–30 per cent or more below their par values.

In a worst-case scenario, a global economic slump longer and deeper than that of the 1930s would result in defaults of some of these senior AAA securities, but there is no reason for such an outcome. The world's workforce has not lost its skills. The machinery and equipment to produce are still there. The underlying drivers of growth and productivity – technological change, education, investment, scope for further globalization of trade in goods and services – have not gone away. A repeat of the 1930s will be a consequence of policy errors that fail to counter the panic, erosion of confidence and lack of trust that underlie the major falls of credit, investment and consumption. With resolute action to end the panic, restore confidence and re-establish trust, all these AAA senior structured securities will be fully repaid.

. . . and helps to explain the course of subsequent events

Panic and collapse of confidence, working through the feedback loops shown in Figure 1.1, also help us understand much of subsequent events. They explain why losses on a relatively small segment of bank lending – US sub-prime mortgages – accounting for less than 2 per cent of the worldwide bank assets, first shook and then destabilized the entire industry. They explain the successive and worsening stages of the crisis.

Chapters 7, 8, 9 and 10 document these events, from the initial losses on sub-prime lending in 2006, through the emergence of problems in global structured securities markets in July and August 2007 to the adoption by the Federal Reserve of its policy of credit easing on 16 December 2008. The course of these events was very different from that experienced in the aftermath of most other credit cycles, for example those in the United Kingdom, the north-eastern United States and Scandinavia in the early 1990s. This banking crisis has preceded rather than followed the economic downturn and, despite accounting systems that emphasize disclosure, has been characterized by continuing deterioration in the accounting valuations of bank assets, protracted emergence of loan losses, and gradual worsening of bank funding problems.

The cyclical timing of this crisis at the beginning rather than the end of an economic cycle is more like that of the Asian banking crises of 1997. Like those crises, it was triggered by a misperception of liquidity risks, and the sudden withdrawal of 'hot money' greatly exaggerated underlying fundamental credit problems. Also, like that crisis, there has been a major problem of contagion, with problems in US sub-prime affecting the markets for mortgage-backed securities worldwide, even though there are no direct economic linkages between US and European housing markets.

The gradual operation of these feedback loops explains the long delay between the first emergence of problems of illiquidity in structured credit and money markets and the global bank run of September and October 2008. Many attribute this run to the failure of the US Treasury and Federal Reserve to engineer a rescue of Lehman Brothers, forcing it to seek Chapter 11 bankruptcy protection. But the global run was an accident waiting to happen. Underlying confidence was being eroded by the continued weakening of global economic activity and further declines in the valuation of structured credits and worsening of bank funding problems.

There were, as Chapter 8 documents, very serious deficiencies in the regulation, risk management and governance of some banks and other financial institutions. Any list of poorly managed firms would include UBS, Citigroup, Merrill Lynch, AIG, Fannie Mae and Freddie Mac in the United States together with the Royal Bank of Scotland and HBOS in the United Kingdom. Excessive risk taking by these and other large firms greatly contributed to the severity of the crisis. But they were not its root cause. The underlying source of problems was the widespread failure to prepare for the end of the consumer and housing market boom and the practice, common among both poorly run and well-run institutions alike, of borrowing short to hold long-term consumer and corporate-backed structured credit securities. It is this maturity mismatch and the triggering of the resulting feedback loops that explains why, when the consumption slowdown eventually came, there has been such a rapid collapse in financial market liquidity, traded credit prices, and the supply of bank credit.

Chapter 9 discusses central bank operations, looking in particular at the role of the central bank as 'lender of last resort'. The major central banks responded robustly to the run of September and October, effectively taking on the job of intermediation between banks that had formerly been undertaken through money market interbank loans. The money markets migrated onto the books of the central banks because they offered interest rates on reserves and were willing to accept collateral for lending that was no longer acceptable for repo in a private contract between two banks.

Chapter 9 also looks at some of the limitations of central bank actions. Central banks can provide liquidity – that is, increase the balances available for circulation within the reserve accounts held by commercial banks at the central banks. If they abandon interest rate targeting and shift to unorthodox implementation of monetary policy, they can increase these balances to any level they choose, using them to purchase any available financial assets. This can increase the amount of credit in the economy, but only through bypassing the normal role of commercial banks in credit assessment (the banks hold reserves with the central bank and the central bank determines the destination of the credit). It does not provide any funding for commercial bank loans.

The continuing deterioration in credit, global output and employment in late 2008 and early 2009 is ominous. There is no reason to believe that the feedbacks in Figure 1.1 have ceased to operate and that we have reached the end of the credit contraction and the consequent contraction of spending, output and employment. The global economy will contract sharply through 2009 and the write-downs of bank assets and loan losses will continue to mount.

Some say that a sharp contraction in mortgage and personal lending is unavoidable, a necessary correction to the unsustainable borrowing and current-account deficits of many countries. This is another expression of panic. There is no need for such a damaging credit collapse to happen immediately. While it is true that the borrowing by households in the deficit countries, and the corresponding current-account surpluses in countries such as China, Japan and Germany, have been unsustainable, this imbalance does not have to be corrected immediately. Rebalancing of the global economy can and should take place gradually over a period of years, through increasing expenditure and imports into the surplus countries and increasing output and exports from the deficit countries. But this outcome requires a re-establishing of confidence in banks and a return of the short-term money that has been withdrawn from the credit markets.

Restoring confidence

The key to re-establishing confidence is to break into the feedback loops that are driving the contraction of credit and output. One frequently proposed way of doing this is to move away from strict 'mark to market' accounting rules, at least for the duration of the crisis. However, abandoning mark to market is a bad idea, because this is often the first and most reliable indicator of problems such as trading losses, and it ensures that banks respond quickly to these problems. One way forward, but one which accountancy standard-setters seem unwilling to contemplate, is to report two measures of values for illiquid markets, one based on opinions about market prices (what I have called 'hypothetical' market prices) and another based on a judgement about the likely cash flow returns from an invest-ment. Banks could be required to use one approach for valuation of their balance sheet and income (with the requirement that they also report the alternative valuation method in notes to their accounts and produce alternative calculations of key balance sheet and income vari-ables such as capital and trading gains and losses).

Accounting changes will not change everything. More important is for governments to make explicit their commitment to shoulder the worst potential losses of the banks. In fact, as chapters 2 and 10 docu-ment, government policy in the United States, the United Kingdom and other countries has been shifting in this direction. These policies are politically controversial (many dislike what they perceive as a bank 'bail-out'). The detailed arrangements have been in flux. They will probably change again in coming months. But the principle is correct, providing sufficient government support to ensure that the banks can continue to lend to all creditworthy borrowers.

Why must this be the job of government? Private enterprise and financial markets have proved themselves over hundreds of years to be highly effective at wealth creation. Free markets, despite their many inefficiencies and injustices, have the great advantage of allowing indi-viduals and companies to pursue the economic opportunities available to them. No better way has been found to harness the initiative and enterprise necessary to growth and economic prosperity. But markets do not cope well with major economic shocks. They are very good at providing protection against individual risks – for example, damage to houses and motor cars, accident, illness or veterinary bills. But no private-sector institution is big enough or powerful enough to provide insurance against a large global 'systemic' disturbance. Only governments can provide the disaster insurance necessary to restore stability to the global financial system.

Several examples of private-sector disaster insurance are described in Chapter 8. These include the credit default swap protection of senior credit instruments provided by the monoline insurance companies and by AIG, and the guarantees on mortgage default provided by Fannie and Freddie. In the face of a major credit downturn, investor confidence in the value of these guarantees collapsed and the institutions that provided them were sucked into the whirlpool of credit write-downs.

Government is different because the value of its guarantees does not depend on investor confidence. It rests instead on the coercive powers of government, which can raise taxes and command economic resources. Therefore only government can stand aside from the whirlpool and offer insurance against a systemic shock such as that underlying the global banking crisis.

Government-backed support for the banking system

The issue, then, is the practical one of how this support is best provided. One widely accepted blueprint is the response of the governments of Finland, Norway and Sweden to their banking crises (briefly examined in chapters 3 and 10). Those countries in their different ways moved to recognize bank losses, provide new funds to recapitalize their banks and sometimes take them into public ownership.

This blueprint does not exactly fit the banking problems at the beginning of 2009. In this current crisis the major concern for banks is not, as in Scandinavia, losses already incurred, but the potential for large losses yet to come. Worries about future losses underlie the illiquidity of structured credit and the resulting withdrawal of short-term 'hot money'. Worries about future losses also underlie the current unwillingness of banks to lend and the resulting sharp decline in credit, output and employment.

The reason for this is that the underlying credit impairment of bank balance sheets is a long way from having completely run its course. As economic conditions deteriorate further, almost any bank asset could eventually become impaired. This means that the Scandinavian solution is not directly applicable; it is simply not possible to decide how much new capital banks need or to isolate and value 'bad assets' and transfer them if necessary out of the banks, when we are still so far from the bottom of the recession.

Even now, in March 2009, policymakers seem very confused about this point. The economic team of the Obama administration, led by Treasury Secretary Timothy Geithner, have very recently announced public–private partnerships for purchasing illiquid structured credit assets and loans and removing them off bank balance sheets. The main justification for this approach seems to be the unwillingness of Congress to approve any more funds for supporting banks, once the current TARP fund is exhausted. But these public–private partnerships seem unlikely to succeed in restoring the health of bank balance sheets. If the pricing is too low then the support will end up doing more to boost the returns of hedge funds and private equity funds than to help bank balance sheets. More importantly, even if the pricing is high enough to benefit the banks, the overall scale of the programme appears too small to make a real difference.

Because the concern is about future losses, other approaches have to be adopted that avoid any artificial attempt to value illiquid assets. This is why governments have been turning to ex ante rather than ex post support (i.e. promising when and if losses are realized). For example, there have been a number of experiments with insurance rather than purchase of bad assets as a tool for strengthening bank balance sheets. Chapter 10 documents some of the initiatives of this kind adopted by the Federal Reserve and the US Treasury. More recently, on 19 January 2009, the UK government announced a very similar initiative, its 'asset protection scheme', and protection has since been agreed under this scheme for both Royal Bank of Scotland and the merged Lloyds-TSB HBOS group. Other similar deals have been use in Europe, the government of the Netherlands having insured safe but undervalued assets of ING.

These initiatives are far from perfect. One problem has been lack of transparency. At least in the case of the US and UK insurance arrangements the credit quality of the insured assets is unknown, so it is unclear whether the premiums paid in return for this insurance have been high enough to compensate for the additional risk to taxpayers. In any case, what is the additional risk to taxpayers? If these bank assets were not insured, the taxpayer would still have to absorb losses in the event that the banks became insolvent and were unable to repay depositors in full.

Still, initiatives of this kind, protecting banks from the impact of declining asset values, without removing all their ownership claims, are a promising way of restoring bank balance sheets. A particularly clever implementation of such an 'ex ante' sharing of returns was the deal between the Swiss government and UBS agreed in October 2008. As described in Chapter 8, this deal transferred problem assets from the UBS balance sheet, at something close to current market prices, into a fund in which both UBS and the Swiss government have an interest. UBS would have been reluctant to sell assets outright at these prices, because they will have perceived mark to market prices in a situation of extreme market illiquidity as an undervaluation of what these assets were really worth. The deal got around this reluctance by offering UBS a share of the 'upside' returns, in the form of an option to purchase the equity in the fund. Similar deals, offering shareholders options to acquire assets in the event of economic recovery and rising prices, could yet play a critical role in ensuring that other banks agree to further support for their balance sheets at an acceptable cost to taxpayers.

Whatever the detailed criticisms of current initiatives, it is clear that some form of government intervention is needed to break into both of the feedback loops shown in Figure 1.1. This can be achieved through a combination of support for existing bank assets (either insurance or a Swiss-style jointly owned fund) with large-scale recapitalization, so that the bank is effectively free of risk of default. It is, however, critical that these measures are taken on a very large scale. Being half-hearted and not fully protecting the banks will mean failing to stop these feedbacks.

The critical argument in favour of carrying out these measures, and doing so on a much larger scale than they have been pursued in the crisis hitherto, is that they are win-win policies. As explained at the close of Chapter 10, the feedback loops illustrated in Figure 1.1 create powerful negative economic externalities. The rational business deci-sions of individual institutions to sell assets or reduce lending create large costs for others. By charging banks appropriately for insuring and recapitalising, on sufficient scale to break into these feedback loops, the government can both make a profit on behalf of taxpayers and offer shareholders substantial capital gains when the value of bank shares subsequently recovers.

Insurance of senior structured credit securities

Government-backed guarantees are also a promising tool for dealing with the wholesale and money market funding problems on the liability side of bank balance sheets. One possibility is for government to provide transferable guarantees on the safe, senior AAA-rated tranches of mortgage- and other loan-backed securities – the tranches that are protected from the first 25 per cent or so of losses on the underlying mortgage pool. Again, there has to be a first loss – so investors have to carry perhaps the first 10 per cent of defaulted interest or principal repayments. The government-backed insurance then makes up any further shortfalls of principal or interest, again subject to some loss-sharing arrangement.

As for any insurance there should be a premium on all these guarantees. A premium of 40 basis points – that is, 0.4 per cent per annum – would be appropriate for the senior structured credit tranches. It does not sound like much but, because the underlying cash flows are secure, the insurance can still make a healthy profit while again creating substantial capital gains for holders of these assets.

If the insurance is transferable then the guaranteed senior tranches of mortgage-backed or other structured securities will be marketable and hence can be sold to other banks or investment funds. With a market for these securities they can also be pledged as collateral in money markets, so that instead of selling the insured tranches to long-term investors, banks can hold them on their balance sheet and use them for short-term funding. In this respect such insurance is like the asset swaps already offered by central banks, but with the crucial difference that it is available for the life of the security, so that the bank can be sure that the underlying loan pool can be financed on a permanent basis.

An important benefit of insuring the structured securities is that their accounting valuations will take account of the government guarantees and be raised upwards to reflect the 'floor' on value created by government insurance. This in turn will provide an immediate large capital boost to banks worldwide; if the full $4.98 billion of the AAA senior securities are insured, then the benefit to bank capital could be as much as $600 billion as the liquidity losses as shown in Table 2.3 are reduced, so reinforcing the government capital injections that have already been made and putting them in a much stronger position to restart their lending (in practice, because of amended international financial reporting standards, banks might have to sell these assets to realize these gains). This is as big a boost to bank capital as all the different programmes of recapitalization announced across the world in October 2008.

Government-backed insurance guarantees and unorthodox monetary policy

Government-backed reinsurance of extreme credit loss complements unorthodox monetary policies, such as the 'credit easing' announced by the US Federal Reserve on 16 December 2008. A central bank can shift from the 'orthodox' approach to monetary policy – of setting a target for short-term interest rates and using its monopoly power over the supply of reserves to enforce that target – to an 'unorthodox' policy where it can expand its balance sheet effectively without limit, using the new funding this creates to purchase securities or other financial assets. The Federal Reserve is now operating monetary policy this way, using its balance sheet to purchase credit-risky assets such as Fannie and Freddie MBS, ABS and commercial paper and, more recently, government bonds. The Bank of England has recently begun shifting to a similar approach. Since March 2008 it has been using its balance sheet to purchase both government bonds and corporate debt.

Central banks are still novices in the application of such unorthodox approaches to monetary policy. There is considerable debate about whether it is more effective for them to purchase government bonds or private-sector credit-risky assets. But if the central bank purchases credit-risky assets (i.e. a 'credit easing') then government-backed guarantees against extreme credit losses is a useful complementary policy. Usually central banks are legally barred from exposing themselves to substantial credit default risk, so a central bank can purchase credit-risky assets only when covered by explicit insurance against credit losses. For example, because the Federal Reserve Act limits such acquisitions, the US government is using TARP funds to provide this insurance and so support the Federal Reserve policy of credit easing through purchase of ABSs and other structured securities.

Unorthodox monetary policy is unlikely to be sufficient to prevent a collapse of credit and economic activity, without the substantial commitment of public funds to directly support the banking system. The reason is that central banks can only purchase tradable loans and securities. Unorthodox monetary policy can provide credit directly to large companies (through purchase of commercial paper and corporate bonds), but it does little to supply credit to smaller businesses or to households that cannot issue their own securities.

The central banks will eventually have to return to an orthodox policy of targeting interest rates as the economy recovers, in order to choke off rising inflation. This will require a reduction of bank reserves and the sale of the government bonds and the credit-risky securities acquired during the previous period of unorthodox balance sheet expansion. With the US and the global economy so weak, the central banks may not have to do this anytime soon, but they still have to plan ahead and work out how it will sell down its credit portfolios. Since investor confidence in credit-related assets is unlikely to be restored quickly, it may prove essential for any government guarantees to be transferable along with the security to the new private-sector purchaser. This is less of an issue for the Bank of England, at least to date, since its security purchases have been focused on government and good-quality corporate bonds.

Presentation and expectations

Government support for the banking system is controversial. Politicians and journalists immediately misinterpret any such measures as some form of bail-out that will protect banks from past mistakes and cost taxpayers a lot of money.

These concerns miss the point. The idea is not to give banks money (that would indeed be a bail-out) but rather to invest in banks in order to obtain a return. Government needs to do this because private investors are scared and will not provide funds. But government should not hesitate to do so because they, alone, have the deep pockets that will allow them to make good returns from these investments and stabilize the financial and economic system to boot.

In any case, the government has to protect bank depositors in the event of a macroeconomic disaster. So the ex ante arrangement where banks receive insurance protection or put illiquid assets in a separate fund, sharing the losses and returns with government when they are eventually realized, imposes little additional burden on taxpayers. In the event of a major economic slump taxpayers will have to cough up, whether or not through these schemes. So additional taxpayer exposure is limited and the objective of stopping the downward spiral of falling confidence and reduced lending is achieved with little fiscal burden. Money on the table now means much less money to be spent later on.

In order to banish the fear that is now undermining our financial system and our economy, the management of expectations is critical. Once investors, consumers and companies regain their faith in recovery, then the insurance of bank assets is not so necessary. They will see how undervalued are financial assets and the many opportunities there are for borrowing, lending and investment.

But what matters most is that governments and central banks, worldwide, express their backing for the banking industry, not just in words but in action, through both recapitalisation and guarantees, and on a sufficient scale to reverse the cumulative erosion of confidence in the banking industry and the contraction of credit. A poker analogy is in order. Ultimately government, with its powers of coercion, has all the money and all the cards. Like a player with a strong hand in the popular televised version of the game, *Texas Roll'em*, now is the time for the public authorities to go 'all in', putting every cent available to them on the table to force the doubters to fold. Such a forceful policy response will both make money for taxpayers and end the cumulative collapse of credit.

Without this response we will be looking at a precipitous decline in consumer spending, with savings rates in the United Kingdom, the United States and other borrowing countries jumping by more than 5 per cent. Allowing for knock-on 'multiplier' effects of contracting income, this could mean falls of global output of as much as 10 per cent, a decline which can only be slowed, not stopped, by using fiscal stimulus, and then only a partial recovery. This will not be a recession but a permanent and damaging slump with appalling economic consequences.

Politicians and officials need to state repeatedly that the programmes of public lending and guarantees and asset purchase, which can only grow much larger in the months ahead, are made not because banks are weak but because they are misunderstood. Banks play a critical role in creating money and credit, a role that government cannot replace. In almost all cases bank and credit assets are of far better quality than market pricing and share valuations suggest. The large majority of bank assets, mortgages, personal loans, corporate loans and structured credit securities are of good quality. With a comprehensive and global effort to back these bank assets, and, where necessary, to supplement bank lending with directly provided public credit, the global credit collapse will be ended and an economic slump avoided.

This does not mean a rapid return to consumption-led growth. Even with the required support for the banking system, recovery of the global economy will be painfully slow, taking many years if not decades. But without support for the banking system we face a very much worse outcome.

Such policies may sound extreme, but even a cursory examination of previous banking crises, such as that provided by Chapter 3, shows that this is what the public authorities do in a crisis, providing massive support to restore confidence in the banking system (so, for example, the Thai government provided explicit guarantees to banks amounting to 40 per cent of national income, and the Swedish and Finnish governments provided legal guarantees of bank liabilities on an even bigger scale).

Political obstacles to support of the banking system

Limiting the impact of the credit crisis requires substantial government support for the banks. But there are major political barriers to providing this support. One barrier is a lack of political consensus about what needs to be done. The idea of providing taxpayer support to the banks is attacked as rewarding bankers for failure and as a bail-out of bank bond holders and shareholders. There is also concern about the impact of bank support on public-sector finances (a serious barrier to both the insurance of bank assets and the nationalization of banks, because these measures greatly increase public-sector accounting-sector liabilities).

When capital markets and banks are in disarray, politicians seek to take the place of the market, for example providing emergency loans to keep troubled companies going in the face of a steep economic downturn. This is an understandable short-term response, but politicians and civil servants are no better than bankers at assessing risks and deciding which businesses are commercially viable and which are not. And, unlike bankers, their decisions to provide public-sector loans are often made on political rather than commercial grounds, for example to support employment among voters in a particular, electorally critical district. Anything other than short-term public sector loans to industry should be avoided.

Politicians are skilful at criticism and passing blame, but impatient with the nitty-gritty details of policy measures. Congressional committees in the United States and parliamentary committees in the United Kingdom have devoted many hours to hostile interrogation both of bankers and of the officials responsible for dealing with the crisis. These committees have expressed extreme scepticism about the quality of bank assets and suspicion of most of the policy measures used to address the crisis. This is healthy democratic debate, but it is also a startling contrast to the way in which Norway, Sweden and Finland handled their banking crises. In those countries there was from an early stage cross-party political agreement on the broad thrust of policy, and both government and opposition politicians were involved in the oversight of public support of the banking system.

Politicians are right to be concerned about the impact of bank support on public-sector finances. But this concern often translates into an unhelpful 'wait and see' attitude. Politicians would generally rather wait until banks have fallen into deep trouble and support is unavoidable before committing public funds. This is a sensible approach to most elements of public expenditure. It is right to delay a decision in order to establish whether an expense is really necessary. But this approach is most unhelpful when dealing with the kind of feedback loops illustrated in Figure 1.1. Breaking these feedback loops depends on early rather than late intervention, and on providing support to banks in an unstinting rather than niggardly manner. Paradoxically, the caution of politicians about the use of public-sector funds to support banks will likely lead to a much greater level of support being required when they finally agree to do so.

A further political barrier has been the controversy created by bonus payments to executives of those banks receiving large sums of public money. These bonus payments are distasteful but, as discussed in

Chapter 8 in the context of the AIG support, the issue of bonuses is not central to restoring stability to the financial system and the economy. The sooner this is put to one side the better (my own preference would be to insist that a substantial share of bonuses, say 60 per cent, being used for charitable purposes rather than being stopped altogether.)

If the barriers to obtaining a domestic political consensus on dealing with the crisis are large, then the barriers to achieving a similar consensus at international level are formidable. One outcome of the global run on the banks of September and October 2008 has been the establishment of the 'G20' group as a forum for discussion and decision-making among the world's leading economies, both developed and emerging. The G20 (actually nineteen countries plus representation from the European Union to reflect the views of the twenty EU countries that are not directly represented – a total of 39 countries in all) covers a huge diversity of political and economic interests. The second meeting of the G20 leaders has been scheduled for 2 April 2009, after this book goes to press. But the early indications are that this meeting will do only a small amount to improve the global response to the current crisis.

There are deep differences as to the appropriate extent of fiscal stimulus in response to the crisis. There is justified scepticism about whether fiscal expansion will deal with the longer-term problems of the financial system and excessive household indebtedness. In any case most countries would prefer that the larger share of stimulus (and hence taxpayer burden) is carried by others, not themselves. There is greater consensus on the need to introduce much stricter regulation of financial markets and institutions, but this is a classic example of shutting the stable door after the horse has bolted. While improved regulation may help a little to re-establish confidence, it will do relatively little to deal with the current credit market downturn, and introducing new financial regulation in a hurry without adequate thought and consultation could well damage rather than support bank lending and credit.

The one form of concerted action that is clearly and urgently needed is substantial public support for banks in the form of both asset protection and recapitalization. Such co-ordinated support for banks in many countries will be essential to limiting the contraction of world demand, without creating unmanageably large fiscal deficits. But as I write, in mid-March 2009, it is unclear whether the G20 meeting in London of 2 April will even discuss this issue.

The future of banking

The priority goals of government response to the credit crisis are to maintain the supply of credit to households and corporations and to restore bank access to wholesale funding. This can happen eventually with the commitment of government and central bank balance sheets to support of the banking system. But once the banking system and credit market are revived there will be not be a return to business as usual.

What, then, will the future of banking be like? One vision – which really would ensure that banking becomes boring again – is of a return to 'utility banking'. According to this view, banks should focus on basic services such as payments, deposits and the safer forms of lending. It is also argued that banks should be under much stricter regulation and supervision.

It is both unlikely and undesirable that all banks switch to such a utility business model. It is unlikely because most of the world's larger banks are now involved in investment banking, and it is not possible to run investment banks as providers of basic utility services. As we saw in Chapter 10, one dramatic consequence of the banking crisis has been the end of the specialized investment bank, with all the US broker dealers either acquired (Bear Stearns, Merrill Lynch), failed (Lehman) or converted into commercial bank holding companies (Morgan Stanley, Goldman Sachs). Now all large investment banking is pursued on the European model, by subsidiaries of larger conglomerate banks that also offer corporate and retail banking services. There are only a few relatively small independent investment banks left, focused mostly on advisory work.

A return to utility banking is also undesirable because we need, more than ever, financial intermediaries that are prepared to take risks, to lend to the entrepreneurs who will create future wealth or to provide financial services to those with relatively little wealth or uncertain incomes. Utility banking could mean going back to a stagnant economy with far fewer economic choices for the less well-off.

But there is still an essential insight to be gained from the proposals for utility banking. The purest form of this proposal is that known as 'narrow' banking or 'limited purpose' banking, an idea promoted in the 1930s by leading US economists Irving Fisher and Frank Knight and supported since by many others, including Milton Friedman. The idea is that in order to make bank deposits and banks entirely safe, deposits should be secured only against very low-risk assets, such as short-term Treasury bills and central bank reserves. There is then no need for government-backed insurance of bank assets or liabilities.

Risky bank assets such as mortgages, credit cards, small business and corporate lending can be separately financed though mutual funds. Banks can originate these loans, manage the mutual funds, and earn a management fee, but the risk is not on their balance sheets. Banks that are too small to operate their own mutual funds can originate and sell loans to larger funds.

The merit of narrow banking is that it highlights the need for the systemic risk inherent in illiquid bank lending to be mutualized and held directly by household investors, either directly or in their pension and insurance plans. But the best way to promote this vision is not necessarily to ban deposit-taking banks from holding illiquid loan assets altogether. The experience of intervention in other markets is that altering relative prices is a more effective form of intervention than imposing quantity controls or banning certain activities altogether.

So, instead, it is appropriate to introduce a relatively expensive charge for systemic risk insurance, not just in response to the current crisis but as a permanent measure. This charge should be compulsory whenever such assets back transaction deposits or other short-term funding, but voluntary whenever such assets are held in mutual funds or are backed by long-term bonds. The charge could be varied over time to ensure that the aggregate quantity of deposits and other short-term bank funding does not grow to a level that threatens financial stability.

This is a more appropriate vision of the future of our banks. At root, in case we have forgotten, all banks are social institutions, a voluntary arrangement by a group of individuals to pursue their mutual interest. Even if their equity is owned by a small group of shareholders or traded on public markets, a bank would not exist without the commitment of funds by retail and wholesale depositors. Banks, in order to be stable, must protect these depositors, whether, as in the extreme circumstances such as we now face today, turning to the state for depositor protection or, more appropriately, ensuring that risks are mutualized and shared by all investors.

In short, all banking, whatever its legal form of ownership, is mutual banking and has wide social responsibilities to fulfil. The suggestion that bank decisions should be driven by high salaries and the pursuit of short-term profit is fundamentally inconsistent with the nature of banking as an activity.

This is not to say that bankers should not be well paid or, when they have created wealth, receive good bonuses on top of their salaries. But it is to say that bankers, unlike professionals in other industries, have much wider responsibilities than to their shareholders and management alone.

Banks should, and hopefully will, get unstinting support from government to see them through the present crisis. The quid pro quo is that banks will have to recognize that they are fundamentally different from other industries. That stability and the interests of both retail and wholesale depositors are as important as profit. That serving customers and ensuring that they operate a long-term viable business is more important than a short-term increase in their share price. And that there will be major changes in both the conduct and regulation of banking in the years to come.

What does this mean in practice? Within the investment banking divisions of the large global banking institutions, there will be a return to core activities: securities issuance where banks bring new issues of corporate bonds and equities to the market, advisory work on mergers and acquisitions, and brokerage and trading, where they conduct financial trades both for clients and on their own behalf.

Credit structuring activities will eventually revive, although these will be focused on the simplest balance sheet securitizations described in Chapter 4, executed on a fee basis to raise funds for commercial banks. Banks will need to control risk taking, avoiding the excessively risky structures such as the ABS-CDOs and not acting like investment funds, holding large amounts of structured credit assets financed out of short-term borrowing.

Government and regulators will want to impose a good deal of quality control on these structuring activities, especially if the relatively risky transaction deals reappear. One framework for imposing control may be to impose a similar compulsory government-backed insurance as that which might be used to encourage narrow banking. Again, this is a permanent extension of one of the insurance measures that can be used to address the current crisis. It might be compulsory for all financial institutions to insure tranches of structured securities or other medium- and long-term securities, whenever they are financed using short term funding. The premia could be based on ratings of the underlying assets, and the ratings themselves might be subject to a quality check either by supervisors or by an appointed independent assessor. This may prove helpful in discouraging maturity mismatch and restoring bank access to wholesale funding on a permanent and stable basis.

Opportunities for investment banks in emerging markets will also re-emerge after the crisis, and there could turn out to be a considerable demand for their services. There will be ongoing and large-scale structural change in many of these economies as they adjust to the changes in the world economy, and therefore a lot of work on mergers and acquisitions, corporate advisory and securities issuance as well as in the development of asset management services for the growing investment and pension funds in these countries.

Many of the major international banks have large and profitable corporate banking operations, providing payments, cash management and a range of other services to larger companies. There is no obvious reasons why these activities should be greatly different after the crisis.

The biggest question marks are not about these investment or corporate banking activities, but about the future of conventional retail banking. This is because we have reached the limits of the policy of the past twenty-five years of maintaining growth of demand through increased consumer borrowing in the United States and other countries. Chapter 2 notes the link between the world's current-account imbalances, the high levels of consumer borrowing, especially mortgage debt, in the deficit countries and the reliance on wholesale funding of the banks that supplied these mortgages and consumer loans, as their lending outstripped their retail deposit base. Going forward, the best that banks can hope for in the deficit countries is stability in the stock of household debt in relation to income, not a further increase in borrowing at a much faster rate than incomes.

One old problem has emerged with a vengeance in this crisis, and it will not go away even when the banking industry recovers. This is the regrettable tendency for banks operating in mature markets to seek growth through acquisition, especially overseas in markets that they do not fully understand. The extreme UK example is RBS, a well-run, efficient and profitable domestic operation and one of the largest banks in the United Kingdom since the smaller Royal Bank of Scotland conducted a very successful takeover of the much larger NatWest bank. Had RBS stuck with domestic corporate and retail banking it would still be celebrated as a success and would not now be in majority government ownership.

What undid RBS was its overseas acquisitions, especially its purchase of a large part of the Netherlands bank ABN-AMRO (with the Belgian-French bank Fortis and the Spanish bank Santander acquiring other parts of the bank). RBS paid far too much in a cash-only deal, and the strain this put on the RBS balance sheet is the main reason why it eventually ended up with the UK government holding the majority of its shares.

The fate of RBS is a salutary warning for other banks, once the credit crisis is over. The drive to increase earnings, through acquisition and merger, is very seductive, but – because of the complexity of banks and the importance of internal culture to their operations – few such deals are totally successful and too many are disasters. Retail banks in sluggish domestic markets may be tempted to push once again for growth through overseas acquisitions.

The problem that led to the downfall of RBS is all too common in banking – a lack of checks and balances on the decisions of a headstrong executive and excessive pressure from banking analysts and shareholders for growth of balance sheet, revenue and profits. The consequence is a downplaying of the risks to which banks expose themselves as they try to meet investor expectations.

Investors and senior management will have to adjust to more realistic expectations of the future growth and revenues in retail banking. Chief executives will have to accept that they are democratic leaders who have to build a consensus among senior management for strategy and change, and not despots who wield unlimited power. This does not mean there are no opportunities for expansion. There may be considerable further development of consumer credit and mortgage markets in the current-account surplus countries such as Germany, Japan and many emerging markets (a development that would be very welcome for correcting the global current-account imbalances). This requires many institutional changes (for example the development of credit referencing agencies who keep track of the individual repayment histories on previous borrowing) and will face substantial cultural and other barriers. But if such a development does take place there will be considerable demand for the international transfer of banking skills from the mortgage and consumer credit banks in the deficit countries such as the United States and the United Kingdom.

These deficit countries are now going to have to grow their output and incomes instead of their expenditure. Banks will play a role here, but it will be a very different kind of banking, perhaps with much greater focus on the provision of credit to small and medium-sized companies. This is a challenging area of business, this form of business credit being much riskier than mortgage lending, and banks in the United Kingdom, for example, with relatively easy pickings in consumer lending, have not always paid such attention to these customers as they might. They may dispute this conclusion, but my impression is that they can do much more to develop the range of services and loan facilities to the smaller businesses and entrepreneurs on which many of the hopes for future growth of income and employment will be pinned.

Another key role of banks will be in the development of invoicing, transaction and payment technologies, at both national and international level. It is a reflection on the barriers to change and the inertia of the industry that banks have done relatively little to exploit the opportunities of applying information technologies to making these processes as low-cost, convenient and global as possible. Reductions in transaction costs, including costs of payments, make a considerable contribution to growth. So banks can be expected to fulfil to a much greater degree than in the past their social obligation to do everything they reasonably can to promote improved use of information technology across all of the industry.

Finally, reflecting the need for banks to fulfil their wider responsibilities to customers and society as well as to shareholders, there will be major changes in bank governance, disclosure and regulation. There is a broad consensus on the need to improve oversight and regulation, but this must be thought through carefully. The majority of financial institutions have not been so badly run. It would be a mistake to burden the entire industry with intrusive oversight and a costly burden of regulatory compliance, such as were introduced by the US Sarbanes-Oxley Act. It would be a still greater mistake if new regulations inhibit bank risk-taking and reduce the availability of credit, especially to the enterprises that will be the source of future income growth.

One change, recognizing that the banks are in effect public–private partnerships, will be to require government-appointed representation on the boards of banks, with responsibility for ensuring that banks do not put taxpayer funds at excessive risk.

There will also be a shift to more qualitative risk management, with an emphasis on business plans and scenarios that can be understood and discussed by generalists, with less emphasis on quantitative models. The newer capital regulations, such as the Basel II international agreement on bank capital regulation with its emphasis on quantitative modelling of risks, now look misplaced. While banks will undoubtedly continue to use quantitative models for assessing risks and return and making business decisions, these models are ill suited to identifying and managing systemic risk. A fundamental point, although one that is often overlooked, is that systemic risk cannot be quantified. Regulators will have to ask banks to hold considerably more capital than they have been used to doing in the past.

The goal must be not to reduce risk but to ensure that banks are aware of the risks they are taking, that the decision to take these risks is broadly supported by the institution and by shareholders, and that they hold enough capital and obtain sufficient return on these risks. There will be much debate over how to achieve this goal. One approach that may be worth pursuing is setting common accepted standards for simplifying and communicating financial positions and risk exposures – that is, the positions of every institution should be made very transparent to the outside world. Portfolios should be tracked and widely publicized on a product-by-product basis, so that everyone is aware, perhaps with some delay, when an institution takes an extreme position. That way there would be an alert to the dependence of banks worldwide on the insurance written by, say, AIG or the extreme positions in restructured CDOs of both Merrill Lynch and UBS.

The biggest change of all will be a transformation of the culture of both investment and commercial bank management, from a preoccupation with short-term growth and meeting the numbers to instead placing greater emphasis on long-term development and customer needs. This is another example, perhaps the most important example, of where there is an absence of trust in the industry. Banks have turned to short-term finance because long-term equity and bond investors neither understand nor trust banks. They have been reluctant to provide them with long-term funds and have become used to assessing their performance using inadequate short-term measures of returns and revenue growth, with inadequate allowance for risks or any attention to the long-term sustainability for these returns.

We need a better relationship of trust and understanding between investment management professionals and the banking industry. One simple change that would help would be a rearrangement of the desks in investment management, so that a single banking desk holds all bank-issued securities, whether these are equity, hybrid debt (bonds with an option to convert into equity), long-term bonds or structured securities. These desks would then be focused on the quality of underlying bank assets rather than on short-term measures such as return on equity. Banks would no longer be incentivized to reduce capital, increase leverage, in order simply to increase return on equity. The desk would see this for what it is, a meaningless rearrangement of bank liabilities that does not change the underlying assets or risk exposures.

More idealistically, one can envisage a relationship where investment managers listen to the bank and understand its business model, its longer-term goals and how it can achieve them. The role of the chief executive would be to persuade investors to accept an analysis of what opportunities are realistically available and to support expansion where this is warranted, but to accept low growth with high dividends if there are few opportunities for expansion, and not pressurize for expansion when the opportunities to do so are really not there. This is idealistic; in the real world expansion and revenue growth are always what create the big pay-offs for management, regardless of the risks involved. But we can at least hope to lower the expectations of investors for revenue growth and persuade them to take a reasonably long-term view of banks, looking through the next credit cycle and focusing on long-term, sustainable revenues, wherever those may be found.

Further reading

There is a lively debate on many blogs and web pages about the appropriate way of handling the current crisis. The Economists' Forum (http://blogs.ft.com/economistsforum/) is an excellent source for these discussions. A number of contributions have already been referred to in the notes on further reading to the introduction and chapters 1 and 10. My own analyses can be found there and on the Cass web pages www.cass.city.ac.uk/cbr/activities/bankingcrisis.html.

Willem Buiters's blog is a further source of inventive and resourceful ideas. I have not discussed the 'good bank' proposal he describes on that blog (see http://blogs.ft.com/maverecon/2009/01/the-good-bank-solution/ and other postings) because, attractive as that proposal is, I believe that it is not operational. This is because of the European Convention on Human Rights and equivalent US statutes. The removal of good assets would force a fire sale of remaining bad assets, and shareholders and bond holders would be able to claim compensation for the resulting loss below their 'fundamental' value. So the 'good bank' proposal founders for exactly the same reason as the earlier proposals for purchasing bad assets from the banks, the problem that it is simply not possible to establish a fair value for the bad assets in illiquid markets.

There is also a great deal now being written about what the new financial architecture will look like once the crisis is over. One important policy proposal widely debated among policymakers is having arrangements for so-called contingent capital – money kept aside in some form of lock box, off balance sheet – that can be called on to replenish bank capital in the event of a systemic crisis. This proposal is developed in the 2008 Jackson Hole paper of Anil Kashyap, Raghuram Rajan and Jeremy Stein, 'Rethinking capital regulation', at www.kc.frb.org/publicat/sympos/2008/KashyapRajanStein.03.12.09. pdf. The biggest drawback is that it is unclear how easy it will be to persuade other institutions to provide the contingent capital. It could be that this capital is government-provided, in which case the proposal is, in effect, rather like having a permanent system of government-backed insurance against extreme disaster losses.

A lot of attention will continue to be paid to bank capital regulations. One promising idea is put forward by Charles Goodhart and Avinash Persaud, 'A proposal for how to avoid the next crash', *Financial Times*, 31 January 2008, at www.ft.com/cms/s/0/dd1e1132-cf9f-11dc-854a-0000779fd2ac.html, who suggest making capital requirements countercyclical, by relating them to the growth of lending. This suggestion and a number of other ideas for improving financial regulation are developed in the 2009 ICMB-Geneva report on the World Economy, 'The Fundamental Principles of Financial Regulation', by Markus Brunnermeier, Andrew Crockett, Charles Goodhart, Avinash D. Persaud and Hyun Shin (downloadable from http://www.voxeu.org/reports/Geneva11.pdf). A number of other papers and analyses are being published at the time of the spring 2009 meeting of the G20 in London on 2 April; for example the chairman of the UK regulator, the Financial Services Authority, is publishing his own report on the future of financial regulation on 18 March and reportedly recommending a much tougher approach to the regulation of financial activities in London.

A lively argument in favour of limited purpose banking is given by Chamley and Kotlikoff on the Economists' Forum (http://blogs. ft.com/economistsforum/2009/01/putting-an-end-to-financial-crises/).

Glossary

AAA, AA, and Aaa, Aa, etc.	Credit agencies use these letters to summarize their opinion about the ability of an issuer to make all the promised payments on a bond or structured security. The scale of one major agency, Moody's, runs Aaa, Aa, A, Baa, Ba, B, Caa, Ca, C, D (from their strongest rating Aaa to default D). Other agencies use the scale AAA, AA, A, BBB, BB, B, CCC, CC, C, D. Chapter 4 provides a brief introduction to these ratings.
A, B and C mortgages	These are the US mortgage-industry conventions for rating the credit risk of residential mortgages. A mortgages are the safest ('prime'), while B and C mortgages are of lower quality ('sub-prime'). These ratings are based on borrower characteristics including income and credit history, summarized in a standardized score known as FICO, and on loan characteristics such as the loan-to-value ratio and loan-to-income ratio.
ABCP	Asset-backed commercial paper. This is similar to commercial paper, but it is issued by conduits or structured investment vehicles (SIVs) holding loans, structured credit securities or other credit assets. The ABCP market is an important source of funding for asset-backed securities (ABS) and thus for the financing of credit cards, vehicle lending and other common forms of retail commercial bank lending. It has also been used to finance MBS.
ABS	Asset-backed security. A security backed by a portfolio of loans, such as credit card receivables,

341

vehicle or small business loans. The market convention is that the term 'ABS' is not applied to a security backed by either mortgages (this is instead a mortgage-backed security or MBS) or tradable corporate loans (this is instead a collateralized loan obligation or CLO).

ABS-CDO   ABS collateralized debt obligation. This is a collateralized debt obligation or CDO in which the underlying securities are tranches of either asset-backed or mortgage-backed securities. This is a complex and risky instrument, and most tranches of these instruments are now failing to repay.

ABX indices   Traded insurance contracts, each providing cover on the repayment on tranches of 20 selected US sub-prime MBS (they are called indices because the cover is for more than one MBS) for a period of five years.

The ABX indices are a bit confusing because there are many different versions. Four 'rolls' were launched, 0601 (covering MBS issued in late 2005 and early 2006), 0602 (covering MBS issued in mid-2006), 0701 (covering MBS issued in late 2006 and early 2007) and 0702 (covering MBS issued in mid 2007). Within each roll there are indices for tranches of different seniorities, so ABX-HE-0601-AAA is protection on 20 senior AAA tranches, ABX-HE-0601-BBB is protection on 20 mezzanine BBB tranches and so on.

Instead of regular premium payments the ABX contract operates with a single upfront payment. Thus a price of 80 for, say, the ABX-HE-0701-AAA means that a protection buyer must pay 20% of the par value of the AAA index in order to purchase protection against any default index over the five years from 2007 to 2001. At the time of writing the ABX BBB tranches are trading at less than 5, indicating that the market is expecting to lose on average around 95% of the par value of the underlying securities.

Alt-A   Alt-A are A mortgages provided to US borrow-
             ers that are 'non-conforming', i.e. do not satisfy
             all the credit quality criteria required to qualify
             for a guarantee from the US government agen-
             cies Fannie Mae or Freddie Mac. Their credit
             quality is better than sub-prime mortgages, which
             are classified B or C. The most common reasons
             for an A mortgage being non-conforming and so
             classified as Alt-A is a high loan-to-value ratio or
             some weaknesses in credit history. Alt-A should
             not be confused with jumbo loans, which are also
             A loans, but non-conforming because the size of
             the loan exceeds the maximum allowed for agency
             guarantee.

ARM   Adjustable rate mortgage. A mortgage on which
             the interest rate varies up and down instead of
             being fixed. In some countries including the United
             States the interest rate on adjustable rate mort-
             gages are conventionally set using a market refer-
             ence interest rate such as Libor. In other countries
             such as the United Kingdom banks often set the
             interest rate on an adjustable rate mortgage on a
             discretionary basis.

Basel I   Basel I is an agreement made by a committee
             of central banks and bank regulators (the Basel
             Committee on Banking Supervision or simply
             the Basel Committee for short) on the capital
             adequacy of internationally active banks. Basel I
             was first agreed in 1988 and came into force in
             1992. The Basel I rules are fairly simple and have
             been adopted by most bank regulators worldwide
             for their domestic banks as well as those operating
             internationally.

Basel II   Basel II is the successor to Basel I, finalized in
             2006 after several years of consultation and intro-
             duced in many countries by the end of 2007. The
             Basel II rules are much more complex than those
             of Basel I, in some cases using quite sophisticated

	mathematical models, in an attempt to match bank capital requirements closely to bank risk.
basis point	A basis point is one hundredth of 1 per cent, so, for example, 0.4%=40 basis points. Basis points are widely used in financial markets in order to quote interest rates and prices with greater precision.
capital	In banking and financial markets the term 'capital' is used to mean the difference between the value of assets and the amount of debt used to finance those assets. Applied to a bank, capital (or equity capital) is the amount of money contributed by shareholders in order to finance the bank's assets. See also 'leverage' (increasing leverage allows the financing of more assets with a given amount of capital).
CBO	Collateralized bond obligation. A tranched security backed by a portfolio of corporate bonds.
CDO	Collateralized debt obligation. A tranched security backed by a portfolio of tradable debt. CDO is a general term. Within the category CDO are included various different types of structure depending on what tradable debt is held; for example a CLO holds tradable loans, a CBO holds bonds, and an ABS-CDO holds ABS and MBS.
CDO^2	Collateralized debt obligation squared. A tranched security backed by a portfolio of CDO tranched securities. This is a complex and risky structure. In most cases even the most senior tranches are now failing to repay.
Chapter 7 bankruptcy	The section of the US bankruptcy code applied when a company is liquidated and all its assets sold to repay its debtors.
Chapter 11 bankruptcy protection	The section of the US bankruptcy code that allows an indebted firm to obtain protection from its creditors while it is being reorganized.
Chapter 15	The section of the US bankruptcy code applicable

bankruptcy	when an insolvency involves debtors and assets in more than one country. Used for the Bear Stearns funds because their bankruptcy proceedings took place under Cayman Islands law, where the funds were registered. Chapter 15 prevented debtors pursuing these assets simultaneously through the US courts.
CLO	Collateralized loan obligation. A credit structure issuing tranched securities of different seniorities and holding a portfolio of tradable loans.
CMBS	Commercial mortgage-backed security. A tranched security backed by a portfolio of commercial mortgages, secured on offices, shops or multi-family residences.
commercial paper or CP	Short-term paper, of maturity up to one year, issued by a private company. The issue of commercial paper usually requires an underwriting facility from a commercial bank standing ready to purchase the paper as it matures, if necessary. Without such underwriting to guarantee the ability to refinance the commercial paper when it matures, then it can be difficult to get investors to hold commercial paper. See also ABCP.
conduit	An off balance sheet vehicle established by a bank to hold asset-backed and mortgage-backed securities, themselves backed by loans taken from the bank's balance sheet. See Chapter 6 for a more detailed description.
coupon	The regular payment made to an investor on a bond or structured security. The coupon is quoted as a percentage of a 'par' value. In the case of a conventional bond, the par value is fixed at the time of issue and is equal to the amount of repayment of principal at maturity. In the case of a structured security, principal can be paid back during the life of the security (according to the rules contained in the documentation of the

structure), and so the par value can decline over time. The 2-A-1 note issued by CWABS-2006-19 described in Chapter 4 is an example.

credit rating

The opinion of a credit rating agency on the ability of an issuer to repay a security. See 'AAA, AA, and Aaa, Aa, etc.'.

credit spread

The difference between the market rate of interest (the yield) paid on a safe and widely traded bond, such as those issued by the US Treasury or the UK or German governments, and the relatively higher rate of interest paid on a riskier bond of the same maturity. Riskier bonds offering high-credit spread include both corporate bonds and structured credit securities (Table 4.1 illustrates how credit spread – i.e. the coupon relative to Libor – increases along with the riskiness of the structured credit).

currency forward market

The market for buying and selling currencies where the actual currency exchange takes place at a designated future date. An example of a six-month currency forward exchange would be an agreement made in January 2010 to exchange €100 for ¥12,500 in July 2010. The agreement is an 'off balance sheet' commitment and so may not appear in accounts and statistics.

ERM

(European) Exchange Rate Mechanism. The agreement among many European countries in the early 1990s to peg their exchange rates against a basket of European Union currencies known as the ECU. This was a precursor to full European monetary union and the creation of the euro in 1999. German unification in 1990 pushed up interest rates for all countries in the ERM and the system eventually failed, in autumn 1992, with first the forced withdrawal of the United Kingdom and then the subsequent withdrawal of several other countries.

Exploding ARM	A form of adjustable rate mortgage widely offered to sub-prime borrowers in which the interest rate is set at an adjustable rate for the first two or three years of the mortgage and then switches to a relatively high fixed rate (these were often labelled something like 2:28 or 3:27 to indicate that the adjustable rate period was 2 or 3 years and the fixed rate period 28 or 27 years). The intention behind these contracts was to force the sub-prime mortgage holder to refinance, hopefully by that time having built up equity and able to qualify as an Alt-A or prime borrower.
FDIC	Federal Deposit Insurance Corporation. It operates the US bank deposit insurance scheme and also regulates and supervises a number of large federally chartered banks that are members of the scheme.
Fed funds rate	The federal funds rate (or Fed funds rate for short) is the overnight interest rate in the market for borrowing and lending of US commercial bank reserves with the Federal Reserve. As explained in Chapter 9, the main determinant of the Fed funds rate is the amount of reserves supplied by the Federal Reserve; when they supply more reserves banks have less need to borrow reserves and the Fed funds rate falls.
FHA	Federal Housing Administration. Now part of the US Department of Housing and Urban Development, the FHA was created by Congress in 1934 to insure mortgages especially for certain deserving groups and to help support the US mortgage market. It has provided insurance to borrowers such as military veterans and the elderly. Before the current housing crisis it had been entirely self-financing, earning enough money on premiums to cover all losses.
GAAP	Generally Accepted Accounting Principles. US GAAP are the rules for company accounting statements applicable to US companies.

GDP   Gross domestic product. A measure of all the
                       income (including wages, rent and profit) gener-
                       ated by economic activity in a country.

GNP   Gross national product. A measure of all the
                       income (including wages, rent and profit) earned
                       by residents of a country. It is not quite the same
                       as gross domestic product, because residents of a
                       country can earn income such as rent or profit, or
                       even wages, from economic activities in another
                       country.

GSE   Government sponsored enterprise. These are com-
                       panies created by the US Congress and operating
                       with a public purpose. Some – such as Sallie Mae,
                       which guarantees and finances student loans,
                       and also Fannie Mae and Freddie Mac before
                       the crisis – are in private ownership. Others,
                       such as Ginnie Mae, which finances government-
                       guaranteed mortgages (e.g. for military veterans
                       or from other special programmes), are govern-
                       ment-owned. GSE-issued bonds are regarded as
                       almost as good in credit quality as those issued by
                       the US Treasury itself.

haircut   The difference between the amount of money
                       lent in a repo contract and the true market value
                       of the security sold and then repurchased. This
                       represents the amount of protection offered to the
                       lender of the money. A haircut of 10% means that
                       the lender is safe from financial loss, should the
                       security not be repurchased, as long as the value
                       of the security falls by no more than 10%. As
                       structured credit securities have become less and
                       less liquid in the crisis, their prices have become
                       more volatile and less meaningful, so haircuts
                       have risen substantially. See also 'repo'.

hedge fund   Hedge funds are lightly regulated investment funds
                       that are not allowed to accept retail investors.
                       Hedge funds follow a number of different invest-
                       ment strategies (LTCM, described in Chapter

3, followed a strategy known as convergence trades).

IFRS
International Financial Reporting Standards. These are the rules for company accounting statements now applied to most companies outside the United States.

IMF
The International Monetary Fund, based in Washington, DC, is one of the international institutions created at the Bretton Woods conference of 1948. It was set up to help support a system of fixed exchange rates. Nowadays 185 countries are members of the fund, but a small number of the wealthiest countries, such as the United States, provide most of its finances and have most influence on its decisions. World exchange rates are now floating, rather than fixed, so the role of the IMF has evolved to that of providing advice and finance to countries that face financial difficulties. It also provides authoritative economic and financial research and analysis on the international economy and on many individual countries.

impairment
An accounting measure of the future loss.

investment-grade securities
Investment-grade securities are those conventionally rated as BBB or better (or Baa or better by Moody's – see 'AAA, AA, and Aaa, Aa, etc.'). Speculative-grade securities are those rated below investment grade.

IPO
Initial public offering, when shares in a company are first sold on the stock market, making it a public rather than a private company. Investment banks play a key role in IPOs, finding investors willing to buy the new stock and establishing an initial price. For this work they can earn substantial fees.

jumbo mortgage
See 'Alt-A'.

junk bonds
The widely used pejorative term for bonds rated at below investment grade (also known as

speculative-grade bonds). These bonds were pioneered in the 1980s by the firm Drexel Burnham Lambert and their star employee Michael Milken. They were widely used for the financing of US private equity deals. A number of scandals involving insider trading weakened the firm, and then a downturn in the market for speculative-grade bonds, to which they were excessively exposed, pushed Drexel Burnham Lambert into bankruptcy in 1990.

leverage and leverage ratio
In banking and financial markets, leverage is the practice of using borrowed funds to provide a share of the total finance for an investment. The leverage ratio is the ratio of the total investment to the investors' own contribution (or equity). The phrase 'financial gearing' is also sometimes used to mean the same thing as leverage. The net gearing ratio is the ratio of total borrowed funds to the investors' own equity.

leveraged loans
Leveraged loans are a form of syndicated loan tailored for the financing of private equity transactions. They are long-term loans, usually of ten to twelve years' maturity, and often with relatively low repayment of principal in the years before maturity. The use of leveraged loans allows a private equity fund to finance many more transactions than if it had to provide all the purchase cost from its own resources.

Libor
Libor (often stated in capitals as LIBOR) is the daily British Bankers' Association index of average London Inter-Bank Offered Rates, as reported to them by a panel of London banks active in the London money markets.

margin
An amount of money or other collateral that has to be placed into an account at the time that a derivative contract such as a credit default swap is written. In order to protect dealers in these instruments from failure to repay, customers are

required to make additional payments into the margin account, corresponding to changes in the mark to market value of the derivative contract they have purchased (if it loses value then they must make additional payments into the margin account). As described in Chapter 8, large margin payments, based on mark to market values in markets that had become suddenly very illiquid, was what led to the failure of AIG.

mark to market The practice of valuing securities or other financial instruments according to the latest financial market prices. This is not usually entirely straightforward, since only some securities are actively traded on a daily basis, so mark to market is more often done by reference to prices of other, hopefully comparable, securities.

MBS Mortgage-backed security. A credit structure issuing tranched securities of different seniorities and holding a portfolio of mortgages. There are two main types of MBS – RMBS, backed by residential mortgages secured on family housing, and CMBS, backed by commercial mortgages secured on offices, retail shops and malls, and multi-family housing.

mergers and acquisitions Mergers are where two companies join together voluntarily to create a single company, with newly issued shares replacing the shares of each company. An acquisition is when one company purchases all the shares of another company either for cash or using newly issued shares. Relatively large numbers of mergers and acquisitions take place during economic booms and are a source of substantial revenues to the investment banks that provide advice and financing for these deals.

mezzanine tranches Mezzanine tranches are the next to most senior tranches of a structured credit security. They are typically issued with an investment-grade rating, but of less than AAA, and can often be recognized by the inclusion of the letter M in their name (for example the M-1 notes issued by CWABS-2006-19 described in Chapter 4).

money market
mutuals

Mutual funds that operate in money markets, holding short-term money market assets such as wholesale bank deposits, asset-backed commercial paper and treasury bills. Money market mutuals are rated by the credit rating agencies and normally achieve the very highest AAA ratings. In normal market conditions money market mutuals are able to hold a mixture of short- and medium-term paper and so achieve better returns than bank deposits or other short-term money market instruments. As mentioned in Chapter 10, money market mutuals got into serious difficulties in September and October 2008, with massive withdrawals leading to their mark to market valuations falling below the value of invested funds (so-called breaking the buck) and triggering yet further withdrawals.

money markets

The different markets where money is borrowed and loaned short term, for periods of up to one year. These include the Treasury bill market, the repo market, the unsecured interbank market, and in the United States the Federal Funds market.

monoline

An insurance company that specializes in insuring financial securities, such as municipal bonds or structured credits. See Chapter 8 for a description of these firms and their recent problems.

mutual funds

An investment fund in which all investors share equally in the returns according to their share of the total investment. The two common types are closed end funds, where investors can realize their ownership only by selling to a new investor, and open end funds, where the management are ready to buy and sell assets in order to meet investor withdrawals. Mutual funds can invest in many different types of asset, including shares, bonds,

	loans and money market instruments (see 'money market mutuals').
NYSE	The New York Stock Exchange, the largest exchange in the world for the trading of equities.
OECD	Organisation of Economic Co-operation and Development. The club of rich developed countries, based in Paris, which provides economic research and policy analysis for its members and supports dialogue on matters of mutual economic interest.
off the run	See 'on the run'. A reference to US bonds or other securities which are no longer on the run.
on the run	A reference to US bonds or other securities which have recently been issued and so are still being actively traded.
OPEC	Organization of the Petroleum Exporting Countries, of which many of the world's largest oil producers are members. It sets production quotas for its members in an attempt to gain some control over world oil prices.
OTC	Over the counter. An arrangement for conducting trades outside an exchange, with most trades conducted through established dealers who buy and sell from customers. OTC traded contracts are more flexible than exchange-based trading and so are used whenever customers require the terms of each contract to be tailored to their own specific requirements.
paper	A casual term used to refer to all forms of securities issued in financial markets, both short-term bills of less than one year maturity and longer-term bonds of more than one year maturity.
par value	The notional value of a bond or structured security used for calculating coupon payments. See also 'coupon'.
pass-through	A security backed by loans or bonds that is *not* tranched, so that all payments of interest and principal are shared equally among security

	holders, rather like what happens with a mutual fund.
principal	See 'coupon'.
repo	A sale and repurchase agreement. This is a binding legal contract in which a security is sold and then bought back, usually for a slightly higher price, a short period later (the duration of a repo can be anything from overnight to one year or more). A repo is effectively a form of secured lending, since if the owner of the security fails to repurchase, the buyer can sell it to someone else in order to recover their money.
RGE Monitor	Roubini Global Economics Monitor, the website operated by Nouriel Roubini providing economic analysis and commentary.
RoE	Return on equity. A standard measure of return on an investment. It is the earnings, after any tax, of a company or vehicle, expressed as a proportion of the value of the equity or residual claim.
savings and loans	Savings and loans, sometimes called thrifts, are specialized US mortgage lending and saving institutions, operating under different charters and different regulations than commercial banks. Federally chartered savings and loans are supervised by the Office of Thrift Supervision. There was a financial crisis during the 1980s in the US savings and loan industry, triggered by high interest rates at the beginning of the decade. Regulators failed to make a decisive intervention and this allowed losses to get much bigger. Protecting depositors in failed savings and loans eventually cost the US taxpayer about 2 per cent of GNP.
SEC	Securities and Exchange Commission. The regulator of all the issuing and trading of securities in the United States, including bonds, equities and structured securities. It was established by the 1934 Securities and Exchange Act.

SEC 10-K	The 10-K report is an annual report which the SEC requires from companies issuing securities in the United States. The 10-K must cover a number of required items such as financial statements and remuneration of senior executives. 10-K reports can be downloaded without charge from the SEC Edgar website and are usually also available on the submitting companies' own websites.
senior tranches	'Senior' means, in a financial context, having the first claim on repayment. Senior tranches are the most senior notes issued by a loan or structured credit security.
SIV	Structured investment vehicle. An off balance sheet fund that purchases high-yield credit assets and finances them through the issue of short-term asset-backed commercial paper – ABCP.
speculative-grade securities	See 'investment-grade securities' and also 'junk bonds'.
structured credit securities	A general term used to refer to any securities backed either by loans or tradable debt.
syndicated loans	Syndicated loans are large-value loans to companies or sovereign borrowers, provided by a group or syndicate of banks. Nowadays syndicated loans are tradable, so lenders can sell part or all of their share to new lenders. See also 'leveraged loans'.
thrifts	See 'savings and loans'.
toxic assets	The slang phrase used to refer to any assets held by a bank that are of uncertain value and so might cause big declines in profits or capital. These declines can be either because of a decline in their mark to market values or because of high levels of provision for impairment.
vanilla	An easy to understand financial instrument in which the payments to an investor depend in a simple way on underlying reference assets. MBSs and ABSs are vanilla instruments. CDOs are rather less vanilla because of the underlying

collateral management. Restructured securities such as ABS-CDOs and CDO^2 are very far from being vanilla.

write-down · A reduction in the value of a bank asset because of a fall in its market value or mark to market accounting valuation.

yield to maturity · The implied rate of interest at which an investment in a security at the current market value would exactly repay all future promised payments of coupon and principal. This is the same as 'internal rate of return' on an investment project.

zero-coupon bond · A bond that does not pay any coupon but instead makes only a single payment of principal on its maturity date.

zero-coupon yield · The yield to maturity on a zero-coupon bond. The zero-coupon yield varies, both with the time to maturity and the credit riskiness of the borrower.

Index